# New Frontiers of Corpus Research

# LANGUAGE AND COMPUTERS: STUDIES IN PRACTICAL LINGUISTICS

## No 36

edited by Jan Aarts and Willem Meijs

# New Frontiers of Corpus Research

Papers from the Twenty First International Conference on English Language Research on Computerized Corpora
Sydney 2000

edited by

Pam Peters
Peter Collins
and Adam Smith

Rodopi

Amsterdam - New York, NY 2002

The paper on which this book is printed meets the requirements of "ISO 9706:1994, Information and documentation - Paper for documents - Requirements for permanence".

ISBN: 90-420-1237-4 (bound)


Printed in The Netherlands

## Contents

**Corpus-based language description**

# Introduction: new frontiers of corpus research

*Pam Peters, Peter Collins*† *and Adam Smith*

Macquarie University †University of New South Wales

This volume presents a selection of papers from the 21st ICAME conference (International Computer Archive of Modern and Medieval English), which was held over Easter 2000 at Macquarie University in Sydney, Australia. It was the first ICAME conference to be held in the southern hemisphere, and designed to provide fresh perspectives on corpus linguistics through their application in places bordering on the Indian and Pacific oceans. This put a focus on Asian speech communities who use English as a second language, as well as antipodeans whose usage both reflects and varies the norms of native-speaker Englishes in the northern half of the world. The conference featured several papers on the discourse of younger users of English, and on its form and use in communicating via electronic and telephonic media, as well as print. The conference agenda also included papers from ICAME's established areas of strength, with new research into English grammar, discourse and the lexicon.

All these frontiers are documented in the present volume. Fresh correlations between genre and language variation are identified. Diachronic change and English language history are illuminated with data from standard and newly created corpora. The methodology of corpus creation, and tools for interrogating and manipulating corpus data, are features of various papers below. Some of the greatest technical challenges come from the data contained in historical corpora, though the computational techniques developed there have application to modern non-standardized English.

The three sections of this volume group together papers with broadly similar focuses:

- new corpora and new speech communities
- historical and regional studies
- corpus-based language description

Such headings are not of course discrete, and in reviewing the papers from each section we will note comparable themes and issues in the other sections – to provide the print equivalent of hypertext links for the interested reader. For ease of reference, the papers in each section are ordered alphabetically by their authors' surnames.

## 1. New corpora and new speech communities

Classic standard corpora such as the Brown, LOB and BNC are of course intended to represent a broad spectrum of usage (within the broadly defined region), rather than narrowly defined communities of users. Their existence allows a second generation of corpus builders to concentrate on specifiable groups of English-users, not necessarily native speakers, and on the functions of English discourse for them.

One such corpus is profiled in McEnery's paper on the 100 Corpus (a collection of telephone calls to the operator for information and services). The highly goal-oriented nature of the exchanges makes for lexical convergence and a limited range of politeness strategies. Brekke's paper also focuses on a corpus of relatively constrained discourse, comprising economic-administrative texts. His particular interest is in developing a term bank of English and Norwegian economic terminology for Norwegian business. The research will help to achieve a realistic balance between the pressure to use English business terms, and the desire to avoid losing those available in Norwegian. Both McEnery's and Brekke's papers highlight actual or potential links with industry for corpus research.

Other papers in the first section feature special-purpose corpora of new English-speaking communities, especially in Asia. The usage of Chinese learners is captured in the papers by Drave (from Hong Kong) and He Anping (from Guangzhou), in aspects of spoken and written discourse. Drave's paper describes the elements of vague language found in the English of Chinese and native-speakers e.g. *sort of, and so on*, and *about* with a precise number. He Anping shows that the techniques of 'vaguification' are quickly taken up by language learners, although the repertoire of Chinese speakers of English is smaller and less varied than that of native English speakers. By contrast, He's paper shows that the particle *so* is overextended in the writing of Chinese students of English, probably because it parallels the Chinese particle 'gum' which has wide-ranging discourse functions. The interactive discourse of Singaporean students (mostly of Chinese origin) produces a few local idioms, in Ooi's analysis of a corpus of internet relay chat (IRC). But most of the IRC lexis involves truncated English words and phrases found in global netspeak (e.g. *pls* 'please', *gd* 'good', *lol* 'laugh out loud', *gtg* 'got to go').

The standard corpora of English have tended to embody the usage of middle-aged to older writers, because of their dependence on published material. The usage of younger writers and speakers of English has remained largely hidden, and so papers focusing on their discourse are a welcome development. Ooi's paper is one such, as is Minugh's with its profile of students' written language from a corpus of college newspapers in the USA, Canada, the UK, Ireland, Australia, South Africa and New Zealand. Minugh's analysis shows both their conforming side and some of their more outrageous detail in the use of slang such as *shag, ass, techno, fave*. In between those extremes, we note that these younger writers make more use than their elders (in data from Brown, Frown, LOB and FLOB) of such things as *albeit* and *snuck* rather than *sneaked*. Generational differences like this are the stuff of language change, as demonstrated by Lehmann [section 2].

Compiling corpora of spoken language is notoriously labor-intensive, yet eminently rewarding for researchers if strategically planned. The construction of the corpus of spoken Dutch is detailed by Oostdijk in the final paper of this section. The project is a major step towards describing the varieties of Dutch spoken in the Netherlands and Flanders (though not South Africa), and in many contexts, public and private. Oostdijk's work, like that of McEnery and Brekke, has strong links with European industry.

## 2. Historical and regional studies

The papers contained in this section have a common interest in changes in English usage over anything from several decades to a few centuries, using standard and ad hoc corpora of different kinds. Johansson's study of pied piping constructions surveys their use from 1150-1500 in data from the Helsinki corpus, demonstrating their frequency in nonfiction and religious writing rather than fiction. Hoffmann's paper traces the grammaticalization of complex prepositions such as *in spite of* from 1600 to the present day. By using texts from Project Gutenberg as well as the Zurich English Newspaper corpus (ZEN), Hoffmann covers their development in both literary and nonliterary sources. The Chadwyck Healey CD-ROM of Early English Prose Fiction provides Gotti with an experimental foil for his study of canting terms derived from Head's glossary (1673), and additional documentation for approximately one third of the terms investigated. The sociolinguistic limitations of the electronic literary canon are evident, though the print medium has always put bounds on the social range of expression that is documented for posterity. Even Minugh's college newspapers [section 1] show this.

Several of the papers in this section are concerned with the way in which language change reflects social change. Gender roles are examined by Markus through a corpus of letters written in the 15th and 17th centuries, using a set of interpersonal elements. Markus's study shows some differences in the positioning of male and female correspondents two centuries apart, which seem to reflect aspects of their respective cultural and social contexts. Holmes and Sigley highlight 20th century changes in women's roles, and in the ways in which women are perceived (or at least talked about). They use comparative data from standard New Zealand, British and American corpora, to show that significant changes have taken place in the last thirty years.

The last three decades is also the span of time in which Lehmann traces the decline of zero subject relative constructions (ZSRs) in spoken British and American English. Their decline – and the restoration of surface subject relative constructions (SSRs) – seems to be associated with younger speakers, at least in Britain. In the US this is less clear-cut but they may there be attributable to immigrant language substrates such as Spanish and German, which use fully articulated relative constructions. Increased use of SSRs by British speakers, like use of the progressive [see Smith's paper in section 3], shows that spoken language does not always tend to prefer the minimal construction

Technical problems in dealing with historical corpora are the focus of Schneider's paper on normalizing the nonstandard spellings of words and especially names for machine-handling of texts in the ZEN corpus. His pseudo-phoneticization serves its purpose for automatic disambiguation of variant forms in 17th and 18th century newspapers, and will add to the battery of techniques for historical corpus linguistics – as would the tagging procedures mentioned by Markus in connection with his handling of 15th century texts.

## 3. Corpus-based language description

The papers included in this section are mostly multimodal studies, using corpora of spoken and written languages or multiple genres (e.g. imaginative, news, conversation, etc.), or else some kind of triangulation between contemporary corpora and contemporary speakers of the language. Divergences between the latter sources serve as input to de Haan's study of the status of *whom*. His data include some outspoken comments to the effect that *whom* is 'dead', from an e-mail discussion group involving academic linguists (the professional counterparts perhaps of Ooi's IRC participants [section 1]). But de Haan finds corpus evidence that *whom* still operates in the regular way in specific linguistic and stylistic contexts, in keeping with the comments of standard grammars. In Kjellmer's study of the semantics of *eventual*, a small survey of English-speakers underscores the direction of his findings from both corpus and other lexicographical material, that the word has two kinds of meaning in contemporary English, one associated with finality and the other with potentiality. The restoration of the second meaning may suggest continental influence on insular English – the reverse of the force that Brekke [section 1] has to reckon with.

Generic contexts make for differences in usage, as shown in Facchinetti's multifaceted study of the modal meanings for *can* and *could*, based on a 10% sample of texts from ICE-GB. The use of 'ability' *can* is concentrated in the spoken medium, while epistemic *could* is common in academic writing. There is generic variation in temporal specification of the present perfect, shown in Schlüter's study to be more extensive (typically by means of prepositional phrases) in expository writing, but restricted to one word (a temporal adverb) in conversation and fiction [cf. the large difference between fiction and nonfiction in Hoffmann's study of complex prepositions: section 2]. The correlation of genre with distribution emerges also in Smith's paper on the progressive in contemporary English. His findings suggest that it has spread from a base in spoken English to more frequent use in written English, and is now attaching itself to stative verbs, in defiance of its canonical use (in standard British English) with verbs of dynamic meaning.

The genres used in corpus compilation are a given in many projects, although valid questions may be raised about them in the search to explain anomalous linguistic findings. Rayson et al.'s paper uses the four 'text types' of the BNC sampler (informative writing, imaginative writing, conversation, task-oriented speech) in describing the distribution of parts of speech. The findings for adjectives conformed to expectation, in occurring more often in writing and especially informative writing, than speech. However there were exceptions for most other grammatical categories, where the findings for the categories of 'task-oriented' speech were closer to writing than expected, and those for imaginative writing were more speech-like. The hybridity of 'imaginative writing' (its mixture of narrative and dialogue) would explain the latter finding. [The heterogeneous nature of corpus text categories is also an issue for Johansson, section 2.]

In spoken discourse (as in written) the distribution of elements may be predictable only up to a point. Mindt's paper on the patterns of falling intonation documents the typical pattern of declination across individual texts and speakers, but also shows how this can be varied to support the speaker's purpose at particular points in the discourse. The implications for the unit of declination are the open questions in all this. Are the bounds of the declination unit set by the intonation pattern, or does the discourse itself frame the pattern?

## Conclusion

ICAME conferences at their best keep raising questions about the structure of discourse, changes in the nature of English grammar and its lexicon, and about the communities of people who use the language for diverse purposes. The titles of the first and last papers in this volume are curiously apt in expressing the overriding function of corpus linguistics: to be a *Clearinghouse* for ideas and research into the English language, and to be *Ever moving on*.

Pam Peters, Peter Collins, Adam Smith Sydney, Australia 2002

# New corpora and new speech communities

# TERMINEC: a clearinghouse for economics text and terminology

*Magnar Brekke*

Norwegian School of Economics and Business Administration

## Abstract

*The paper presents early results of a 3-year project to establish an English – Norwegian text-and-term database (TERMINEC) representing the special languages of about 30 Economics/Administrative subdomains, sampled from textbooks, research articles and newspaper/journal material. Initial sampled text for each language will be of the order of half a million words, to be expanded by regular monitoring. The English-language textbank is approaching 20% of this volume and already allows pilot testing of available software for text bank operation, term extraction and management. By trawling through a subset of this preliminary test corpus we are able to make a number of observations about the lexical makeup of the three subcorpora. Although the current holdings are far too small to produce representative results, they demonstrate some of the types of lexical-terminological knowledge that can be extracted from raw text through the study of frequency ranking and contamination, lexical weirdness ratios, collocations and multi-word sequences. TERMINEC will thus be able in the future to take on the role of clearinghouse and reference point for professional communication.*

## 1. Introduction: why a clearinghouse?

Globalization is all the rage these days, and nowhere is the impact felt more acutely than in the financial sector. National borders are no longer barriers to the free and rapid movement of capital, any more than they keep out the accompanying language of international business, i.e. English. As a result other languages and cultures, particularly 'lesser used' varieties like Norwegian with 4 million speakers, are placed under heavy pressure to either adapt or die as vehicles of professional communication. The threat of special domain losses is a real one.

What makes **special languages**[1] special is precisely their close involvement of the objects and processes of the real world. In handling the special lexical units used by domain experts, linguistic knowledge is necessary but not sufficient, since these units (collectively known as terminology) represent the essential concepts needed for defining, developing and communicating the knowledge that constitutes a given domain. When more than one national language is involved, the communication problems are aggravated, not only because countries and domain experts differ in their linguistic/terminological traditions and practices, but also because they may differ in their world view, their material and social cultures as well as their conceptualizations thereof. For example, the linguistic knowledge that the Norwegian term equivalent to the English *Bill of Exchange* is *veksel* (cf. Ger. *Wechsel*) is of limited use to someone lacking knowledge of the world in which such items play important roles.

Developing an interface which facilitates communication across national and domain borders is a challenge even under conditions of symmetry and relative stability; under conditions of asymmetry between the communication partners (say, English-Norwegian) and in times of rapid changes (say, economic globalization) it would appear to be an almost impossible task. If the subject matter is a moving target, tracking it by conceptual and linguistic means would be even more so. New concepts are being created in the professional community and migrate towards general usage, sometimes even grabbing front page headlines: *unit-link*, *derivatives* and *hedge funds* have recently enjoyed such instant attention. *Hedge funds* started life as the stuff that Nobel prizes are awarded for, then burst into the popular genres of the tabloid press, and has no doubt found its way into the textbook genre as well. At the time of writing *e-business* is very much in vogue (along with almost any noun with an *e-* prefix), and who knows what next month's financial headlines will bring?

This implies that simply registering the constitutive concepts of a given domain, including their manifestation through the terminology of one or more national languages, is not done once and for all. What is required is a more or less continual monitoring of the entire life cycle of any given term, from creation through extension and expansion to disuse and eventual death. The above are random examples of an ongoing process which is in fact quite normal, although the speed and intensity may vary with the times and the subdomain. Ideally the new or altered terms would need to be absorbed by writers, their underlying concepts defined and systematized by domain experts and terminologists, standardized by professional bodies, and their usage documented through carefully vetted citations. At the receiving end of this process would be speakers of other languages (be they experts, journalists or textbook authors) who would ideally have to establish procedures for finding or creating equivalent terms and determine appropriate usage.

What has just been sketched in broad strokes is the complicated multilingual interface of cross-domain specialist communication. Fortunately the rapid development of Information Technology has placed tools within our reach which may enable even a lesser spoken language to cope, partly at least, with such major challenges (cf. Brekke et al. 1996). This presupposes a will to place cultural and terminological self defense on the political agenda by implementing policies to ensure that the interface with English is being handled with seriousness and professionalism, in the form of a clearinghouse to which domain experts, terminologists, linguists, translators and writers of various categories can turn for reference and documentation.

This paper describes Project TERMINEC, a three-year effort to establish the foundations of such a clearinghouse, intended as a resource database for Norwegian and English special language as used in economic-administrative domains (with possible later inclusion of French, German and Spanish). What follows below is first a description of the basic project architecture and design features along with the subdomains and text categories to be included. Based on the holdings as of April 2000, results are then presented of a pilot project probing the text bank for distinct lexical profiles through 'Tales of the Unexpected': frequencies, quirks and collocations form the basis of a preliminary search for viable term candidates. Lastly an indication of the main uses as well as problems and preliminary conclusions round off the exposition.

## 2. TERMINEC: design features

### 2.1 Architecture

The foundations of the TERMINEC database are formed by two parallel text corpora, one English, one Norwegian, of representative text from about 30 economic-administrative subdomains, and a parallel term database whose contents are largely derived from and dynamically linked to the text corpora. One of the pillars is thus a **textbank**, a representative corpus of indexed whole texts in the chief genres associated with didactic, expository and popularizing text types. The other pillar is a **termbank** holding domain-constitutive terms mapped to their respective concepts and conceptual hierarchies, classified as to subdomains, cross-referenced to synonyms, other language equivalents etc.

There will be dual linkage of terms and authentic segments in the textbank, allowing source inspection and evaluation by user. The focus is on the identification of key concepts, establishing conceptual hierarchies, definitions, terminological representations, Norwegian-English equivalence problems and contrastive phraseology. The aim is to facilitate the representation, learning, teaching and dissemination of relevant domain knowledge, to monitor changes in and development of the subdomain languages and to document all through authentic citations.

### 2.2 The material

The textual basis for the envisaged corpus can be conceived of as a matrix taking didactic (e.g. textbooks), expository, (e.g. research articles) and popularizing material (e.g. newspaper and journal articles) as column headings. Three simple reasons underlie the selection of just these three text types: they all play a central role in the study and teaching of economic-administrative text, as well as research underlying these. Each can be expected to manifest clear contrasts with the other two, along interesting parameters, and an abundance of representative authentic text samples is readily available. This is not the case for transactional text, which is central in business communication, otherwise an obvious fourth candidate for inclusion in the project. The study of business communication is clearly in need of a broader empirical foundation and thus deserves a project of its own. Approximately 30 economic-administrative domains/subdomains will constitute the rows in this matrix, along the lines suggested in Table 1.

**Table 1:** Tentative economic-administrative domains/subdomains

| |
|---|
| Accounting and Costing, Capital markets, Corporate analysis, Corporate law, Corporate strategy and Ethics, Economic geography, Economic history, Economics, Economy systems and management, EU/EEA law, Finance, Investment, Information systems & management, Law, Macroeconomics, Management, Market communication, Market economics, Market research, Marketing, Mathematics and statistics, Microeconomics, Organization and management, Organizational behavior, Public economy, Quality management, Tax law, etc. |

### 2.3 Sampling criteria

TERMINEC will from the start be equipped with functions and routines which allow continuous maintenance and periodic updating, to preclude its turning into a 'mausoleum' of the special languages and terminology of bygone times. Rather than constituting a closed universe the corpus will gradually, as already foreshadowed, become a 'monitor corpus' reflecting the fact that professional domain knowledge is not fixed once and for all, but rather flows dynamically through communication between living users.

Ideally every text sample should be a complete whole, but for copyright reasons the user will not be able to download entire texts but only paragraphs, enough to render a given term unambiguous in its co-text (on the order of one screenful). As regards textbooks a given title will only contribute one text, as far as possible a whole chapter, sampled alternatively from the first, middle or last third of the book. The question of representing non-linguistic material (formulae, graphs, illustrations etc.) is still open; as a minimum the location of such material will be marked in the text (a la BNC), but the digital storage of multimedia elements is currently making such great strides that it may not be considered a problem very much longer.

After this brief outline of the overall plans, and before wading too deep into the ocean of available domain text (cf. Brekke 2000a), it might be worth trying to catch a glimpse of the potential benefits that can be expected to accrue from the envisaged textbank/termbank. At the time of writing the text bank holds about 100,000 words in 32 texts over eight subdomains. For test purposes we have selected a subset of three subcorpora from subdomains listed in Table 1: Economics (where we have selected one scholarly (SCHOL) and one popularizing (ECO) subcorpus, and Organizational Behavior, where we have picked a didactic (OB) subcorpus).

## 3. Empirical interlude: probing the pilot corpus

### 3.1 Occurrence phenomena

In the following we will explore a set of heuristics with a view to revealing the lexical profiles of three selected subcorpora in terms of a) their top 100 frequency lists, particularly with reference to the 'contamination' of higher (function word) frequency bands by lexical words, b) their lexical deviation from general language text (or 'weirdness'), c) their respective use of shared items (namely **role** and **growth**), d) their respective lexical uniqueness (as viewed via **productivity**, **groupthink** and **slowdown**). We will also consider differences in collocational patterns of the same lexical items before looking briefly at the results of an attempt at automatic term extraction. The general idea has been to approach the corpora from the angle of the ordinary corpus-oriented linguist dependent on commercially available software rather than that of the computational linguist designing his/her own tools. Hence the research instrument used here is the suite of corpus workbench programs known as SystemQuirk.[2]

### 3.1.1 Frequency ranking and contamination

It is generally the case that in a large general corpus (say, of 100 million words) the top frequency bands down to about rank 100 are occupied by function words, and that any contamination by content words in these ranges is likely to represent special and noteworthy cases. Similarly the number of content words which contaminate the higher function word bands of a given subcorpus could give a clue to its relative lexical deviation from a general corpus. In the case of a special language corpus the size can be far smaller than that required for a general corpus (see Ahmad and Rogers 1994 and endnote), but the 'normal' level of contamination would have to be established for smaller corpora.

As indicated in Table 2 the size of three subcorpora selected is about 15,000 words, with a total of nearly 50,000 for the entire test corpus. Of the three subcorpora OB is the least contaminated one in that there are only 29 content words among the 100 most frequent words (column 3). ECO is slightly more contaminated (34) while SCHOL is the most contaminated of the three (48 content words among the 100 most frequent), indicating perhaps the increased term density to be expected in research writing.

**Table 2:** TERMINEC test corpus; basic statistics.

| SUBCORPORA | WORDS | CHAR. | cw>fw | AWL | SENT. | WPS |
|---|---|---|---|---|---|---|
| ECO (news mag.) | 16848 | 87966 | 34 | **5.22** | 865 | **19.48** |
| OB (textbook) | 17434 | 93519 | 29 | 5.36 | 702 | 24.83 |
| SCHOL (j. article) | 14102 | 79016 | 48 | *5.60* | 487 | *28.96* |
| Total test corpus | 48384 | 260501 | | 5.38 | 2054 | 23.56 |
| Current holdings | 101311 | 510009 | | 5.34 | 4737 | 21.39 |

(The abbreviations appearing in the header row of Table 2 should be read as follows: CHAR. = characters, AWL = average word length, SENT. = number of sentences, WPS = words per sentence. Bold figures: lowest, italics: highest values). Table 2 thus makes clear that ECO, the news magazine text, has the shortest words and the shortest sentences, scoring considerably lower than OB, the textbook text. This is perhaps a little surprising in view of the semi-specialist readership assumed for *The Economist.* SCHOL, the journal article, contains the longest words and the longest sentences of the three pilot subcorpora, entirely consistent with the general expectation of an article written for a scholarly readership.

A standard frequency count of each subcorpus was performed and the results down to rank 100 arranged in a parallel synopsis (see Table 3). For practical reasons a superficial form of 'lemmatization' was undertaken, whereby the singular and plural form of nouns referring to the same concept (e.g. *group/groups*) were lumped together. Perhaps slightly more questionably, forms derived from the same stem (e.g. *economy/economic/economics*) were also subsumed under a single lexeme and their frequencies added up. As a result the top 100 table represents somewhat more than 100 word forms.

**Table 3:** TERMINEC frequency synopsis, top 100 items; content words boldface.

| *bd* | *frq* | *ECO-ITEMS* | *OB-ITEMS* | *SCHOL-ITEMS* |
|---|---|---|---|---|
| 1 | 1–10 | the of to and in a/an that is it for | the **group/s** of to a/an and in is that are | the of and in to a/an is **brenner** that as |
| 2 | 11–20 | as are this be have on by has but with | **member/s** or be for as more by it with **individuals** | for by on this it **capital** with has **market/s capitalist/s** |
| 3 | 21–30 | **internet** at their **america** not more than will **new** from | on this we **work** their they **decision/s** can have **organization/s** | be **crisis/es** are his which **financial** not **economic investment** from |
| 4 | 31–40 | **country/ies share/s economy year/s market/s fund/s** or they **growth price/s** | **norm/s role/s** when **task/s** if from one than but who | have **theory growth economy capitalism profitability class/es** or between **profit** |
| 5 | 41–50 | **productivity** its so one may **investor/s** been all **firms bank/s** | **performance** at not **status** these will **be-havior** its what other | been **development** at **fixed new** more long **credit system** such |
| 6 | 51–60 | **business company/ies** up other over if can such many would | **people** you has was each which all **cohesiveness** so **social** | other **finance bank/s production competit-ion** its also **relations accumulation contribution/s** |
| 7 | 61–70 | **economic** these much about most was which even also now | those **high** may **employees** there **time** together because been others | **state industrial approach** but can **analysis/es** they since **rate** one |
| 8 | 71–80 | **technology high risk** only **investment capital** because could **japan** there | would **conflict management** were within first like should **stage technique/s** | there over **marx restructuring** their if **based role international** us |
| 9 | 81–90 | into some **big** out **commerce** pension them **american** mr less | between how **instance** two up any do he his **process** | than these what **account falling term** was **world** no **squeeze** |
| 10 | 91–100 | do **long costs average** what **world inflation** no should **money** | likely many some **decisions expectations formal size** where about **important** | **theoretical short press economics historical** thus **productive** all most he |

On the other hand no purpose was served by listing proper names and other spurious items occurring in the relevant texts, and so the lists were purged of items like *Internet* (rank 21), followed by *America* (rank 24, in a British journal!) – it is no doubt a sign of the times that these two were the highest ranked content words in ECO – with *Japan* in 79th place. In the SCHOL list we chose to ignore the item *Brenner* (which turns out to be the name of the author against whom this long polemical article is directed) but decided to keep *Marx* for reasons which will become clear. On the whole we claim that the slight inaccuracies introduced by such editing will not substantially affect the generalizations attempted in the following.

In order to enhance the synoptic view of lexical uniqueness and overlap in the three subcorpora the content words of Table 3 were extracted and arranged in what might be dubbed a 'Venn table', a tabular representation of all the logical possibilities for overlap among three different categories (represented by the three subcorpora), see Table 4.

**Table 4:**'Venn table' of unique and shared content words among the top 100 items in all three corpora.

<table>
<tr><th>ECO</th><th>OB</th><th>SCHOL</th></tr>
<tr><td>country/ies, share/s, year/s, fund/s, price/s, firm/s, business, company/ies, technology, risk, big, commerce, pension, mr, long, costs, average, inflation, money</td><td>group/s, member/s, individuals, work, decision/s, organization/s, norms/s, task/s, performance, status, behavior, people, cohesiveness, social, employees, time, conflict, management, stage, technique/s, instance, process, decisions, expectations, formal, size, important</td><td>capitalist/s/m, crisis/es, financ/ial, theory/etical, profit/ability, class/es, development, fixed, new, credit, system, competition, relation, accumulation, contribution/s, state, industrial, approach, analysis/es, rate, Marx, restructuring, based, international, account, falling, term, squeeze, short, press, historical</td></tr>
<tr><td colspan="2">high</td><td></td></tr>
<tr><td></td><td colspan="2">role</td></tr>
<tr><td>capital, bank/s, economy/ic/s, growth, invest/or/ment,</td><td></td><td>market/s, new, product/ion/ive/ity, world,</td></tr>
<tr><td colspan="3">(none)</td></tr>
</table>

Examining first the unique content word sets (Table 4, first row, leftmost box, items ordered by descending frequencies), the ECO list reads like a concept inventory of international finance and business economics. The appellation *Mr* probably reflects the style of person-oriented news reporting. The OB frequency list is rather striking in that the content word *group/s* has penetrated all the 'normal' function word bands with the sole exception of *the*, which keeps its top position by a wide margin (1097 vs. 611). OB's lexical set obviously takes us into a subdomain of the social sciences, while the SCHOL frequency list (rightmost box) brings us back into a domain reminiscent of that of ECO. In quick succession we encounter terms familiar to students of the theory and practice of economics: perhaps the only remarkable feature here is the prominence of *Marx* (rank 73), which seems to cluster conceptually with e.g. *capital/ism/ist/s, profit/ability* and *class/es* to suggest a subject matter intimately involved with Marxist economic theory.

These were the corpus-specific content words among the top 100 items in each subcorpus (cf. Brekke 2000b). At the other extreme we should find the items shared by all three, which were none (last row of Table 4). Of greater theoretical significance, however, is the high number of SCHOL terms overlapping with the ECO list (second row from bottom, this is the one category where a 'Venn table' is inferior to the more space-consuming Venn diagram): about a dozen items which are cognates and/or share root/stem among the top 100 words point to a high degree of semantic and conceptual congruence in the two subcorpora, indicative of a shared domain and partially overlapping subdomains.

The third row from the bottom contains the item *role*, the only content word in the top 100 frequency table (rank 32) which OB shares with SCHOL (where *role* is ranked 78th)); *role* also appears in ECO but with much lower frequency. The fourth row from the bottom is occupied by the adjective *high*, the only content word in the top 100 list that SCHOL (with rank 62) shares with ECO (in rank 72).

The Venn-style frequency tabulation of our three subcorpora has thus highlighted an outstanding fact: except for the two items *role* and *high* there is no lexical overlap among the top 100 items between OB and the other two. The obvious implication is that the OB subject matter is equally far removed from the technical terms, concepts and the associated knowledge base of the bustling business world of ECO and the lofty academic argumentation of SCHOL.

We have now pursued the top-down perspective on the comparison of three subcorpora of the TERMINEC test corpus and identified the general lexical affinities of ECO and SCHOL, leaving OB in its own lexical niche as far as the 100 or so most frequent words are concerned.

### 3.1.2 'Weirdness'

An alternative measure of the lexical 'differentness' of a special language subcorpus can be calculated by comparing the frequency of selected items with their expected likelihood of occurrence in a general reference corpus, yielding a special language/general language ratio or 'weirdness ratio' as produced by SystemQuirk. A special corpus item not occurring in the general reference corpus will thus be assigned an infinite ('infl') ratio and is thereby flagged as either a typing error, a neologism, or a special-domain term candidate, as are also items with very high SL/GL ratios.

A preliminary comparison of the three subcorpora provides interesting clues to their respective lexical profile. ECO reveals as many as 148 infl-items (i.e. not present in the general reference corpus), while OB has 64 and SCHOL 61 such. The implication is that in comparison with general language text ECO has a considerably larger set of special domain terms than the other two subcorpora. Our investigation needs to probe considerably deeper if the real significance of these clues is to be revealed.

### 3.1.3 Shared items: lexical overlap

The incidence of shared items in the three subcorpora (not just among the top 100) turns out to be insignificant, with two exceptions: the items *role* and *growth*. These are shared by all three corpora and with high frequencies in two of them. Table 5 indicates that *role* is marginal in ECO but strongly present in OB and SCHOL with a likely occurrence of 2,638 and 1,914 per million, respectively, and respective SL/GL ratio being above 17 and 10, which would put them (unlike ECO) at some distance from general language text. The item *growth* is marginal in OB but strongly present in ECO and SCHOL: its likely occurrence would be 3,739 and 4,041 per million, respectively, with a SL/GL ratio of almost 44 and over 40, respectively.

**Table 5:** Incidence of shared items

| *TEST ITEMS>* | *role* | | | *growth* | | |
|---|---|---|---|---|---|---|
| *SUBCORP.* | *frq* | */mill* | *SL/GL* | *frq* | */mill* | *SL/GL* |
| **ECO** | 3 | 178 | 1.16 | 63 | 3739 | 43.96 |
| **OB** | 46 | 2638 | 17.24 | 2 | 114 | 1.34 |
| **SCHOL** | 27 | 1914 | 10.62 | 57 | 4041 | 40.32 |
| **BNC written** | 18080 | 14.92 | | 12857 | 139.08 | |
| **bnc c&f** | 167 | 25.04 | | 2533 | 379.85 | |
| **bnc social** | 317 | 26.01 | | 2138 | 175.44 | |
| **WWW** | 9.6m | | | 9.8m | | |

For an indirect comparison (Table 5, bottom half) the item *role* has a likely occurrence of almost 15 per million in the British National Corpus[3] (and about 25 per million in its social as well as in its commercial and financial subdomains (c&f)), while the item *growth* has a likely occurrence of about 139 per million in the BNC (and almost 380 in commercial and financial subdomains, over twice that of social subdomains at 175). Both items are well represented in AltaVista's index as of April 2000 (9.6 and 9.8 million occurrences, respectively) and thus of very wide and varied usage.[4]

A general picture of the TERMINEC test corpus is now emerging: the two shared items *role* and *growth* reveal a statistical behavior which tentatively places ECO texts close to general usage in the case of *role*, and OB close to general usage in the case of *growth*. By the same token *role* is over-represented in OB and SCHOL (as well as in the social and commercial and financial subdomains of the BNC), while *growth* is even more over-represented in ECO and SCHOL (as well as in commercial and financial subdomains). But on the whole the degree of lexical overlap between ECO, OB and SCHOL has been shown to be quite modest.

### 3.1.4 Distinctive items: lexical uniqueness

In the preceding section we have tried to characterize the possible relatedness of the three subcorpora in terms of lexical overlap. We will now consider the opposite aspect, their unrelatedness in terms of distinctive lexical items with a significant presence in only one of them. Table 6 brings out the relevant figures for the items *productivity*, *groupthink*, and *slowdown*.

**Table 6:** Distinctive items

| *TEST ITEMS>* | *productivity* | | | *groupthink* | | | *slowdown* | | |
|---|---|---|---|---|---|---|---|---|---|
| *SUBCORP.* | *frq* | */mill* | *SL/GL* | *frq* | */mill* | *SL/GL* | *frq* | */mill* | *SL/GL* |
| **ECO** | 60 | 3561 | 234.63 | 0 | | | 4 | 237 | inf |
| **OB** | 21 | 1204 | 79.31 | 130 | 1456 | inf | 0 | | |
| **SCHOL** | 18 | 1276 | 71.36 | 0 | | | 16 | 1134 | inf |
| **BNC written** | 1933 | 20.28 | | 0 | | | 143 | 1.59 | |
| **c&f** | 399 | 59.83 | | 0 | | | 47 | 7.05 | |
| **social** | 331 | 27.16 | | 0 | | | 7 | 0.57 | |
| **WWW** | 2.2m | | | 7k | | | 114k | | |

*Productivity*, with 60 occurrences, ranks as item no. 41 on the ECO frequency table and thus among the top 100, making it not unique but about three times as common in ECO as in the other two. This is confirmed also by *productivity* having a three times higher likelihood of occurrence (3½ vs. 1¼ thousand occ. per million words) and a roughly three times higher weirdness ratio in special text, in ECO than in the other two. In the BNC general written material the likelihood of occurrence is 20 per million, while in the commercial and financial subdomains that figure is close to 60 (as compared with 27 for social). In other words, on the assumption that ECO represents a good sampling, the item *productivity* is a characteristic but not unique representative of *Economist* text. It occurs about 2.2 million times on the WWW.

With *groupthink*, however, we are in a very different situation. It is not among the top 100, is one of the 64 infl-items in OB (i.e. not present in the general reference corpus) and has a likelihood of occurrence of about 1,500 per million there, and is absent from the other two subcorpora and from the 100 million words of the BNC. The WWW interestingly has about 7 thousand occurrences. The overall pattern points to an item unique to the OB subdomain and a likely member of its professional jargon.

The item *slowdown*, finally, is absent from OB, is found 4 times in ECO but comes into its own in SCHOL with a significantly higher occurrence (almost 1,150 per million) even though it fails to make the top 100. It is one of the 61 infl-items in SCHOL. It is relatively rare in the BNC material but with a likelihood of 7 per million in commercial and financial subdomains. On the WWW it is found about 114 thousand times. All in all the occurrence profile of *slowdown* makes it a fairly good indicator of the lexical domain of the SCHOL text.

So far we have considered the occurrence of lexical items somehow characterizing the three subcorpora using simple and established techniques. We will now try to approach their lexical co-occurrence patterning by briefly surveying some of their collocations, a far less conventionalized procedure.

## 3.2 Co-occurrence phenomena

### 3.2.1 Identifying collocations

A considerable effort has gone into the search for statistical methods and measures that serve to bring out the co-occurrence patterns of specific lexical items in general as well as special text (e.g. Church et al. 1991, Lebart et al. 1998). However, as pointed out most forcefully by Stubbs (1995) the transfer of statistical techniques from mathematics to linguistics is not straightforward. Any measure of deviation from a norm (or expected situation) which assumes a totally random occurrence of the units under investigation will necessarily distort the description of the statistical evaluation of lexical units in text, whose occurrence is dictated by rigid syntactic norms. A random occurrence of words in successive strings would be rejected by any speaker of any language as representing a text of that language, even with perfect word recognition.

Despite such serious shortcomings there can be no doubt that the most commonly used statistical measures (e.g. MI, log likelihood, log-log, cf. Oakes 1998) can yield important insights into collocational patterns, and that such patterns in turn reveal very specific usage conventions of a given subdomain. Table 7 displays salient content word collocates of the five test items.

**Table 7:** Content word collocates among the top 20 collocates of the five test items

| *TEST ITEMS* | **ECO** | **OB** | **SCHOL** |
|---|---|---|---|
| ***role*** | small, relatively, redefined, **play**, banks, employers, find | expectations, perception, identity, individual, behavior/s, conflict/s, divergent | credit, mediating, **play, played, pivotal,** finance, stock, market, system, international, **important** |
| ***growth*** | **productivity, economic,** faster, output, high, increase, boost, **gdp** | **rate**, personal, groups, rated, person, income, higher, sex, companies, mixed, use | theory, new, **economic,** growth, low, capital, market/s, path, economy, **population** |
| ***productivity*** | **growth** gains, **manufacturing, improvements**, figures | group, cohesiveness, related, **low**, norms, performance, **high**, suggestions, influences, productivity | fall, **levels, higher, increase**, rising, market, investment, **growth**, wages |
| ***groupthink*** | | phenomenon, disease, groups, demonstrated, appears, characteristics, deadly, called | |
| ***slowdown*** | **sharp,** years, germany, recession, **productivity,** 1972, **growth,** ubiquitous, japan | | long, boom, least, followed, crisis, recent, global |

Boldface items are among the respective top 20 collocates (log-log) in the BNC.

### 3.2.2 Top collocates of shared items

In the case of the two shared items selected for the present study, Table 7 (top section) establishes the top 20 collocates of *role* and *growth* within a window of +/- 3 units to the left and right of the node, as expressed through a 'mutual expectancy' ratio ranging from 1 to –1. Boldface items in Table 7 also figure among the top 20 collocates of those nodes in the BNC material.

There are overlaps in the set of collocates in the three subcorpora: with *role* both ECO and SCHOL have *play/ed* as a collocate, with *growth* they both have *economic* high on the list, and ECO shares with OB the adjectival *high/er*. But the differences are much more interesting and informative as regards the word combinations characteristic of a given subdomain. In the ECO subcorpus only 7 of the 20 top collocates of *role* are content words. Noun collocates are *banks* and *employer*, the predicates *find* and *redefined* are prominent, as are the modifiers *relatively* and *small*. The ECO collocates of *growth* include the nouns *productivity*, *output* and *gdp*. It collocates closely with the verbs *increase* and *boost* and the adjective *faster*.

Moving next to the OB subcorpus the content word set of *role* collocates contains two adjectivals, *individual* and *divergent*, while the rest are nouns: *expectations*, *perception*, *conflict/s*, *identity* and *behavior/s*. The set of *growth* collocates comprises *rate/d*, which is also in the BNC but not in ECO or SCHOL. It is the obvious second member of the term *growth rate*. *Person/al, groups, income* and *companies* seem well motivated members (whereas the inclusion of *sex* calls for further investigation!).

It now remains for us to deal with shared items in the SCHOL subcorpus. Top *role* collocates are the nouns *credit, finance, stock, market* (including the term *stock market*) and *system*; the adjectivals *mediating, pivotal, international* and *important*. The *growth* collocates, in addition to *economic/economy* which SCHOL shares with ECO and *market/s,* which *growth* also shares with *role*, are the following nouns: *theory*, *capital* (also as part of *capital market*), *path* and *population*; interestingly enough *growth* also collocates with *growth*, which prompts a quick look at the text:

(1) productivity growth and wage growth have declined.
(2) low growth and high growth equilibria

One adjectival stands out with *growth*, namely *new*, but no verbs are noteworthy.

### 3.2.3 Top collocates of distinctive items.

If we proceed now to a charting of the top 20 content word collocates of *productivity*, *groupthink* and *slowdown* (cf Table 7, lower half), which we found distinctive of the vocabulary of ECO, OB and SCHOL, respectively, it cannot escape notice that in ECO only five of the top 20 collocates of *productivity* are content words (all nouns) and none of them with especially high ratios. But three of them are also among the BNC top 20, namely *growth, manufacturing* and *improvements*, in addition to *gains* and *figures; growth* as a collocate of *productivity* is also shared with SCHOL.

Since ECO does not contain the OB-item *groupthink* it has of course no collocates either, but ECO does have some occurrences of *slowdown*, the distinctive SCHOL item. Here an interesting point emerges, namely the high ratios in ECO expressing a close collocability of *slowdown*, especially with the adjectival *sharp*; less so with *ubiquitous*. *Slowdown* in ECO further collocates with the nouns *productivity*, *years* and *recession*, the country names *Germany* and *Japan* (not surprisingly for a text written in the aftermath of the Asian financial crisis in the late 90's) and the year *1972*.

The OB subcorpus should be a prime arena for *groupthink* and associated items, which is indeed the case, although all ratios are quite low (.07). Top *groupthink* collocates are the nouns *phenomenon*, *groups* and *characteristics*, plus the rather surprising *disease*, not to mention the adjective *deadly*. In the predicate category we find *appears*, *demonstrated* and *called*.

But the OB subcorpus also contains the distinctive ECO item *productivity*, which collocates with the singular *group* as well as with the nouns *cohesiveness, norms, performance, suggestions, influences* (N/V) and, more intriguingly, *productivity* itself; here is the textual basis:

(3) cohesiveness influences productivity and productivity influences cohesiveness

The predicate *related* turns up here, as do the adjectives *low* and *high* (also on BNC's top 20 list).

Turning finally to the SCHOL subcorpus, only seven content words are among the top 20 collocates of the distinctive item *slowdown*, with quite low ratios. We find here only two nouns, *boom* and *crisis*, the adjectivals *long, recent* and *global*, the predicate *followed* and the quantifier *least*. As noted earlier SCHOL also contains the item *productivity*, which now collocates with *growth* (shared with ECO) and *high/er* (cf. *high* in OB), and with *increase* and *levels*; all four are among the BNC top 20 collocates for *productivity*. Additional nouns are *fall* (V?), *market, investment* and *wages*, and the single predicate *rising*.

Taking an overall retrospective view of the collocates of the three distinctive items surveyed here, many share certain domain-related semantic fields. Thus under *productivity* ECO and SCHOL, in addition to sharing *growth*, are clearly associated via items like *gains, improvements, fall, levels, increase* and *rising*. Under *groupthink* nothing links it to the ECO and SCHOL subdomains, whereas under *slowdown* (where *growth* and *productivity* turn up again) we may have semantic links between *recession* and *boom/crisis*. Whether *ubiquitous* and *global* should be thus linked is a moot question.

### 3.3 From single items to multi-word terms

SystemQuirk offers, on an experimental basis, a tool for ferreting out possible terminology candidates, among sequences of content words that are uninterrupted by function words and fixed expressions which are unlikely to be part of terms. Table 8 lists the 30 most frequent such multi-word sequences in the three subcorpora.

Although the need for further refinement of the stop-list employed by SystemQuirk here is rather obvious, one must admit that a domain expert will recognize a number of automatically extracted term candidates among the examples that we have sorted into the top row. Those in the second row must be considered more undesirable output or noise, while the third row contains downright junk, largely caused by the program's inability to handle genitive *'s* once it has been split from its noun, probably not a serious problem.

**Table 8:** Subdomain multi-word term candidates

| ECO | OB | SCHOL |
|---|---|---|
| capital markets, pension funds, mutual funds, life insurers, information technology, institutional investors, share prices, retail sales, cost savings, world bank, foreign aid, emerging economies, supply chain, short term, | group members, work group, group development, delphi technique, group decision, social loafing, group size, nominal group technique, role perception, related norms, work groups, electronic meetings, role conflict | financial system, fixed capital, class conflict, capitalist crisis, mainstream economics, profit squeeze, productive forces, capitalist competition, smithian marxism, feudal crisis, profit squeeze approach, political economy, labour relation, |
| see charts, less than, past decade, this year, on average, recent years, since America, point out, but there, this survey, other countries, but even, poorest countries, | evidence indicates, more likely, this section, great deal, same time, we found, more complex, each other, individual members, other words, other hand, other group members, given situation, larger groups | falling profitability, other hand, so on, other words, same token, this respect, this connection, united states, not least, at least, competitive struggle between capitals, long downturn, world economy |
| s economy, b2b e, s gdp | s performance, s members, s task | s contribution, s account, s approach, s theory, |

### 3.4 Retrospective overview

By trawling through a subset of the preliminary test corpus destined for inclusion in a future TERMINEC text bank, we have in the preceding section made a number of observations about the lexical makeup of the three subcorpora, and some of the more salient similarities and differences among them. Although the current holdings are far too small to produce representative results, the experimental assaying they allow through the use of frequency ranking and contamination, lexical weirdness ratios, collocations and multi-word sequences has demonstrated the types of lexical-terminological knowledge that can be extracted from raw text and refined into useful representations. As the number of texts and subdomains in the TERMINEC text bank increases, so do the odds for uncovering more interesting and revealing generalizations about the form and content of special language genres in parallel languages.

We now return to the general theme by briefly considering the uses of the planned textual/terminological resource bank.

## 4. Future dissemination and use

It is assumed that the problems currently being debated regarding intellectual property rights to electronically stored material will find an acceptable solution for source text, database entries as well as derived user-oriented products. At the outset the TERMINEC material will be accessible for graduate and doctoral research and for academic papers. It will likewise form the basis for student-oriented bilingual domain glossaries with definitions, as well as genre-related material for learning and teaching.

Both textbank and termbank will be SGML conformant, adhering as far as possible to the TEI guidelines, which allows interactive access via a Web-browser or ftp downloading. In addition all or parts of the termbank may be distributed on CD-ROM. Printed versions are possible, but the main emphasis will be on interactive use via electronic networks.

This will take full advantage of the dynamic aspects of electronic media, allowing e.g. fuzzy matching of any search to the nearest form. All searches will be logged to allow a study of user behavior and user needs, with a view to enhancing the intuitiveness of the user interface. Following an unsuccessful search, the user will be asked to report unfound terms and submit a relevant text segment with source reference, and will have a chance to include responses or comments. It will be considered whether users also should be invited to join an 'official' discussion group. Success in engaging the user in such dynamic interaction will not only provide a way of monitoring a continuous growth of the collection but may also create greater user identification with the termbase, which in turn may have a standardizing effect.

A well-documented and web-accessible clearinghouse for English-Norwegian economics text and terminology as envisaged here would establish a point of reference not just to facilitate student learning, but also for empirically based term formation and possibly standardization, thus providing Norwegian export oriented corporations with a much needed quality assurance of the linguistic interface. The same would hold for the State's administrative and political cooperation with the outside world, as well as for the global language industry, which depends on the availability of multilingual databases and some form of translation. The realism of trying to stem the flood of English usage in conducting the professional affairs of people whose normal mode of communication is something other than English is highly debatable, but the virtue of avoiding linguistic domain losses in Norwegian is not.

## Notes

1 English lacks a term as precise as the German *Fachsprache* for referring to the variety of language used in an occupational domain.

2 SystemQuirk: http://www.mcs.surrey.ac.uk/Research/CS/AI/SystemQ/

3 BNC: http://info.ox.ac.uk/bnc/
BNCweb: http://escorp.unizh.ch/ or hmlehman@es.unizh.ch or sebhoff@es.unizh.ch

4 There is no obvious explanation at hand for the discrepancies in the figures for occurrences per million words between the BNC and the TERMINEC test corpus. Perhaps these are distortions introduced into any investigation by small samples, in which case it would be a clear indication that even a sample size of 15,000 words of special language text would be grossly inadequate for the present purposes.

**References**

Ahmad, K. and M. Rogers (1994). 'Computerised terminology for translators: the role of text'. In M. Brekke, O. Andersen, T. Dahl and J. Myking (eds) *Applications and implications of current LSP research*. Bergen: Fagbokforlaget. 840–851.

Brekke, M., J. Myking and K. Ahmad (1996). 'Terminology management and lesser-used living languages: a critique of the corpus-based approach'. In *Proceedings of 4th International Congress on Tterminology and Knowledge Engineering* (TKE '96). Vienna: Indeks Verlag. 179–189.

Brekke, M. (1999). 'TERMINEC: the dual linkage of text and terminology'. In *Proceedings of 5th International Congress on Terminology and Knowledge Engineering* (TKE '99). Vienna: Indeks Verlag. 330–342.

Brekke, M. (2000a). 'From the BNC to the cybercorpus: a quantum leap into chaos?'. In Kirk, J. (ed.) *Corpora galore: proceedings of the 19th ICAME Conference*. Amsterdam: Rodopi. 227–247.

Brekke, M. (2000b). 'On the lexical identification of domain focal text and terminology'. *Proceedings of COMLEX 2000*. University of Patras, Greece. 55–58

Church, K. et al. (1991). 'Using statistics in lexical analysis'. In Zernik, U. (ed.) *Lexical Acquisition: Exploiting on-line resources to build a lexicon*. Hillsdale, New Jersey: Lawrence Erlbaum Associates. 115–164.

Lebart, L., A. Salem and L. Berry (1998). *Exploring textual data*. Dordrecht: Kluwer Academic Publishers.

Oakes, M. (1998). *Statistics for corpus linguistics*. Edinburgh: EUP.

Stubbs, M. (1995). 'Collocations and semantic profiles. On the cause of the trouble with quantitative methods'. *Functions of language* 2(1): 1–33.

# Vaguely speaking: a corpus approach to vague language in intercultural conversations

*Neil Drave*

City University of Hong Kong

**Abstract**

*This paper presents findings from the initial stage of an ongoing, corpus-based study into the forms and functions of vague language in intercultural conversations. The corpus consists of 30 hours of naturally occurring conversation in English between native speakers of English (NSE) and native speakers of Cantonese (NSC), recorded in Hong Kong. A concordancing program was used to identify all examples of the three main types of vague language and to detect major distributional patterns in a sample of the most frequent items. It was found that, while NSE participants use more vague language than NSC participants, the range of different types was similar for the two groups of speakers, as were major collocations. However, there were important functional differences, notably the greater NSE exploitation of vague language for affective and interpersonal purposes. These are illustrated using the example of* stuff.

## 1. Introduction

This paper reports on ongoing research into the functions of vague language in a corpus of intercultural conversations in Hong Kong.[1] The research derives from an interest in two areas, vague language and intercultural pragmatics, and seeks to address gaps in both areas of research and to find ways in which the study of one can illuminate the study of the other. The study is corpus-based and draws upon familiar work in Gricean pragmatics and Conversation Analysis to inform the explanation of usage differences between native speakers of Cantonese and of English as they converse in English.

In this paper, I first define vague language and briefly summarise relevant research. I go on to describe the corpus of conversations used in the study and present some preliminary findings from the quantitative phase in which a small selection of exemplars were studied using concordancing software. I then look more closely at one vague language exemplar and conclude with some brief remarks on the relevance of corpus methods for researching conversational pragmatics.

## 2. Vague language

Vague language (hereafter VL) may be defined as that which modifies a linguistic item, phrase or utterance to make its meaning less precise (cf. Channell 1994: 20). In this study VL comprises a closed set of items which are inherently or purposively (Powell 1985: 31) vague in that it is impossible to paraphrase their meaning in a precise (non-vague) fashion. Various terms have been used in the literature to refer to VL, with one influential early study calling it 'approximation' (Prince et al. 1982: 85).

Vagueness as defined here has a certain degree of semantic overlap with hedging, since both are concerned with conveying the relationship between a speaker/writer and the matter of an utterance/statement, which places both within the domain of epistemic modality (Hyland 1998: 44). For our present purposes, it may be convenient to think of VL as a sub-category of hedging (cf. Hyland 1998) since VL is more specifically concerned with propositional precision or exactness.

It is necessary to make a distinction between VL, a concern of linguists, and vagueness, a concern of philosophers, and in so doing to work with a natural-language conception of what is vague rather than a logical one. The basic framework for types of VL has been adopted with minor modifications from the seminal work of Channell (1983, 1985, 1990, 1994) and includes the following types of VL:

- Number approximations
  A word or phrase is added to a precise figure to signal a vague reading e.g. *about* 12, 5 *or* 6
  A sub-category of 'partial specifiers' indicates that the approximation is either more or less than the named figure e.g. *at least* 20, *under* 100
- Non-numerical vague quantifiers (indeterminate)
  Vagueness is indicated by vague words or phrases rather than by using numbers e.g. *several* people, *a lot of* books
- Vague category markers
  A vague 'tag' is added to a lexical item (usually a noun) in order to indicate that this item exemplifies a category (natural or otherwise) e.g. fish *or something*, lectures *and so on*
- Placeholder words e.g. *thing*, *stuff*
  These words stand on their own as replacements for other, more specific nouns.

Different researchers favour different terms for these VL types. For example, Overstreet (1999) calls category markers 'general extenders' because they are non-specific and function to extend otherwise grammatically complete utterances. Overstreet also emphasises the interpersonal function of such items over the categorisation function (*contra* Channell 1994). While I too adopt this kind of approach, for various reasons I have chosen to retain Channell's terminology.

While these types of VL share the property of propositional imprecision (this is their 'family resemblance' in Wittgensteinian terms) it is quite possible for the same VL items to perform different specific functions and for similar functions to be instantiated using different lexis. I therefore follow Hyland (1998: 186) and others in viewing the typology of VL expressions as consisting of several fuzzy categories with protean boundaries.

The major function of VL is to tailor conversational contributions to the perceived informational needs of the other participant(s) so as to maintain and enhance the ongoing relationship. Specific functions include:

- Filling lexical gaps (where a speaker cannot recall a word or where one does not exist in the language)
- Filling knowledge gaps (memory lapse)

- Emphasising (and de-emphasising) certain information
- Deliberately withholding specific information
- Conveying tentativeness
- Conveying an evaluation of, or expectation about, a proposition
- Maintaining an atmosphere of friendliness, informality or deference.

There are epistemic (propositional) and affective meta-functions here: changing the degree of specificity of discourse may reflect knowledge or vocabulary limitations on the part of the speaker, but also contributes to the overall tenor of the conversation and thus to the achievement and maintenance of interpersonal goals. It is very difficult to determine which of the functions (or motives) is in evidence for any single VL item, but this list of functions is nevertheless a necessary, preliminary heuristic for approaching the study of VL.

Previous studies, from which the preceding frameworks were derived, have provided a useful start in describing the scope of reference of VL items in L1 conversation, and situating them broadly within a Gricean pragmatic framework of information manipulation (Grice 1975). However there is much more to be said about where and why VL is used; in other words, about the strategic uses of VL in naturally occurring conversations, for promoting politeness and intersubjectivity (cf. Drave, Cheng and Warren 1996; Overstreet 1999) and for managing asymmetries of knowledge (Drew 1991: 21), particularly in intercultural interaction. In the following section, I describe the aims and methods of the study as a whole, before moving on (in section 4) to talk about the preliminary quantificational findings which are the main focus of this paper.

## 3. Aims of the research

The central concern of this research is to determine whether intercultural conversations in Hong Kong exhibit vagueness, to discover the nature of vagueness exhibited, and to determine its effect on communication. Intercultural conversations are here restricted to conversations in English between adult native speakers of English (hereafter NSE[2]) and adult native speakers of Cantonese (NSC), recorded in Hong Kong. The approach is mainly lexical but any implications for discourse coherence will also be considered at a later stage.

While there has been a great deal of work on intercultural interaction (e.g. Piirainen-Marsh 1995), very few studies qualify as useful and defensible discussions of naturally occurring casual conversation. If there is a corpus at all, rarely is the corpus large enough to shed light on interesting linguistic patterns and often the data are so unnatural as to be of limited use for drawing conclusions about how real people behave in the real world (because they are role-plays, for example). This study attempts to rectify these inadequacies using a large corpus of naturally occurring data, as described in the following section.

## 4. Corpus

The corpus for this study was selected from the Hong Kong Corpus of Conversational English (HKCCE), a growing body of intercultural conversational data held at the HK Polytechnic University (for details, see Cheng and Warren 1999). The recordings were done by members of the research team (including myself) and research assistants. The majority selected for my corpus were recorded in 1997 and 1998 in food courts and restaurants (i.e. they are private conversations in public places) using digital mini-disc recorders. Participants' permission was obtained before the recording began, in line with the guidelines on ethical research promulgated by the HKPU and City University of Hong Kong, and personal details were collected using a short pro-forma.

The details of the corpus are:

- Number of words: 182,518 (NSE 98,310, NSC 84, 208)
- Hours: approximately 30
- No. speakers: 222 (NSE 104, NSC 118)
- No. conversations: 84
- Transcribed (using a modified version of Jefferson's well known conventions)

This is a small corpus compared to many published ones, but for a project of this size it would seem to be large enough. It is unparsed and untagged, except that when using the concordancing program *Wordsmith Tools*, I have identified whether each VL item was spoken by an NSE or NSC.

The conversations in the corpus for this study are considered to be intercultural in the sense that at least one participant was born in Hong Kong and is a native speaker of Cantonese, and at least one other was not born there and is a native speaker of English. Prevailing opinion seems to be that any general notion of 'culture' is of limited use when it comes to explaining the moment-by-moment behaviour of participants in interaction (Sarangi 1994, 1995; Shea 1994; Scollon 2001): in other words, even if culture can be identified as a variable in interaction, how is it operationalised and how can one identify its effects? It would seem necessary to adopt an open-minded and socio-critical approach to conversations in which members of different language groups come together and to be wary of ascribing all differences in language to cultural differences, even when these can be relatively easily identified. This 'non-essentialist and action-oriented' perspective on culture (Sarangi 1994: 416) is a necessary antidote to a neo-Whorfian (Gumperzian) one, which claims that differences in linguistic behaviour are always due to differences in cultural practices. The choice of the term intercultural should therefore be regarded as a convenience rather than as programmatic, intended to indicate only that there are two groups of speakers with different first languages.

## 5. Quantitative findings

This section presents illustrative preliminary findings from what might be called the piloting phase of the wider research, in which concordancing methods were tried on a small sample of data. The aims of this phase were to compare the two sets of speakers in terms of the amount and types of VL they used, as well as to try out concordancing methods on a small sample of data to determine whether to apply them to the whole data set. Due to space limitations, only four kinds of findings are reported here:

(i) Amount of VL used by NSE and NSC
(ii) Types of VL used by NSE and NSC
(iii) Patterns: collocation and clustering
(iv) Functional differences between NSE and NSC: the case of *stuff*

### 5.1 Amount of VL used by NSE and NSC

It seems that NSE are 'vaguer' than NSC. A frequency count of the number of VL expressions (tokens) which occur more than once revealed that NSE used approximately 1500 in total (59%), while NSC used around 1050 (41%). The total number of lexical items which form part of vague expressions was also counted: in number approximations, for example, the number itself was discounted so that *about 50* was counted as one word while *50 more or less* was counted as three words. It was found that approximately 3.4% of the NSE's word total is vague, compared to around 2.7% for NSC. The range of vague expressions (types) was similar, however, with only two used exclusively by NSE.

This means that around 3% of the words in the corpus form part of vague expressions, a relatively small proportion compared to similar research but understandable given the narrower scope of the present work. In Nikula's (1996) study of pragmatic force modification in Finnish-English conversations, 9.7% of words were found to have a modifying function, but the range of devices at issue was much larger in her study since it included modal verbs and other hedges. Kennedy (1987) found that around 14% of words perform a quantifying function, but this figure includes non-vague quantifiers.

### 5.2 Types of VL favoured by NSE and NSC

It was expected that NSE would use VL which NSC did not. The findings were contrary to expectations, with very few VL items being used exclusively by one group or the other and the rank orders of the most frequent items virtually identical. Neither NSE nor NSC use the full range of VL items available in English: of the 150-odd possible VL items, roughly half did not occur at all and seven occurred only once. As an example, a comparison of the most frequently used VL of the type 'number approximation' is given below (Table 1).

**Table 1:** Most frequently occurring number approximations, in descending order

| VL item<br>(Overall number of occurrences in brackets) | NSE | NSC |
|---|---|---|
| *about* n<br>(225) | *about* n (128) | *about* n (97) |
| n *or* m*<br>(167) | n *or* m * (102) | n *or* m (65) |
| *maybe* n<br>(70) | *maybe* (37) | n *to* m (33) |
| n *to* m<br>(35) | n *to* m (17) | *maybe* (18) |
| Overall % | 55% | 45% |

* *Note: n = first number, m = second number e.g. 15 or 20*

The rank order here is identical except for *maybe* and *n to m*, whose rankings are reversed. The rankings for all other exemplars were very similar, which suggests that there are very real similarities between the VL usage of NSE and NSC participants, especially in the matter of preference for certain VL exemplars. While on the whole the NSE participants use more VL, there is no indication that they are using items which the NSC do not know. One explanation for this is that Cantonese has a large number of vague quantifying and other expression expressions: in a recent focus group discussion on this issue, I found that all but the most obscure and infrequent English VL has a Cantonese equivalent. The one interesting difference is that the NSC use 'etcetera' as a vague category marker while NSE do not. One might speculate that NSC carry over this genre-inappropriate item (a written, rather academic lexical item) because of the greater emphasis placed on writing in the Hong Kong education system (cf. De Cock et al. 1998).

### 5.3 Patterns: collocation and clustering

To determine whether it would be a useful approach for all the data, I decided to look at the collocational patterning associated with the most frequently used VL items by selecting the top two numerical and non-numerical approximators, as well as the most common category marker and placeholder. It was thought that this might illuminate interesting similarities or differences in the kinds of things which are 'vaguified' (collocations) and whether the two sets of speakers used similar vague phrasing (clusters). This exercise might be described as a piloting stage designed to determine whether it might be useful to adopt this approach for all VL exemplars. The findings are reported below, beginning with the numerical approximator *about*.

### 5.3.1 *About*

It was found that the type of lexical item which most often immediately follows *about* is a simple number (in the range 1–30) for both groups of participants, with the numbers 2 and 1 being the most common for NSE and NSC respectively. In the second position to the right of *about* the most common items are usually either time lexis ('years', 'minutes', 'hours') or a larger, base-ten enumerator ('100', '1000'). The concordancing program also revealed the relatively high frequency of the phrase *about the same* for both NSE and NSC (Table 2).

**Table 2:** Clusters *about*

| NSE | NSC |
|---|---|
| *about the same* | *about the same* |
| *about an hour* | *for about one* |
| *about two hours* | *about I think* |
| *about two years* | *about ten years* |

Both NSE and NSC display some use of idiomatic patterns (clusters), the most frequent being the same for both sets of speakers. All the NSE clusters, apart from the first, concern periods of time, whereas the NSC clusters are more varied.

### 5.3.2 *N or m*

The second most frequent numerical approximator was *n or m* (where *n* and *m* represent numbers). The collocation patterns are very similar for both sets of speakers and concern periods of time and money, with references to dollars occurring in both the first and second positions to the right of the vague expression. For both groups of speakers, right collocates which immediately follow *n or m* either refer to periods of time ('years', 'days', 'months') or round, base-ten enumerators ('100', '1000'), supporting Channell's (1990: 101) claim that reference point (round, particularly base ten) numbers are more likely to be vaguified than others. In the second position to the right of *n or m*, 'ago' commonly occurs, indicating that this expression is often used to manage recall of events in the past.

Channell (1994: 56) identifies constraints on the kinds of numbers which may be combined using *n or m*, suggesting, for example, that where the *n* number is a multiple of 10, the *m* number will be 10 above. She also notes that the difference between the two numbers increases along with the size of the numbers. The clusters here (Table 3) seem to conform to the suggested norms apart from *ten or eleven*, but it is easy to imagine a circumstance in which this would be perfectly acceptable.

**Table 3:** Clusters *n or m*

| NSE | NSC |
|---|---|
| *two or three* | *three or four* |
| *three or four* | *five or ten* |
| *four or five* | *one or two* |
| *an hour or* | *or thirty dollars* |
| *one or two* | *ten or eleven* |
| *six or seven* | *ten or twenty* |
| *half an hour* | *two or three* |

### 5.3.3 *A lot of*

This was the most frequent non-numerical approximator. The most frequent collocations were 'people', 'money', 'things' and 'work' for both groups, with the addition of 'places' for the NSC. Clusters were also very similar (Table 4). Clearly, there are grammatical and other similarities here, such as the head nouns relating to people and money, the only difference being the NSC reduplication in *lots and lots of* and the higher NSE ranking for the (hedged) *quite a lot of.*

**Table 4:** Clusters *a lot of*

| NSE | NSC |
|---|---|
| *a lot of people* | *a lot of people* |
| *quite a lot of* | *a lot of er* |
| *have a lot of* | *a lot of money* |
| *a lot of money* | *have a lot of* |
| *and a lot of* | *lots and lots of* |
| *a lot of the* | *quite a lot of* |

### 5.3.4 *Many*

This was the second most common non-numerical approximator. 'Not' as a left collocate ranks more highly for the NSE than for the NSC group. It is perhaps overly formal to use *many* as a determiner in a positive statement, except where premodified (Berry 1997: 106). The concordancer revealed that it is far more likely to be used in the negative ('not many'), in questions ('how') or with the intensifer 'too': there were no other collocates for the NSE, but in the NSC data, the verb 'have' also appeared as a collocate. One possible conclusion to be drawn from this is that the NSC may be less aware of usage constraints. However, the fact that the phrase 'I could have *many*' occurs as a common NSE cluster shows that this conclusion may be unwarranted (Table 5). Right collocates were identical for both groups: 'people', 'things', 'years', 'times', 'kinds' and 'choices' (in rank order).

**Table 5:** Clusters *many*

| NSE | NSC |
|---|---|
| *there are so many* | *I could have many* |
| *there are many many* | *I don't know how* |
| *I could have many* | *many many kinds of* |
| *I don't know how* | *many many times I* |
| *many many kinds of* | *many times I have* |

### 5.3.5 Partial specifiers, category markers and placeholders

There were no significant correlations for partial specifiers (*more*, *less*), vague category markers or placeholders. This may be due to the small number of exemplars of each type but perhaps also demonstrates that these forms can be used with all topics; they are freely combinable and give rise to fewer fixed patterns. The fact that they are relatively semantically empty makes them less amenable to concordancing analysis than more specific lexemes. Table 6 presents the clusters for the most common category marker, *or something.*

**Table 6:** Clusters *or something*

| NSE | NSC |
|---|---|
| *or something like that* | *or something like that* |
| *or something of that* | ___ |
| *something of that nature* | ___ |

There is some difference in the clustering here with the NSE using a cluster which the NSC do not. Table 7 presents clusters for the most common placeholder, *thing*.

**Table 7:** Clusters *thing*

| NSE | NSC |
|---|---|
| *that kind of thing* | *that kind of thing* |
| ___ | *that sort of thing* |
| ___ | *this kind of thing* |

The NSC display more variety in this case. No clusters occurred more than twice for *sort of.*

Once again, there would seem to be a remarkable similarity in the most frequent collocates, suggesting that, at least for these VL items, NSE and NSC are being vague about similar things. Number approximations naturally (by definition) expect a following number, but in the R2 position (i.e. two words to the right of the node word) one would expect considerable variation since it can be occupied by anything which can be quantified. Yet the most frequently occurring items are almost identical for the two sets of speakers; they overwhelmingly concern time, people, places, work and money. There does not seem to be any support for the claim that fixed expressions are more fixed for native than they are for non-native speakers (*contra* De Cock et al. 1998).

On this evidence, quantification using concordancing software is useful for getting an overall picture of how much VL is used by each type of speaker (NSE, NSC). However, an emphasis on frequency, as is necessitated by a quantitative approach to data analysis, can mask potentially interesting infrequent cases, and overemphasise repeated combinations of words in the immediate linguistic context. Since concordancing is based on high frequencies, it tends to focus on popular (i.e. high frequency) items, which might give learners of a language fewer problems because there will have been more exposure to them during the language learning process. Problems in VL usage might therefore be hidden by a concentration on high frequency items. Again, given that several types of VL are semantically empty and grammatically unrestricted, much of importance is also not amenable to collocational analysis. To find out more about how NSE and NSC actually use VL, it is necessary to look in more detail at the linguistic context of utterances, but with the attitude that even single instances can be revealing about speaker attitudes and motivations. Lack of space precludes a detailed discussion of all the VL in the corpus, but as an illustration of this more qualitative approach I use the example of *stuff* in the following section.

## 6. Usage: the example of *stuff*

Although the figures presented above seem to suggest a great deal of similarity in usage, we need to look more deeply into the functions and usage of VL before drawing conclusions. To that end, I examine below one VL exemplar, the category marker and placeholder *stuff*. The range of functions, epistemic and affective, performed by the VL in the NSE and NSC data are presented in order to illustrate the differences in usage between the two groups of speakers. There is obviously a limit to what can be understood from a single line of concordance printout, but I hope that this will be enough for the reader to at least get a sense of what is happening. The NSE participant is identified by use of a capital letter and the NSC by the use of a lower case letter.

### 6.1 NSE (54 occurrences)

The NSE uses *stuff* in a wide range of linguistic environments (with nouns, in lists, attached to clauses and so on), and as a placeholder

(1) which is quite nice if you like juicy stuff a: right B: but yeah I'm gonna h

and a category marker:

(2) B: some people got aunts and uncles and stuff there a: no no no I know I don't k

There is ample evidence of *stuff*'s usefulness as a compensator for linguistic inadequacy (or lack of knowledge) for example:

(3) this a a from six bottom you mix tiger stuff shark and snake in it is quite exp

The speaker may not have a clear idea of what he is talking about, or does not have the appropriate vocabulary, since the topic is Chinese medicine.

There is reference to categories that are readily accessible (though not necessarily lexicalised in English), for example clothing:

(4) walking around in shorts and T-shirts and stuff b: yea they are local people but

The mention of two category members allows one to infer which category is meant, perhaps 'very casual wear'.

*Stuff* compensates when the speaker lacks specialised scientific terminology:

(5) now you know because there's this beef stuff that you can get [diseases from [t

Encephalitis, BSE and 'Mad Cow Disease' are all possibilities here: the speaker has either forgotten or does not know the correct term.

VL can be useful as a circumlocutory device by a speaker who is not quite sure of what she wants to say:

(6) ul of sugar a: ((laughs)) B: all that stuff er you know when you look at for t

Several speakers use *stuff* to create what might be called fuzzy, ad hoc categories (after Barsalou, cited by Channell, 1994: 122):

(7) n something with their B: Bible memory stuff and see how we could a: really

Notice that even though there is no obvious category invoked by 'Bible memory *stuff*', there is no communication breakdown and speaker 'a' seems to understand what is meant.

The adjunctive *stuff* is used to convey the sense that there is more that might be said:

(8) about women when they're together and stuff= B: =and I know men are like

Speaker B is making some general comments on male-female relationships and feels that she does not have to go into greater detail to make her point.

Another use found here is for de-emphasising an item of information for rhetorical purposes so as to emphasise contrasting (more precise or well explained) information:

(9) the lunch they will simply to have some stuff fill their stomach. For dinner you

The contrast here is between lunch, a quick meal where getting full is the priority, and dinner, more leisurely and enjoyable.

*Stuff* can be used to convey a variety of stances such as incredulity,

(10) r the world or where do they get this stuff this stuff b: I don't know from US

as well as defensiveness,

(11) Nike (.) I'm not very good on that stuff A: anyway he went there after school

for deference or politeness through mitigation or softening, as in this case where potentially face-threatening advice is given,

(12) g right A: there is a lot of things or stuff you need to learn about B: quite

And pejoratively, often for humorous dismissiveness:

(13) A: I mean I don't wear that sportswear stuff particularly c: but there't a time

*Stuff* occurs at certain points within the discourse where the speaker takes stock of the general trend of what has been said and attempts to generalise. This is often preceded by a deictic:

(14) class so (.) mm A: you need to do that stuff I think= b: =mm (.) huh A: but ar

*Stuff* is also used in combination with deictics when the intended referent is easily identifiable:

(15) the case B: yea I would it leave that stuff on the floor d: you you won't get

Finally, there are many examples of what Hyland (1998: 150) calls 'harmonic combinations', where VL co-occurs with hedging or other VL types, for example 'kind of':

(16) t you you took A yea they keep track of stuff [ so it's kind of a neat system b

Thus there is tremendous variety in the uses to which *stuff* is put. It is grammatically flexible and can be used to convey, or reinforce, many different emotions. Overstreet (1999: Ch. 5) demonstrates that VL is useful not only epistemically for categorising and giving the 'right' amount of information but also for a range of interpersonal functions which suggest that speakers share knowledge and assumptions. The message is that specificity is unnecessary, and this suggestion of mutual familiarity enhances conversational rapport. The 'basic' use may be to compensate for lexical or other deficiencies (placeholder function) or to suggest that one could say more but prefers to suggest it instead, but *stuff* is obviously multi-dimensional. It does not work in isolation of course, but achieves these effects in combination with other verbal and non-verbal messages.

### 6.2 NSC (19 occurrences)

There are not as many examples from the NSC data so one would not expect such a great variety of functions. However, even taking this into account, the relative homogeneity of the data is noteworthy, as is the fact that *stuff* is never used as a category marker.

There is often a lexical item or phrase to replace *stuff* , for example:

(17) hose and [anatomical [and physiological stuff A: [yeah [yeah

*Stuff* could easily be replaced with 'subjects' here and does not seem to convey any sense of dismissiveness.

Sometimes an acceptable word (synonym) occurs within the lexical environment:

(18) a: =I I I like analysing data analysing stuff I like this so I_ I I just try my

In some cases there is linguistic (agreement) error,

(19) use) b: shall I go and get one of those stuff erm anyway A: yea okay thanks (pau

or redundancy (or at least nothing added to the core meaning):

(20) ax it off anyway m: how about the cover stuff do you have any A: yes [that's

The speaker is referring to the cover of a magazine so it is difficult to see what the addition of *stuff* adds to the message here. Once again, there is no reason to believe that the speaker is using the word pejoratively.

The use of *stuff* in the following example could be compensation for lack of intimate knowledge of the nature of the business (self-protection, since her elaborations are equally vague):

(21) firm yeah (.) working on communications stuff (.) so ah B: like what a: like t

On this evidence, it seems that NSC do not employ the full range of functions for which *stuff* can be used. Scrutiny of these utterances in context reveals that they are very much epistemic uses of VL and seem relatively unmotivated by affective concerns.

Similar findings have emerged in a preliminary look at occurrences of *sort of*. All of the functions of *sort of* noted by Aijmer (1984) occur in the NSE data, but only two can be found in the NSC examples. Holmes (1988) identifies epistemic and affective meanings of *sort of*, the latter within the tradition of politeness research, all of which are in evidence in the speech of the NSE. In contrast, the NSC make less affective use of *sort of* and there seem to be fewer harmonic combinations. Holmes's (1988) conclusion is that discourse type rather than speaker sex (her original object of investigation) largely determines the frequency of occurrence. My work suggests that, for intercultural interaction, another variable may be the native language of the speaker. The nature of these influences remains to be explored in greater depth.

## 7. Conclusion

On the strength of this preliminary work, it seems that the figures on preferred types of VL suggest a greater similarity than do the overall quantities (which show clearly that NSE participants are 'vaguer' than NSC), and the more detailed functional analysis. It is in this last area where the NSE emerges as the more skilled user of the language, making full use of this flexible linguistic resource. Note that there is little evidence here of NSE accommodation or of NSC communication strategies. There is also no evidence that the NSC inaccuracies and limitations hinder conversational cooperativeness or prevent the achievement of conversational goals, and while there are linguistic problems it is rather difficult to say whether there are also pragmalinguistic or sociopragmatic ones (Thomas, 1983: 91).

Various explanations are possible for the differences noted above. One is that the first language of the NSC participants interferes with their performance in English. This seems unlikely since Cantonese has a range of expressions which are functionally equivalent to both the placeholding and category marking functions of *stuff* (D. Li, personal communication 14 February 2001). There may of course be register restrictions on such forms in the first language which might preclude their use in the situations which arise in these data. Another possible explanation is an educational one. Perhaps it is the case that prevailing pedagogical methods do not allow for sufficient exposure to native language models which contain VL, such as informal conversation. Proving that these factors influence the acquisition of VL is a complex undertaking however, requiring the collection and analysis of additional data, and so is outside the scope of the present study.

For the next phase of the research it will be necessary to complement the approaches and methods described above, where the NSE and NSC data are essentially being treated as separate corpora, with one more in line with current thinking about best practice in the analysis of conversation. There is a need to take into account participant reactions to utterances (Schegloff 1992: 101) and to look at conversations in their entirety. The question is not only which *linguistic* environments cause people to use vague language, but which other environments do so, how these environments become instantiated and with what consequences. An interpretative framework is needed to aid understanding of a lexical item, and this may be very difficult to assemble from concordance lines alone: each line may have to be expanded to take into account larger chunks of discourse, up to and including the whole conversation. There can be no doubt that corpora of naturally occurring data are the best way forward for studies of conversation and, as de Beaugrande (1996) argues, it would be difficult to see how meaningful pragmatics research, which focuses on the various functions performed by utterances in different contexts, could be conducted in any other way.

## Notes

1 The research is being undertaken for a Ph.D. at City University of Hong Kong, under the supervision of Professor Chris Candlin.

2 For simplicity, the abbreviations 'NSE' and 'NSC' refer to both single speakers and groups of speakers.

## References


Aijmer, K. (1984). '"Sort of" and "kind of" in English conversation'. *Studia Linguistica* 38.2:118–128.

Beaugrande de, R. (1996). 'The "pragmatics" of doing language science: the "warrant" for large-corpus linguistics. *Journal of Pragmatics* 25:503–535.

Berry, R. (1997). *Collins Cobuild English guides 10: determiners and quantifiers*. London: Harper Collins.

Channell, J. (1983). *Vague language: some vague expressions in English*. Unpublished Ph.D. dissertation, University of York, UK.

Channell, J. (1985). 'Vagueness as a conversational strategy'. *Nottingham Linguistic Circular* 14: 3–24.

Channell, J. (1990). 'Precise and vague quantities in academic writing'. In Nash, W. (ed.) *The writing scholar: studies in the language and conventions of academic discourse*. Beverly Hills: Sage. 95–117.

Channell, J. (1994). *Vague language*. Oxford: Oxford University Press.

Cheng, W. and M. Warren. (1999). 'Facilitating a description of intercultural conversations: the Hong Kong Corpus of Conversational English'. *ICAME Journal* 23:5–20.

De Cock, S., S. Granger, G. Leech and T. McEnery. (1998). 'An automated approach to the phrasicon of EFL learners'. In Granger, S. (ed.) *Learner English on computer*. London: Longman. 67–79.

Drave, N., W. Cheng and M. Warren. (1996, July). 'Inexplicitness in conversations: a comparative study of native and non-native speakers of English'. Paper presented at the 5th International Pragmatics Conference, Mexico City.

Drew. P. (1991). 'Asymmetries of knowledge in conversational interactions'. In Markovà, J. and K. Foppa (eds) *Asymmetries in dialogue*. Hemel Hempstead: Harvester Wheatsheaf. 21–48.

Grice, H. P. (1975). 'Logic and conversation'. In Cole, P. and J. Morgan (eds), *Syntax and semantics 3: speech acts*. New York: Academic Press.

Holmes, J. (1988). '*Sort of* in New Zealand women's and men's speech'. *Studia Linguistica* 42.2:85–121.

Hyland, K. (1998). *Hedging in scientific research articles*. Amsterdam/Philadelphia: John Benjamins.

Kennedy, G. (1987). 'Quantification and the use of English: a case study of one aspect of the learner's task'. *Applied Linguistics* 8.3:264–286.

Nikula, T. (1996). *Pragmatic force modifiers: a study in interlanguage pragmatics.* Jyväskylä, Finland: University of Jyväskylä.

Overstreet, M. (1999). *Whales, candlelight, and stuff like that: general extenders in English discourse.* New York: OUP.

Piirainen-March, A. (1995). *Face in second language conversation.* Jyväskylä, Finland: University of Jyväskylä.

Powell, M. J. (1985). 'Purposive vagueness: an evaluative dimension of vague quantifying expressions'. *Journal of Linguistics* 21:31–50.

Prince, E., J. Frader and C. Bosk. (1982). 'On hedging in physician-physician discourse'. In Di Pietro, R. (ed.) *Linguistics and the professions.* Norwood, NJ:Ablex. 83–97.

Sarangi, S. (1994). 'Intercultural or not? Beyond celebration of cultural differences in miscommunication analysis'. *Pragmatics* 4.3:409–427.

Sarangi, S. (1995). 'Culture'. In Verschueren, J., J.-O. Osteman and J. Blommaert (eds) *Handbook of pragmatics 1995.* Amsterdam/Philadelphia: John Benjamins. 1–30.

Schegloff, E. (1992). 'On talk and its institutional occasions'. In P. Drew and J. Heritage (eds) *Talk at work: interaction in institutional settings.* Cambridge: CUP. 101–134.

Scollon, R. (2001). 'Intercultural communication and ethnography: why? And why not?' In Barron, C., N. Bruce and D. Nunan (eds) *Knowledge and discourse: language and ecology in theory and practice.* London: Longman.

Shea, D. (1994). 'Perspective and production: structuring conversational participation across cultural borders'. *Pragmatics* 4.3:356–389.

Thomas, J. (1983). 'Cross-cultural pragmatic failure'. *Applied Linguistics* 4.2:91–112.

# On the discourse marker *so*

*He Anping*

South China Normal University

## Abstract

*This study is triggered by the overuse of* so *in Chinese EFL learners' written English. It is based on a number of English corpora including the discourse of both native English speakers and learners of English in China. The discoursal use of* so *is investigated in terms of frequency distribution, sentence position and associated patterns. Comparison is also made between* so *in spoken English and its equivalent in spoken Chinese. The writer invokes four possible explanations for the overuse and inappropriate use of* so *by the Chinese EFL learners: 1) learners' unawareness of the stylistic impact in written language, 2) limitations in learners' exposure to English, 3) preference for the simpler/early-learned strategy, and 4) negative transfer from learners' mother tongue.*

## 1. Introduction

This is a corpus-based analysis of the word *so* in terms of its grammatical, discourse and pragmatic functions. The study was triggered by the overuse of *so* in Chinese EFL learners' written English. Some previous corpus studies have found the overuse and misuse of English connectives in EFL learners' written English (Tribble and Jones 1990; Field and Yip 1992; Milton and Tsang 1993; Field 1993, 1994; Granger and Tyson 1996). The causes of this problem were traced to negative transfer from learners' mother tongues, the influence of EFL teaching materials and teaching method, etc. The present study investigates this phenomenon in a number of corpora containing Chinese learners' written and spoken English, native English speakers' written and spoken English, and the equivalents of *so* in spoken Chinese as well. The assumption is that the overuse and inappropriate use of *so* by Chinese EFL learners may be due to their unawareness of the stylistic differences between written and spoken English and negative transfer from their mother tongue.

## 2. Relevant theory and concepts

*So* is a frequently used word in English with multiple functions and meanings. People often use it but may find it difficult to explain its exact meaning. According to the *Longman Dictionary of Contemporary English* (1997: 1363), *so* is first an adverb which means 'in this/that way' and indicates manner. One of its adverbial uses is similar to that of *thus* and *therefore,* which are used in more formal contexts. The second role of *so* is as a conjunction used to connect two clauses. It means 'therefore' or 'that's why', and indicates a logical outcome. The dictionary also highlights the different uses of *so* in spoken and written English. In the British National Corpus and the Longman Lancaster Corpus, the tokens of *so* in spoken data are about three times those of the written data. *So* in spoken English has the special function of getting someone's attention, asking a question about what someone has just said, showing that the speaker has understood something, or that the speaker does not think something is important, etc. The position of *so* shifts to sentence-initial, indicating a linking between two utterances. These kinds of usage indicate that *so* has in some ways lost its original meaning and become a discourse marker or a pragmatic particle instead. It has developed from a grammatical connector to a discourse item, serving one or more of the following discourse functions that are summarized by Schiffrin (1987) and Schleppegrell (1991) in their studies of discourse markers:

- bracketing units of talk
- enabling the speaker to hold the turn
- indicating continuation
- permitting the speaker to provide extra material
- doing metatextual work
- serving as a thematic link

(cited by Stenström, 1998:133)

Such a process of change can be illustrated in the following examples from the *Longman Dictionary of Contemporary English* (1997: 1363):

(a) Why does life have to be **so** complicated? (adjective modifier)
(b) The passport was found to have passed its expiry date and ***so*** to be void (consequential linker)
(c) I heard a noise **so** I got out of bed and turned the light on. (resulting connector)
(d) **So**, how long do you think you'll be staying in England? (question initiator, attracting listener's attention)
(e) A: I've decided to leave.
B: **So** what are you going to do?
(turn taking signal, connecting the previous turn)
(f) **So**, I lied. They can't put me in prison for that! (attitudinal signal: the speaker doesn't think something is important)
(g) **So**! You've got a new girlfriend, huh? (attitudinal signal: the speaker has just found out something about someone)

These examples illustrate three aspects of change in *so*:

(i) The functional development of *so* from content word to function word:
content word (adverb) → adverbial connector → function word (conjunction) → discourse marker → pragmatic particle
(ii) The positional movement of *so* from local modifier to global modifier:
before a word (modifying adjective) → before a part of a sentence (linking two constituents) → before a clause (connecting two sentences) → before a turn (connecting two turns)
(iii) The meaning development of *so* from concrete to abstract:

'in such a way' → signaling consequential result →signaling continuum of the previous utterance →signaling continuum of the previous turn

The issue to be examined in this study is whether Chinese learners of English are aware of the grammatical and pragmatic development of *so* or whether current English teaching materials in China have made their learners notice these changes.

## 3. The present study

This study focuses on the connective use of *so* with meanings similar to *so that* ('with the result that'), *thus* ('in this way') and *therefore* ('for that reason'). It uses MicroConcord software to investigate *so* in a number of corpora, including:

- LOB-J Section J of LOB, the British written English in the 'Learned' category
- LLC1-2 Sample 1 and 2 of the LLC corpus, British spoken English
- EFL-1[1] Written English by Chinese middle school students
- EFL-2 Written English by English majors in Chinese universities
- SEC Spoken English by Chinese English learners, i.e. English classroom interaction between teachers and students in Chinese middle schools
- EFL-1 textbooks, English teaching materials in Chinese middle schools
- SC[2] Spoken Chinese (Cantonese) conversations by Chinese families on topics of daily life.

The procedures of the study are first to investigate *so* in terms of its frequency distribution, its position in a sentence and associated patterns, using LOB-J, EFL-1 and EFL-2, so as to reveal the overuse and inappropriate use of *so* by the Chinese EFL learners. The second step is to compare the frequency of *so* with that of *so that*, *therefore*, and *thus* in LOB-J, LLC1-2, EFL-1, EFL-2 and EFL-1 textbooks. This is to find out if the EFL learners' overuse of *so* shows an informal and spoken style in their written English, which could be further traced to the influence of their English teaching materials and performing strategy. The third step is to compare *so* in the spoken English corpus (LLC) and the equivalents of *so* in the spoken Chinese corpus (SC), to find out whether the EFL learners' overuse of *so* could be due to negative transfer from their mother tongue. The study concludes with some possible causes for Chinese EFL learners' overuse and inappropriate use of *so* in written English.

### 3.1 Investigation of English *so*

In this section data on *so* is extracted to establish its frequency, sentence position and associated patterns, using LOB-J, LLC1-2, EFL-1, EFL-2 and EFL-1 textbooks.

### 3.1.1 Frequency of *so*

**Table 1:** Frequency of connective *so* in corpora of written English

| Corpora | Total words | Tokens of *so* | /1000words |
|---|---|---|---|
| LOB-J | 160,000 | 59 | 0.33 |
| EFL-1 | 167,816 | 646 | 3.9 |
| EFL-2 | 158,341 | 355 | 2.2 |

Table 1 shows the overuse of *so* in Chinese students' written English. It is about 7 to 10 times that of native English speakers (3.9:0.33, 2.2:0.33). When doing the error tagging of EFL-2, a native English-speaking teacher identified quite a number of cases in which *so* is unnecessarily or unreasonably used (see Extract 1).

**Extract 1:** Instances of inappropriate *so* in EFL-2 corpus

| | |
|---|---|
| cause I missed my family very much. | ***So*** [wd5,-s] , at that night I was |
| because I'm writing about feminism, | ***so*** [wd5,-s] I have to think that's some |
| now, because I have changed my job, | ***so*** [wd5,6-0] I have moved to Room 216, |
| locked in the workshop by their boss | ***so*** [wd5,-s] what they could do was |
| down because of uncooperation. | ***So*** [wd5,-s] it made great fun not only to |
| it was a wonderful day. | ***So*** [wd5,-s] my roommates and other new f |
| if we want success at once. | ***So*** [wd5, -s] we must have good basis. When |
| but you can not do. | ***So*** [wd5,-s] you must practise every day, |
| we can make it well at once. | ***So*** [wd5,-s] "Practice Makes Perfect". |
| but we can't speak English, | ***so*** [wd5,-s] we can't talk with foreign pe |
| will be delicious, isn't it? | ***So*** [wd5,-s] when we have some difficulties |
| practice makes perfect" is a truth. | ***So*** [wd5,-s] we should make [wd3,-1] it in |
| the more practice, the more perfect. | ***So*** [wd5,-s] we ought to increase our dail |
| keep practising it and use our heads. | ***So*** [wd5,-s] we can make it perfect. <BAND |
| understand it and grasp at it. | ***So*** [wd5,-s] you will do it perfectly. For |

(Note: [wd5, -s] is an error-tag which means an oversupply of a word in the sentence. Other error-tags not being discussed in this study have been stripped off.)

The error tagger identified the above instances of *so* as redundant or as having no grammatical meaning at all.

### 3.1.2 Position of *so*

Table 2 compares the position of the connective *so* in the native English speakers' and the Chinese learners' written English. It shows that native English speakers tend to embed *so* within a sentence (78%>22%), while the Chinese EFL learners tend to put *so* in sentence-initial position (78%>44%>22%). This is particularly striking in the EFL-1 corpus, which includes the work of Chinese middle school students. Their English proficiency may be expected to be lower than the English majors in Chinese universities (EFL-2), and they prefer to use *so* in sentence-initial position.

**Table 2:** Position of *so* in corpora of written English

| | **Initial *so*** | **%** | **Embedded *so*** | **%** | **Total** |
|---|---|---|---|---|---|
| LOB-J | 13 | 22 | 46 | 78 | 59 |
| EFL-1 | 503 | 78 | 143 | 22 | 646 |
| EFL-2 | 155 | 44 | 200 | 56 | 355 |

Here are examples of native English speakers' use of *so* from LOB-J:

**Extract 2:** Instances of embedded *so* in LOB-J

| | |
|---|---|
| when my parents have gone out | ***so*** I can get peace to watch |
| artists of the School of Paris, | ***so*** I shall praise her work here in |
| about are not now remembered | ***so*** I was fortunate that among the few |
| from torch, 10 is twice as big | ***so*** it goes at 20 \0cm., 15 is half |
| 15 is half as big again | ***so*** it goes at 30, and 20 is twice 10 so |
| goes at 30, and 20 is twice 10 | ***so*** it goes here at 40. |
| among our basic industries, and | ***so*** it may be well to deal, first |
| suspected that at the time, | ***so*** it was only a matter of answering one |
| erefore,**[FORMULA**], and | ***so*** the charge in the capacitor at time |
| is at most finite, and | ***so*** the number of adjoint functions is at |
| simultaneously or in succession, | ***so*** the number of reports of methods exceeds |
| exact duplicate of the apparatus | ***so*** the subject could work with |
| than the chordwise loading, and | ***so*** the wing and its wake are replace |

Comparing Extract 2 and Extract 1, it is clear that native English speakers use *so* as an intra-sentence connector. It links a consequential result within a sentence, usually with reasoning in the first part. Chinese EFL learners however tend to use *so* as an inter-sentential connector. It does not introduce a consequential result but just loosely links the current sentence with the previous one(s), hence the frequent occurrence of capitalized *so*. This preferred position of *so* in EFL learners' English indicates it is more like a discourse marker than a syntactic conjunction.

### 3.1.3 Sentence patterns associated with *so*

As for the syntactic structure immediately after *so*, the pattern '*so* + subordinate clause (phrase) + main clause', as in '*so after* ...', '*so if* ...', '*so when* ...', occurs quite often in the Chinese middle school English learners' corpus (see Extract 3), but seldom in the native English speakers' corpus (see Extract 2).

**Extract 3**: Patterns of '*so* + subordinate clause/phrase + main clause' in EFL-1 corpus

| | |
|---|---|
| catching. but I don't like football. | ***So after*** a while, I go into the room and |
| my living of study is very busy. | ***So after*** class we should have some fun to |
| But there were many people there, | ***so after*** my classmate bought the English |
| two fairies's words was correctly. | ***So after*** that the Emperor changed into a |
| another company's generations. | ***So after*** the meeting he was given this blac |

| | |
|---|---|
| hard. I was very lazy in my study. | ***So after*** the test, they could smiled aloud |
| that nobody could recognize them. | ***So after*** they got the invention, they didn't |
| ause there was much homework to do. | ***So if*** I wanted to have a good time in the |
| in English can improve our English. | ***So if*** we want to learn English well, we |
| stories very much but she can't read. | ***So when*** ever her father comes, she always |
| could hardly go through the street. | ***So when*** I got to our classroom. I already |
| y head low when I did my homework. | ***So when*** I knew the examination was coming, |
| --- daisy; Oct. --- dahlia ... . | ***so when*** someone birthday, his friend bought |
| tried their best to control the fire. | ***So when*** the firefighters arrived, they had |
| not the right men from government. | ***So when*** the other people were worrying about |
| of basketball is stronger than us. | ***So when*** the match began, they played at |
| Festival, we all enjoyed ourselves. | ***So when*** we returned to the school it is |
| ut sometimes swimming is dangerous. | ***So when*** you swim in the sea, you must be |

In LOB-J, for which the word count is similar to that of EFL-1 (see Table 1), there are only 2 instances of '*so* + *if* clause'. There is no instance of '*so* + *after* clause' or '*so* + *when* clause'. This again demonstrates that EFL learners seem to use *so* more as a marker organizing discourse structure than as a local conjunction within a sentence. The result is consistent with the findings reported by Tribble and Jones (1990: 69), who conclude that 'using adverbial connectors sentence initially (*not only so but also yet, therefore, thus, however,* etc) is a common phenomenon in Chinese students' written English as well as in other non-native English speaking students'. The question of whether this inappropriate use of *so* is a reflection of the English spoken style in EFL students' written English prompted the present writer to further investigation of the corpora, as discussed in the next section (3.1.4).

### 3.1.4 Frequency of *so, so that, thus, therefore* in five corpora

Some previous studies have found that the overuse of *so* in Chinese EFL learners may be due to inadequate teaching materials and mixed attitudes towards coherence in students' writing (Milton and Tsang 1993), or perhaps the learners' lack of awareness of the stylistic differences between spoken and written English. This is confirmed in the present corpus investigation by the frequency distributions of *so, so that, therefore, thus* in the five corpora shown in Table 4.

**Table 4:** Distribution of *so, so that, therefore* and *thus* in five corpora

| Types of data | Total words | *so* | *so that* | *therefore* | *thus* |
|---|---|---|---|---|---|
| LOB-J | 160,000 | 59 | 78 | 110 | 109 |
| LLC1-2 | 140,000 | 492 | 47 | 15 | 0 |
| EFL-1 textbooks | 114,000 | 123 | 26 | 18 | 5 |
| EFL-1 | 167,816 | 646 | 75 | 0 | 1 |
| EFL-2 | 158,341 | 355 | 50 | 64 | 52 |

(Note: EFL-1 textbooks refers to *Senior English for China* (Books 1–3). They were published by PEP and Longman in 1996 and are most popularly used by senior middle school students in mainland China.)

In Table 4, the total number of tokens of *therefore, thus* and *so that* is about 1.5 to 2 times that of *so* in LOB-J (110 > 109 > 78 > 59); while *so* occurs much more than any of the other three expressions in LLC1-2 (492 > 47 > 15 > 0). This sharp contrast indicates that *so* is a stylistic feature of informal spoken English while *therefore, thus* and *so that* are features of formal written style.

In the EFL-1 and EFL-2 corpora, there is an even larger proportion of *so* than any of the other three expressions (646 > 75 > 0 > 1 and 355 > 50 > 64 > 52). It thus reflects an informal or spoken style in these Chinese learners' written English, particularly in that of the middle school learners (EFL-1's 646 : EFL-2's 355). As to the influence of Chinese EFL learners' exposure to English, Table 4 shows that EFL-1's English textbooks, the current major source of English exposure to Chinese middle school students, have a frequency of *so* 5 to 20 times that of *so that, therefore* and *thus* (123 > 26 > 18 > 5). This indicates that *so* is the early occurring and dominant consequential connective in middle school English teaching materials. Moreover, the word *so* is simple in pronunciation and spelling, and it is also quite similar to the phonetic realization of its Chinese equivalents 所以 (*suoyi /so:i/*). Chinese EFL learners may be influenced by such early and frequent exposure to *so* and thus find its use comes easily. Yet this finding might only relate EFL learners' overuse of *so* to their informal writing style. Whether it is related to transfer from their Chinese language needs to be analyzed by comparing the English corpus with the Chinese one.

### 3.2 Investigation of the Chinese equivalents of *so*

The Chinese equivalents of *so* can be 所以 (*suoyi*), 于是 (*yushi*), 那么 (*name*), 噉 (*gum*, in spoken Cantonese). In this section, a smaller corpus of spoken Chinese (Cantonese) named SC is used to investigate *gum* (噉) in terms of its frequency, its position and the sentence patterns associated with it. SC is a 117,000-word corpus of casual conversations made by five native Chinese speaking families (see endnote 2). It has been chosen for comparison with LLC1-2, which are also daily conversations between people who are familiar with each other. Another corpus named SEC (spoken English of Chinese teachers and students) is also used for comparison. The reason for choosing the Cantonese 噉 (*gum*) as the Chinese equivalent of *so* for the comparative study is that the speakers in SC, SEC and EFL-1, EFL-2 are mainly from Guangdong (a province in South China) whose local dialects are mainly Cantonese.

#### 3.2.1 Frequency and functions of 噉

**Table 5:** Frequency of *so* and its Chinese equivalents

| Corpus | Size | Tokens of *so* | requency /1000 words |
|---|---|---|---|
| LLC1-2 | 140,000 | 492 | 3.5 |
| SEC | 211,579 | 1144 | 5.4 |
| SC | 117,842 | 770 | 6.6 |

In Table 5, the 770 tokens of 噉 (*gum*) in SC do not include their adverbial usage, whose pronunciation is Cantonese tone 3, such as in 噉大 (*gum dai* = 'so big') or 噉多 (*gum do* = 'so many'). It only includes its usage as a connective, which is Cantonese tone 2. The result shows that the frequency of 噉 (*gum*) in SC is nearly two times that of *so* in LLC1-2 (6.6 > 3.5). A closer examination of the instances of 噉 (*gum*) in the following examples reveals that its position is more flexible than *so*. Its associated patterns are more varied than *so* as well. 噉 (*gum*) not only functions as a conjunction, but also a mood auxiliary, a hesitation filler or a conversational particle that signals the beginning or the termination of an utterance. In a sense, 噉 (*gum*) has gone even further than *so* in the process of pragmaticalization, because of its more flexible position and the various moods it conveys. Here are some examples showing the discourse and pragmatic use of 噉 (*gum*) in spoken Cantonese. The English below the Cantonese symbols is a gloss of each word while in the brackets is a free translation of the whole Chinese utterance.

- 噉 (*gum*) as an embedded connector, occurring with another cohesive connector, serving as a strengthener, as in:

(1) 因为 我老母 喺 香港:人 女 噉*所以* 多啲中国文 整来啦
because my mother is Hong Kong daughter so therefore more Chinese come (P)
(As my mother is the daughter of a Hong Kong citizen, there is more Chinese in her speech.)

(Note: (P) indicates a Cantonese conversation particle serving as a mood auxiliary. The same is to the other Chinese examples below.)

- 噉 (*gum*) as a hesitation filler and terminator, occuring in the middle or at the end of the utterance, serving as a boundary marker, as in:

(2) 我我唔喺读咗读咗一年 中学． 两样都 噉．两样都一样一半 噉*啦*
I I am not read read one year middle school. both are **so**. both are one type one half **so** (P)
(I just studied in the middle school for one year, both are…both are half and half.)

- 噉 (*gum*) as a turn taking marker, occurring at the beginning of a turn, serving as a turn starter, as in:

(3) 甲：好彩 无乜嘢点咬倒 乙：噉 唔喺 好紧要姐: 佢着咗 裤 架嘛
fortunate nothing was bitten **so** is not very serious (P) he has worn trousers (P)
(A: Fortunately he's not actually bitten. B: Well. It's not that serious because he's worn trousers.)

- 噉 (*gum*) as utterance final, occurring with another particle, serving as a mood auxiliary in Chinese. e.g.,

(4) 嗰度好彩 嗰嗰佬喺.喺大家喺乡里 噉*呢*:我哋话俾佢听打咗针架 只狗
that fortunate that man is. is we all are fellow countrymen **so** (P) we tell him

listen had injection (P) that dog
(Fortunately that man and we are fellow countrymen! We told him that the dog had had an injection.)

The above examples show the discoursal functions of the Chinese 噉 (*gum*). It originated as an adverb, meaning, 'in such a way' or 'to such a degree'. Its latter meaning often makes it a continuation of the previous statement, and so it gradually becomes a conjunction or a logical connector in connected speech. When it was put into such a syntactic slot, 噉 (*gum*) continues to develop the new function based on its original adverbial meaning and its connective function. It was further used as a discourse organizer to initiate an utterance within a turn, or to initiate a turn at a turn transaction boundary, i.e. when the second speaker takes a turn from the current speaker (as in examples 1 and 3 above). It is also used as a means of continuing the previous speakers' topic, a means of getting someone's attention (as in examples 2 and 3), or a means of emphasizing one's mood in speaking, or as a filler to hold the floor (as in examples 2 and 4). In all these uses, it becomes independent either from its previous clause or from its following clause. Its meaning is bleached in the process, into a discourse marker or conversational particle in spoken discourse. In the SEC corpus, i.e. the English classroom interaction of Chinese middle schools, there are many instances of *so* as follows:

(a) ***so*** now let's start the game…
(b) let's go on . come on ----- ***so*** ----- are you ready .
(c) ok ***so*** . can you ***so*** are you clear about that
(d) a child . and maybe children . ***so*** ask her ask the wife to help…
(e) yeah . ***so*** I I know . ***so*** at that time . her mother…
(f) very considerate . ***so*** . m .. ***so*** . and her friend…
(cited from SEC)

Here *so* is more often used as a pragmatic particle in the discourse of classroom conversation. It can be regarded as a framing marker of classroom activity transactions as in example (a), a take-off point for further talk as in (b), an initiator of an utterance as again in (b), a topic initiator as in (c), a turn initiator as in (d), or a pause filler in speech as in examples (e) and (f). Its frequency in SEC is much higher than in LLC1-2 (see Table 5, 5.4 > 3.5), indicating an influence from the Cantonese 噉 (*gum*).

### 3.2.2 Position of 噉 (*gum*)

In the LLC1-2 corpus, the connective *so* is mostly tone unit-initial, in other words, it occurs initially in an utterance (see Extract 4 below). The Cantonese 噉 (*gum*), however, not only occurs at the start of an utterance but also at the middle or end of an utterance (see the Chinese examples in 3.2.1).

**Extract 4:** Retrieval of *so* in spoken English (LLC)

/ 1 5 23 3510 1 1 B 11 ^just **so** I`d :get the i:d\ea#

/ 1 5  22 3390  1 1 C  11  **so** I`d ^better not 'say any |more about :th\ose#
/ 1 8  77 8020  1 1 C  11  **so** I`m ^terribly |\envious# -
/ 1 3  12 1960  1 1 A  11  **so** I`ve got this ^fabulous mach\ine#
/ 1 4  7711910  1 2 A  11  ^**so** I`ve se|lected :three or 'four 'passages
/ 1 7  69 6260  1 1 B  11  ^**so** it was 'to re|lease - 'twelve m\asters#
/ 1 9  64 6170  1 1 A  11  and \@! ^**so** it was de:c\/ided#
/ 1 5  52 7860  1 1 A  11  **so** it ^d\oes 'seem#
/ 110 109 8690 1 1 b  20  **so** it was the sheer printing
/ 1 5  61 9230  1 1 A  11  ^**so** it |r\eally#
/ 1 4  14 2060  1 1 A  11  ***so** - \@! . it ^looks _very |g\ood#
/ 112  47 4540  1 1 D  11  **and** ^**so** it _goes |\on#

### 3.2.3 Patterns associated with 噉 (*gum*)

In spoken English, *so* is often preceded by *and* (e.g., … *and so* …) and followed by a noun or a pronoun which is the subject of the following clause (e.g., …*so I* … or *so it* …. ). In Cantonese, 噉 (*gum*) is often followed by another adverbial connector, such as 噉但喺 (*so but*...) , 噉如果 (*so if* …), 噉而家 (*so now*...), 噉所以 (*so therefore* ...). For example:

(5) 我知：噉但喺做唔倒八十七题啦嘛喺唔喺呀
I know: **so but** can't do 87 item (P) isn't it (P)
(I know, but I can't do 87 exercises, can I?)
(6) 不过佢话有 study 啵.噉如果佢 study 噉未得 啰
but he said has s study (P) . **so if** he study **so** is good (P)
(But he said he's studied. If he's studied, that's good.)
(7) M: 退退休 或者你 又 稳 啲嘢 做吓 架啦喺嘛
re retired or you again find something to do (P) isn't it
F: 噉而家噉嘅情形你喺唔喺退休呀
**so now** such situation you have or not have retired (P)
(M: When you are retired you will find something to do again, won't you?
F: So in the present situation are you retired or not?)
(8) GP: 做牧师 呀 钱 又唔多 啦
be clergy man (P) money is not much (P)
GM: 噉所以 呢嗰阵时 喺好艰难 架
**so therefore**(P) at that time is very difficult (P)
(GP: He's a clergyman and didn't have much money.
GM: So it's very difficult at that time.)

The frequent occurrences of 噉所以 ('so therefore'), 噉因为 ('so because'), 噉如果 ('so if'), 噉而家 ('so now'), 噉等阵 ('so after') in spoken Cantonese may transfer to EFL learners' written English; hence the frequent occurrence of similar patterns such as 'so after…', 'so if…', 'so therefore…' in Chinese EFL learners' written performance (see Extract 3), because they may use *so* as a discourse marker instead of a clause connector. Some previous studies have also found this negative transfer of L1 at a discourse level. Ringbom (1998: 198) claims that 'use of metatextual phrases, connectors, hedges and other argumentative patterns will frequently reflect L1-usage', because the learner may 'unconsciously assume that the way we talk or write about experience is not subject to between-language variation' (Kellerman: 1995: 141).

## 4. Conclusions

This is a data-driven analysis supported by a number of corpora: written and spoken, native speaker and non-native speaker, learners' performance and teaching materials and learners' mother tongue data. It began with analysis of the frequency and position of *so* in the native English speakers' corpora and those of the Chinese EFL learners. The contrasting results reveal the inappropriate use of *so* in the EFL corpora involving learners with higher and lower English proficiency. It thus draws attention to the changing functions of *so* in spoken English and Chinese. This is an aspect of the grammar of spoken language which has long been neglected in Chinese EFL teaching and learning. For the teaching focus has always concentrated on written grammar, with little on spoken English analysis. The overuse and inappropriate use of *so* in their written English could be due to:

(i) learners' unawareness of the stylistic impact of *so* in spoken and written English, hence a spoken style in their written English;
(ii) limitations in middle school learners' exposure to English, i.e., the source of teaching materials is orally and informally orientated;
(iii) learners' learning/performing strategies, i.e., the inclination to use or preference for using the early-learned or simpler means of expression.
(iv) L1 transfer, i.e. the highly frequent use of the pragmatic particle of 噉 (gum) in Chinese (Cantonese) with some positions and associated patterns different from its English equivalent *so*, which may lead to the inappropriate use by EFL learners.

### Notes

1 EFL-1, EFL-2, SEC and EFL-1 textbooks are sub-corpora of *Corpora of English Education in China* built in the School of Foreign Studies, South China Normal University, Guangzhou, China. For details contact heanping@scnu.edu.cn.

2 The corpus of SC (spoken Chinese) contains transcriptions of the daily conversations of five native Cantonese speaking families. Acknowledgement is given to Prof. Sikhung Ng for his kind permission to use some of the data from his project *Stereotyping of Elderly People and Cross-Generation Communication* at the Victoria University of Wellington, New Zealand.

**References**

Field, Y. (1994). 'Cohesive conjunctions in the English writing of Cantonese speaking students from Hong Kong'. *Australian review of applied linguistics* 17.1: 125–139.

Field, Y. and L. M. O. Yip (1992). 'A comparison of internal conjunctive cohesion in the English essay writing of Cantonese speakers and native speakers of English'. *RELC Journal* 23.1: 15–28.

Granger, S. and Tyson, S. (1996). 'Connector usage in the English essay writing of native and non-native EFL speakers of English'. *World Englishes* 15: 19–29.

Kellerman, E. (1995). 'Crosslinguistic influence: transfer to nowhere?' *Annual review of applied linguistics* 15: 125–150.

*Longman dictionary of contemporary English* (1997). Beijing: Foreign Language Teaching and Research Press.

Milton, J and E. S. C. Tsang (1993). 'A corpus-based study of logical connectors in EFL students' writing: directions for future research'. In Richard Pemberton and Elza S. C. Tsang (eds) *Studies in lexis*. Hong Kong University of Science and Technology, Language Center.

Ringbom, H. (1998). 'Verbs in the ICLE corpus'. In Antoinette Renouf (ed.) *Explorations in corpus lingusitics*. Amsterdam: Rodopi.

Schiffrin, Deborah (1987). *Discourse markers*. Cambridge: CUP.

Schleppegrell, M. (1991). 'Paratactic *because*'. *Journal of pragmatics* 16: 323–337.

Stenström, A-B. (1998). 'From sentence to discourse: *cos* (because) in teenage talk'. In Andreas H. Jucker and Yael Ziv (eds) *Discourse markers – descriptions and theory*. Amsterdam: John Benjamins.

Tribble, C. and G. Jones (eds) (1990). *Concordances in the classroom*. London: Longman.

# Lexis, indirectness and politeness in operator calls

*Tony McEnery, Paul Baker and Christine Cheepen*[†]

Lancaster University [†]British Telecom Laboratories

## Abstract

*This paper presents work undertaken for British Telecom on their corpus of calls to the operator: the so-called 100 Corpus*[1]*. Our aim in analysing this corpus was to explore the distinctiveness of the language used by both the caller and the operator in the corpus. In achieving this goal we have, from time to time, compared the 100 Corpus to other corpora: the spoken and written sections of the British National Corpus*[2] *(BNC), and a corpus of operator-caller conversations from a train booking office.*

## 1. Introduction

Telephone-based transactional dialogues (TTDs) are an increasingly common part of everyday life in many parts of the world. TTDs can be identified as dialogues conducted via the telephone, within which some exchange is transacted, either of services or of support. While the web is taking on an increasingly important role in the selling of products from train tickets to insurance, telephone sales and support will remain an important aspect of commercial life for the foreseeable future. In this paper we report on some work undertaken to examine the nature of such dialogues. The paper is written along the lines that our investigation took, and as such is divided into three parts. Initially, we investigate the lexis of the corpus, in order to examine the hypothesis that it makes use of a distinctive and constrained lexicon. Second, we demonstrate how, by the application of a relatively novel form of corpus annotation, mismatches in sense and force can be revealed in the speech of the operator. The final strand of research is concerned with the construction of commands, looking specifically at how indirectness and the use of mitigators realises politeness in the corpus. While the results of our investigation only yield a somewhat preliminary investigation of TTDs, the results are nonetheless interesting, as they show that TTDs, at least by comparison to writing and face-to-face spontaneous dialogues, have a range of distinctive features.

### 1.1 The 100 Corpus

The 100 Corpus is composed of orthographic transcriptions of calls to the telephone operator service in the UK. For the purposes of this paper *calls* can best be described as '*ongoing and developing sequences of actions*, actions that systematically get formed up into "calls"' (Whalen 1990: 6). These calls form the basis of a TTD – in the 100 Corpus users are telephoning in order to transact an exchange of information. While work on TTDs does not abound, there has been some work done on calls in general, especially within the framework of Conversation Analysis (CA). For example,

Zimmerman (1984) and Whalen and Zimmerman (1987) used a CA approach to the exploration of the discourse grammar behind calls to the emergency services. While we employed some of the techniques of CA to analyse the role of questions and politeness within the 100 Corpus, we rooted our initial investigation of the corpus in a lexically driven approach, hypothesising that operator-caller transactions are distinctive in that they utilise a relatively constrained set of lexical items. Following work undertaken previously in examining IBM manuals as a sub-language (McEnery and Wilson 1996), we decided to examine tendencies towards a lack of lexical diversity in the 100 Corpus.

## 2. Lexis

We began our investigation by calculating a simple type-token ratio for the 100 Corpus and comparing it to the same figures for the written and spoken sections of the BNC. The first problem we faced was that the 100 Corpus contains a high number of numerical *hapax legomena*. The 100 Corpus as a whole is made up of 94,641 tokens. However, when numerical tokens are removed, this figure falls to 74,629, meaning that around 30% of the 100 Corpus is composed of numerals. Compare this to the BNC, where cardinal (tagged CRD and including here those words tagged CRD-PNI) and ordinal (tagged ORD) numbers account for 2,193,315 tokens in the corpus, or roughly 2.19% of the tokens of the corpus. Numbers are clearly of inordinate importance in the 100 Corpus. This is not surprising considering that many calls to the operator will lead to the operator asking the caller for the phone number that they are calling from, or for the number of a line which they are reporting as being faulty. However, the individual numbers are very rarely used more than once. As a consequence, when calculating our type token ratio we excluded numbers. In order to compare the lexis of the 100 Corpus to writing and spontaneous speech, we developed small subsets of the BNC spoken and written data identical in size to the 100 Corpus. Numbers were also filtered out of the BNC data, so that comparisons between roughly 74,000 words of spoken and written general British English and 74,000 words of the 100 Corpus were possible. Table 1 below summarises the findings:

**Table 1:** Type-token ratios of the 100 Corpus and the BNC spoken and written subsets

| Corpus | Size in tokens | Types | Ratio (types/tokens) × 100 |
|---|---|---|---|
| 100 | 74,629 | 2,489 | 3.34% |
| BNC (spoken) | 74,000 | 4,751 | 6.42% |
| BNC (written) | 74,000 | 9.317 | 12.59% |

From the table above it appears that lexical innovation, in the sense of words as yet unseen in the corpus being identified as the data is processed, is significantly lower in the 100 Corpus than for the BNC data. Such a conclusion is difficult to make sense of, given a type token ratio of this sort – is the growth steady, does innovation grow as we observe more data, or does innovation die away as more data is observed? In order to explore these questions we mapped the identification of new types by the number of tokens observed onto a graph for each of the three corpora, as shown in Figure 1 below.

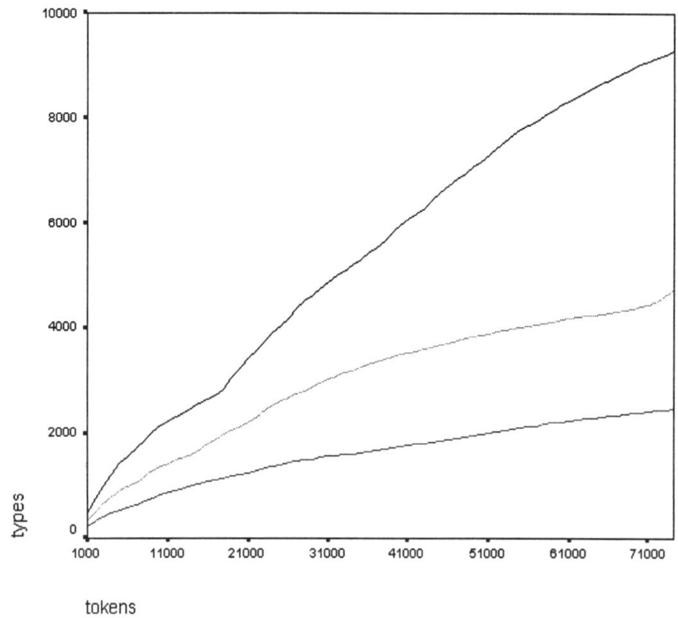


**Figure 1:** Type-token ratios for written and spoken BNC data, and the 100 Corpus, showing the written BNC (top line), the spoken BNC (middle line) and the 100 Corpus (bottom line)

Figure 1 shows cumulative type-token ratios for the written BNC, spoken BNC and the 100 Corpus data. While steady, the addition of new types in the 100 Corpus data is markedly less frequent than in the BNC data. While the data is too limited to observe or comment upon closure of the lexicon, it is at least clear from the above graph that the lexis is prone to much more repetition. Lexical innovation is markedly suppressed in the 100 Corpus. A hypothesis we explored in order to explain this was that the operators were working to a script, meaning that the tendency not to innovate lexically was caused by most of the utterances of the operator being scripted. However, when we enquired as to whether this was the case it became clear that no script was involved. Another hypothesis which may account for this suppression of lexical innovation in the 100 Corpus was that the exchanges were short – hence within them greetings, farewells and other such formulaic utterances were, as a proportion of the data, high in number. When we examined the average length of turn for the exchanges in the corpus we found evidence to support this claim. There are a total of 8,859 turns in the corpus, giving a mean length of utterance of 10.68 words. Those turns make up the 650 TTDs in the corpus, giving an average length for each TTD of 13.63 turns. As ever, one must be cautious when using simple averages, so we mapped the lengths of the TTDs in turns onto a bar chart, so that we could better observe the distribution of TTD lengths. Figure 2 below shows that bar chart.

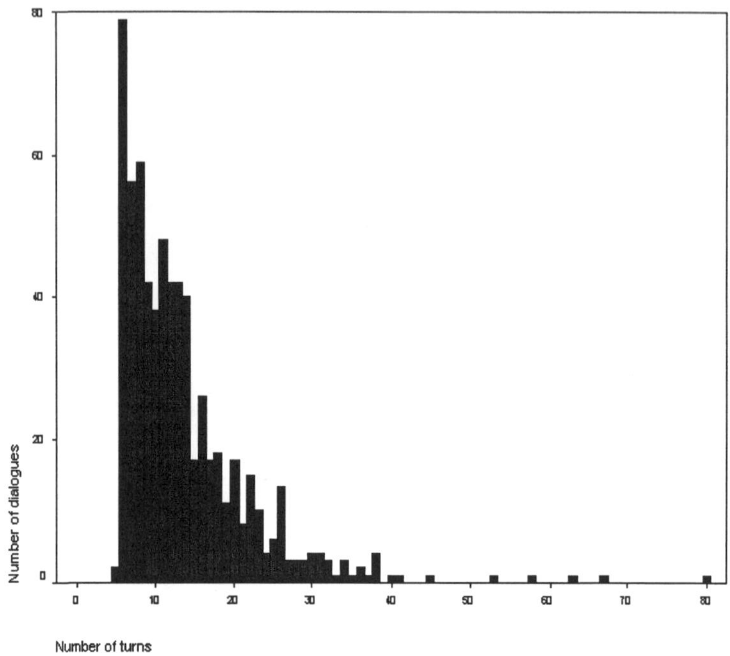


**Figure 2:** Turn length in the 100 Corpus

The data shown in Figure 2 clearly cluster around lengths 6–15, a relatively narrow range, with the arithmetic mode occurring at the beginning of that range, i.e. 6. Given that the TTDs begin and end with a greeting/farewell, and that typically both the caller and the operator produce one each of these, we have a situation within which the calls that have the mode number of turns (6) will typically contain a greeting and a farewell from the operator and a greeting and a farewell from a caller. To give a concrete example of this Table 2 below shows the lexis of greetings in the opening of each of the 650 TTDs in the corpus. Table 2 shows that 40% of the calls in the corpus contain lexis associated with greeting in the first turn of the caller, with 'hello' being very common in this position.

In such circumstances, at least one explanation of why the 100 Corpus seems to be subject to less lexical diversity than the BNC data it was compared to seems identifiable. To add further weight to this hypothesis we wished to explore the spoken section of the BNC in order to find average turn lengths and patterns of interchange to compare them directly to the TTDs. However, the beginnings and ends of conversations are not as clearly delineated in face to face conversations as in TTDs, and consequently the task proved not to be feasible in the time available to us.

**Table 2:** The lexis of greetings in the telephone corpus

| Greeting | Occurring as first word(s) | Occurring within first 12 words |
|---|---|---|
| hello | 201 | 288 |
| hi | 55 | 76 |
| good morning | 6 | 23 |
| good afternoon | 1 | 12 |
| good evening | 0 | 15 |
| how are you | 1 | 2 |
| morning | 1 | 1 |
| **Total** | **265 (accounting for 40% of initial utterances)**[3] | **417** |

Following on from this investigation, we decided to explore another hypothesis that may explain the relatively constrained nature of the lexis in the 100 Corpus – the variety of topics discussed is limited, and hence the need for a wider vocabulary is removed. In order to begin to explore this, we firstly categorised the TTDs in the 100 Corpus. We identified 41 different types of call. Of these 41 types of call, the ten most common (which account for 78.3% of the TTDs) are shown in Table 3 below.

**Table 3**: The ten most frequent types of call

| Type | Number of TTDs | Percentage of total TTDs |
|---|---|---|
| Caller wants the operator to check a number is working. | 139 | 21.40 |
| Caller wants to place a wake up call. | 120 | 18.50 |
| Caller wants to find a number (but doesn't ask for Directory Enquiries). | 72 | 11.10 |
| Caller wants to report a fault. | 34 | 5.20 |
| Caller has a number and wants to know the address the number is at. | 29 | 4.50 |
| Caller asks to be transferred to Directory Enquiries. | 27 | 4.20 |
| Caller wants area code. | 27 | 4.20 |
| Caller wants to be transferred to another service (not Directory Enquiries). | 25 | 3.80 |
| Caller is receiving silent/ malicious calls. | 18 | 2.80 |
| Caller wants time/date. | 17 | 2.60 |

The TTDs do, as one may expect, relate to the limited range of services offered by the company being contacted, and the overwhelming majority of calls relate to ten distinct services. Note also that each TTD is typically made to access one service only – of the 650 TTDs in the corpus, only 10 have a caller asking for more than one service. Under such circumstances, we should expect lexis to be less diverse than in spontaneous conversation where almost anything could be discussed. The task-oriented nature of the TTDs is once again visible if the top 100 tokens of the 100 Corpus are compared to the top 100 of the spoken and written BNC. In Figure 3 below, the words appearing in those top 100 lists are placed in a Venn diagram, showing areas of similarity and difference between the three corpora.

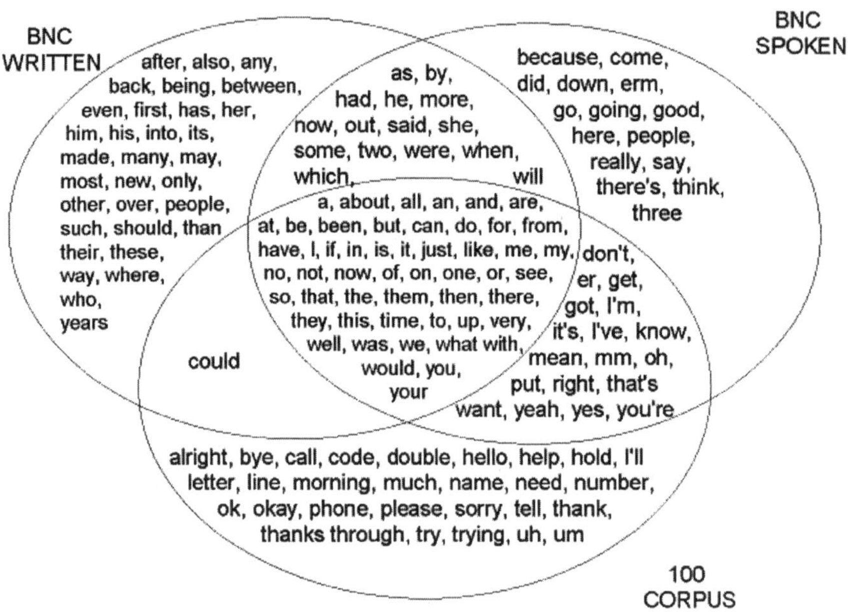


**Figure 3:** The 100 most frequently occurring words in the spoken and written BNC and the 100 Corpus

This figure in itself is a fascinating reflection of the nature of transactional telephone corpus data. The words in the diagram which only appear frequently in the 100 Corpus (those at the bottom segment of the figure) seem to reflect the task-oriented nature of the TTDs (e.g. *need, trying, call, help, code, line, number, phone*) or are associated with discourse management (e.g. *tell, sorry, hello, bye, ok, alright*). We developed a further hypothesis on the basis of this data. As well as being characterised by a low level of lexical innovation, TTDs can be identified by the profile of lexis in its top 100. In common with other genres of spoken and written English, **function words** abound, belonging to closed-class grammatical categories (prepositions, pronouns, conjunctions, articles, determiners, modal verbs etc.). These words are commonly found with high frequency in almost all genres of language. However, **discourse markers** should also feature strongly, as these are common in spoken interactions; indeed they are identified by Stenström (1990: 137–8) as small words or expressions that are peculiar to spoken discourse, while 'its interactive and pragmatic functions prevail over its "ordinary" grammatical function'. These include mitigators such as *just* (Holmes 1984: 36), hedges (Quirk et al 1985: 1114), politeness markers e.g. *please*, news-receipts e.g. *oh* (Atkinson 1992: 208), greetings e.g. *hello* (Aijmer 1996: 2), and hesitations *er, um*[4]. Finally, and most characteristic of TTDs, are **context-specific words**, a category composed (mainly) of nouns and verbs which are specific to the particular conversational context and reflect its task-oriented nature. In the case of the 100 Corpus data, words such as *call, telephone, phone* etc. fall within this category.

While these three categories of words could be applied easily to the 100 most frequent words in the 100 Corpus, we further hypothesised that the appearance of similar sorts of discourse markers and function words would be characteristic of all types of transactional operator/caller conversations, whereas each genre would also have a relatively stable and unique set of context-based words. To test this hypothesis we compared the 100 most frequent words in the BT corpus with the 100 most frequent words in another TTD corpus we were developing called the Gemini Corpus. The Gemini Corpus is a corpus of TTDs taken from a telephone train ticket booking company, While smaller than the 100 Corpus, (it contains 24,482 tokens, from 26 TTDs) we assumed that the lack of lexical innovation in TTDs should allow us to carry out this broad comparison of frequent lexis in both corpora. The results are shown in Table 4 below.

**Table 4:** Comparison of the most frequent words in the BT and train-booking call data

| **Type** | **Words occurring in the top 100 of the Gemini corpus but not the 100 Corpus** | **Words occurring in the top 100 of the 100 Corpus but not the Gemini corpus** | **Words occurring in the top 100 of both corpora** |
|---|---|---|---|
| **Function words** | your from going any out want non before which would will (11) | they through I've got I'll been try was trying could what's are know see don't about actually put getting all an we mean (23) | the you to a and is for that I it's on do there's with I'm so be of if in it get at there then me can you're but not as this have that's what or one (37) |
| **Discourse markers** | like aha afternoon (3) | oh sorry um hello okay uh thanks moment alright (9) | now thank bye yes just yeah right please ok no good well er (13) |
| **Context-specific** | {station}[5]card ticket time train credit pounds letter smoking {business} date | {business}double line {town} code call zero engaged check calling phone | name number hold (3) |

| | | | |
|---|---|---|---|
| | return travelling available book arriving October quality tickets seat reference Virgin journey purchase fare class travel advance day (29) | ringing operator (13) | |

The number of discourse markers and function words occurring in the most frequent 100 words of both files is 50: the corpora therefore have half of the most frequent words in common with each other. However, only 3 context-specific words are found in the top 100 words in *both* files. This distribution of common lexis bears out our hypothesis – the corpora are similar to general English in the sense that function words abound. Similarly, they show a clear affinity with spoken language by their use of discourse markers, many of which are shared. However, their task-oriented nature becomes clear when we see that both corpora have significant task-oriented lexis in their top 100, and this is typically not shared between the corpora (though we could hypothesise that the lexis would be shared if the services being provided were similar).

In order to see if this feature was common to spoken texts *per se*, and not just to operator/caller conversations, we carried out the same comparative process on the top 100 words in the spoken BNC data and found that most of the top function words in the 100 Corpus were also found in the top 100 words of the spoken BNC. However, the spoken BNC is made up of many more function words and fewer discourse markers than the 100 Corpus (as can be seen in part in Figure 3).

To summarise, in the purely lexical phase of our investigation of the corpus we examined six hypotheses related to the nature of the lexis of the 100 Corpus and TTDs in general.

(i) The 100 Corpus makes use of a distinctive and constrained lexicon.
(ii) A possible explanation of hypothesis (i) is that the operators are working to a script, meaning that the tendency not to innovate lexically is caused at least in part by most of the utterances of the operator being scripted.
(iii) A further possible explanation of hypothesis (i) is that in the 100 Corpus the exchanges are short – hence within them greetings, farewells and other such formulaic utterances are, as a proportion of the data, high in number.
(iv) A further factor weighing against lexical innovation is that in TTDs the variety of topics discussed is limited, and hence the need for a wider vocabulary is removed.
(v) TTDs can be identified by the profile of lexis in their top 100 words.
(vi) The appearance of similar sorts of discourse markers and function words would be characteristic of all types of transactional operator/caller conversations, whereas each sub-type of TTD will also have a relatively stable and unique set of context-based words.

Our investigation of the corpus provided support for all of these hypotheses except hypothesis (ii). This proved to be untrue when we investigated the practices of the BT telephone operators. With this characterisation of the lexis of TTDs in place, we decided to move our focus away from the purely lexical, and start to explore the nature of the interaction that takes place in TTDs. This led us to an examination of directness and indirectness in the 100 Corpus, as described in the next section.

## 3. Verbal response modes

While exploring the corpus for the purposes of discovering the goal of each TTD, we noticed that such features as indirect requests appeared, to our intuition at least, to be common in the TTDs. We were faced with a challenge in trying to add weight to this observation. Some work on the annotation of directness and indirectness in spoken corpora has been reported, however, e.g. by Leech, McEnery and Wynne (1997). We decided to undertake an experimental annotation of a subsection of our data in order to explore the feasibility of a more quantitative approach to characterising directness/indirectness in the 100 Corpus. In order to achieve this annotation we used the 'verbal response mode' annotation of Stiles (1992: 14–23) as reported in Leech, McEnery and Wynne (1997: 91–4). The advantage of this scheme is that a broad speech act label is applied twice to any given utterance – once to annotate the sense of the utterance, and then again to annotate the force of an utterance. Hence if an utterance appears to have the sense of a question, but the force of a command (e.g. '*Can you shut the window?*' spoken to cause somebody to shut the window) then this mismatch between the sense and force of the utterance can be captured by this twofold process of annotation. The speech act labels provided by Stiles and used by us are few in number and are outlined in Table 5 below.

**Table 5**: The eight classes of interaction Stiles discovered in patient/doctor interaction

| | |
|---|---|
| Disclosure (D) | Reveals thoughts, feelings, perceptions or intentions. |
| Edification (E) | States objective information. |
| Advisement (A) | Attempts to guide behaviour, suggestions, commands, permission, prohibition. |
| Confirmation (C) | Compares speaker's experience with others; agreement, disagreement, shared experience. |
| Question (Q) | Requests information or guidance. |
| Acknowledgement (K) | Conveys receipt or receptiveness to other's communication; simple acceptance; salutations. |
| Interpretation (I) | Explains or labels the other; judgements or evaluations or the other's experience/behaviour. |
| Reflection (R) | Puts other's experience into words; repetitions, restatements or clarifications. |

### 3.1 Method and findings

We annotated 14 TTDs from the 100 Corpus, using Stiles' system, but adding the classification U for cases which we thought were truly unclassifiable. We were only able to encode a subset of the corpus as the process of applying the annotations was highly time consuming, with much discussion necessary for the application of what, at times is a rather subjective analysis. Nonetheless, we were satisfied by the end of the process that the annotation, while necessarily subjective, was at least consistent as a result of the careful discussions and the development of case law that each analysis entailed.

The 14 conversations contained 93 operator turns and 73 caller turns. Figure 4 below gives an example of one of the files to demonstrate the annotation undertaken. Following that, Table 6 shows the distribution of turns in terms of sense and force for both callers and operators in the 100 Corpus.

```
A.1: %name
B.2: <44:48.664>yeah [KK] hello [KK] em can you put me
through em tell me which number I need to ring em # for a
new telephone line [QA] you know in in a new property [EA]
<44:60.964>
A.3: sorry [KQ] you want to have a new telephone line
installed into your property madam [RQ]
B.4: no [KD] i've got a telephone line already in [EE] i
just want it con... <connected?> reconnected [ED]
A.5: okay [KK] if you just hold on the line [AA] i'll i'll
put you through to <?> customer service [EE] and they
should be able to do that # help you [EE] okay [QQ]
B.6: thank you [KK]
A.7: #<3.8s> ringing for you now [EE] thank you [KK]
<ringing>
B.8: thanks [KK]
```

**Figure 4:** A sample analysis of a file

**Table 6:**Frequencies for caller/operator discourse categories
First number = caller frequencies. Second number = operator frequencies

| | | FORCE | | | | | | | | |
|---|---|---|---|---|---|---|---|---|---|---|
| | | D | E | A | C | Q | K | I | R | U |
| SENSE | D | 5-9 | 14-5 | 1-8 | 0-0 | 0-2 | 3-7 | 0-0 | 0-0 | 0-0 |
| | E | 3-0 | 38-22 | 0-9 | 0-1 | 0-1 | 0-3 | 0-0 | 0-0 | 1-0 |
| | A | 0-0 | 0-0 | 3-5 | 0-0 | 0-0 | 0-0 | 0-0 | 0-0 | 0-0 |
| | C | 1-0 | 0-0 | 0-0 | 0-0 | 0-0 | 0-0 | 0-0 | 0-0 | 0-0 |
| | Q | 0-0 | 0-0 | 11-9 | 0-0 | 6-13 | 0-0 | 0-0 | 0-1 | 0-1 |
| | K | 1-0 | 1-0 | 0-0 | 11-6 | 0-0 | 48-79 | 2-1 | 0-0 | 0-0 |
| | I | 0-0 | 0-0 | 0-0 | 0-4 | 2-0 | 3-3 | 1-3 | 0-0 | 0-0 |
| | R | 1-0 | 1-0 | 1-0 | 0-0 | 0-0 | 0-0 | 0-0 | 3-37 | 0-0 |
| | U | 0-0 | 0-0 | 0-0 | 0-0 | 0-0 | 0-0 | 0-0 | 0-0 | 3-1 |

With reference to Table 6, it is clear that utterances of the sense K, Q, D and E represent the majority of the utterances analysed. Of these, K, and more specifically utterances with the force of K predominate – it is clear that acknowledgement/back-channelling is important in this dialogue type. In terms of looking for a match between sense and force, K, R and E type utterances typically have an identical sense and force – in other words there is little in the way of mismatch in form and function for these utterances. On the other hand, while questions are frequently both questions in sense and force, there is a majority of cases where utterances with the sense of a question are actually functioning as advisements. Below are a couple of examples from the data to show this type of utterance:

```
B.2: <22:24.999>yeah [KK] can you check a number for me [QA]

A.9: sorry [DD] mam [KK] can you just confirm me that number again
     please [QA]
```

In each case, while we have an utterance in the form of a question, there is an attempt to guide behaviour – an imperative of sorts. Apparent questions have the intention of an imperative. In the first example the caller wants the operator to check a number – they are not asking the operator whether they are capable of checking the number. In the second example the operator knows the caller can confirm the number - this is an indirect request for the caller to do so. Considering that advisements of this sort are where actions are being requested of the caller or operator, it is clearly a focus for politeness phenomena. It is therefore most notable that looking at the advisement column/row we see a minority of cases where advisements appear clearly and unambiguously as advisements (AA). Clearly, with such a small sample it is difficult to draw strong conclusions about the formation of advisements in the 100 Corpus. But nonetheless, we have some persuasive evidence in this small sample to suggest that advisements in the corpus tend to be indirect, and that an important form for advisements is as a question. This is a hypothesis we will follow up in detail in our fourth section. For the moment, we shall simply note that the Stiles analysis reveals an important degree of indirectness in the data analysed, and that questions seem to be realised indirectly specifically to form advisements.

However, we have so far only analysed the data as a whole. How, if at all, does the speech of the operators differ from that of the callers with respect to directness? In terms of noticeable differences, the operator produces more KK and RR[6] utterances, and the caller produces more EE and DE utterances. This observation in itself is interesting – the caller is producing a relatively high volume of objective information, and this is strongly linked to speech acts with the sense of a disclosure. On the other hand, the operator is producing a higher volume of acknowledgements and is frequently reformulating and repeating the callers' statements. To return to the main theme of this section, questions in both the case of the operator and caller show striking similarities. Both use QQ and QA speech acts as their main sense of Q-based speech acts. Although there is a small (and at this stage statistically untestable) difference between the two, we might hypothesise that the purpose of forming indirect questions by both the operator and caller may be identical and most likely relates to some politeness phenomenon focused on advisements. Again, we will not labour this point as it will be studied in some depth in the following section. For the moment, it is sufficient to say that the Stiles analysis was illuminating both in terms of what it told us about the dialogues as a whole, and what it told us about the language of the callers when contrasted with the language of the operators. One thing it does bring to the fore is politeness in the TTDs. In order to pursue this strand of research, we decided to return to reconsider the lexical level, and to begin to explore the relationship between directness and lexical markers of politeness with respect to one important type of utterance in the TTDs – requests from the operator to the caller to hold the line.

## 4. Politeness requests

One of the most common occurrences in the dialogue concerns the operator asking the caller to 'hold the line'. This requires the caller to co-operate by waiting patiently for a possibly unspecified (sometimes lengthy) amount of time while the operator attempts to resolve the caller's problem or locate an answer to their question. Consequently we decided to examine the ways in which this request was formed in order to examine politeness strategies in the data. This request takes a number of forms, and is a good basis for a study of politeness, as it involves the force of the utterance as a command (or advisement under Stiles' 1992 verbal response modes system).

There are 283 cases of such a request in the corpus, all of which were analysed for this part of our study. In Table 7 below, a taxonomy of types of requests to hold the line is presented, together with a list of the relative proportions of each sort. Of these request types, only the bare imperatives are unambiguously direct. All of the other types, as will be discussed, are, to some degree, indirect imperatives.

**Table 7:** Taxonomy of request strategies

| *Type* | *Description* | *Count* | *%* |
|---|---|---|---|
| Bare imperative | A bald imperative, with no indirectness, e.g. 'hold the line'. | 137 | 48% |
| Deletion | A fragment is produced in which the verb is absent, e.g. 'just a moment'. | 70 | 26% |
| Conditional *if-* | The request to hold the line is couched in a conditional 'if .... then' statement, e.g. 'if you could hold the line...' | 51 | 18% |
| Prediction | This is a weakened imperative having a declarative form, e.g. 'I will be one moment'. | 13 | 4% |
| Question | An indirect form of imperative, couched as a question e.g. 'could you hold the line'. | 12 | 4% |
| | **Total** | **283** | **100%** |

The table suggests that politeness is not being marked in a solely lexical fashion in the majority of these requests. Rather there is a tendency for the force of an utterance to be different from its sense[7] – it is only truly the case with bare imperatives that we have a simple unambiguous case of sense and force being identical. To consider each case in more detail, **bare imperatives** are the most common category (although it should be noted that 52% of utterances were not bare). The most common forms are 'hold on', 'hold the line' or 'bear with me'. An interesting point, however, is that the use of lexical markers of politeness is notable if the bare imperative is used – many of these bare imperatives are softened with the mitigators *please* (48% of the cases) and/or the mitigator *just* (30% of the cases). So, in terms of examining the politeness of operator speech, this study suggests that if the direct form is used, then politeness is marked lexically by a mitigator. However, lexical marking of politeness is less likely when politeness is marked via indirectness. The relationship between mitigators and directness will be discussed later in section 5.1.

The **deletion** type of utterance is distinguished by the absence of a verb: so 'one moment' implies perhaps 'wait one moment', or 'hold the line just one moment'. By omitting the verb the operator lessens the literal force of the utterance (Levinson 1983: 270) while at the same time keeping the meaning intact. Additionally, **interactional optimism** is used to placate the caller further. To elucidate, Levinson (1983: 274) discusses **interactional pessimism** whereby a speaker asking a question will use one or more mitigators e.g. 'I don't suppose that you would by any chance be able to lend me some cash, would you?' However, the cases in this category take the opposite tack of using interactional optimism. By attempting to minimise the amount of time the caller will have to wait (a 'moment', a 'minute' or a 'second') then the imposition incurred from the imperative appears lessened. There is clearly more indirectness in this approach to the formation of a request than in the bare imperative category.

The sole pattern used for the **conditional *if*** form of request is 'If you <possible premodifying mitigators> <bare imperative> ....' in all 51 cases. It is notable that the outcome implied by the conditional statement is often deleted in the speech of the operator – in only 36 cases (70% of the cases studied) is the outcome stated. Otherwise it is simply deleted. Perkins (1983: 124) argues that such *if* forms have the force of a 'polite concession towards the addressee, who is not expected to refuse the speaker's request'.

Predictions of the length of time the speaker is going to have to wait contain patterns of interactional optimism similar to the *deletion* category. Here the focus is on the operator rather than the caller. The operator side-steps the task of forcing the caller to directly acknowledge that he/she will have to wait, by framing the utterance not as an imperative, nor as an interrogative but as a *declarative*, which does not require a response (other than waiting). Again the effect is a minimisation of imposition and a notable indirectness in question formation.

Finally, as Stiles (1992: 105–6) points out, **question forms** are often idioms for requests, having an indirect force, and sense/force discrepancy often reflects conflicting interpersonal pressures. A request made in the form of a question is a hearer-based felicity condition[8] (FC), rather than a speaker-based FC such as 'I want more ice cream'. In short, it is an indirect form of request, and it is this indirectness which is a marker of politeness in the utterance. However, directness and indirectness are only one mechanism for marking politeness. As noted, lexical elements form an important component of interactional pessimism in the form of mitigators. To what extent do these interact with different types of request? Does directness lead to the use of mitigators and indirectness remove the need for them? In order to explore this interaction between directness and mitigation, we explored the relationship of mitigators to the different types of request to hold the line.

## 4.1 Mitigators

The most common mitigators used in 'hold the line' type utterances are *please* and *just*. What became apparent during our study was that while *please* may be limited to certain types of request – indeed in our study *please* is clearly related to directness, with the direct form of request frequently using *please* and the more indirect forms using it less often, as noted in the list below – other mitigators could occur in any category of request to hold the line.

| **PLEASE**[9] | |
|---|---|
| Bare imperative | 66/137 (48%) |
| Conditional *if…* | 21/51 (41%) |
| Deletion of *wait…* | 19/70 (27%) |
| Question | 4/12 (33%) |
| Prediction | 0/13 (0%) |

Stiles (1992: 175) notes that *please* is a contraction of 'if you please' and is used to turn declarative and interrogative forms into imperatives. *Please* is used most frequently to soften the bare imperative form (48% of the time), although it is also used with the conditional *if-* (41%) and question forms (33%). This finding supports Aijmer (1996: 166) who also noted that *please* occurs especially frequently in telephone conversations in the London-Lund corpus.

It is fair to say that the mitigator *just* is in fact a key means of establishing politeness by minimising imposition, regardless of the directness of request type in the data we analysed. With this said, a further discussion of mitigators is clearly useful.

| **JUST** | |
|---|---|
| Conditional *if…* | 38/51 (75%) |
| Deletion of *wait…* | 38/70 (54%) |
| Bare imperative | 41/137 (30%) |
| Question | 4/12 (33%) |
| Prediction | 1/13 (8%) |

*Just* has a minimising effect similar to specifying the length of time as 'a second'. By acting as a 'downtoning intensifier' (Aijmer 1996: 169) *just* 'seeks to imply that the force of the item concerned is limited' (Quirk et al 1985: 598). So by down-playing the inconvenience entailed in the utterance e.g. 'if you just hold the line' the operator attempts to lessen the imposition caused by making the caller wait. *Just* occurs most frequently in conditional *if* constructs, but is also popular in utterances where the command verb is deleted e.g. 'just a minute'. Unlike *please*, *just* was not highly correlated with directness, a finding which is in contrast to Aijmer (1996: 169) who notes '*just* characteristically modifies imperatives and was unusual with forms such as *can you/would you*'.

Finally, the addition of 'for me' (usually at the end of the utterance) is another mitigator used in the 100 Corpus. This mitigator personalises the request/command e.g. 'could you hold the line for me?' and is most popular when used with questions or conditional *if* constructs.

| **FOR ME** | |
|---|---|
| Bare imperative | 9/137 (7%) |
| Conditional *if*... | 11/51 (21%) |
| Question | 5/12 (42%) |

If we assume bare imperatives to be the most direct form of request, it is clear to see that some mitigators are used more typically to soften direct requests, while other mitigators, for example *for me*, are used with more indirect forms of request. Hence, while preliminary, there is evidence here that there is a connection between mitigator choice and directness – it is not simply the case that one form of politeness excludes another. Rather, different forms of mitigation (interactional pessimism) complement indirectness (e.g. interactional optimism) and directness.

## 5. Conclusion

The study undertaken on TTDs in this paper is wide ranging. From an initial lexical approach, where our focus was upon defining the characteristics of the lexis used in TTDs, we moved to a series of more focused studies examining smaller subsets of the corpus data. In carrying out our more focused studies, we found ourselves returning to the lexical level and beginning to demonstrate the inter-connected nature of lexical and non-lexical marking of politeness in the 100 Corpus. TTDs represent an interesting area of study, for as noted at the beginning of this paper, they are an increasingly frequent event in everyday life in the UK and other countries. The work presented here, we hope, also demonstrates the linguistic interest that may lie in TTDs.

## Notes

1 The corpus was named after the telephone number used to dial for operator services. It is also known as the Oasis corpus.

2 The BNC is a 100,000,000 word corpus of written and spoken British English from the early 1990s. Approximately 90% of the corpus is made up of written material and approximately 10% is made up of spoken material. The corpus covers a broad range of text types and speakers. Because of its size, it is useful in our study as being representative of contemporary British English.

3 The other 60% of initial utterances consisted of hesitation words (27%), assertions (15%), commands (7%), hedges (3%), names (1%) and others (7%).

4 Many of these markers occur in multi-word units e.g. ‘I'm sorry’, ‘thank you very much’, and so a discourse marker can include function words. For the purposes of this analysis, we have only included single words such as *thank* and *sorry* which tend always to be used for discourse purposes.

5 Words found in curly brackets refer to prototype tags, so in the 100 Corpus and the train-booking corpus, whenever a word which referred to a proper name was mentioned, it received a tag such as {name} or {station}.

6 Many of the RR utterances from the operator are repetitions of numbers spoken by the caller.

7 Sense here refers to the surface meaning of an utterance – so ‘can you hold the line?’ has the sense of a question, asking whether a caller is capable of waiting. The force of this utterance – its meaning interpreted in context – is different, as it has the force of a command to hold the line and is not a question at all.

8 Felicity conditions: proposed by Austin (1962) are conditions relating to utterances that must be met if the utterance is to ‘succeed’ e.g. saying ‘I divorce you’ will not succeed as an utterance in the UK as there is no such procedure entrenched in British law.

9 In presenting the use of mitigators in the corpus, we follow each of the category labels with two numbers. The first relates to how often the mitigator in question is used with this form of request to hold the line. The second number is how many times this type of request to hold the line is used.

## References

Aijmer, K. (1996). *Conversational routines in English.* London: Longman.

Atkinson, J. M. (1992). ‘Displaying neutrality: formal aspects of informal court proceedings.’ In Drew, P and J. Heritage *Talk at work.* Cambridge: Cambridge University Press. 199–211.

Austin, J. L. (1962). *How to do things with words.* Oxford: Clarendon Press

Holmes, J. (1984). ‘Modifying Illocutionary Force’. *Journal of Pragmatics* 8.3: 345–65.

Leech, G., A. M. McEnery, and M. Wynne (1997). ‘Further levels of annotation’. In R. Garside, G. Leech and A. McEnery (eds) *Corpus annotation.* London: Longman. 85–101.

Levinson, S. C. (1983). *Pragmatics.* Cambridge: Cambridge University Press.

McEnery, A. M. and A. Wilson (1996). *Corpus linguistics.* Edinburgh: Edinburgh University Press.

Perkins, M. R. (1983). *Modal expressions in English*. London: Frances-Pinter.
Quirk, R., S. Greenbaum, G. Leech, and J. Svartvik (1985). *A comprehensive grammar of the English language*. London: Longman.
Stenström, A-B. (1990). 'Lexical items peculiar to spoken discourse'. In Svartvik, J. *The London-Lund corpus of Spoken English: description and research*. Lund Studies in English 82. Lund: Lund University Press. 137–75.
Stiles, W. B. (1992). *Describing talk.* New York: Sage.
Whalen, J. and D. Zimmerman (1987). 'Sequential and institutional contexts in calls for help'. *Social Psychology Quarterly 50.2*: 172–85.
Whalen, J. (1990). *Processing 'emergencies' in 9-1-1 communications*. Unpublished paper. Department of Sociology, University of Oregon.
Zimmerman, D. (1984). 'Talk and its occasion: the case of calling the police'. In D. Schiffrin (ed.). *Meaning, form and use in context: linguistic applications*. Georgetown University Roundtable on Language and Linguistics. Washington D.C: Georgetown University Press. 210–28.

# The Coll Corpus: towards a corpus of web-based college student newspapers

*David C. Minugh*

University of Stockholm

**Abstract**

*Unlike major English-language corpora hitherto released, on-line college student newspapers provide an unexplored record from much younger writers. In these newspapers, 20-year-olds address their peers in a situation that largely parallels standard newspaper writing as regards formal correctness and time pressure. Nearly unconstrained by outside intervention or house style sheets, they deal with a range of university student interests, including creative writing. This preliminary version of the Coll Corpus consists of one issue each of nearly all 300-plus college and university newspapers available on the Web as of spring 1999, with a total of 3.88 million words. Although American English (AmE) dominates, the resultant geographical distribution is relatively well matched to actual population ratios. In its present form, the corpus already allows exploration of numerous lexical and semantic features along temporal and geographic dimensions. Given its on-line accessibility, future versions should be easily expandable by several orders of magnitude.*

## 1. Introduction

The successful completion of (for their time) very large corpus projects, such as the Brown Corpus and its British successor the LOB Corpus, or, more recently, the COBUILD Bank of English and the BNC, inevitably entails one major drawback: precisely because such corpora are so very useful, there is a very real danger that research at the time becomes concentrated on those particular corpora; in a sense, they come indirectly to define what a corpus 'should' be. The title of the 1998 ICAME volume, *Corpora Galore*, thus serves not merely to indicate its wide-ranging contents, but also as a salutary reminder of the need for many different types of corpora and corpus investigations.

One of the more important potential sources of major 'accidental'[1] corpora consists of the annual CDs released by various newspapers. In particular, 'quality' newspapers have always formed a major component of large corpora, but only recently has research begun into their potential use as stand-alone corpora.[2] Their role as daily reading in middle-class households makes them particularly interesting, although they are clearly somewhat restricted in scope and subject.[3]

The corpus to be presented in this paper continues this tradition of seeking ways of finding additional sources of large-scale corpora. It is somewhat similar to standard newspaper corpora, but innovative on several accounts, as specified below.

## 2. The choice of corpus

Although detailed descriptions of English have traditionally been centered upon the standard of written educated British English, increasing emphasis from the 60s onwards has been placed upon opening up this descriptive world to more of the many varieties of English that actually exist. This in turn makes increasingly difficult the Chomskyan demand for reliance on native-speaker intuition.[4] After all, few indeed are the speakers of English who can provide us with reliable intuitive data about e.g. both British and American English.[5]

By its very nature, the collective enterprise called the English language thus seems to cry out for a corpus linguistics approach. But how are the appropriate corpora to be found or created, and how much are they to be shaped? The first large-scale answers, such as Brown and LOB, were designed and sampled corpora with a clearly defined geographical base, and their relevance as reference corpora lives on, not least thanks to FROWN and FLOB.

Our generation's megacorpora, however, have broadened the base, perhaps most notably with the BNC's inclusion of the COLT subcorpus of spoken teenage British speech. Nevertheless, the available multimillion-word corpora, as well as all available newspaper CDs, clearly consist of relatively formal written English, to an overwhelming extent written by established reporters and columnists, which unavoidably leads to the conclusion that these corpora decisively reflect the language of educated middle-aged and older writers.

It should, however, also be imperative to seek out further ways of investigating the language of the coming generation, as well. If we go back to Chomsky's claims about intuition, it would seem that few academic linguists qualify as native speakers in the under-25 bracket. Let us therefore instead begin with the question of how corpus linguistics may be used to investigate this rather different major segment of English, and do so throughout the English-speaking world.

It seems clear that the written production of under-25s now takes place primarily in two contexts: that of the Internet and that of the educational system. It is probable that the home pages and chat rooms of the Net may be one source that bears more than a passing resemblance to some of the COLT exchanges (although perhaps with a rather larger male dominance), but the present paper will not pursue this more casual side of the Internet.

In the second context, that of the educational system, the only texts that are both abundant in number and aimed at the writers' peers (rather than their teachers) are student newspapers. Since secondary schools are frequently expected to act in loco parentis, they are normally held accountable for the contents of their student publications, which places certain limits on their freedom. This by no means totally disqualifies them from our interest, since many of the phenomena to be discussed in this paper could also be examined there, such as the use of modals, gender-related language choices and much more. A more serious objection is that adult editors (primarily the English teachers at the school in question) may also intervene when it comes to the language itself, and demand a more 'correct' (i.e. more formal) style than their students.

College and university editors, on the other hand, have almost complete freedom in all such respects, and the Coll Corpus is therefore based on student newspapers from tertiary educational institutions. A typical claim to uncensored freedom may be seen in the proud disclaimer of the student online newspaper from Auburn, Alabama, the *Aumnibus*:

(1) No content on this page or following pages has been reviewed or approved by Auburn University Montgomery, and the *Aumnibus* is solely responsible for its content. ... The *Aumnibus* is the student newspaper of Auburn University Montgomery and is produced entirely by students with no censorship from the faculty advisor or the administration.

A few caveats: particularly for colleges financed and run by religious communities, this freedom may be somewhat more limited, but as regards the key question of the freedom of the press, it has been assumed that this freedom is fundamentally not at issue in the Coll Corpus catchment areas.[6] As regards the age of the contributors, it is possible that a few of those involved are older students, but given the standard pattern of Western education, it can safely be assumed that the vast majority of contributors are under 25. (Possible exceptions include stories from the 'Police Blotter'[7] and, more pertinently, letters from professors and statements by the university or college administration.) There are a fair number of letters to the Editor and freelance articles, but it is clear that a large amount of this material is written by students of journalism, and especially in the smaller papers, only a few writers may be represented. On the other hand, since literally hundreds of newspapers are involved, no individual writers or publishing-house norms can dominate.

Since many corpus questions require large or very large amounts of data, it is highly desirable that these texts already be easily available in electronic form. That condition is fulfilled by college and university student newspaper publications on the Internet. The Coll Corpus is thus designed to explore the possibility that online university and college student newspapers may provide us with a large enough corpus to study the evolving language of the next generation, as it seeks to find a voice that speaks to its own, untrammeled by the restraints of publishing houses or copy-editors, and containing a wide variety of writing. Certain universities, particularly in the U.S., have a strong religious orientation or political commitments, and their tightly-reasoned theological or economic discussions may be expected to balance some of the more scurrilous parodies and hedonistic aspects of other schools (names withheld by request).

One major drawback of choosing a corpus of this kind is that it is not immediately comparable with designed corpora, even their 'journalistic' sections, or with the larger corpora such as the BNC (an objection that also holds for commercial newspaper CDs). The Coll Corpus will in addition almost certainly contain an unusually high component of parody and language playfulness, since its newspapers are considerably less stereotyped than commercial newspapers, and there is a significant component of student creative writing, both poems and stories. Nor is it likely that a full regional balance can be easily maintained, as will be discussed below.[8] Nevertheless, the advantages of having large-scale access to young people's written language makes the project well worth doing.

## 3. Collecting the corpus

The technical criterion for inclusion was that the student newspaper already be online, i.e. freely available on the Internet. The initial search for such papers quickly turned up several important search paths, including a relatively accurate listing of over 200 American college newspapers, complete with Web addresses; unfortunately, it has not been updated since May 1999. Canada was also relatively easy, but finding sites in other countries turned out to be a time-consuming task, not least because such compilations do not yet seem to exist.[9] Yahoo's layered searches sometimes help, but more often than not contain no information about the student newspapers that actually do exist on any given campus. Moreover, many official university websites either do not acknowledge their own student publications or bury the links to them in a page several levels down, under '/campus life/student union/activities' or the like. In the end, the Coll list nevertheless embraced some 300 websites available in spring 1999, and there is every likelihood that this list will grow fairly rapidly over the next few years.

The method of collection used for the first version of Coll was embarrassingly primitive, yet relatively effective: with the Web and Microsoft Office open at the same time, a cut-and-paste technique sufficed in most cases.[10] In this first version, the entire Coll Corpus of some 3.9 M words was collected on a Pentium or a Pentium II PC, with a number of texts being downloaded via modem.[11] The entire corpus in its current form takes up only 55 megabytes and thus fits easily onto a Zip disk, and can be effortlessly handled by WordSmith running on a Pentium. Thus, no sophisticated machines, software or technical expertise are actually required to assemble or explore such a corpus. This is a point that deserves reiteration: it is fully possible for individual researchers and students working with modest means to collect their own net-based corpora. This is not to claim that access to such expertise or machines would not improve the resultant corpus – on the contrary, one of the major goals of this paper is to arouse interest among those better qualified to work with storing and organizing data of this sort, so as to produce a faster, more user-friendly environment for queries. Nevertheless, it should be emphasized that even without expertise, it appears fully possible to create thoroughly useable multimillion-word corpora within only a month or two!

As indicated above, all publications had to be student-run to qualify for inclusion, and thus not be official organs of or derived from outside the college or university. Therefore, all articles specifically labelled as being provided by wirepress services or reprinted from commercial newspapers were excluded; on the other hand, supplements containing, e.g. arts sections consisting of student fiction, were included, as were university documents published in these student newspapers.

The time factor turned out in fact to be extremely difficult to control. Some student newspapers are published daily, others weekly or monthly, some sporadically, and yet others simply leave on their website the last issue posted by a Web-oriented editor, even though he may have graduated three years ago![12] Many of the online papers that publish more sporadically retain material from issue to issue, giving priority to updating the news and sports sections. One specific drawback of the present material is that it was gathered during the late spring and early summer, a time when many papers post only partial editions, or the (somewhat special) graduation issue from June.

As regards the past, some papers offer back issues from as far back as 1995 or 1996, which can imply 50–100 issues for a weekly, while others offer only an archive search for the past, while yet others apparently post only the current issue; a few have been withdrawn from the Net, and others that are claimed to be there never quite reached the online stage.

Looking to the future, there are various 'Watch this site' signs, occasionally with comments such as that the site was last updated in January 1998. In addition, there are literally thousands of colleges whose student papers are not yet online, and many may be expected to add net versions as time goes on. Where issues have disappeared, it may prove possible to contact the newspaper directly and obtain back files that way. A very few student papers have closed sites accessible to students only, but the politics of alumni financial support to education, at least in the United States, virtually guarantee that most sites will remain open. Finally, there is always the threat of technological change that could close this window of textual opportunity, such as conversion to purely graphic files.

As with all corpus research, a knottier problem is that of permission to use the material. In its current state, the Coll Corpus has simply been collected, and thus is not yet available to the research community at large. However, a first E-mail request to 150 newspapers for permission to include it in a publicly-available corpus resulted in a dozen granting permission at once and one more after a follow-up letter; none refused permission. It may thus be assumed that gaining permission may be an onerous task, but should on the whole not prove impossible.

In this initial version of the Coll Corpus, each publication is represented by one issue only. The entire issue is included, but links backwards are not followed, even where the reader is invited to via hotlinks.[13] It will subsequently be possible to greatly expand the corpus by relaxing this restriction (admittedly at the cost of loss of representativity). One potential solution is to establish both a balanced monitor corpus and a much larger, geographically-skewed 'kitchen-sink' corpus.

The average issue contains about 10–15,000 words, with the largest being just over 30,000; the shortest is the terse statement from the University of Southwestern Louisiana:

(2) Due to budget problems, *The Vermilion* will no longer be placed online.

Geographically speaking, no area of the United States failed to be represented, but that is not true of the entire English-speaking world (see below). In all, as Table 1 indicates, 288 newspapers are represented, heavily skewed in favor of the U.S (where the figures are presented by U.S. Census regions). This distribution is nevertheless not strikingly out of line with the population figures for the traditional, relatively monolingual English-speaking world.

**Table 1:** The geographical distribution of online college student newspapers

| Country | Total wds | % wds | Target % | Pop. (M) | Papers | Avg. size |
|---|---|---|---|---|---|---|
| | | | | | | |
| United Kingdom | 368,803 | 10 % | 20 % | 80 | 26 | 14,185 |
| Australia | 48,965 | 1 % | 4 % | 18 | 4 | 12,241 |
| New Zealand | 23,671 | 1 % | 1 % | 3 | 2 | 11,836 |
| Canada | 401,614 | 10 % | 6 % | 25 | 35 | 11,475 |
| United States | 2,980,289 | 77 % | 67 % | 270 | 215 | 13,862 |
| Ireland/Eire | 28,552 | 1 % | 1 % | 4 | 3 | 9,517 |
| South Africa | 25,963 | 1 % | 0 % | 2 | 3 | 8,654 |
| **Totals:** | **3,877,857** | | | **402** | **288** | **11,681** |

| US breakdown: | Total wds | % wds | Target % | Pop. (M) | Papers | Avg. size |
|---|---|---|---|---|---|---|
| | | | | | | |
| New England | 363,799 | 12 % | 5 % | 13 | 23 | 15,817 |
| Middle Atlantic | 573,085 | 19 % | 14 % | 38 | 22 | 26,049 |
| East North Central | 547,370 | 18 % | 16 % | 44 | 42 | 13,033 |
| West North Central | 270,415 | 9 % | 7 % | 19 | 28 | 9,658 |
| South Atlantic | 450,238 | 15 % | 18 % | 49 | 32 | 14,070 |
| East South Central | 111,969 | 4 % | 6 % | 17 | 10 | 11,197 |
| West South Central | 165,891 | 6 % | 11 % | 30 | 19 | 8,731 |
| Mountain | 199,744 | 7 % | 6 % | 17 | 13 | 15,365 |
| Pacific | 297,778 | 10 % | 16 % | 43 | 26 | 11,453 |
| **US Totals** | **2,980,289** | **100 %** | **100 %** | **270** | **215** | **13,862** |

In the geographical sense, this is a paper about a future corpus, rather than the present-day possibilities: for many types of comparison that demand large corpora, such as low-frequency lexical items or constructions and most idioms, numerous areas of the English-speaking world are not yet sufficiently represented by student online newspapers, although that situation will inevitably change.

## 4. The content of student newspapers

Nearly all student papers offer five major sections:

(i) news, often divided into campus news and general news
(ii) editorials, op-eds and Letters to the Editor
(iii) sports (with a major component of women's sports)
(iv) features (including feature pieces, columnists and the odd horoscope)
(v) arts and entertainment (including film, CD, theater reviews)

Other areas that may be represented include:

(vi) university policy documents, decisions, visions and speeches

(vii) community news, including the 'Police Blotter'
(viii) 'Greek news', i.e. news from the world of fraternities and sororities
(ix) classified advertisements
(x) publication policies, presentation of staff and E-mail response slots

Given the relative uniformity of writer and reader age and social status, it is clear that this corpus cannot approach the breadth of the BNC or COBUILD corpora, but that should not affect many of the comparisons that it will permit. It is the latter that will now be discussed.

## 5. Analyzing the material

Since the corpus merely consists of text files, the primary method of querying the corpus has been WordSmith searches. To enable comparisons, the results have been normalized to instances per million, which also facilitates comparison with the corresponding 1 M word corpora from the 1960s (Brown, LOB) and 1990s (Frown, FLOB).[14] In consequence of the small size of the Irish, Australian, New Zealand and South African components (taken together, they comprise less than 4% of the corpus material), they have normally been included with the UK component to form the category 'non-North American'. In addition, there are potential comparisons to be made with the BNC and COBUILD corpora.

### 5.1 Modal verbs[15]

The figures for the modals (per million words) are presented in Table 2. As might be expected, the frequencies for the major modals continue to develop along the lines indicated by the 60s to 90s Brown/LOB to Frown/FLOB shifts, with *can*, *will* and the contracted *'ll* all gaining, while *could*, *would* and particularly *must* and *might* are even less frequent. The increasing reluctance to use *may* shown in Frown is only partially supported here,[16] and the gain by *will* is much larger than anything indicated by the standard corpora.

**Table 2:** The major modal verbs (per 1 M words)

| | | | | | COLL | | | |
|---|---|---|---|---|---|---|---|---|
| Item: | Brown | Frown | LOB | FLOB | US | Non-US | Non-NAm | Canada |
| | | | | | | | | |
| Tokens | 1,000,000 | 1,000,000 | 1,000,000 | 1,000,000 | 2,763,781 | 956,891 | 500,336 | 456,555 |
| Conversion | 1.00 | 1.00 | 1.00 | 1.00 | 0.36 | 1.05 | 2.00 | 2.19 |
| | | | | | | | | |
| **CAN** | **1,913** | **1,997** | **1,801** | **1,999** | **2,242** | **2,767** | **2,784** | **2,749** |
| can | 1,751 | 1,737 | 1,655 | 1,772 | 1,936 | 2,357 | 2,380 | 2,330 |
| cannot | 252 | 193 | 318 | 240 | 135 | 134 | 104 | 166 |
| can't | 162 | 260 | 146 | 227 | 306 | 411 | 404 | 418 |
| **COULD** | **1,762** | **1,655** | **1,729** | **1,766** | **1,084** | **1,161** | **1,243** | **1,071** |

| | | | | | | | | |
|---|---|---|---|---|---|---|---|---|
| could | 1,589 | 1,472 | 1,604 | 1,564 | 969 | 1,056 | 1,129 | 975 |
| couldn't | 172 | 180 | 122 | 198 | 111 | 103 | 110 | 96 |
| could've | 1 | 3 | 3 | 4 | 4 | 2 | 4 | 0 |
| **MAY** | **1,392** | **940** | **1,422** | **1,208** | **1,135** | **1,067** | **1,043** | **1,093** |
| **MIGHT** | **671** | **639** | **781** | **642** | **353** | **414** | **470** | **353** |
| might | 671 | 639 | 776 | 641 | 353 | 413 | 468 | 353 |
| mightn't | 0 | 0 | 3 | 0 | 0 | 0 | 0 | 0 |
| might've | 0 | 0 | 2 | 1 | 0 | 1 | 2 | 0 |
| **MUST** | **1,016** | **670** | **1,114** | **816** | **484** | **439** | **452** | **425** |
| must | 1,009 | 663 | 1,094 | 803 | 483 | 436 | 446 | 425 |
| mustn't | 5 | 6 | 18 | 6 | 0 | 3 | 6 | 0 |
| must've | 2 | 1 | 2 | 7 | 0 | 0 | 0 | 0 |
| **OUGHT** | **68** | **50** | **104** | **58** | **17** | **14** | **20** | **7** |
| ought | 68 | 50 | 103 | 58 | 17 | 14 | 20 | 7 |
| oughtn't | 0 | 0 | 1 | 0 | 0 | 0 | 0 | 0 |
| **SHALL** | **257** | **150** | **354** | **199** | **17** | **43** | **60** | **24** |
| shan't | 1 | 1 | 5 | 2 | 0 | 0 | 0 | 0 |
| **SHOULD** | **896** | **791** | **1,284** | **1,148** | **890** | **904** | **947** | **856** |
| should | 874 | 757 | 1,259 | 1,115 | 843 | 852 | 901 | 797 |
| shouldn't | 22 | 28 | 25 | 29 | 46 | 49 | 44 | 55 |
| should've | 0 | 6 | 0 | 4 | 1 | 3 | 2 | 4 |
| **WILL** | **2,335** | **1,996** | **2,348** | **2,381** | **4,558** | **4,009** | **3,392** | **4,685** |
| will | 2,230 | 1,845 | 2,240 | 2,284 | 4,398 | 3,786 | 3,196 | 4,433 |
| won't | 105 | 151 | 108 | 97 | 160 | 223 | 196 | 252 |
| **WOULD** | **2,840** | **2,565** | **2,783** | **2,438** | **2,061** | **1,896** | **1,895** | **2,175** |
| would | 2,711 | 2,418 | 2,673 | 2,308 | 1,936 | 1,894 | 1,763 | 2,037 |
| wouldn't | 129 | 141 | 107 | 128 | 117 | 134 | 132 | 136 |
| would've | 0 | 6 | 3 | 2 | 9 | 1 | 0 | 2 |
| **'LL** | **429** | **469** | **505** | **402** | **434** | **626** | **640** | **611** |

These changes, together with the effective vanishing of *ought* and *shall*, and the literal disappearance of *shan't*, point to a familiar major problem (Mair 1998:153–54): is there an actual change in the language, or merely a wider acceptance of less formal registers? More precisely: since relatively informal texts are to a greater extent being published today than a generation ago, we may merely be noting a shift in taste as to what gets published, rather than a real change in the norms of the printed language (formal texts would thus still be formal in the same way – but there would be fewer such texts).[17] In the present case, this is complicated by the possibility that these young speakers have not yet mastered the more formal English used by their elders, but will do so in the coming decades.[18] It nonetheless seems likely that after several years of college or university education, these writers in their early 20s are not likely to change their writing habits, with the obvious exception of those that enter fields with archaizing demands, such as the law. Yet, if informal styles are indeed expanding into areas previously reserved for formal styles, a point which the much higher ratio of *can't* to *cannot* would seem to indicate, how are we to interpret the surprisingly low number of instances of *'ll*, a form that would seem to be an obvious feature of a less formal style? This question will be discussed at length in section 6, below.

### 5.2 Lexical comparisons across the varieties

Table 3 provides statistics, normalized to per 1 M words, for a few of the traditional British/American vocabulary distinctions. The first group is that of the *-st* and *-s* endings in *amid* etc. While Americans (and Canadians) continue to completely reject *whilst* and only occasionally use *amongst*, it seems as if young Americans are accepting *towards* and actually prefer *amidst* – since this data is in sharp contrast to both Brown and Frown, it is a point worth investigating further.

Traditional BrE/AmE distinctions such as *windscreen/windshield*, *lorry/truck* and *nappy/diaper* provide few surprises, especially as the latter pair is not normally part of college life! As for other, less well-known lexical distinctions, the limitations of a 'small' corpus become apparent: 4 M words are insufficient for such lexical items as *gazump*, *blindside*, or *schlep(p)*; here, corpora of at least an order of magnitude larger are necessary, not least in order to check distribution between varieties.[19] This claim would appear to be contradicted by the extraordinary number of American instances of the British slang term *shag*; they derive, however, almost entirely from reviews of a film called *The Spy Who Shagged Me*, featuring such forgettable characters as Felicity Shagwell and Ivana Humpalot.[20]

Unlike the data seen for the established corpora, in the Coll Corpus, all areas of English appear to be abandoning the mutated vowels in the comparative *elder/older* and superlative *eldest/oldest*. Only derivatives such as *village elders* appear to be surviving.

**Table 3:** Comparisons of Coll and the established corpora. Vocabulary I

| | Brown | Frown | LOB | FLOB | US | Canada | Non-NAm | Non-US |
|---|---|---|---|---|---|---|---|---|
| Conv. factor | 1.00 | 1.00 | 1.00 | 1.00 | 0.36 | 2.19 | 2.00 | 1.05 |
| | | | | | | | | |
| **Br/Am:** | | | | | | | | |
| *amid* | 14 | 17 | 9 | 18 | 6 | 7 | 16 | 11 |
| *amidst* | 3 | 2 | 5 | 8 | 11 | 4 | 12 | 8 |
| *among* | 369 | 451 | 304 | 249 | 247 | 197 | 92 | 142 |
| *amongst* | 4 | 1 | 43 | 51 | 9 | 24 | 122 | 75 |
| *toward* | 385 | 360 | 14 | 11 | 137 | 53 | 12 | 31 |
| *towards* | 64 | 17 | 316 | 293 | 66 | 158 | 192 | 176 |
| *while* | 679 | 727 | 580 | 742 | 972 | 990 | 873 | 929 |
| *whilst* | 0 | 0 | 65 | 54 | 0 | 2 | 218 | 115 |
| | | | | | | | | |
| *elder* | 7 | 10 | 15 | 9 | 2 | 0 | 2 | 1 |
| *older* | 93 | 125 | 102 | 84 | 64 | 77 | 50 | 63 |
| *eldest* | 5 | 9 | 15 | 19 | 1 | 0 | 4 | 2 |
| *oldest* | 14 | 17 | 11 | 19 | 18 | 18 | 16 | 17 |
| | | | | | | | | |
| *windscreen* | 0 | 0 | 3 | 8 | 0 | 0 | 6 | 3 |
| *windshield* | 6 | 6 | 0 | 0 | 3 | 0 | 0 | 0 |
| *lorry* | 0 | 1 | 20 | 16 | 0 | 0 | 6 | 3 |

| | | | | | | | | |
|---|---|---|---|---|---|---|---|---|
| *truck* | 83 | 104 | 13 | 21 | 37 | 20 | 10 | 15 |
| *nappy, -ies* | 0 | 0 | 1 | 1 | 0 | 0 | 2 | 1 |
| *diaper* | 3 | 3 | 2 | 0 | 3 | 4 | 0 | 2 |
| *Pampers* | 0 | 4 | 0 | 0 | 0 | 0 | 0 | 0 |
| *Huggies* | 0 | 0 | 0 | 0 | 0 | 0 | 0 | 0 |
| | | | | | | | | |
| *date rape* | 0 | 0 | 0 | 0 | 1 | 11 | 6 | 8 |
| *acquaintance r* | 0 | 0 | 0 | 0 | 1 | 0 | 0 | 0 |
| *gazump* | 0 | 0 | 0 | 0 | 0 | 0 | 0 | 0 |
| *blindside* | 0 | 1 | 0 | 0 | 0 | 2 | 0 | 0 |
| *shag* | 0 | 0 | 1 | 2 | 15 | 15 | 50 | 33 |
| *schlep* | 0 | 0 | 0 | 0 | 1 | 2 | 0 | 1 |

**Table 4:** Gender ratios in Coll and other current corpora. (Items in **boldface** indicate the most gender-neutral ratios for each category.)

| Term | *Coll* | *BNC* | *NYT 96* | *IND 99* | *LAT 96* |
|---|---|---|---|---|---|
| | | | | | |
| *he/she* | 2.14 | **1.79** | 2.41 | 3.01 | 2.28 |
| *his/{her/hers}* | 1.79 | **1.32** | 2.26 | 2.75 | 2.20 |
| *spokesman/-woman* | 2.24 | 6.43 | 2.26 | 3.75 | **1.95** |
| *spokesman/-person* | **0.77** | 15.66 | 138.14 | 24.00 | 36.97 |
| *man/woman* | 2.42 | 2.68 | **1.87** | 2.92 | 2.05 |
| *men/women* | **0.48** | 0.97 | 1.05 | 1.32 | 0.95 |

In the area of gender and lexis, it is hardly surprising that the ratios from the spoken part of the BNC are relatively consistently among the most gender-neutral ones, since it was balanced for speaker gender.[21] To a noticeable extent the Coll Corpus also appears to have more material about women than normal newspapers, as seen in Table 4. In Coll, *spokesperson* actually outnumbers *spokesman*, perhaps heralding a permanent change in our language. On the other hand, the terms are by a full order of magnitude more common in regular newspapers, indicating that this is a term firmly entrenched in the larger world of (male-dominated) politics. Certain other omissions are more startling, such as the extraordinarily low search results for *acquaintance/date rape* (4 and 11 instances, respectively, for the entire Coll Corpus).

## 5.3 Lexis and syntax

As for items touching on grammar (Table 4), *snuck* continues to gain ground on *sneaked*, although here too a larger corpus would be desirable. There is, however, enough material to continue an earlier investigation (Mair 1998: 150) on the British willingness to accept *prevent* + V-*ing* without the preposition *from*:

(3) It is, however, a skill worth acquiring; the more fixations you have, the more there is to prevent you from being bored. Which is good. [Leicester University, *Ripple*]
(4) This should be done twice as the double lining prevents the custard leaking through and sticking to the tin. [University of Manchester, *Grip*]

Interestingly enough, the BrE college data is not nearly as conclusive as is the shift between LOB and FLOB would seem to indicate. Canadians, like Americans, seem not to be taking part in this shift. Since this change is not of American origin, it should be of particular interest to monitor the possible spread of this new structure to other areas of the English-speaking world; the present type of corpus offers one future way to do so.[22]

**Table 5:** Comparisons of Coll and the established corpora. Grammar I.

| | | Brown | Frown | LOB | FLOB | US | Canada | Non-NAm | Non-US |
|---|---|---|---|---|---|---|---|---|---|
| Conv. factor | | 1.00 | 1.00 | 1.00 | 1.00 | 0.36 | 2.19 | 2.00 | 1.05 |
| *sneaked* | | 6 | 2 | 1 | 1 | 1 | 0 | 0 | 0 |
| *snuck* | | 1 | 0 | 0 | 0 | 2 | 2 | 2 | 2 |
| | | | | | | | | | |
| *prevent + from* | | 50 | 36 | 37 | 22 | 46 | 39 | 36 | 38 |
| *prevent -from* | | 0 | 2 | 7 | 20 | 0 | 2 | 18 | 10 |
| | | | | | | | | | |
| *if...would have* | | 0 | 1 | 1 | 0 | 3 | 4 | 0 | 2 |
| | | | | | | | | | |
| mand. subj: | | | | | | US | Other | UK | Can |
| mand. | active | 45 | 64 | 2 | 22 | 54 | 55 | 41 | 22 |
| | passive | 59 | 36 | 10 | 22 | 22 | 16 | 31 | 2 |
| *should* | active | 8 | 5 | 50 | 38 | 4 | 0 | 5 | 4 |
| | passive | 6 | 4 | 31 | 29 | 2 | 8 | 5 | 4 |

A shift in the hypothetical past *if*-clause that is now quite common in spoken American involves the double marking via *would*:

(5) Sprint coach and drill sergeant, Coco James, who is faster than a two-legged cow, summed up the meet with these words: 'The team performed admirably under the conditions, and if we would have had preliminaries we would have done better.' [University of Minnesota (Morris), *The University Register*]

This pattern was noted more than a decade ago by Quirk et al. (1985: 1011n.c), and has consistently been stigmatized in e.g. American college entrance exams.[23] Despite its nearly ubiquitous presence in the spoken form, it is strikingly rare in these college texts, with only 7 US and 2 Canadian instances (normalized to 3 and 4, respectively).

The mandative subjunctive v the *should* forms was a point dealt with in some detail by Marianne Hundt (1998: 159–75), building inter alia on Johansson and

Norheim's (1988: 27–36) earlier work with the Brown and LOB corpora. Examples (6) and (7) represent the two choices under consideration:[24]

(6) Those two candidates, who lost big at the straw poll, can demand that Bush come clean all they want. [Iowa State University, *Iowa State Daily*]
(7) Buhrow recommends that engineers who aspire to become brewmasters should take classes in biology, biochemistry, cereal chemistry, microbiology and fluids while earning their undergraduate degrees. [University of Iowa, *Hawkeye Engineer*]

With their data as a jumping-off point, it may be noted that the present student data, while not as striking as the data from those corpora, clearly indicates that the mandative subjunctive is strongly preferred by Americans and Canadians over the *should* construction. But it should also be noted that even in BrE college texts, the mandative form is far more common than the *should* form, in sharp contrast to LOB and even FLOB. Moreover, a breakdown into active v passive forms indicates that the active now dominates, unlike the data from the previous corpora, which suggested that the (presumably more formal) passive was the more likely of the two.

**Table 6:** The *way* construction

| Source | Corpus size | Verb totals | Verb types | Hapax legomena | Hapax % |
|---|---|---|---|---|---|
| | | | | | |
| BNC | 100 M | 6129 | 566 | 321 | 57 % |
| BN | 44 M | 1549 | 205 | 129 | 63 % |
| Coll | 4 M | 231 | 85 | 61 | 72 % |

The *way* construction, with various verbs that can fit in the V slot, e.g. 'She wisecracked/clawed/slithered/smiled her way through the crowd', is an example of a construction that can be investigated in a corpus of this magnitude.[25] As Table 6 indicates, the pattern is the same as that found in larger corpora, such as the BNC, with the expected higher percentages of single instances in smaller corpora. With no less than 85 different verbs to choose from in Coll, there is nevertheless ample evidence of how variable the construction may be, including such creative surprises as:

(8) [The] album kicks, shouts and pouts its way through an adrenalised journey into no-compromise techno. [University of Edinburgh, *Edinburgh Student*]

## 6. A question of formality

The above are only a small sample of the types of searches that may be run on this material. Another aspect worth examining is that of formality. This is a question that has repeatedly been raised, not least by Mair and Biber in numerous publications.[26] For the Coll Corpus, this is particularly acute, since student publications may exhibit a larger component of informal styles than many others. Some of the various types of evidence are presented in Table 7.

**Table 7:** Formality in Coll and the established corpora.

| | Brown | Frown | LOB | FLOB | US | Canada | Non-NAm | Non-US |
|---|---|---|---|---|---|---|---|---|
| Conv. factor | 1.00 | 1.00 | 1.00 | 1.00 | 0.36 | 2.19 | 2.00 | 1.05 |
| | | | | | | | | |
| **Formality:** | | | | | | | | |
| *albeit* | 2 | 10 | 4 | 16 | 9 | 9 | 22 | 16 |
| *lest* | 17 | 10 | 3 | 8 | 3 | 0 | 4 | 2 |
| *whereas* | 0 | 0 | 0 | 0 | 0 | 0 | 0 | 0 |
| *behove* | 0 | 0 | 0 | 1 | 0 | 0 | 2 | 1 |
| *behoove* | 1 | 2 | 0 | 0 | 1 | 0 | 0 | 0 |
| *granted [that]* | 8 | 7 | 1 | 4 | 13 | 9 | 4 | 6 |
| *whether it be* | 3 | 1 | 7 | 0 | 9 | 4 | 6 | 5 |
| | | | | | | | | |
| *on* | 6,719 | 6,898 | 6,912 | 7,122 | 7,189 | 7,272 | 7,469 | 7,375 |
| *upon* | 493 | 196 | 407 | 243 | 168 | 177 | 180 | 179 |

Beginning with a series of formal items, such as *lest* and *albeit*, the present data matches that from FLOB, confirming that *albeit* is now well-established in BrE, while *lest* is nearly absent from the college corpus. Of the 9 instances of the latter, only 5 may be said to have been used in a serious context, that of a Biblical or political quote (examples (9) and (10)), while the others range from the dubiously serious to the clearly playful (examples (11) and (12)):

(9) Perhaps owing to the unfortunate Christian dictate of 'judge not, lest ye be judged,' we have managed to bind our moral development to the shallowest of circles with this fatuous standard. [Carnegie Mellon University: *The Tartan Online*]

(10) When the Government breezed into office 12 months ago, they did so with the largest majority of any Labour government, lest we should forget. [Edinburgh University: *The Edinburgh Student*]

(11) Parents avert your eyes lest something within this column sends you into a conniption fit. [Virginia Tech: *Collegiate Times*]

(12) For example, one of my personal faves . . . er, favorites, is *jook*. It's Bahamian for *stab*. So let this be a warning: beware lest ye happen to commit a verbal offense in my presence, for I may, perforce, be overcome by the insatiable need to jook you. [Princeton University: *The Daily Princetonian*]

Of the 40 instances of *albeit*, on the other hand, only (13) and (14) appear to be at all playful. Examples (15) to (17) illustrate its use (in a wide range of subject areas) as an alternative to *although*:

(13) Living in Clinton for a year, albeit in some sadistically altered former barn whose stability has always been in question, has provided me with a sense of connection and familiarity with this place that campus life never could have supplied. [Hamilton College: *SpecOnline*]

(14) The soldier in me finally became too much, and I, the Black Hand, changed the course of history with one simple, albeit strategic, pinch. 'Fire in the hole!' I bellowed. [University of Wisconsin (Milwalkee): *The Post Online*]

(15) I'm as giddy as a little school girl, albeit a school girl with a self inflicted SLAYER tattoo. The real kicker on this one is that they re playing with the gnarly NOMADS, the triple-guitared QUADRAJETS and Missoula natives gone-west-coast-big-time, FIREBALLS OF FREEDOM. [University of Montana: *Montana Kaimin*]

(16) Western Australian students still go on bar crawls; they still have clubs and societies; and they still have student newspapers. (albeit full of corporate advertising. Eds) [University of Newcastle: *Opus*]

(17) If a bum shoulder wasn't going her keep her out though, a new position wouldn't either. The new position, albeit less stressful than catcher, was nonetheless quite taxing on Slone's injury. [University of Chicago: *Chicago Maroon*]

Thus, of the two, *lest* may well function as a sign of parody or playfulness, unless in a direct quote, whereas *albeit* is clearly still part of the normal range of the English in the Coll Corpus.[27]

One example which deserves closer consideration is the uses to which *thou/thee/thy/thine* are now put. Since this pronoun is increasingly no longer a natural part of our life, except in prayers to God, its use is becoming confined to quotes, parody or otherwise 'exuberant' language; the high value for 'pseudo-archaic' (as in (20)) is a direct indication of this latter pattern.

**Table 8:** Uses of *thou* and related forms, per million words

| Abbrev | Type per M: | Coll | BNC | 94 Ind |
|---|---|---|---|---|
| | | | | |
| **Q** | Quote | 1.0 | | 3.85 |
| **PQ** | Pseudo-quote | 1.25 | | .35 |
| **I** | Idiom | .75 | | .48 |
| **PI** | Pseudo-idiom | 0.00 | | .58 |
| **A** | Archaic | .75 | | .68 |
| **PA** | Pseudo-archaic | 1.25 | | .18 |
| **D** | Dialect | 0.00 | | .48 |
| **S** | Song | 0.00 | | .40 |
| **M** | Meta-comment | 0.00 | | .10 |
| **Totals:** | | 5.00 | 20.09 | 7.08 |

(18) Compiling the *Best of the Blotter* for State Of The Gate, I saw that a map of Africa had been stolen from Alumni, as well as some combination door handles. Come on, people. I seem to remember a neat quote from my Western Traditions reading (which I actually did) – something about 'Thou shalt not steal.' Somebody important said that – hmm – could it have been God?!?! [Colgate University *The Colgate-Maroon*]

(19) Are we forgetting that The United States of America kicks some serious a**? We are already on the most bitchin' continent, so why not explore it and discover just why this country tis of thee is such an oh so sweet land of liberty. [California State Univ, Chico, *The Orion Online*]

(20) Tune in next year to find out: Will I ever get a piece of ass? Will someone eventually kick my ass? Is it wrong to covet thy neighbors ass? And, of course, will I ever get my sammiches, ass? Ya know, if you say 'ass' enough times, it really starts to sound stupid. [University of North Dakota, *The Digital Student*]

Among other indications of formality, the continuing decrease in use of *upon* is also clearly seen in this corpus. The formal structure, *granted [that]*, does, however, seem to be holding its own. Another point of comparison is provided by the subject-operator inversion with an introductory adverbial such as *hardly* or *no sooner*. It seems clear that the Coll use of this type of construction is within the normal range of the comparison corpora.

**Table 9:** Introductory negative adverbials with subject-operator inversion, per 4 M

| per 4 M wds | Coll | Ind 93[28] | Brown | Frown | LOB | FLOB |
|---|---|---|---|---|---|---|
| Hardly | 0 | 2 | 8 | 4 | 0 | 4 |
| Never | 29 | 21 | 44 | 8 | 16 | 36 |
| Scarcely | 0 | 0 | 0 | 0 | 0 | 0 |
| Seldom | 2 | 3 | 0 | 4 | 0 | 0 |
| No longer | 10 | 1 | 8 | 12 | 8 | 4 |
| No sooner | 2 | 5 | 20 | 4 | 12 | 4 |
| Not until | 3 | 0 | 16 | 12 | 4 | 12 |
| **Totals:** | 46 | 32 | 96 | 44 | 40 | 60 |

**Table 10:** Comparisons of Coll and the established corpus: Vocabulary II.

| | Brown | Frown | LOB | FLOB | US | Canada | Non-NAm | Non-US |
|---|---|---|---|---|---|---|---|---|
| Conv. factor | 1.00 | 1.00 | 1.00 | 1.00 | 0.36 | 2.19 | 2.00 | 1.05 |
| | | | | | | | | |
| **Informality:** | | | | | | | | |
| | | | | | | | | |
| *its (correct)* | | | | | 1616 | 1,172 | 1,279 | 1,228 |
| *its (error)* | | | | | 35 | 44 | 142 | 95 |
| **error %** | | | | | **2%** | **4%** | **11%** | **8%** |
| *it's (correct)* | | | | | 1615 | 2,103 | 2,093 | 2,097 |
| *it's (error)* | | | | | 25 | 35 | 78 | 57 |
| **error %** | | | | | **2%** | **2%** | **4%** | **3%** |
| | | | | | | | | |
| *ain't* | 44 | 57 | 0 | 13 | 15 | 20 | 26 | 23 |
| | | | | | | | | |
| *bloody hell!* | 0 | 0 | 0 | 1 | 0 | 0 | 2 | 1 |

| | | | | | | | | |
|---|---|---|---|---|---|---|---|---|
| *damn!* | 28 | 40 | 21 | 24 | 31 | 44 | 62 | 53 |
| *fuck!* | 0 | 10 | 0 | 9 | 4 | 20 | 52 | 37 |
| *shit!* | 0 | 17 | 0 | 5 | 10 | 46 | 110 | 79 |

The most striking instances of how any increase in informality can nevertheless maintain barriers against specific socially stigmatized forms are to be seen in the cases of *its/it's* and *ain't*. A comparison of over 6,000 instances of *its/it's* resulted in an error rate of only 2% for the American writers; the British students are clearly less concerned about this error, as their contribution produced an 11% error rate for *its* (instead of the correct *it's*), although insertion of a gratuitous apostrophe was at a much lower rate, 4%. This particular pair of mistakes is of special interest, as it will not be picked up by computer spelling checkers. Finally, students are considerably more reluctant to use *ain't* than a variety of swear words, with only *fuck* still clearly being on at least some North American taboo lists.

## 7. The future

The examples examined above raise a number of problems, not least the general issue of (in)formality, a matter that needs considerable attention, as people become increasingly empowered to reach others via electronic media such as the Internet.

This preliminary version of the student online newspaper corpus has a number of flaws, the most serious being that copyright permission has not yet been obtained, which precludes release in its present form. The next step is therefore to see to it that the corpus becomes official, publicly available, improved and augmented, in preparation for further synchronic and diachronic studies over the next few years, particularly as more university and college students from the other major varieties of English begin to go electronic on the scale now seen in the United States. Our young people are providing us with a wealth of living data, even as they reshape the language we are handing over to them – it is merely up to us to learn to listen to them.

## Notes

1 I would distinguish among **designed corpora** created by linguists (e.g. Brown, BNC), **accidental corpora** (e.g. newspaper CDs with search engines designed to retrieve news content) and **opportunistic corpora** (e.g. the Nixon Watergate tapes).

2 See the author's paper at the 1994 TALC conference (Minugh 1997: 67–82). Cf. the brief comments by e.g. Svartvik (Thomas and Short 1996: 9) or the more extensive discussion in Sinclair (Melchers and Warren 1995: 17–33).

3 The Sunday issues and suburban supplements are considerably more varied in this respect.

4 Chomsky's celebrated lack of interest in corpus linguistics, and his preference for the data of native-speaker intuition alone, have of course been noted and objected to by corpus linguists; see e.g. Stubbs (1996: 23 ff.) or Ch. 1 of McEnery and Wilson (1999). and references therein. A more general discussion may be found in e.g. Chapter 1 of Van Valin and LaPolla (1998).

5 Obviously, speakers of local dialects may also be proficient users of standard varieties, and there are considerable numbers of e.g. BrE speakers who are also well acquainted with the English of, for example, the Indian subcontinent, the Caribbean or various areas of Africa.

6 Australia, Canada, New Zealand, the Republic of Ireland, South Africa, the United Kingdom and the United States. Censorship is of course always a potential issue, although the very fact that the Coll material is available on the Net mitigates against it.

7 Local crime notes.

8 See also the discussions in e.g. Ch. 2 of Kennedy 1998.

9 *The Roving Reporter* at http://www.cpxnet.com/College_newspapers.html. For Canada, see http://www.edu.gov.on.ca/eng/relsites/Collnews.html. For Great Britain, coverage is provided by http://www.mediauk.com/studentmedia/print/. For Australia, the site to watch for future online publications is http://www.yap.com.au/publications/.

10 Technical details: the multiple column layout of many web pages caused considerable difficulties, but in nearly all cases could be overcome by copying small segments one at a time. Even pages that appeared non-copyable could usually be copied by working with the coding-page version of the display. Only PDF files from Adobe Acrobat were unobtainable by this method.

As Knut Hofland (Bergen) was kind enough to point out, a recent discussion on the Linguist List noted several programs that can more fully automatize this Collection process: see his link via http://www.hit.uib.no/corpora/2000-1/0358.html.

11 Technical details: all texts are stored by Word as .txt files, one per newspaper, grouped by state and then region. For search purposes, the regions (US, UK, etc.) are represented individually, as well as in one duplicate directory including all the files. Each file can also be accessed separately. Searches were conducted via Word or WordSmith, but can of course be carried out with other programs, such as WordCruncher. File sizes were all calculated via Word's 'Word Count' function.

12 The word *he* is used advisedly, most webmasters being male; there are a great many female reporters and editors, however, so that the corpus itself is probably considerably less gender-skewed than commercial newspapers.

13 This feature is otherwise a major advantage of online publishing, as ongoing controversies can be presented from the original article onward, with hotlinks to each editorial, article or letter to the Editor.

14 It should continually be borne in mind that these four corpora of written English cover a wider range of text types than the present corpus (although not as wide as either COBUILD or the BNC), so that the comparisons presented here must be treated with a certain reserve.

15 Untagged versions of the four reference corpora were used, as the Coll Corpus is merely raw texts. This means that items such as *can* are given *in toto*, rather than merely instances of the verb, and are thus exaggerated, compared to items such as *should* or *would*, which have no noun homonyms.

16 Much of the Coll Corpus was gathered during the spring of 1999, hence the frequent references to May.

17 This problem is similar to the 'apparent-time' question of language change, as treated in e.g. Chapter 3 of Labov (1994).

18 Cf. e.g. Croft (2000: 72–73) on the distinction between competence (of the individual) and convention (of the speech community).

19 Of the three, only *blindside* (from American football) is not in the *Collins* or *Macquarie* dictionaries; *gazump* is not in *Webster's* 10th ed. Idioms were not investigated here, but their frequency range appears to be 1–10 per 10 M (*Cobuild Dictionary of Idioms* 1995: v,xvii, confirmed in Minugh 1999), which also indicates that the present corpus is as yet far too small for such areas.

20 The specifically American sense of *shag*, 'to practice catching fly balls', a baseball term, occurs twice in the American material, and the 'shag rug' sense once.

21 Aston and Burnard 1998: 33. This is apparently not the case for the much larger, written section (Aston and Burnard 1998: 28–31).

22 In this perspective, the current relative paucity of data from many English-speaking areas should be weighed against the fact that only a very few of the Coll student newspapers online in the United States seem to go back further than 1997.

23 In one such handbook, Brownstein and Weiner (1978: 336,338) provide a practice exercise where 'If he would have listened to me, he would not have applied for that position' is corrected as follows: 'Sequence of tenses requires that the verb in an *if*-clause be in the past perfect tense. Correction: *If he had listened to me...*'.

24 Other choices also exist; see Hundt (1998) and the references therein.

25 Cf. especially Goldberg (1995) on this construction (in the Fillmorean sense).

26 See Biber, Conrad and Reppen (1998) for an overview.

27 The ratio is 40/1532 for *albeit/although*. For the Brown/Frown/LOB/FLOB (at 4 million words), the ratio is 32/1540.

28 January 2 – February 6, which is roughly 10% of the nearly 40 M words in that year's CD.

**References**

ACE Corpus (1999). *ICAME Collection of English Language Corpora*, 2nd ed. CD. Bergen: HIT Centre.

Aston, Guy and Lou Burnard (1998). *The BNC Handbook*. Edinburgh: Edinburgh University Press.

*Bank of English* (1991). Birmingham: COBUILD/ Birmingham.

Biber, Douglas, Susan Conrad and Randi Reppen (1998). *Corpus linguistics: investigating language structure and use*. Cambridge: CUP.

*British National Corpus* (1995). Oxford: Oxford Computing Centre.

Brown Corpus (1999). *ICAME Collection of English Language Corpora*, 2nd ed. CD. Bergen: HIT Centre.

Brownstein, Samuel and Mitchel Weiner (1978). *How to prepare for college entrance examinations*, 9th ed. Woodbury, New York: Barron's.

*Collins COBUILD Dictionary of Idioms* (1995). London: Harper Collins.

*Collins English Dictionary* (1998) 4th ed. London: Harper Collins.

Croft, William (2000). *Explaining language change: an evolutionary approach*. Harlow: Longman.

Frown Corpus (1999). *ICAME Collection of English Language Corpora*, 2nd ed. CD. Bergen: HIT Centre.

FLOB Corpus (1999). *ICAME Collection of English Language Corpora*, 2nd ed. CD. Bergen: HIT Centre.

Goldberg, Adele (1995). *A Construction Grammar approach to argument structure*. Chicago: University of Chicago Press.

Hundt, Marianne (1998). 'It is important that this study (*should*) *be* based on the analysis of parallel corpora: On the use of the mandative subjunctive in four major varieties of English'. In Lindquist et al. 159–175.

Johansson. S and E. H. Norheim. (1988). 'The subjunctive in British and American English'. *ICAME Journal* 12: 27–36.

Kennedy, G. 1998. *An introduction to corpus linguistics*. London: Longman.

Kirk, John (ed.) (2000). *Corpora galore: analyses and techniques in describing English*. Amsterdam: Rodopi.

Labov, W. (1994). *Principles of linguistic change: I, internal factors*. Oxford: Blackwell.

Lindquist, Hans, Staffan Klintborg, Magnus Levin and Maria Estling (eds) (1998). *The major varieties of English*. Växjö, Sweden: Acta Wexionensia.

LOB Corpus (1999). *ICAME Collection of English Language Corpora*, 2nd ed. CD. Bergen: HIT Centre.

McEnery, Tony and Andrew Wilson (1999). *Corpus linguistics*, 2nd ed. Edinburgh: Edinburgh University Press.

*Macquarie Dictionary* (1997). 3rd ed. New South Wales: Macquarie Library.

Mair, Christian (1998). 'Corpora and the study of the major varieties of English: issues and results'. In Lindquist et al. 139–157

Melchers, Gunnel and Beatrice Warren (eds) (1995). *Studies in Anglistics*. Stockholm: Almqvist and Wiksell.

Minugh, David (1997). 'All the language that's fit to print: using British and American newspaper CD-ROMs as corpora'. In Wichmann et al. 67–82.

Minugh, David (1999). 'You people use such weird expressions: the frequency of idioms in newspaper CDs as corpora'. In Kirk. 57–71.

Quirk, Randolph, Sidney Greenbaum, Geoffrey Leech, and Jan Svartvik (1985). *A comprehensive grammar of the English language*. London: Longman.

Sinclair, John (1995). 'Corpus typology: a framework for classification'. In Melchers and Warren. 17–33.

Stubbs, Michael (1996). *Text and corpus analysis*. Oxford: Blackwell

Svartvik, Jan (1996). 'Corpora are becoming mainstream'. In Thomas and Short. 3–13.

Thomas, Jenny and Mick Short (1996). *Using corpora for language research*. Harlow: Longman.

Trudgill, Peter and Jean Hannah (1994). *International English*, 3rd ed. London: Arnold.

Van Valin, Robert D. and Randy J. LaPolla (1997). *Syntax: structure, meaning and function*. Cambridge: CUP.

Wells, John (1982). *Accents of English*, 3 vols. Cambridge: CUP.

Wichmann, Anne, Steven Fligelstone, Tony McEnery and Gerry Knowles (1997). *Teaching and language corpora*. London: Longman.

# Aspects of computer-mediated communication for research in corpus linguistics

*Vincent B Y Ooi*

National University of Singapore

## Abstract

*This paper suggests that an important frontier for corpus linguistics to reach is the ability to handle more precisely the discourse of imagined/virtual/on-line communities on the World Wide Web and their attendant linguistic expressions. Computer-mediated communication, exemplified by the Internet Relay Chat/'I Seek You' genre, brings the global world together every day and has proved to be immensely popular. Such types of discourse present a challenge to corpus linguistics, whose agenda should then include refining appropriate computational tools, and linguistic theories, in order to provide a more thorough investigation of such new linguistic patterns. This paper examines aspects of this agenda to measure new electronic textualities within the paradigm of corpus linguistics. It compares the ability of two well-known corpus taggers to handle such texts, and discusses some of the lexicogrammatical patterns that emerge from an Internet Relay Chat corpus.*

## 1. Introduction

Computer corpus linguistics of the twentieth century has been concerned with the robust description and analysis of orthodox texts (e.g. transcriptions of spoken dialogues, books, magazines and newspapers) in their electronic form. These texts reflect the traditional and familiar modes of writing and speech that have been documented in grammar books and dictionaries, and there has been the assumption of a somewhat strict dichotomy between speech and writing. Since the advent of the World Wide Web in the 1990s, it will be the task of linguistics and semiotic theory to analyse the mega corpora within the Web, in which the dynamic enmeshing of text, sound and graphics/video increasingly becomes the order of the day. Within the textual mode alone, computer-mediated communication, made via a hybrid of speech, writing, graphics and orthography, has become a very popular mode of communication, especially among the younger generation. This mode, involving the computer as the instrument of communication (hence 'computer-mediated communication'), will be unfamiliar to those who claim to be 'computer illiterate', and might even befuddle those who have some knowledge of the computer but who would prefer to use the telephone and direct face contact for closer communication.

Such new modes of communication force us to reflect on our current models of language which are based much more on the written than the spoken mode. McCarthy and Carter (2000: 281), for instance, say that the current 'adherence to the kinds of functions we find in writing and our neglect of functions peculiar to speech creates an imbalance in favour of a type of syntax that ultimately derives from the monologic page rather than the dialogic spoken word. One only has to consider the different distribution in speech and writing (of non-minimal response tokens in everyday

English conversation, e.g. *absolutely!*) to see that something is going on in speech that is distinct from what typically occurs in writing.' McCarthy and Carter stress that it is through analysing a well-compiled corpus that the central and typical aspects of each mode can be compared more adequately with the other. Similarly, it would seem well worth the effort to devise and gather well-sampled corpora typifying the new modes of communication, so as to understand their central and typical aspects and work towards the larger goal of unravelling the complex relationship between traditional forms of writing and speech, as well as between these traditional forms and the newer modes of communication, such as computer-mediated communication on the Web (see Herring 1996, Goodman and Graddol 1997). As the Web becomes a part of everyday life for most peoples in the world, 'virtual', 'on-line' or 'imagined' communities deserve an understanding on their own terms, in their creation of new texts and genres. It will be some time before we can throw away the keyboard in favour of voice and direct internet conferencing, and such new modes are here to stay at least for a while.

In this paper, I would like to sketch aspects of this agenda to understand computer-mediated communication (henceforth 'CMC', the broad term given to such new modes of communication on the Web) within the paradigm of corpus linguistics. This agenda involves complementing a 'pen-and-paper' (largely 'qualitative') approach with an 'electronic' (largely 'quantitative') approach. In order to achieve this, a CMC corpus, preferably one that is maximally representative of the central and typical aspects being measured, should first be compiled. As CMC is very wide in its remit, for this exercise I would like to narrow the discussion in this paper to an aspect of CMC known as Internet Relay Chat (or 'IRC'). Second, such an electronic corpus should be run through by existing part-of-speech software, in order to identify any unknown lexico-grammatical features, and to train the software for future analysis of such modes of communication. Third, once the right annotation has been done (which is of course dependent on whether there are resources for serious post-editing), the corpus can be subjected to various linguistic and statistical analyses.

In Section 2, I first present an overview of CMC and what is generally known about IRC. Section 3 then runs the IRC data through two well-known pieces of robust corpus linguistic software, in order to better understand some of the parameters of this new genre. Section 4 goes further into interfacing annotated IRC corpus data with linguistic tools that can search, count and sort, not for their own sake, but for gleaning various linguistic features (see Ooi 2001). Robust linguistic programs are used to understand new types of electronic textuality, and point to parameters which these programs should address if they are to be customized for these new purposes.

## 2. An overview of computer mediated communication

This section aims to provide the context for our discussion: I would first like to sketch what CMC entails, and where IRC fits into this spectrum of speech and writing. According to Herring (1996: 1) CMC refers generally to communication that takes place between human beings via the instrumentality of computer. For Morris and Ogan (1996), CMC is:

(a) one-to-one asynchronous communication, such as e-mail;

(b) many-to-many asynchronous communication, such as Usenet, electronic bulletin boards, and Listservers that require the receiver to sign up for a service or log on to a program to access messages around a particular topic or topics;
(c) synchronous communication that can be one-to-one, one-to-few, or one-to-many and can be organized around a topic, the construction of an object, or role playing, such as MUDS (Multi-User Dungeons and their various transformations as MOOs [or more commonly nowadays 'Multi-User Domains'], MUCKs ['Multi-User Character Kits'], and MUSHs [Multi-User Shared Hallucinations']), Internet Relay Chat ('IRC') and chat rooms on commercial services; and
(d) asynchronous communication generally characterized by the receiver's need to seek out the site in order to access information, which may involve many-to-one, one-to-one, or one-to-many source-receiver relationships (e.g. Web sites, gophers [data retrieval programs], and FTP sites [for data transfer]).

CMC can therefore be divided broadly into two modes: synchronous ('instantaneous/ real-time') and asynchronous ('non-realtime'). Asynchronous CMC, which predisposes the mode to be more like writing, can include both e-mail (as mentioned earlier) and Short Message Service ('SMS') for mobile phones. Synchronous CMC, which predisposes the mode to be more like speech, can include not only text but also voice, images and sound; it also requires participants to be reciprocally present at the same time during the interaction. If synchronous CMC is more speech-like, it is also conversational. On this point, Eggins and Slade (1997: 19–20) make a distinction between pragmatic and casual conversation. The motivation for pragmatic (or directed) conversation is to achieve clearly defined goals for participants, and it tends to be shorter in terms of the number of turns. Casual (or non-directed) conversation refers to 'interactions which are not motivated by a clear pragmatic purpose, and which display informality and humour.' On the other hand, Poster (1997: 139) points out that synchronous CMC (such as computer conferencing) is not always very much like face-to-face speech. Poster notes that 'problems do arise over matters such as taking turns and keeping the discussion going'; participants must continually 'be as explicit as possible about what they are saying, and frequently clarify their statements by the use of metastatements.' According to Poster, computer conferencing easily becomes 'talk about talk' by virtue of the fact that it upsets the conventions of ordinary speech. In addition, Poster thinks that power relations (such as institutional status, personal charisma, rhetorical skills, gender and race) which normally govern face-to-face speech are minimized in computer conferencing; decentralization of power is the norm. While such ideological questions associated with CMC are interesting, they are not within the remit of this paper. Instead, we may notice that synchronous CMC vis-à-vis such internet technologies as IRC (currently at http://www.mirc.com/irc.html) and ICQ ('I Seek You', currently at http://web.icq.com/index) are primarily concerned with bringing people together mainly for chatting and casual conversation. The difference between the two is largely that ICQ alerts the user to a predefined group of friends or fellow users the moment they are logged on-line, and chatting can be restricted to this in-group of users. ICQ, simply put, is 'essentially IRC between people who have a pre-existing relationship' (Mar 2000: 152).

While typifying synchronous CMC and largely casual conversation, neither IRC nor ICQ relies on voice or video in the traditional way. Instead, simultaneity, prosody and gestures are conveyed through the use of emoticons, other orthographic devices and in-built program features. Emoticons or iconic faces are graphic representations of emotions, and are an economical way of making known one's feelings in CMC. They also involve less typing skill and time. Other orthographic devices include the use of capitalization and other punctuation marks to signal the features of casual conversation: humour, appraisal, intimacy, attitude etc. In-built program features may be designed to allow the chat window to be viewed in various multi-view formats. Sound can also be conveyed in terms of a (i) Laugh Out Loud sound event (functioning to convey a loud laugh), (ii) Keystroke Sound event (functioning to convey the keystrokes of a typewriter), and (iii) Beep Users event (functioning to get the user's attention by beeping him/her. In addition, there is an Emote Icon to convey emotions and feelings such as shock, irritation and disgust; the Action Icon is also able to signal responses to utterances (e.g. *cough, laugh, scream, drool, hug, grin* etc). Ellipsis and abbreviations are also pervasive as in spoken discourse (McCarthy and Carter 2000: 14), since there is a large amount of shared knowledge and common conventions among participants. In this brief overview, we should also be aware of the danger of oversimplifying CMC as simply 'speech-like' or simply 'written-like'. According to Yates (1996: 46), CMC is more like written discourse in terms of type/token ratio and lexical density, but more speech-like in terms of pronoun and modal auxiliary use. Such language choices of speech and writing are exemplified through the language of IRC, whose linguistic 'context of situation' is outlined in Mar (2000) in terms of the well-known Hallidayan concept of Field, Mode and Tenor.

Notwithstanding the dangers of dichotomizing speech and writing and thus simplifying their complex nature, like Schulze (1999: 72), I find the following diagram (see Fig. 1) by Lenke and Schmitz (1995: 120) useful in capturing where CMC modes of discourse such as IRC and e-mail stand in relation to the traditional types of communication:

In Figure 1, we note an unfilled lower-left quadrant, in which there are no forms of local asynchronous communication. According to Schulze (1999: 73), 'asynchronous communication always requires the additional (effort) of storing and retrieving any utterances. Furthermore, it does not allow direct interaction between interlocutors. In the case of local communication, these disadvantages can be avoided.' Turning to the position of IRC in this spectrum, Schulze rightly observes that 'IRC was not only the first form of remote, synchronous communication providing the many-to-many mode, [but] it also was the first form of synchronous communication in written form to become widespread' (Schulze, 1999: 73). According to both Lenke and Schmitz (1995: 120) and Schulze (1999: 73), this situation resulted in IRC being a hybrid between the synchronous forms of spoken speech and the asynchronous written medium.

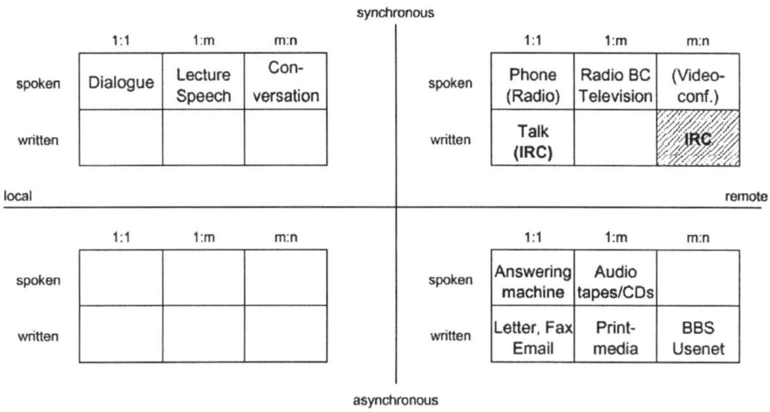


**Figure 1**: Classification of the form of communication on IRC – the attributes considered include the following: synchronous/asynchronous, spoken/ written, local/remote, and one-to-one/one-to-many/many-to-many (Lenke and Schmitz 1995: 120; also in Schulze 1999: 72).

## 3. Annotating a corpus to measure electronic textuality

How might IRC as a hybrid of speech and writing be handled by corpus linguistic programs? Part-of-speech annotation (or 'grammatical tagging') programs such as CLAWS (Garside and Smith, 1997) and AUTASYS (Fang 1996) are arguably the most robust programs available to the corpus linguistics community. Both are probabilistic taggers that employ stochastic information for the disambiguation of different tags assigned to a word form. There are a few differences between the two taggers, though. AUTASYS uses three tagsets: LOB ('Lancaster Oslo Bergen'), ICE ('International Corpus of English'), and SKELETON (derived from the ICE tagset). CLAWS, Version 4, currently uses Lancaster University's C7 tagset. At the disambiguation stage, CLAWS first uses morphological information such as prefixes and suffixes to predict possible tags associated with a wordform. The default selection is a nominal item for unknown words whose tag cannot be determined correctly. AUTASYS instead relies on a lexicon of approximately 80,000 wordforms which, if not found, will then trigger a set of morphological rules. The default selection is either a common noun or adjective for unknown words whose tag cannot be determined correctly. So, when the following innocuous sentence *John loves Mary* and its variant in lower caps are subjected to CLAWS and AUTASYS respectively, the following output is obtained:

(1a) ^ John_NP1 loves_VVZ Mary_NP1 ._. [CLAWS]

(1b) ^ john_NN1 loves_VVZ mary_NN1 ._. [CLAWS]

(1c) John <tag N(prop,sing)> loves <tag V(montr,pres)> Mary <tag N(prop,sing)> . <tag PUNC(per)> <#000000> [AUTASYS]

(1d) john <tag N(prop,sing)> loves <tag V(montr,pres)> mary <tag N(prop,sing)> <tag PUNC(per)> <#000000> [AUTASYS]

The point to be noted here is that (1b) somehow provides the wrong output for *John* and *Mary* probably because of the lower case, i.e. NP1 represents a proper noun, whereas NN1 represents a singular common noun. Thus, the CLAWS tagger – and other taggers in general – works best with the proper mix of upper and lower case. However, this fact does not augur well for IRC texts which have certain hybrid properties that predispose them to be treated as, at best, a new English genre (or two sub-genres) and, at worst, not English at all. A lot of CMC language does not distinguish between upper and lower case, and would thus predispose CLAWS to make mistakes. Thus, to the extent that the invitation to try out English running text (up to a maximum of) 300 words at one go is made (see the CLAWS demo program currently at http://www.comp.lancs.ac.uk/ucrel/claws/trial.html), it would seem manifestly unfair to subject CLAWS, and indeed AUTASYS too, to the likes of English-like CMC. The current version of CLAWS is demonstrably successful, in that it has analysed the 100-million word British National Corpus (see Aston and Burnard 1998), which is no mean feat: 10 million words of spoken texts and 90 million words of written texts typifying contemporary British English (and, to some extent, U.S. English as well). Thus, CLAWS has been largely trained on written texts, not spoken ones. However, as the World Wide Web continues to exert a profound influence on everyday life, it is likely that, if there is a next edition of the BNC, computer-mediated language will constitute part of its range of texts and so CLAWS can be trained further in this manner. Also, how is it that CMC users all over the world continue to generate such text happily and seemingly understand one another (in English)? We might expect communication to break down and the whole genre to sink into disuse. However, this is manifestly not the case, and we must somewhat conclude that well-known instances of computer-mediated communication also do (somewhat) constitute 'English running text'.

### 3.1 A part-of-speech analysis of IRC/ICQ texts

From the preceding section, we may suppose for a moment that such taggers as CLAWS and AUTASYS are to be retrained to analyse English-like CMC such as IRC. What would the issues then entail? In order to answer this question, let us first take a look at a typical conversational exchange in IRC/ICQ, which is dyadic:

(2a) <archangel> Great to see U again :)
(2b) <CutiePie> Me 2 … Busy but still got enough time for R & R….How abt U, William???

A possible concern here is the nicknames that are contained within angled brackets, a feature that is currently treated in most taggers as SGML ('Standard Generalized Mark-up') tags. Other concerns include the following: (2a) contains the letter U to replace the personal pronoun *you* and the smiling emoticon (or 'smiley'); (2b) contains the numeral 2 to replace the adverb *too* phonologically, and the abbreviations *R & R* and *abt* stand for *rest and recreation* and *about* respectively. The lexicon for these taggers would need to be extended to contain comprehensive listings of emoticons and abbreviated terms.

In order to explicate the nature of IRC further, Figure 2 contains an edited series of exchanges between 3 participants on a Singaporean channel that will be abbreviated simply as #cybercafe. The exchange is on a mentoring programme in a particular school, and our point of entry is when user <archangel> joins the discussion:

** Now talking in #cybercafe **
** archangel has joined #cybercafe **

<archangel> wat are u guys tokking about?
<Cyclops> Iris is talking about her experiences at her mentoring sessions…
<archangel> oic, pls continue…
<CutiePie> as I was saying, my school does mentoring in groups…b4 the first session, we split ourselves into groups of guys and gals, instead of the teech doing 4 us…
<Cyclops> Wow …gd idea. So how's the outcome?
<CutiePie> *grin* … trust me, you'll have fun, but you must get to know 1st lor…
<archangel> sorry…I'm feeling confused. What mentoring?
<Cyclops> Sher, you still remember the mentoring program that I was in last year?
*** Tink ….A light bulb lights up in archangel ***
<archangel> Oh….now I get the picture lol.
<CutiePie> We just chitchat. Get to know each other better…we can have so much fun tt sometimes 2 hours just seems so short. ;)
<Cyclops> guys, I gtg do my things, see ya' around…byezz

**Figure 2:** A short conversational exchange in IRC (text from *The Ridge*, August September 2000)

Even in this short exchange, it is apparent that the three participants have equal opportunities for turn-taking, although it seems that one particular participant uses more declarative clauses (providing information) while the other two interlocutors tend to employ interrogative clauses (seeking information). The following glossary may assist the uninitiated IRC/ICQ reader in deciphering this conversational exchange: *wat*='what'; *tokking*='talking'; *oic*='Oh, I see'; *pls*='please'; *b4*='before'; *teech*='teacher'; *4*='for'; *gd*='good'; *grin*= in-built program feature to express this gesture; *lor*=a Colloquial Singaporean English emphatic discourse particle; *tink….*=in-built program feature to express this act; *lol*='Laugh Out Loud'; *tt*='that'; gtg='got to go'; *byezz*='bye'

Owing to constraints of space, the respective CLAWS and AUTASYS output for the text in Figure 2 will not be shown in this paper. However, as expected, neither tagger can handle emoticons and extra-linguistic acts (such as *lol*, **grin**, **tink**). While non-standard spelling is also undecipherable (e.g. *wat* is wrongly tagged as a singular common noun by both programs instead of the correct *wh*-determiner tag), morphological endings provide a good clue to the wordclass (e.g. *tokking* is correctly tagged by both programs as an *-ing* participle verb). However, a morphological clue may prove to be a double-edged sword, and both programs are remarkably similar in treating *oic* ('Oh, I see') wrongly as an adjective, probably because the ending is the same as an adjectival term as *heroic*. Similarly, the abbreviation *pls*='please' is treated as a plural noun probably because it resembles a noun suffix. For *b4*, CLAWS treats it as an unknown word, while AUTASYS bravely treats it as a singular common noun, instead of applying the prepositional tag. Also, this instance of *before* indicates the prevalence of conflating phonology with orthography. Another instance is the preposition *for*, which is tagged as a numeral, since the orthography is *4*. Clearly the lexicon in these programs will need to be modified in order to handle CMC language. A term such as *teech* ('teacher') is, however, correctly analysed as a singular common noun. Even if the lexicon in these programs did not contain this term, the occurrence of the term immediately after the determiner gives the correct cue to treat it as a noun. Another abbreviation to note is *gd* for the adjective *good*. In this case, AUTASYS has tagged this correctly, whereas CLAWS for some reason treats it as a unit of measurement (i.e. NNU). It is perhaps an understatement to say that abbreviations abound in IRC/ICQ because of the need for rapid typing in real-time discourse (and probably some measure of laziness too!). Thus, *tt* is the abbreviation for *that*, and *gtg* for *got to go*.

Discourse markers, which are prevalent in conversation, are also very much part of the genre of IRC/ICQ. Such markers include *oh, well, and, but, or, so, coz, now, then y'know, I mean* etc. (see Eggins and Slade, 1997: 37). The item in Figure 2 that is probably not transparent to most Western readers is the emphatic discourse particle *lor*, which is found in Colloquial Singapore English, together with other particles such as *lah, leh, meh*, etc. (see Higgleton and Ooi 1997: 707).

Yet the current versions of CLAWS and AUTASYS have actually been quite successful in assigning the correct tags to the other parts of the text in Figure 2. This is because the structural features of this text do not differ from those that these taggers have been trained on (British National Corpus, International Corpus of English-British component etc). However, there are many other IRC/ICQ texts that do not conform to standard English structures, and indeed many violate concord agreement (e.g. 'tt fucker scold my mother'='that fucker scolds/scolded my mother'). We would therefore expect to see a cline of success, ranging from standard written texts (most success) to very casual conversation (least success).

## 4. Interfacing a tagged corpus with search-retrieval-sort programs

A tagged corpus is only as useful as the search-and-sort perspectives that can be done on it. In order to illustrate this point, a reasonably large corpus is first needed, and I would therefore like to utilize a corpus of IRC that is currently available on the Web (http://www.linguistik.uni-erlangen.de/~max/Tree/irc.en.html). This corpus, compiled by Markus Schulze in March 1998[1], contains 28345 lines (around 900KB), inclusive of system messages, and comprises the IRC channels Australia (2424 lines) cybercafe (1865 lines), london (11130 lines), scotland (12304 lines) and 20+ (622 lines). Schulze (personal communication) chose these channels as a sampling of different varieties of English, including Australian, Scottish, British and non-native ones. In his own analysis of the corpus, Schulze (1999) includes information on the contextual factors involved (i.e. IRC users by profession, age and gender), and explicates the various nonverbal and paraverbal cues involved that are meant to create 'a perceived presence (or virtual presence) of interlocutors' (of which many of the features in Section 3 of this paper have the same objective). As an instance of nonverbal cues, he interestingly demonstrates that 'smileys' (positive emoticons) occur 1308 times, compared to 'frowneys' (negative emoticons) which occur only 192 times: his interlocutors are clearly a friendly bunch of people. As an instance of paraverbal cues, Schulze analyses the preference for reduplication (e.g. 'hiii!!!' is responded to by 'HELOOOOOOOOoo'), upper case (to indicate 'shouting' and other prosodic effects), and pauses (to give the impression of interlocutors keying in what they actually would speak).

In order to complement Schulze's analysis, and following the approach outlined in Section 3, I have run both AUTASYS and CLAWS on his corpus, but have not done any post-editing work (which would be time-consuming) on the annotated corpus. This methodology of first annotating a raw corpus with linguistic information allows us to derive search, retrieve and sort this information later. As my comments regarding AUTASYS will be similar to CLAWS, and to economize on space, we will confine our discussion to only the CLAWS output, which uses the C7 tagset (currently available from the following URL: http://www.comp.lancs.ac.uk/ucrel/claws7tags.html).

As mentioned elsewhere (Ooi 2001), UNIX tools such as *grep* and *awk* are fairly useful in grouping the various linguistic tags assigned by the part-of-speech tagger. For instance, using these tools, the top 25 nouns, verbs, adjectives and adverbs for the Schulze corpus figure respectively as follows (see Table 1):

**Table 1:** Top 25 CLAWS-tagged nouns, verbs, adjectives, adverbs respectively in the Schulze corpus

| **Nouns** | | **Verbs** | | **Adjectives** | | **Adverbs** | |
|---|---|---|---|---|---|---|---|
| channel_nn1 | 7220 | has_vhz | 6377 | hi_jj | 527 | now_rt | 1014 |
| emailaddress_nn1 | 3912 | joined_vvn | 3910 | good_jj | 249 | here_r | 1382 |
| signoff_nn1 | 1684 | is_vbz | 2127 | sorry_jj | 111 | just_rr | 335 |
| scotfife_null | 1445 | left_vvn | 1996 | nice_jj | 109 | how_rrq | 266 |
| change_nn1 | 907 | known_vvn | 774 | old_jj | 85 | well_rr | 224 |
| mode_nn1 | 904 | do_vd0 | 598 | sure_jj | 66 | there_rl | 221 |
| centime_null | 625 | s_vbz | 553 | krystal_jj | 61 | where_rrq | 217 |
| leaving_nn1 | 550 | are_vbr | 481 | new_jj | 59 | then_rt | 206 |
| noha_null | 408 | was_vbdz | 386 | great_jj | 58 | ok_rr | 200 |
| inkie_null | 370 | m_vbm | 361 | bad_jj | 55 | why_rrq | 187 |
| wull_null | 309 | been_vbn | 346 | happy_jj | 55 | up_rp | 184 |
| lol_nn1 | 303 | have_vh0 | 344 | wrong_jj | 55 | out_rp | 147 |
| billabong_null | 294 | be_vbi | 343 | cool_jj | 53 | too_rg | 134 |
| nicks_null | 287 | know_vv0 | 238 | dead_jj | 53 | really_rr | 131 |
| time_nnt1 | 283 | kicked_vvn | 237 | big_jj | 51 | back_rp | 126 |
| scotland_null | 262 | seen_vvn | 210 | fine_jj | 49 | so_rg | 109 |
| scotland_np1 | 241 | did_vdd | 192 | english_jj | 47 | never_rr | 106 |
| juel_null | 228 | can_vm | 187 | shy_jj | 41 | still_rr | 106 |
| ping_nn1 | 226 | know_vvi | 177 | other_jj | 39 | again_rt | 101 |
| jaki_null | 225 | reset_vvn | 162 | right_jj | 39 | too_rr | 100 |

| | | | | | | | |
|---|---|---|---|---|---|---|---|
| mctavish_np1 | 218 | will_vm | 151 | real_jj | 38 | am_ra | 96 |
| dwiezel_null | 215 | go_vvi | 143 | funny_jj | 37 | very_rg | 95 |
| timeout_nn1 | 210 | am_vbm | 139 | ok_jj | 35 | only_rr | 90 |
| centime_nn1 | 209 | see_vv0 | 134 | free_jj | 34 | please_rr | 85 |
| connection_nn1 | 207 | have_vhi | 120 | mean_jj | 34 | ago_ra | 81 |

Let us first examine the nouns in Table 1: it is perhaps unsurprising that *channel* emerges as the top noun, with people signing in and out (hence *signoff* being the third top noun) of the channel continually. Figure 3 shows an edited concordance listing for the term, using the WordSmith Tools suite of lexical programs (N.B.: a fuller description is available from its developer's website: see http://www.liv.ac.uk/~ms2928/wordsmith/). The Schulze corpus shows a high number of system messages indicating that the user *has joined*, *has left* or *has been kicked off* the channel (by the system).

| N | Concordance |
|---|---|
| 1 | **_FO aggelos_NN2 has_VHZ been_VBN kicked_VVN@ off_II channel _NN1 #london_FO by_II Cass_NP1 (_( No_UH )_) |
| 2 | _UH ***_FO ag_NN1 has_VHZ been_VBN kicked_VVN@ off_II channel _NN1 #London_FO by_II IMC_NP1 (_( [_( nc_NN |
| 3 | _NULL centime_NN1 was_VBDZ last_MD on_II IRC_NP1 channel _NN1 #scotland_FO 31_MC minutes_NNT2 ago_RA ._ |
| 4 | has_VHZ joined_VVN address_NN1 )_) has_VHZ joined_VVN channel _NN1 #london_FO _NULL **fary**_FO |
| 5 | FO waw.pl_NNU "_" on_II waw.pl_NNU "_" on_II channel _NN1 #cybercafe_FO by_II `_" Guus_NP1 `_" _N |
| 6 | hannel_NN1 #SCOTLAND_FO _NULL is_VBZ this_DD1 channel _NN1 full_JJ of_IO brazen_JJ drafters_NN2 ?_? _ |
| 7 | VVI a_AT1 chat_NN1 ***_FO coronita_NN1 has_VHZ left_VVN channel _NN1 #australia_FO _NULL which_DDQ of_IO u |
| 8 | VV0 na_TO chat_VVI ***_FO Tommy_NP1 has_VHZ left_VVN channel _NN1 #london_FO _NULL fucking_VVG faggots_ |
| 9 | _NULL cheers_VVZ ***_FO josch_NN1 has_VHZ left_VVN channel _NN1 #scotland_FO ***_FO GrahamS_NP1 (_( email- |
| 10 | @ ,_, cheers_VVZ ***_FO chatgal_NN1% has_VHZ left_VVN channel _NN1 #cybercafe_FO _NULL superBop_NN1 :_: |

**Figure 3:** Edited concordance listing of *channel* in the Schulze corpus (using Mike Scott's WordSmith Tools)

Apart from this term in Table 1, many of the top nouns, or those not recognised by the tagger (hence 'null'), have to do with user nicknames, which figure so prominently probably because of the same users signing in regularly to the channels concerned. The top 12th phrase, *Lol* ('Laugh Out Loud') has been tagged incorrectly as a noun. Nevertheless, this phrase is an important feature of IRC discourse (as discussed in Section 2). The term *email address* is actually a generic term for the individual e-mail addresses, inserted (by Schulze presumably) to protect the identity and privacy of the users concerned.

In addition to single nouns, a tagged corpus allows the search for compound nouns (see Figure 4) by specifying the pattern *_NN* *_NN*:

| N | Concordance |
|---|---|
| 1 | _JJ r_ZZ1 u_ZZ1 ?_? _NULL 28_MC ,_, u_ZZ1 ?_? ***_FO Mode_NN1 change_NN1 "_" -b_ZZ1 *_FO !_! *@rmetcalfe.demo |
| 2 | t_RG 300_MC wavs._NNU _NULL its_APPGE my_APPGE kinda_NN1 thing_NN1 i_ZZ1 collect_VV0 them_PPHO2 _ |
| 3 | :_: **39;10000;TOOLONG_FO _NULL with_IW similar_JJ sound_NN1 quality_NN1 _NULL that_CST 's_VBZ true_JJ |
| 4 | Tue_NP1 Mar_NPM1 3_MC 13:14:39_MC 1998_MC )_) ***_FO Mode_NN1 change_NN1 "_" -sm-k_ZZ1 it_PPH1 !_! "_" on_II ch |
| 5 | about_RG 3_MC days_NNT2 _NULL seems_VVZ the_AT record_NN1 companies_NN2 are_VBR n't_XX happy_JJ bout_N |
| 6 | ;_NULL 7DIGGITY_FODOGS_NN2 1alike_FO to_II his_APPGE web_NN1 site_NN1 -_- 12http_FO :_: //surf.to/liberty_FO |
| 7 | ith_IW ?_? _NULL (_( 7th_MD Sphere_NN1 )_) XDCC_NPFile_NN1 Server_NN1:_: [_( Open_JJ ]_) :_: /ctcp_ |
| 8 | _FO AllEars_NN2 has_VHZ left_VVN channel_NN1 #london_FO IRC_NN1 log_NN1 ended_VVD Fri_NPD1 Mar_NPM1 6_MC 09: |
| 9 | fuck-all_DB is._NNU ***_FO Signoff_NN1 :_: Pantahan_NP1 (_( Ping_NN1 timeout_NN1 )_) ***_FO Mode_NN1 change_NN1 "_" |
| 10 | ULL french_JJ fries_NN2 ***_FO Signoff_NN1:_: mrm16_FO (_( Ping_NN1 timeout_NN1 )_) _NULL thanks_NN2 aussuze_V |

**Figure 4:** Edited concordance listing of some significant compound nouns in the Schulze corpus (using Mike Scott's WordSmith Tools)

While significant compound nouns do not figure very much in this corpus, combinations such as *IRC log* (a record of the user's IRC session) and *ping timeout* (system logout) point to the range of genre-specific terms that are bound to turn up in a larger, and perhaps more representative, corpus of IRC.

Turning to the verbs, the top verb is a singular primary auxiliary verb (*has_VHZ*) which is immediately followed by the past participle form (see Figure 5). As indicated earlier, most instances of the perfective aspect in this corpus have to do with system messages detailing the status of certain users: *has left* (a particular channel), *has been kicked off* (the channel), *has joined* (a particular channel) – phrases that a learner of this genre would do well to master in order to understand what is going on in the interaction.

| N | Concordance |
|---|---|
| 1 | o_UH!_!)_)***_FO`_"00d00_FO(_(emailaddress_NN1)_) has_VHZjoined_VVNchannel_NN1#scotland_FO _N |
| 2 | ff_NN1:_: bst_RA(_(Error_NN10_MC)_)***_FOeega-_NN1has_VHZ left_VVNchannel_NN1#australia_FO _NULL* |
| 3 | L 1,14I_MChave_VH01,114Returned._FO***_FODrew_NP1has_VHZleft_VVNchannel_NN1#Scotland_FO***_FOSign |
| 4 | ,1_MF1,9/1,1_MF1,9/11,1_MF4_MC***_FOmelanie-_NN1has_VHZleft_VVNchannel_NN1#london_FO _NULL1, |
| 5 | _RRLO_UH**11;4991;_NULL_: P_ZZ1***_FOsasha_NN1has_VHZchanged_VVNthe_AT topic_NN1on_IIchannel_NN |
| 6 | C-4_NN114/02/98_MFadvertising_NN1)_)***_FOvalih_NN1has_VHZleft_VVN channel_NN1#CyberCafe_FO _N |
| 7 | _VH016_MCsongs_NN2already_RR***_FOLordSena_NP1has_VHZ left_VVNchannel_NN1#scotland_FO*_FOWull_N |
| 8 | )_)***_FOJoCiE_NP1_"16_MC(_(emailaddress_NN1)_) has_VHZjoined_VVNchannel_NN1#london_FO**_FOfugiti |
| 9 | cybercafe_FO**_FOgUY-22_NN1(_(emailaddress_NN1)_)has_VHZjoined_VVNchannel_NN1#CyberCafe_FO**_FO |
| 10 | dolph_NN1***_FOant-it-26_NN1(_( emailaddress_NN1)_)has_VHZjoined_VVNchannel_NN1#scotland_FO _ |

**Figure 5:** Edited concordance listing of *has_VHZ+_VVN* (*'past participle of lexical verb'*) in the Schulze corpus (using Mike Scott's WordSmith Tools)

Doubtless, many other verb patterns such as VBZ (*is*) + VVG ('*-ing* participle of lexical verb') and VM (modal auxiliary, e.g. *will*) + VBI (*be*-infinitive) + VDN (*done*) can be specified in a search of the tagged output, in order to discover significant grammatical patterns.

Turning now to the adjective column in Table 1, we see that *hi*, which has the highest frequency, has been incorrectly tagged as an adjective (or _jj): the correct tag should be *hi_uh*. Thus, we should call up all instances of *_uh* in the corpus to see whether *hi* has also been correctly tagged as *_uh*. Indeed, Table 2 indicates that *hi* is also the most frequently used interjection marker. Other markers in Table 2 express a range of feelings, including approval, surprise, disappointment, and pain. Indeed, this table indicates not only the 'creativity' involved in the choice of non-standard interjections but more so the speaker's desire to signify his/her precise degree of felt emotion and intonational contours by means of the limited orthography that is available on the keyboard:

**Table 2:** Words tagged as *_uh* (interjection) in the Schulze corpus, in order of descending frequency

| |
|---|
| *hi_uh 502; yeah_uh 227; oh_uh 196; hello_uh 173; yes_uh 169; bye_uh 133; no_uh 127; hey_uh 105; hmm_uh 80; well_uh 70; eh_uh 43; yep_uh 42; ah_uh 37; aye_uh 36; wow_uh 27; ha_uh 26; oops_uh 25; ooh_uh 23; ooo_uh 23; ciao_uh 22; oi_uh 22; yo_uh 22; yum_uh 20; ouch_uh 19; huh_uh 18; aha_uh 17; oo_uh 14; ahh_uh 13; ho_uh 13; damn_uh 10; lo_uh 10; mmm_uh 10;* |

*aww_uh 8; dear_uh 8; nah_uh 8; yea_uh 8; hm_uh 7; oooh_uh 7; umm_uh 6; yah_uh 6; aw_uh 5; uh_uh 5; ummm_uh 5; woo_uh 5; ahah_uh 4; ay_uh 4; blah_uh 4; dammit_uh 4; ello_uh 4; ermm_uh 4; haha_uh 4; hallo_uh 4; um_uh 4; cheerio_uh 3; ermmm_uh 3; hah_uh 3; hoo_uh 3; hullo_uh 3; woah_uh 3; ahhh_uh 2; ahhhh_uh 2; ahmm_uh 2; gee_uh 2; humm_uh 2; mariah_uh 2; mm_uh 2; mmmm_uh 2; phew_uh 2; programm_uh 2; samm_uh 2; zzzz_uh 2;aah_uh 1; ahem_uh 1; amen_uh 1; au_uh21 1; bah_uh 1; blimey_uh 1; boo_uh 1; buhahaah_uh 1; cammmmmmmmmmm_uh 1; damnit_uh 1; darn_uh 1; dumm_uh 1; ee_uh 1; emm_uh 1; ermmmm_uh 1; ermmmmm_uh 1; errrmmm_uh 1; goodbye_uh 1; goodnight_uh 1; gosh_uh 1; hahaah_uh 1; hahah_uh 1; hahahhah_uh 1; hemm_uh 1; hemmm_uh 1; leeloo_uh 1; noah_uh 1; oooo_uh 1; pop_uh 1; pow_uh 1; revoir_uh22 1; sh_uh 1; shh_uh 1; tomorrah_uh 1; ugh_uh 1; uhmmmmmmmmmm_uh 1; uumm_uh 1; whee_uh 1; whoops_uh 1; yeahyeahyeah_uh 1; yuk_uh 1; zzz_uh 1*

With *hi* not being really an adjective, the top adjective in the third column is actually *good*; indeed, since adjectives give a measure of the moral and value systems of the virtual community concerned, the third column in Table 1 shows the range of positive and less positive evaluators that the corpus contains. Further, if the pattern *_J* and *_N* is specified, interesting noun phrase collocates that show the range of evaluative markers in the corpus can be obtained (see Figure 6):

| N | Concordance |
|---|---|
| 1 | EVIL_NULL _NULL I_PPIS1 got_VVD a_AT1 cool_JJ pressie_NN1 from_II one_MC1 of_IO my_ |
| 2 | 0_MC *_FO LilStar_NN1 wonders_VVZ how_RGQ tall_JJ DaMo_NN1 is_VBZ now_RT _NULL |
| 3 | MC cases_NN2 of_IO whiskey_NN1 _NULL hi_JJ% JayDee_NN1 _NULL Hey_UH Centi |
| 4 | 145_MC operators_NN2 online_RR ***_FO 2_MC unknown_JJ connections_NN2 ***_FO 8642_MC |
| 5 | alba_NN1 is_VBZ what_DDQ scotland_NN1 's_GE real_JJ name_NN1 is_VBZ _NULL oh_UH ,_ |
| 6 | VBM the_AT vache_NN1 Folle._NP1 _NULL long_JJ time_NNT1 no_RR% see_VV0 :_: )_) |
| 7 | BM I_PPIS1 surrounded_VVN by_II fucking_VVG sad_JJ bastards_NN2 ?_? ?_? ?_? ?_? ?_? ***_F |
| 8 | N1 around_II a_PN121 bit_PN122 with_IW a_AT1 large_JJ trout_NN _NULL Tommok_VV0 :_: |
| 9 | as_II Sebwork_NP1 ***_FO You_PPY have_VH0 new_JJ email._NNU ***_FO The_AT time_NNT1 i |
| 10 | as_II AsHnMaC_NP1 ***_FO You_PPY have_VH0 new_JJ email._NNU ***_FO AgA6_FO is_VBZ no |

**Figure 6:** Edited concordance listing of the *adjectival term+noun* (*_J* *_N*) pattern in the Schulze corpus (using Mike Scott's WordSmith Tools)

Finally, in the use of adverbs, one grammatical pattern stands out when a closer examination of *now* (as the top adverb) is made: *X+is+now+known+as+Y* (see Figure 7). Firstly, it indicates that the here and now constitutes the immediate reality and central importance in the IRC world. Secondly, it indicates the fluidity of identity in the cyberworld, in which the term 'avatar' is now used to designate an online identity (Jordan, 1999: 67) and, indeed, multiple online identities – thus multiple avatars.

| N | Concordance |
|---|---|
| 1 | n_NN1 7-6_MCMC6-3_MCMC ***_FO Scotland_NP1 is_VBZ now_RT known_VVN as_II Wull_NP1 ***_FO Wimp_NN1 is_ |
| 2 | Matb_NP1 agree_VV0 's_VBZ ***_FO topman_NN1 is_VBZ now_RT known_VVN as_II awayeh_NN1 ***_FO Matb_NN1@ |
| 3 | e_PN1 here_RL alive_JJ?_? ***_FO MacKinnon_NP1 is_VBZ now_RT known_VVN as_II Diarmui_NP1 _NULL i_MC1 a |
| 4 | _NULL byee_NN1 all_DB !_! ***_FO wnelson_NN1 is_VBZ now_RT known_VVN as_II Inkie_NP1 _NULL Noha_NP1- |
| 5 | _? _NULL hi_UH all_DB ***_FO SPoCK--_NP1 is_VBZ now_RT known_VVN as_II Ali_NP1 ***_FO Cadete_NN1(_( e |
| 6 | who_PNQS are_VBR ya_PPY ***_FO Noodles_VVZ is_VBZ now_RT known_VVN as_II Plopy_NP1 _NULL Hiya_NP1 |
| 7 | II_VVD asleep_JJ sara_NN1 ***_FO Drmweaver_NN1 is_VBZ now_RT known_VVN as_II Drm-away_JJ*_FO Drm-away_JJ |
| 8 | RT known_VVN as_II Wull_NP1 ***_FO Syphilis_NN1 is_VBZ now_RT known_VVN as_II McTavish_NP1 _NULL I_P |
| 9 | VN channel_NN1#australia_FO***_FO sheila-_NN1 is_VBZ now_RT known_VVN as_II robyn_JJ _NULL kattomatta_ |
| 10 | N channel_NN1#australia_FO***_FO Han-Solo_NN1 is_VBZ now_RT known_VVN as_II han-away_JJ _NULL damissis |

**Figure 7:** Edited concordance listing of *now* in the Schulze corpus (using Mike Scott's WordSmith Tools)

## 5. Conclusion

In this paper, I have suggested that an important frontier for corpus linguistics to reach is the ability to handle the discourse of imagined/virtual/on-line communities on the World Wide Web and their attendant linguistic expressions. CMC, exemplified by the Internet Relay Chat/'I Seek You' genre, brings the global world together every day and has proved to be immensely popular. These new modes of communication are themselves evolving quite rapidly on the Web but, at the same time, stabilising their own forms: for instance, people nowadays are familiar with the notion of an emoticon. While it is arguable whether the Web is truly global in its pervasiveness (since many people do not yet own a personal computer), its overarching presence is felt in everyday life among those who are computer literate. The linguistic phenomena on the Web increasingly pose a challenge to the scope of current language study and register distinctions. For instance, if we consider the four primary registers in Biber et al (1999: 16) – conversation, fiction, news, and academic discourse – we can see that IRC discourse is at once both speech-like and written-like, cutting across a number of traditional distinctions. Such types of discourse present a challenge to corpus linguistics, whose agenda should then include refining appropriate computational tools, and linguistic theories, in order to provide a more thorough investigation of significant linguistic patterns in the virtual – and thus traditionally somewhat 'unreal' – universe. Notwithstanding the philosophical question of which of the two universes is more 'real', the Web may be said to establish the virtual universe as the dynamic mirror of its 'physical' counterpart. In the coming years, corpus linguistics has the exciting agenda of measuring more precisely the multivariate electronic textualities that are readily found on the most dynamic megacorpus of all time, the World Wide Web.

## Notes

1 I am grateful to Markus Schulze for permission to use the IRC corpus that he began compiling in March 1998.

## References

Aston, Guy, and Lou Burnard (1998). *The BNC handbook: exploring the British National Corpus with SARA*. Edinburgh: Edinburgh University Press.

Biber Doug, Stig Johansson, Geoffrey Leech, Susan Conrad, and Edward Finegan (1999). *Longman grammar of spoken and written English*. Harlow: Longman-Pearson Education.

Eggins, Susan, and Diane Slade (1997). *Analysing casual conversation*. London: Cassell.

Fang, Alex C. (1996). 'AUTASYS: Automatic word tagging and cross-tagset mapping'. In Greenbaum, Sidney (ed.), *Comparing English world wide: the international corpus of English*. Oxford: Oxford University Press. 110–24.

Garside, Roger, and Neil Smith (1997). 'A hybrid grammatical tagger: CLAWS4'. In Garside, Roger, Geoffrey Leech, and Anthony McEnery (eds) *Corpus annotation: linguistic information from computer text corpora*. London: Longman.

Goodman, Sharon, and David Graddol (eds) (1997). *Redesigning English: new texts, new identities*. New York: Routledge.

Herring, Susan C. (ed.) (1996). *Computer-mediated communication: linguistic, social and cross-cultural perspectives*. Amsterdam: John Benjamins.

Higgleton, Elaine, and Vincent B. Y. Ooi (eds-in-chief) (1997). *Times-Chambers Essential English Dictionary*. 2nd edition. Edinburgh, Singapore: Chambers-Harrap and Federal/Times Media.

Jordan, Tim (1999). *Cyberpower: the culture and politics of cyberspace and the Internet*. London: Routledge.

Lenke, N. and P. Schmitz. (1995). 'Geschwätz im "Globalen Dorf" – Kommunikation im Internet'. In *Osnabrücker Beiträge zur Sprächtheorie*. 50: 117–41.

Mar, Juliet (2000). 'Online on time: the language of Internet Relay Chat'. In Gibbs, Donna and Kerri-Lee Krause (eds) *Cyberlines: languages and cultures of the Internet*. Australia: James Nicholas. 149–74.

McCarthy, Mike and Ron Carter (2000). 'Feeding back: non-minimal response tokens in everyday English conversation'. In Heffer, Chris and Helen Sauntson (eds), *Words in context: a tribute to John Sinclair on his retirement*. Birmingham: ELR Discourse Analysis Monograph No. 18. 263–83.

Morris, Merrill and Christine Ogan (1996). 'The internet as mass medium'. In *Journal of computer-mediated communication*. 1:4. http://www.ascusc.org/jcmc/vol1/issue4/morris.html

Poster, Mark (1997). 'Communication and new subjects'. In Goodman and Graddol, 137–40.

Ooi, Vincent B. Y. (2001). 'Investigating and teaching genres on the World Wide Web'. In Ghadessy, Mohsen, Robert Roseberry, and Alex Henry (eds) *Small corpus studies and ELT: theory and practice (studies in corpus linguistics v. 5)*, Amsterdam: John Benjamins. 175–204.

Schulze, Markus (1999). 'Substitution of paraverbal and nonverbal cues in the written medium of IRC'. In Naumann, Bernd (ed.) *Dialogue analysis and the mass media*. Tübingen: Niemeyer. 65–82. [also at http://www.linguistik.uni-erlangen.de/~max/Tree/bib.en.html ]

Werry, Christopher C. (1996). 'Linguistic and interactional features of internet relay chat'. In Herring (ed.). 47–63.

Yates, Simeon J. (1996). 'Oral and written linguistic aspects of computer conferencing: a corpus-based study'. In Herring (ed.). 29–46.

# The design of the Spoken Dutch Corpus

*Nelleke Oostdijk*

University of Nijmegen

**Abstract**

*In June 1998 the Spoken Dutch Corpus project was started, a five-year project aimed at the compilation and annotation of a 10-million-word corpus of contemporary standard Dutch as spoken in the Netherlands and Flanders. This paper describes the corpus as it is currently under construction. It discusses more specifically the various considerations that have guided its design.*

## 1. Introduction

Standard Dutch is the official language in the Netherlands and in Flanders.[1] As one of the minority languages in Europe, Dutch is gradually losing ground to English. The availability of the necessary resources has placed the English language and speech technology in the leading position it holds today and has thus further strengthened the position of English for business communication. The fact that, to date, few relevant language resources are available for Dutch represents a serious obstacle for the advancement of Dutch language and speech technology (cf. Bouma and Schuurman 1998). It is against this background that the Flemish and Dutch governments and science foundations decided to jointly fund the compilation of a corpus of spoken Dutch.

The corpus is intended to serve a range of research interests, not just those of language and speech technologists. It addresses the needs of linguists from various backgrounds. Thus far for Dutch, the only more or less substantial data collections have come from written sources. As a consequence, studies of Dutch linguistics in the past have focused on the written language, leaving the spoken language rather poorly documented. Another field in which the corpus will be of significant use is that of education. The insights that can be gained into everyday language use are indispensable for developing Dutch language courses and course materials.

The Spoken Dutch Corpus project aims to compile a ten-million-word corpus which will be orthographically transcribed, lemmatized and annotated with part-of-speech information. For a subcorpus of one million words, more detailed annotations are envisaged, including an auditorily verified broad phonetic transcription and syntactic annotation. A selection of 250,000 words will receive a prosodic annotation. To enable effective access to the speech recordings, the transcriptions will be enriched with pointers into the speech files. The automatic time alignment will be manually checked on the word level for that part of the corpus for which a verified phonetic transcription is available. Audio files will be made available along with the corpus.[2]

## 2. Design considerations

The design of the corpus poses an interesting and complex problem. For Dutch there is no tradition in corpus linguistics such as there is for English. The major corpora currently available for Dutch are written corpora that have been designed for lexicographical purposes. Consequently, there are no examples of (large-scale) spoken language corpora that are intended to serve the diverse purposes that we envisage for the Spoken Dutch Corpus (Corpus Gesproken Nederlands, CGN). When we look at other smaller European languages, the situation is very similar to that for Dutch and there does not appear to be any corpus that can serve as a model. Turning to English then, we see that spoken component of the British National Corpus (BNC; Burnard 1995; Aston and Burnard 1998) is of the same size and has been compiled with similar purposes in mind to the ones pursued with the Dutch corpus. It is therefore worthwhile to consider its design more carefully. Before doing so, however, I shall discuss the pre-conditions that must be observed in the context of the Spoken Dutch Corpus project.

### 2.1 Pre-conditions

The design of the corpus must take into account the following pre-conditions. First, there is the fact that the corpus is intended to serve so many diverse interests that the design must go to great lengths to try and meet the requirements of the various user groups. This is no trivial matter: different user groups with different priorities and requirements are bound to disagree. Second, the design issue is complicated by the fact that we are dealing with spoken rather than with written language data. Speech is volatile and data capture is complex, as it is affected by recording conditions and other factors that are often beyond one's control. Another design consideration is the available budget and the respective contributions by the funding parties. The total budget for the project is fixed at 4.6 M Euro. This should cover all costs involved in recording and collecting the data, and transcribing and annotating it. Two-thirds of the money is supplied by the Dutch, one-third by the Flemish. It has been stipulated that two-thirds of the data should originate from the Netherlands, while one-third originates from Flanders. Finally, the issue of copyright is a major concern as it complicates matters enormously. Since audio files will be distributed along with the corpus, the consent of all speakers is required as well as that of any other parties who hold any rights to the recorded material.

### 2.2 Spoken texts in the BNC

The spoken component of the BNC constitutes approximately ten per cent of the total corpus, i.e. some ten million words. The material comprises two types of data. The first type is referred to as the demographic component, made up of 'informal encounters recorded by a socially-stratified sample of respondents, selected by age group, sex, social class and geographic region' (Aston and Burnard 1998: 31). Data of the second type include 'more formal encounters (meetings, debates, lectures, seminars, radio programmes and the like), categorized by topic and type of interaction' (ibid.) and are usually referred to as the context-governed component. It is worth noting at this point that, as Aston and Burnard point out, 'this dual approach was chosen in the absence of any previous objective measures that might be used to define the target population or to construct a sampling frame for spoken language' (Aston and Burnard 1998: 31).

At the start of the Spoken Dutch Corpus project, the BNC design was contemplated as a possible model, but it soon became clear that there were various reasons why this would not work. For example, the fact that the Dutch corpus is envisaged as a resource for research in the field of speech recognition required that the audio files be made available. Under Belgian and Dutch legislation recordings can only be made with prior consent of all parties involved,[3] which proves a major problem especially with the demographic component. To have people that have been recruited for the project make (surreptitious) recordings of everyone they speak to over a period of two weeks and then obtain the permission of these speakers obviously is out of the question. Another reason for departing from the BNC approach is that there is general agreement that the more detailed the information about the speakers, recording conditions, etc. that is included, the more valuable the corpus will prove to be. Collecting such information from people you happen to record but who are unknown to you seems at best problematic.

After considering the BNC design and sampling strategy, we decided to reject it and come up with a design of our own. This design is described in some detail in sections 2.3 and 2.4 below.

## 2.3 Overall design

The design of the Spoken Dutch Corpus takes into account the various dimensions underlying the variation that can be observed in language use. In the overall design of the corpus the principal parameter is taken to be the setting in which language is used. This leads us to distinguish a number of components, each of which can be characterized in terms of its socio-situational characteristics, such as communicative goal, medium, number of speakers participating, and the relationship between speaker(s) and hearer(s). The specification of each of the components is given in terms of sample sizes, total number of speakers, range of topics, etc. Where this is considered to be of particular interest, speaker characteristics such as gender, age, geographical region, and socio-economic class are used as (demographic) sampling criteria; otherwise they are merely recorded as part of the meta-data.[4] The overall design of the corpus is given in Table 1.

In all, 14 different components are distinguished. The total number of words varies from component to component. Since a full specification is not as yet available for all components, the total number of words per component remains somewhat arbitrary at this point. However, we assume that no adaptations will be necessary. Considerations that have played a role in determining the present sizes of the components are the following:

- there is a great demand for spontaneously spoken language data; this explains the overall bias towards unscripted language;

- interaction is considered to be a typical characteristic of spoken communication; therefore it is felt that dialogues and multilogues should be amply represented in the data;
- certain language varieties display a great deal more variation than others; in order to capture this variation, more heterogeneous components generally are represented in the corpus by a larger number of samples than the more homogeneous ones;
- the sample size differs from component to component; while it is impossible to know what the optimum sample size is, intuitive judgements are brought into play when it comes to deciding what constitutes an appropriate sample. Here the 'natural' length of a spoken text also plays a role: an item in a radio news broadcast is inevitably shorter than the spoken commentary in a television documentary;
- some types of data are easier to collect than others;
- in order to meet the needs of particular user groups some components require a certain minimum amount of data; this is especially true for components that are used for the development of technological applications such as telephone conversations and read aloud text.[5]

**Table 1:** Overall design of the corpus

| | | | | | |
|---|---|---|---|---|---|
| dialogue/ multilogue 8,110,000 | private 6,635,000 | | unscripted 6,635,000 | direct 3,460,000 | conversations (face-to-face) 3,000,000 |
| | | | | | interviews 460,000 |
| | | | | distanced 3,175,000 | telephone conversations 3,000,000 |
| | | | | | business transactions 175,000 |
| | public 1,475,000 | broadcast 750,000 | more or less scripted 750,000 | | interviews and discussions 750,000 |
| | | non-broadcast 725,000 | unscripted 725,000 | | discuss., debates, meetings 375,000 |
| | | | | | lectures 350,000 |
| monologue 1,890,000 | private 40,000 | | more or less scripted 40,000 | | descriptions of pictures 40,000 |
| | public 1,850,000 | broadcast 950,000 | unscripted 250,000 | | spontaneous commentary 250,000 |
| | | | scripted 700,000 | | newsreports, current affairs programmes 250,000 |
| | | | | | news 250,000 |
| | | | | | commentary 200,000 |
| | | non-broadcast 900,000 | scripted 900,000 | | lectures, speeches 275,000 |
| | | | | | read aloud text 625,000 (+ 375,000) |

The approach adopted here yields a highly flexible design and has the advantage that each component may be tailored to the specific needs of one or more special interest groups. Within the framework of the overall design, separate designs are made for each component. Thus sampling criteria may differ from one component to another, and so may the sampling strategy. For a component such as *lectures and speeches* (component 13), material is collected through what is best characterized as 'opportunistic sampling', whereas for other components, such as component 1 (*face-to-face conversations*), stratified sampling is applied.

Here it should be observed that sampling is complicated by the fact that even between two neighbouring countries such as Belgian and the Netherlands, there are cultural differences that may interfere with any straightforward design. While ideally it is possible to have parallel sampling for northern standard Dutch and southern standard Dutch, in actual practice this is not so easily achieved. An example is the recording of lectures. Due to differences between the educational system in Belgium and the Netherlands (esp. higher education), it is impossible to sample the same type of lectures. Lectures in Belgium are usually (prepared) monologues, while in the Netherlands, depending on the number of students, they are generally much more interactive, spontaneous dialogues.

Most data that will be included in the Spoken Dutch Corpus are original in the sense that they do not occur in any other data collection. For a few components, however, it seems advantageous to include data that have been collected in other projects. This is the case for the data that make up component 4 (*business transactions*). Here the fact that such data are normally rather difficult to obtain but very interesting to have has been decisive for including them, despite the fact that no such data are available for Flanders. Also the data that make up components 2 (*interviews*) and 8 (*description of pictures*) originate from another project. By incorporating these data in the much larger Spoken Dutch Corpus, both parties involved have something to gain. Thus, for the Spoken Dutch Corpus, the benefit is that the data come as a properly designed set and have already been collected, thus saving time and money. For the project that supplies the data, the benefit is that the data are included in full, i.e. they are made to conform to the practice adopted by the Spoken Dutch Corpus, which is becoming a de facto standard for Dutch language resources, while the data also receive additional annotations.

Where data are contributed from other projects, the original design is left intact. This conflicts with the stipulation that two-thirds of the data in the Spoken Dutch Corpus should originate from the Netherlands and only one-third from Flanders, at least to the extent that the individual components are concerned. The overall two to one division is restored by adapting the sizes of some of the other components. Table 2 shows the respective contributions by the Dutch and Flemish data to each of the components.

**Table 2:** Respective contributions from Flanders and the Netherlands

| **Component:** | **total number of words** | originating from the Netherlands | originating from Flanders |
|---|---|---|---|
| 1. conversations (face-to-face) | 3,000,000 | 2,000,000 | 1,000,000 |
| 2. interviews | 460,000 | 230,000 | 230,000 |
| 3. telephone conversations | 3,000,000 | 2,000,000 | 1,000,000 |
| 4. business transactions | 175,000 | 175,000 | 0 |
| 5. interviews and discussions | 750,000 | 520,000 | 230,000 |
| 6. discussions, debates, meetings | 375,000 | 245,000 | 130,000 |
| 7. lectures | 350,000 | 240,000 | 110,000 |
| 8. descriptions of pictures | 40,000 | 0 | 40,000 |
| 9. spontaneous commentary | 250,000 | 180,000 | 70,000 |
| 10. newsreports, current affairs programmes | 250,000 | 170,000 | 80,000 |
| 11. news | 250,000 | 170,000 | 80,000 |
| 12. commentary | 200,000 | 140,000 | 60,000 |
| 13. lectures, speeches | 275,000 | 180,000 | 95,000 |
| 14. read aloud text | 625,000<br>*(+ 375,000)* | 415,000<br>*(+ 250,000)* | 210,000<br>*(+ 125,000)* |
| Total | **10,000,000**<br>***(10,375,000)*** | **6,665,000**<br>***(6,915,000)*** | **3,335,000**<br>***(3,460,000)*** |

## 2.4 Selections for which more advanced annotations are envisaged

Once the overall design of the corpus is established, it remains to be decided which part(s) of the corpus should be included in the selection of one million words (or 250,000 words in the case of prosodic annotation) for which more detailed annotations are envisaged. Preferably, the selection should in some way reflect the composition of the full corpus. While it would be straightforward to simply select 10 per cent of each component, two powerful arguments can be raised against this procedure. First, there is the fact that some user groups require certain minimum amounts of data with specific higher level (or more detailed) annotations that exceed the 10 per cent norm. Second, not all types of data can be annotated with the same rate of success and/or at the same expense. Therefore, in the light of users' needs, quality standards to be upheld, and the time and money available, certain types of data are given priority over others. The selections envisaged for each type of detailed annotation are displayed in Table 3.

Two observations can be made here. First, wherever possible, there is overlap between the various selections. The motivation for this is that, in so far as this is feasible, users should have access to a maximally large set of data with a maximum amount of annotation. Second, with the selections for which more detailed types of annotation are envisaged, a similar distribution over the Flemish and Dutch data as that over the entire corpus is aimed for. Here again there are factors that make it impossible to maintain the two to one division that was originally intended for each component. The overall picture for the selections, however, shows that all selections together comprise roughly twice as much data originating from the Netherlands as from Flanders.

## 3. Conclusion

The design of the Spoken Dutch Corpus is a complex matter. It has been guided by a great many factors and considerations. Since the Corpus is perceived as a major resource for various fields of interest, ranging from Dutch linguistics and language engineering to education, for years to come, its design must anticipate the various research interests arising from these fields and provide for them. It is our contention that the compilation of the Spoken Dutch Corpus will yield a resource for Dutch that holds up to international standards. Both with respect to its design and with respect to the nature of the transcriptions and annotations, the corpus conforms to international standards, guidelines and best practice. The corpus will be comparable in size to the spoken component of the British National Corpus. The sophistication of the different transcriptions and annotations and the availability of the sound files place the corpus at the forefront of corpus development. Thus the expectation that the Spoken Dutch Corpus will prove a valuable asset for language and speech technologists as well as linguists from various backgrounds is well-justified.

**Table 3:** Selections for which more advanced annotations are envisaged

| **Component:** | **total number of words in the corpus** | **amount of data and types of annotation (in number of words)** | | |
|---|---|---|---|---|
| | | phon.transcr. + alignment | syntactic annotation | prosodic annotation |
| 1. conversations (face-to-face) | 3,000,000 | 150,000 | 550,000 | 100,000 |
| 2. interviews | 460,000 | 50,000 | 50,000 | 20,000 |
| 3. telephone conversations | 3,000,000 | 300,000 | 100,000 | 50,000 |
| 4. business transactions | 175,000 | 15,000 | 15,000 | 10,000 |
| 5. interviews and discussions | 750,000 | 75,000 | 75,000 | 10,000 |
| 6. discussions, debates, meetings | 375,000 | 35,000 | 35,000 | 10,000 |
| 7. lectures | 350,000 | 35,000 | 35,000 | 0 |
| 8. descriptions of pictures | 40,000 | 5,000 | 5,000 | 0 |
| 9. spontaneous commentary | 250,000 | 27,500 | 27,500 | 10,000 |
| 10. newsreports current affairs programmes | 250,000 | 25,000 | 25,000 | 10,000 |
| 11. news | 250,000 | 27,500 | 27,500 | 10,000 |
| 12. commentary | 200,000 | 25,000 | 25,000 | 10,000 |
| 13. lectures, speeches | 275,000 | 30,000 | 30,000 | 10,000 |
| 14. read aloud text | 625,000 *(+ 375,000)* | 200,000 | 0 | 0 |
| **Total** | **10,000,000** ***(10,375,000)*** | **1,000,000** | **1,000,000** | **250,000** |

**Acknowledgement**

This publication was supported by the Netherlands Organization for Scientific Research (NWO) under grant number 014-17-510.

**Notes**

1 In addition, Dutch is the official first language in Surinam and the Dutch Antilles. However speakers in these countries use Dutch predominantly in formal settings, unlike the Netherlands and Flanders, while the populations are very small (some 360,000 and 240,000 speakers respectively).

2 More information about the Spoken Dutch Corpus project can be found at http://lands.let.kun.nl/cgn/ See also Oostdijk (2000a).

3 This also explains why the Spoken Dutch Corpus only includes the speech of adults: under Belgian and Dutch legislation only adults (18 years and over) can give their consent.

4 See also Oostdijk (2000b).

5 In the field of speech recognition there was a major interest in incorporating a component of read aloud text. Based on experiences abroad with other languages, it was estimated that the data should comprise at least one million words. However it was felt that to include so much scripted text would skew the entire corpus. So it was decided to reduce that part of the data to 625,000 words, in the 10-million-word corpus, and the remaining 375,000 words will be collected as time and money will allow.

**References**

Aston, Guy and Lou Burnard (1998). *The BNC Handbook. Exploring the British National Corpus with SARA*. Edinburgh: Edinburgh University Press.

Bouma, Gosse and Ineke Schuurman. (1998). 'Intergovernmental language policy for Dutch and the language and speech technology infrastructure'. In Antonio Rubio, Natividad Gallardo, Rosa Castro, and Antonio Tejada (eds), *Proceedings of the First International Conference on Language Resources and Evaluation*. Vol. I: 509–513. Granada, Spain.

Burnard, Lou (ed.) (1995). *Users reference guide for the British National Corpus*. Oxford: Oxford University Press.

Oostdijk, Nelleke (2000a). 'The Spoken Dutch Corpus. Overview and first evaluation'. In Maria Gravilidou, George Carayannis, Stella Markantonatou, Stelios Piperidis, and Gregory Stainhaouer (eds), *LREC-2000 (Second International Conference on Language Resources and Evaluation) proceedings*. Vol. II: 887–894. Athens, Greece.

Oostdijk, Nelleke (2000b). 'Meta-data in the Spoken Dutch Corpus'. In Daan Broeder, Hamish Cunningham, Nancy Ide, David Roy, Henry Thompson, and Peter Wittenburg (eds), *LREC-2000 workshop proceedings of the Workshop on Meta-Descriptions and Annotation Schemes for Multi-Modal/Multi-Media Language Resources*. 29–30 May 2000. 21–25. Athens, Greece.

# Historical and regional studies

# Canting terms in the Early English Prose Fiction Corpus

*Maurizio Gotti*

University of Bergamo

**Abstract**

*The paper discusses the use of the Early English Prose Corpus, to identify canting terms and expressions, and verify their meanings in comparison with those given them in contemporary lexicographic works. The analysis finds canting terms and expressions in at least a dozen of the contemporary narrative works included in the Early English Prose Corpus. The meanings found in novels and pamphlets coincide with the definitions of 17th and 18th century dictionaries and glossaries. Quotations found during these searches also provide antedatings of a few terms in earlier sources than those commonly attested, and a few previously unrecorded expressions.*

## 1. Introduction

This paper describes a project designed to find out whether the most frequent canting terms and expressions identified in 17th and 18th century dictionaries and glossaries are present in contemporary narrative works, so as to assess the actual use of these words in the literary compositions of the period and thus increase their degree of reliability. By *canting* we mean the particular jargon spoken by thieves and vagabonds, identified as an 'antilanguage' typical of an 'antisociety', since its speakers' activities were considered criminal for the rest of British society (cf. Gotti 1999).

The Early English Prose Corpus used in this research is a database containing 211 complete works in English prose, from the period 1500 to 1700, by writers from the British Isles; the database is stored on a CD-ROM published by Chadwyck-Healey Ltd. For the purposes of this paper, Richard Head has been selected as a paradigmatic figure to represent 18th century canting lexicographers, as his works are included in the corpus.

## 2. Richard Head's contribution to canting lexicography

In his publications, Richard Head dealt with the main types of criminal figures then characterizing the English underworld, their illicit activities and their secret language. The interest in this topic was not new, as several books and dictionaries dealing with the language and the habits of the underworld had appeared for over a century. However, the Civil War and the subsequent Puritan rule had caused a halt in the production of such publications, and only after the end of the Commonwealth had an interest in rogues and their habits arisen again, testified to by the appearance of many pamphlets and books dealing with the description of the tricks of the various types of underworld criminals and of the different kinds of punishment meted out to them. The influence of this new interest in the underworld on the development of a specific sector of the English literature of that time is pointed out effectively by Rawlings:

> During the late seventeenth century and throughout the eighteenth century, crime provided one of the principal subjects for popular literature. All aspects were covered: the crime itself, the investigation, the trial, the punishment and the life of the offender. The works ranged from newspaper articles through broadsheets and pamphlets to large books, sometimes in several volumes. (Rawlings 1992: 1)

In this revival of the interest in the roguish sector of English society, Richard Head played an important role through two very popular works: *The English Rogue* and *The Canting Academy*. In these publications, Head not only provided a thorough description of the habits of this social class, but also reported the most popular words used in communicating within that context. His justification for this linguistic side of his work was that at this time there was 'little [...] extant in Print of [this] way of speaking, commonly known by the name of Canting. [...] and yet you know how much it is in use among some persons, I mean, the more debauched and looser sort of people' (Head 1673: To the Reader).

It is particularly in the later of the two books that we find a more accurate treatment of the linguistic aspects of the canting world, testified to not only by the inclusion of a specific dictionary, but also of several remarks and comments on the features of this jargon. A first remark concerns the identification of the main users of this language, who are thus outlined:

> There is no profest Rogue whatever, (if he be qualified for his thieving faculty) but must be well vers'd in Canting: and to the intent that they may not fall short of being excellent proficients in all manner of Roguery, they lay the ground work thereof in Canting, for by this they are able to converse with, and understand those of the upper Form of Villany, and by constant frequenting their company, become acquainted with Canting words which are most new, and what are thrown aside as too commonly known, the use whereof if not timely left off, may be the Instruments which may unhappily betray them to their condign punishments. (Head 1673: 2)

Once he has specified the users of this language, Head points out its main characteristics; the first of these is identified in its secret nature, the reason for which is explained by the author:

> I shall endeavour to give you an exact account of these Caterpillars, with their hidden and mysterious way of speaking, which they make use of to blind the eyes of those they have cheated or robb'd, and inform one another with what they have done, or designe to do. (Head 1673: 2)

The secret nature of this language is clearly perceived by its users and is strengthened by the oath that each new member of the underworld is made to take during the ceremony in which he is officially admitted into that society; the wording of this oath is reported by Head:

> I will not teach any one to Cant, nor will I disclose ought of our mysteries to them, although they flaug me to the death. (Head 1673: 4)

Another aspect of this roguish cant pointed out by Head is its high degree of changeability, the reason being thus explained in *The Canting Academy*:

> From these [the Rogues] I understood, that the Mode of Canting alter'd very often, and that they were forced to change frequently those material words which chiefly discovered their mysterious practices and Villanies, least growing too common their own words should betray them. (Head 1673: 56–57)

In order to emphasize the linguistic aspect of his work, Richard Head groups the terms most commonly used by the members of the underworld in a specific dictionary, divided into two sections: 'Canting before the English' and 'English before the Canting' (the equivalent of a bilingual dictionary's sections). The importance of Head's contribution is highlighted by the fact that in these sections he not only reports the canting terms listed in previous publications, but also adds many new ones, so as to make his dictionary 'more compleat than any hath been publisht hitherto' (Head 1673: To the Reader). As several of the terms included in his dictionary will be totally unknown to his readers, Head is aware of the need to emphasize the reliability of his data and reassures his readers:

> I can assure you (the helps being so inconsiderable) the pains I took in the Collection of new Words is unimaginable. (Head 1673: To the Reader)

Moreover, in order to strengthen the reliability of his new terms, Head clearly states that all of them 'have passed the approbation of the Critical Canter' (Head 1673: 57). Indeed, in his collection of material for his new books, Head has not been at all reluctant to contact even rogues and other speakers of cant, and to include them – together with previous canting publications – among his sources for new data, as he himself clearly states in his work:

> I have consulted likewise what is printed on this subject, and have slighted no help I could gather from thence, which indeed is very little; the greatest assistance I had in this discovery, was from Newgate; which with much difficulty I screw'd out of the sullen Rogues, who would not speak a word till I had suppled their tongues with the oil of Barley, or rather thaw'd their obstinate silence with the heat of strong Liquors. (Head 1673: 56)

This great care in collecting data and the differentiation of his sources make Head's contribution to the analysis of canting language very interesting. His innovative canting expressions will constitute the main object of our analysis, which will be based on the text of *The English Rogue*, one of the works included in the Early English Prose Corpus.

## 3. Head's new canting terms

The new canting terms occurring in *The English Rogue* have been grouped in the Appendix; apart from three, all these terms are listed in the 'Canting Vocabulary' included in Chapter 5 of the first part of this text. The entries reported in this dictionary amount to 187, which is a relatively high number if compared to the total of five hundred expressions included in all the different books on cant published between 1535 and 1612. Among the cant expressions that Head provides, 37 are new or have a meaning which is different from the one(s) reported in previous publications, thus demonstrating that his contribution is extremely relevant, at least in quantitative terms. Of these new expressions the great majority consists of nouns (31 out of 37); the rest is made up of adjectives (4) and verbs (2); all the new terms correspond to content words, while grammatical words remain the same as those of the general language. This aspect is a typical linguistic feature of both cant and slang, as several studies on the subject have pointed out; cf. Halliday:

> The principle is that of same grammar, different vocabulary; but different vocabulary only in certain areas, typically those that are central to the activities of the subculture and that set it off most sharply from the established society. (Halliday 1978: 165)

As regards the semantic fields to which Head's new canting terms belong, they correspond to the lexical areas typical of the various underworld activities and of the reality in which their practitioners live. The highest number consists of expressions used to indicate people, and in particular the members of this social class: *Dommerar* = 'A Madman', *Mumpers* = 'Gentile Beggers' [i.e. genteel beggars, who will not accept victuals, but money or clothes], *Quier-Cove* = 'A Rogue', *Quier-Mort* = 'A Pocky Jade' [i.e. a woman or harlot that is syphilitic]. Other terms refer to their aspect, character or condition: *Canke* = 'Dumb', *Damber* = 'Rascal', *Dimber* = 'Pretty'; or to the different representatives of the more general society with whom rogues are in contact: *Culle* = 'A Sap-headed Fellow', *Cully* = 'A Fool or Fop', *Rome-Culle* = 'A Rich Coxcomb' [i.e. a rich fool, simpleton or dupe], *Kinchin Cove* = 'A little man'. A few expressions have been coined to denote parts of the body or diseases: *Cannakin* = 'The Plague', *Prating cheat* = 'A Tongue', *Quarron* = 'A Body'. Other lexemes instead refer to clothes and personal objects: *Calle* = 'A Cloak', *Duds* = 'Goods', *Lurries* = 'All manner of cloaths', *Mish* = 'A Shirt'.

A number of expressions refer to crime and fraud, particularly as regards theft and cheating: *Betty* = 'An Instrument to break a door', *Budge* = 'One that steals Cloaks', *Bulk and File* = 'The Pickpocket and his mate', *Gilt* = 'A Pick-lock', *Kidnapper* = 'A fellow that walketh the streets, and takes all advantages to pick up the younger sort of people, whom with lies and many fair promises he inticeth on board a ship and transports them into forreign plantations', *Nab* = 'To take, or cheat', *Rome-Padders* = 'High-way men', *Shop-lift* = 'One that steals out of shops'. Strictly connected with these are the terms referring to trial, punishment or imprisonment: *Fib* = 'To beat', *Naskin* = 'A Gaol or Bridewell', *Trine* = 'Tyburn' [i.e. the place of execution for Middlesex to 1783].

Several terms refer to actions commonly carried out by members of the underworld: *Dup* = 'To enter'; or to different aspects of their daily lives: *Fogus* = 'Tobacco or Smoke', *Frummagem* = 'Choakt', *Jague* = 'A Ditch', *Pad* = 'The High-way', *Tick-rome* = 'A License'. Two expressions are linked to the semantic area of money and spending: *Deuswins* = 'Two pence', *Tres wins* = 'Three pence'.

## 4. The analysis of the corpus

The Early English Prose Corpus has been comprehensively searched for all words listed in the Appendix, to find any occurrences in other texts than Head's. Of the 37 terms, 25 (two thirds of the canting expressions analysed) appear only in *The English Rogue*. The others (identified by an asterisk in the Appendix), appear also in other texts, although not always with a canting connotation; the seven which have a canting value only in Head's texts are the following:

- *Betty*, which is used as a proper noun in the other texts.
- *Budge*, which appears in other books with the semantic value of 'fur (garment)' or with a verbal function.
- *Calle*, which is used as a graphic variant of the verb *call* or as a noun having the semantic values of 'street' or 'driving' (place where cattle are driven).
- *Gilt*, usually connected with gold covering or to a young prostitute.
- *Mish*, appearing in the expression *mish-mashes* (meaning 'confused mixtures').
- *Nab*: apart from its other canting value of 'head' found in *The English Rogue*, this word occurs in other texts within the expressions *hab-nab* (used as an adjective with the meaning 'random') and *hab nab* (having the adverbial value of 'anyhow').
- *Trine*, appearing in another text in the noun phrase *God Trine*.

The remaining five terms have been found with a canting connotation also in other texts, published either before or after inclusion in *The English Rogue*. In the latter case the occurrence in a later text may be the result of the influence of Head's canting dictionary or a confirmation of its reliability; in the former case – besides providing further evidence for the real existence of these expressions – the texts identified may also be hypothesised as possible sources of Head's neologisms. The canting expressions found in texts published after *The English Rogue* are the following:

- *Bulk and File*: This expression has been found twice in Keach (1684) with the same meaning as Head's.
- *Cully*: This word appears in many texts such as Anonymous (1683a, 1683b, 1683c, 1684), Behn (1685, 1687), Brown (1700), Gildon (1692) and Kirkman (1673a). The 33 occurrences[1] of this term in these texts testify to its popularity in the last quarter of the 17th century and its use not only in canting contexts but also in the standard language – although in colloquial environments and concerning topics connected to the lives of criminals – with its wider double meaning of 'dupe' and 'mate'.
- *Mumpers*, used by Keach (1684) in the following list of canting terms: 'and learn'd the Canting Names, used by the whole Corporation of Thieves and Beggars; as Mumpers, Milkins, Pads, and Room-Padders, Clapperdogeons, Bulk and File, &tc'[2] (Keach 1684: 84).
- *Kidnapper*: This too is a word that became standardised in the period following the publication of *The English Rogue*; indeed, in our analysis of the corpus we

found it included in a quotation drawn from Bunyan's *Pilgrim's Progress* (1684).

- *Pad*, inserted in the expression *Squires of the Pad* (meaning 'Highway-men') in the context of the following lively description of roguish people:

> The persons that meet are generally Men of an Infamous Character, and are in various Shapes, Habits, and Employments. Sometimes they are Squires of the Pad and now and then borrow a little Money upon the King's High-Way, to recruit their Losses at the Gaming-House, and when a Hue and Cry is out, to apprehend them, they are safe in one of these Houses, as a Thief in a Mill, and practise the old Trade of Cross-biting Cullies, assisting the Frail square Dye with high and low Fullums, and other Napping Tricks, in comparison of whom the common Bulkers, and Pick-Pockets, are a very honest Society. (Brown 1700: 106–107)

One of these canting terms has also been found in a text published before *The English Rogue*, and may therefore have acted as a source for Head's dictionary. This term is *Bulk*, which appears twice in Anonymous (1662); it is interesting to notice that in these two quotations – reported below – the author provides a clear context from which the semantic value of this term (i.e. a pickpocket's accomplice) is made evident:

> They have several Forms or sorts of Pick-pockets, they have one fellow alwayes in company when they go about this Employment, whom they call a Bulk, that is, to make some quarrel in the streets, or else obstruct the passage while the Whipsters do the Feat; (Anonymous 1662: 50)

> there was one Bat Rud as He was since informed, who was the Bulk; who observing the man held his Hand in the Pocket where his Gold was, just in the middle of the Lane whitherto they dogged him, overthrew a Barrel trimming at an Alehouse door, while one behind the Grasier pusht him over, who withall throws down Bat who was ready for the fall; betwixt these two, in the ground arose a quarrel, the Pick-pocket demanding satisfaction, while his Comrades interposing (after two or three blowes) in favour of the Countrey-man (who had drawn his hands out of his Fob to defend himself) soon drew out his Treasure; and while he was looking, on the scuffle, some of them had lent him a hand too and Fingered out his Watch. (Anonymous 1662: 77–78)

It is interesting to notice that these occurrences have so far been ignored, as they do not appear as first quotations of the canting term *bulk* in the main diachronic dictionaries of the English language (such as *The Oxford English Dictionary*) or of the language of the underworld (such as Partridge 1949/1961), which commonly quote Head as the innovator.

## 5. The search for orthographic variants

As spelling conventions in the 16th and 17th centuries were not very consistent, the existence of several orthographic variants for the same word was a common phenomenon. Starting from this assumption, a search for the presence of Head's new terms in the Early English Prose Corpus was carried out using the orthographic variants suggested in Partridge (1949/1961). This search, however, gave limited results, as only the following five variants were found:

- *Canniken*, only found in Head with the same meaning as *Cannakin*.
- *Culley*, found in Anonymous (1683c) with the same semantic values as *Cully* (cf. above).
- *Kinchin Co*, used by Head himself in his Second Part (1668) as a variant for *Kinchin Cove*.
- *Room-Padders*, found in Keach (1684) with the same canting meaning as Head's *Rome-padders*.
- *Shop-lifter*, which occurs both in Head (1671b) and Kirkman (1673b) with the same meaning as *Shop-lift*.

In order to find more orthographic variants of Head's neologisms, the searching options of the Early English Prose Corpus were used, and in particular those seeking variant spellings. Of these, the searching option based on a * wildcard (representing any number of characters including none, e.g. *wander**) often proved to be too time-consuming and frequently gave an excessively high number of hits; this was the case, for example, when searching for the following words, which resulted in over 50 hits: *d*mer**, *du*d**, *can*k**, *cul**. Better results were instead obtained when specifying as many known characters as possible, with a minimum of three. Integrating the results with those previously obtained, the following were cases of confirmation of Head's spellings:

- De*wins > Deuswins.
- D?mb?r* > Dimber, Damber.
- Fru*mage* > Frummagem.
- Nask* > Naskin.
- Nas*k?n > Naskin.

- Qu?er*mort* > Quier-mort.
- R?m*-Pad*er* > Rome-padders.

## 6. The unexpected results

The reading of some of the quotations found during the searches above provided the stimulus for further analyses. Indeed, the canting context in which some of Head's new terms were found contained other words and expressions which were worthy of investigation. This was the case with the following quotation taken from Head's text, in which *Mouths* is provided as a synonym for *Cullies* (in the sense of 'dupes'):

(1) … the tricks on Cards, by which they usually cheated their Cullies or Mouths, … (Head 1665: 320)

(2) … the tricks on Cards by which they were wont to cheat their Cullies or Mouths; (Head 1665: 428)

Interestingly, Partridge (1949/1961) reports the first occurrence of this word used in canting contexts with the semantic value of 'a gullible person, a dupe (esp. if an easy one)' in John Poulter's *Discoveries* (1753); *The Oxford English Dictionary* gives the following quotation, which is also taken from a later work than Head's:

(3) 6. *slang*. A silly person; a dupe; **1680** COTTON *Compl. Gamester* (ed. 2) 7 The whole Gang will be ever and anon watching an opportunity to make a Mouth of you.

Another source for interesting observations has proved to be Anonymous (1662). In analysing the quotation containing the term *Bulk*, we came across the word *Rub*; as can be seen in the continuation of the quotation reported above, this is reported as a term used by pick-pockets:

(4) And then there is another ready whom they call the Rub, into whose Hands the prey is conveyed, and he clearly carries it away. (Anonymous 1662: 50)

In Partridge (1949/1961) this term is not even reported; only the verb *to rub* is mentioned with the meaning 'to run away', first occurring in a quotation dated 1688; similarly, this noun – used in a canting sense – is omitted also in *The Oxford English Dictionary*. Another expression reported neither in Partridge (1949/1961) nor in the *OED* is *File-clyers*, given as a synonym of the canting noun *diver* (meaning 'pickpocket') as can be seen from the following quotation:

(5) I had but very little choice, so I listed my self of another Colony or Plantation (but who neither sow nor reap) of the Divers or File-clyers. (Anonymous 1662: 48)

Words with this meaning but different spellings are indeed reported in those two dictionaries, but all appearing in quotations dated later than 1662: Partridge (1949/1961) mentions the spellings *file(-)cloy*, *file-cly*, *foil-cloy* and *foyl-cloy* with B.E. (1698) as the earliest occurrence; *The Oxford English Dictionary* indicates Head (1673) as the first source for the term *Foyl-cloy*.

## 7. Conclusion

The analysis carried out has proved that canting terms and expressions were not limited to 17th and 18th century dictionaries and glossaries, as they were also present in at least a dozen of the contemporary narrative works included in the Early English Prose Corpus. The meanings with which they were explained in lexicographic works coincided with those found in novels and pamphlets.

As regards the particular reliability of Richard Head's reporting of innovative canting terms, the corpus analysed has provided a very limited confirmation, as only five of his 37 new expressions have been found in other texts. These terms generally occur with a canting connotation in works published after they were included in *The*

*English Rogue*, and may therefore be the result of the influence of Head's canting dictionary; indeed, some of them became quite popular in the last quarter of the 17th century and were in use not only in canting contexts but also in the standard language, although generally in colloquial environments and concerning topics connected to the lives of criminals. One of these canting terms has also been found in a text published before *The English Rogue*, and may therefore have acted as a source for Head's dictionary.

By making use of the searching options offered by the CD-ROM adopted, a few orthographic variants of Head's neologisms have also been investigated. Although it has given limited results (as only five variants were identified), this search for variant spellings has proved particularly useful as an analytical practice, as different strategies have been tried out and varying results have been obtained.

The corpus examined has otherwise not proved to be very useful for this analysis, since only a minority of the terms investigated appear in it; thus the CD-ROM used – although a wide database, comprising 211 complete works in English prose – only represents a slice of the Early Modern English of the period, as it is biased towards the standard and the literary.

The reading of some of the quotations found during these searches has also pointed to the occurrence of a few terms in earlier sources than those commonly attested, as well as the presence of a few expressions appearing in canting contexts and not previously mentioned. Many of these innovative forms have been found in Anonymous (1662), which has proved to be a very stimulating source of observations.

## Notes

1 Apart from these 33 occurrences, twelve more concerning the plural form *cullies* have been found in five texts, all of which already mentioned it in connection with the singular form.

2 All of these terms are included in Head's canting dictionary, albeit sometimes with a different spelling.

3 This word appears in the Part 3 of *The English Rogue.*

4 This term does not appear in the canting vocabulary but elsewhere in the text of the first part of *The English Rogue.*

5 This word appears in Part 4 of *The English Rogue.*

6 This term already existed as 'to hang'; Head added the meaning 'Tyburn' to it.

## References

Anonymous (1662). *The life and death of Mrs. Mary Frith. Commonly called Mal Cutpurse*. London: printed for W. Gilbertson.

Anonymous (1683a). *The Dutch rogue*. London: printed by A.M. for Greg. Hill.

Anonymous (1683b). *The London bully*. London: printed by Hen. Clark, for Tho. Malthus.
Anonymous (1683c). *The London jilt*. London: printed for Hen. Rhodes.
Anonymous (1684). *Eve revived*. London: printed by William Downing.
B. E. (1698). *A new dictionary of the terms ancient and modern of the canting crew*. London: printed for W. Hawes, P. Gilbourne and W. Davis.
Behn, Aphra (1685). *Love letters from a noble man to his sister. The second part*. London: printed for the Author.
Behn, Aphra (1687). *The amours of Philander and Silvia*. London: printed and to be Sold by most Book-Sellers.
Brown, Thomas (1700). *Amusements serious and comical*. London: printed for John Nutt.
Bunyan, John (1684). *The pilgrim's progress. The second part*. London: printed for Nathaniel Ponder.
Gildon, Charles (1692). *The post-boy rob'd of his mail*. London: printed for John Dunton.
Gotti, Maurizio (1999). *The language of thieves and vagabonds. 17th and 18th century canting lexicography in England*. Tübingen: Niemeyer.
Halliday, Michael A.K. (1978). *Language as social semiotic. The social interpretation of language and meaning*. London: Edward Arnold.
Head, Richard (1665). *The English rogue*. London: printed for Henry Marsh.
Head, Richard (with Francis Kirkman) (1668). *The English rogue. The second part*. London: printed for Francis Kirkman.
Head, Richard (with Francis Kirkman) (1671a). *The English rogue. The third part*. London: printed for Francis Kirkman.
Head, Richard (with Francis Kirkman) (1671b). *The English rogue. The fourth part*. London: printed for Francis Kirkman.
Head, Richard (1673). *The canting academy*. London: printed by F. Leach for Mat. Drew.
Keach, Benjamin (1684). *The progress of sin*. London: printed for John Dunton.
Kirkman, Francis (1673a). *The counterfeit lady unveiled*. London: printed for Peter Parker.
Kirkman, Francis (1673b). *The unlucky citizen*. London: printed for Anne Johnson.
Partridge, Eric ([1]1949 / [2]1961). *A dictionary of the underworld*. London: Routledge & Kegan Paul.
Rawlings, Philip (1992). *Drunks, whores and idle apprentices: criminal biographies of the eighteenth century*. London: Routledge.

**Appendix**

This appendix lists the terms in *The English Rogue* which are either new or have a new meaning. The words marked with an asterisk appear in the Early English Prose Corpus in the context of other works besides Head's.

BETTY*
BUDGE*
BULK AND FILE*
CALLE*
CANNAKIN
CANKE
CULLE
CULLY[3]*
DAMBER
DEUSWINS
DIMBER
DOMMERAR
DUDS
DUP
FIB
FOGUS
FRUMMAGEM
GILT*
JAGUE
KIDNAPPER[4]*
KINCHIN COVE
LURRIES
MISH*
MUMPERS*
NAB*
NASKIN[5]
PAD*
PRATING CHEAT
QUARRON
QUIER-COVE
QUIER-MORT
ROME-CULLE
ROME-PADDERS
SHOP-LIFT
TICK-ROME
TRES WINS
TRINE[6]*

# In (hot) pursuit of data: complex prepositions in late modern English

*Sebastian Hoffmann*

University of Zürich

**Abstract**

*This paper is a corpus-based study of complex prepositions and their development over the last three centuries. After a general description of the distribution of complex prepositions in fiction and non-fiction, the paper focuses on the question of how complex prepositions become fixed as indivisible units. For this purpose, one of the variable phenomena commonly found during incipient stages of the grammaticalization of complex prepositions is discussed in more detail: adjectival premodification of the nominal element (e.g.* in **hot** pursuit of*). The results show that a proportionally higher number of such instances coincide with the introduction of the corresponding complex prepositions into the language. In the second part of the paper, the development of three individual complex prepositions (*in front of, in (the) face of, *and* on the part of*) is traced both in terms of their frequency and distribution as well as in terms of the changes in meaning that can be observed.*

## 1. Introduction

Complex prepositions are fixed units that are traditionally considered to be indivisible both in terms of syntax and in terms of meaning. Thus, they form the head of a prepositional phrase (PP) and need not be analysed into smaller constituents (e.g. PP -> P + NP + P (+ NP)). Typical examples are shown in (1) and (2):

(1) They went swimming <u>in spite of</u> the rain.
(2) <u>In breach of</u> the protocol, he left the banquet early.

From a diachronic perspective, complex prepositions can be looked at as examples of a grammaticalization process. In the course of time, their syntactic structure became reanalysed as in the typical example *instead of*, which has its roots in the Old English *in stede* plus a genitival NP:

[[in stede] of X] -> [[in stede of] X]

In addition to reanalysis, the formerly concrete locative reference of *in stede* + NP (people and objects) was gradually extended to carry a predominantly substitutive meaning that in Middle English could also be applied to abstract activities. Today, the Germanic word *stede* meaning 'place' is almost exclusively used in *homestead* or in the archaic *in his/her/its stead*. Thus, *stead* has clearly lost its syntactic and lexical independence and *instead of* is a fixed and indivisible phrase. Finally, spelling is another indication of this gradual process with today's standard two-word spelling first occurring in the 16th century. (Cf. Schwenter and Traugott 1995: 247–52.)

Many of today's complex prepositions cannot be traced back to origins in Old English, which suggests that their grammaticalization took place more recently. In the first part of this paper, I am going to present a general overview of the use of complex prepositions in the last three centuries. I will try to assess whether simple and complex prepositions exhibit different general patterns of use and will address the question whether the introduction of new complex prepositions into the language is matched by an overall increase in their frequency of use. In the second part of the paper, I am going to analyse the development and use of three individual complex prepositions in more detail. On the basis of this data, I will try to determine whether common patterns in the grammaticalization of complex prepositions can be observed.

This paper has an exploratory character and is intended as a preparation for further study. As a consequence, the theoretical and methodological aspects involved in a study of complex prepositions (see section 3.2) will receive comparatively little attention.

## 2. Previous work

According to Lehmann (1991: 501), '[t]he formation of new prepositions through the combination of a (mostly relational) noun with either a preposition or a case suffix is one of the most common grammaticalization processes in the world'. Given this observation, it may come as a surprise that complex prepositions have received comparatively little scholarly attention. Indeed, I know of no study that investigates the development of complex prepositions over several centuries in greater detail.

Of the literature available to me, Akimoto (1999) is the only work that offers some information concerning the overall frequency and genre-specific use of complex prepositions from a diachronic perspective. In his data from the Early Modern English period, he found that '[t]he P + NP + P pattern occurs more frequently in essays, such as those of Adam Smith and John Stewart Mill and less frequently in dramas'. (p.217) In addition, Akimoto notes a decrease in the overall number of occurrences by about 30 per cent from the 18th to the 19th century texts, although he does not explicitly discuss this in his paper.[1]

The bulk of Akimoto's study is concerned with the processes of idiomatization, i.e. 'the linguistic process, both synchronic and diachronic, of reorganizing certain phrases into fixed/fossilized expressions, whose meanings have become more or less abstract and undecipherable'. (p.225) In this context, he discusses the shift from concreteness to abstractness, the decategorialization of nouns, rivalry (or fluctuation) of forms and syntactic reanalysis as possible contributing factors. For example, he notes that '[i]n *P* + *NP* + *P* phrases, the definite article *the* was often attached to the nouns in early English and 18th century English. This seems to indicate that the phrases were used more literally than they were used now.' (p.227) Rivalry between different forms can be seen between *in comparison of* and *in comparison with* – the former being more frequent in earlier texts and the latter clearly being the preferred form in the 19th century. Overall, Akimoto (1999) offers many points that invite further study on a larger scale.

Schwenter and Traugott (1995) discuss the grammaticalization of three complex prepositions (*instead of*, *in place of*, and *in lieu of*) and trace their development in the history of English. Their emphasis is on the description of semantic-pragmatic change in combination with a detailed discourse analysis approach which serves to highlight subtle differences in the processes outlined. For example, they observe that the initially locative meaning of *instead of* came to be used in contexts where it reflected the subjective expectations of the speaker/writer about some other person's role or position. However, since

> ... it is no more possible for one person to have exactly the same role as another than it is possible for one place to be exactly where another is ... the speaker implies a mismatch ... and the hearer is invited to make the construction relevant by drawing a subjective inference. Out of repeated uses the expectation (i.e. substitution) meaning was semanticized ... by context-induced reinterpretation. (Schwenter and Traugott 1995: 266)

Schwenter and Traugott (1995: 267) thus convincingly show that a 'detailed examination of historical data in their discourse context' is important for a better understanding of how meanings change. In the present paper, however, where the emphasis is on the overall distribution and use of complex prepositions, such considerations will necessarily have to be backgrounded.

Lehmann (1991) gives an overview of recent grammaticalization processes in German and – among many other aspects – remarks on a new wave of complex prepositions (e.g. *im Zuge*, *im Wege*, etc.) that have been entering the grammar since about 1975. Interestingly, he observes that the 'complex prepositions arise in a narrowly circumscribed set of contexts' (p.503). On the basis of his data, he comments on the relationship between phraseology and grammaticalization: newly formed expressions will not be perceived in isolation by other speakers but always in their specific context. Consequently, they 'will not then spread at once to all kinds of contexts which, given the rules of grammar, would admit it, but will initially be restricted to certain collocations which come close to being phraseologisms' (p.503).

## 3. Material and method

### 3.1 The corpora

At the time of writing, no single suitable corpus is readily available that covers the time between 1650 and today.[2] The following three sources were used to retrieve my data:

- The Gutenberg texts
- The written part of the British National Corpus (BNC)
- The Zürich English Newspaper corpus (ZEN)

#### 3.1.1 The Gutenberg texts

Project Gutenberg's philosophy is 'to make information, books and other materials available [for free] to the general public in forms a vast majority of the computers, programs and people can easily read, use, quote, and search'. (Di Micello 1992) Its archive contains a large collection of non-copyright texts including many works written by British authors in the 17th, 18th and 19th centuries.[3] Of these, I selected about 220 different texts containing approximately 20 million words.

Since these texts were not intended for use in corpus linguistics, they have a number of shortcomings:

- The texts are not necessarily based on the original version published by the authors and may contain some editorial changes or corrections.[4] Often, very little information about the texts is available and their authenticity cannot usually be ascertained. This has potentially serious implications when the Gutenberg texts are used to find constructions which today are ungrammatical but were fully accepted a few centuries ago.[5]

- The spelling may have been corrected to reflect the standards in place at the time when the edition was published. For the corpus linguist interested in grammatical structures, this is of course an advantage because most irregular spellings will have been changed. Given the lack of documentation about the consistency of these changes across different authors and publishers, the possibility of missing some relevant examples in a search based on modern English spelling must however be taken into consideration.[6]

- The collection of texts is not balanced in terms of number of words per time-span or author. Some authors are clearly overrepresented in my set of texts (e.g. Dickens) whereas from other authors only one book could be included.

However, the Gutenberg texts were the only source of data available to me which spans almost three centuries and I believe that a careful evaluation of the data can still yield meaningful results.

The texts were classified on the basis of the date of birth of the author. Thus, I am taking an apparent-time approach, assuming that the linguistic competence of authors does not change greatly once it has been acquired. As a second method of classification, I distinguished between fiction and non-fiction texts.[7] These two categories are admittedly very general labels for genres and a more detailed categorization would be desirable but has to be postponed until a later date. In the remaining part of this paper, the Gutenberg texts will be referred to as the 'Gutenberg corpus'.

### 3.1.2 The British National Corpus (BNC)

The data for present-day English was taken from the written part of the BNC. It comprises about 90 million words from a large range of different genres and registers. (See Aston and Burnard (1998) for a detailed description of the BNC.) The written texts of the BNC are categorized into two major text types: imaginative and informative prose texts. Even though the individual components of these categories are much more varied in the BNC, for the purpose of this paper they are taken to correspond to the general distinction between fiction and non-fiction texts established for the Gutenberg corpus.

### 3.1.3 The Zurich English Newspaper Corpus

The second source for historical data in this paper is the Zurich English Newspaper Corpus (ZEN), with roughly 1.1 million words dating from a variety of British newspapers published between 1671 and 1791. For further information about its composition and a description of its compilation, see Studer and Schneider (2000). Since the texts of ZEN are categorized according to the date of publication rather than the date of birth of the author as in the Gutenberg corpus, direct comparisons between the results gathered from the two corpora cannot be drawn. In addition, ZEN contains a large number of spelling variants and no version with normalized spelling has so far been created (however, see Schneider, this volume). Data retrieved from ZEN will therefore only be of minor importance for this paper.

### 3.1.4 Searching the corpora

The three corpora were searched with perl-scripts and the results were stored in a relational database to allow for easy comparisons between individual complex prepositions across the time-spans and genres. All searches were carried out on a lexical basis. (Given the large extent of standardized spelling in the Gutenberg corpus, it would have been possible to create a version with part-of-speech tags. However, since standard taggers such as CLAWS or ENGCG were designed for present-day English, their precision may be greatly reduced when used on earlier texts and such a step was therefore not considered a viable option. Tagging ZEN in its current form with a standard tagger would clearly produce even more erroneous results.)

## 3.2 The prepositions

### 3.2.1 Compiling a list of complex prepositions

In this paper, only complex prepositions consisting of at least three lexical items are included in the investigation. Thus, prepositions such as *according to* and *instead of* are beyond the scope set for this project. As the lists of complex prepositions found in standard grammars and other relevant sources differ quite considerably, I decided to compile my set of prepositions on the basis of the corpora used. For this purpose, the BNC, the Gutenberg corpus and ZEN were searched for recurrent combinations of the pattern '(simple) preposition – any word – (simple) preposition'. Since simple prepositions form a closed class of items, such a purely lexical search would retrieve virtually all potential three-word complex prepositions in the corpora. The resulting frequency lists certainly contained many items which I could not have found in traditional grammars or other available sources. This is particularly relevant in the case of complex prepositions that have largely disappeared from present-day English, e.g. *in behalf of*, or *on peril of*. An example of the latter can be seen in (3):

(3) After the third cry, he withdrew to one side of the lists, and again proclaimed, that none, on peril of instant death, should dare, by word, cry, or action, to interfere with or disturb this fair field of combat. [Scott (1771): *Ivanhoe*]

The list of complex prepositions compiled with this method contains about 275 items.

### 3.2.2 Methodological considerations

The borderline between complex prepositions and free sequences of adjacent PP-phrases is not easy to determine. No distinctive formal or functional features can be defined and a closer look at standard grammars suggests that lists of complex prepositions are based on intuition rather than precise grammatical criteria.

Quirk et al. (1985: 671–2) offer nine different criteria which help in the distinction between complex prepositions and other, freer combinations. For example, *in spite of* allows no modifications whatsoever (**in the spite of* or **in spite to* or **in spites of*) whereas instead of *in pursuit of* one can find *in the pursuit of* and *in hot pursuit of* etc. They establish a 'scale of cohesiveness' with *in spite of* at one extreme – behaving in all possible ways like a single word preposition – and *on the shelf by (the door)* at the other extreme, allowing all nine types of variation. However, the authors stress that these 'indicators of syntactic separateness' form a gradient scale and consequently offer no opinion as to where the cut-off point should be drawn.

Quirk et al.'s 'scale of cohesiveness' raises further questions: since the majority of complex prepositions clearly allow the insertion of further elements such as premodifying adjectives or determiners, does this not jeopardize the concept of the indivisible unit? Indeed, scholars have questioned the entire grammatical category of complex prepositions. Thus Seppänen et al. (1994: 25) say: 'Introduced into the grammar on the basis of an untenable analysis, the class of complex prepositions as defined by Quirk et al. is empty, and the term itself is thus not helpful in the description of English'.

In a diachronic perspective, the problems of classification become even more pertinent since the syntactic reanalyis from [[P NP] P NP] to [[P NP P] NP] is a covert process. As an inevitable consequence, it is impossible to decide on the grammatical status of many early examples of complex prepositions.

As I mentioned in the Introduction, this paper has an exploratory character. Therefore, all finer considerations of definition and classification will be largely put aside. My list of 275 complex prepositions was thus compiled by looking at example sentences of all items on the frequency list of 'P – any word – P' combinations and deciding for or against inclusion on the grounds of my own intuition. For the present project, I will furthermore take an all-inclusive approach with regard to the earlier texts and categorize all retrieved instances of the 275 combinations as complex prepositions.

## 4. Results

### 4.1 Overall distribution

As a first step, I will be concerned with the development of the overall use of complex prepositions over the centuries. Figure 1 shows the frequency of the 275 complex prepositions over the time periods of 1700–1749, 1750–1799, and 1800–1849 (birth date of author) and in the written part of the BNC in both fiction and non-fiction texts.

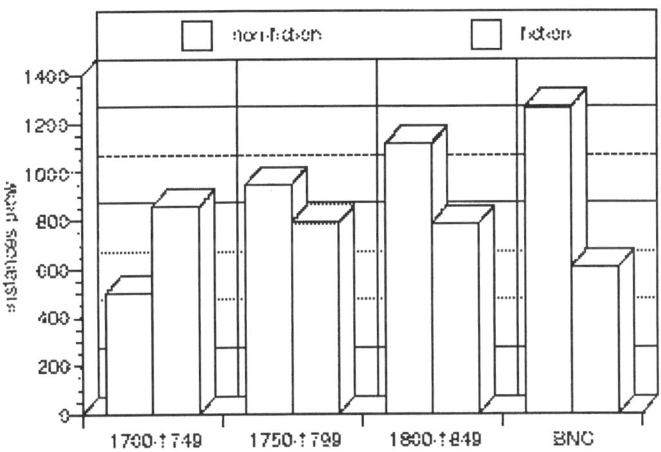


**Figure 1:** The overall frequency of 275 complex prepositions in the Gutenberg Corpus and the BNC (non-fiction = informative texts, fiction = imaginative prose); number of tokens: Gutenberg: 14,845, BNC: 101,371

Interestingly, one can observe an opposite trend in the two major genres. Whereas there is a clear increase in the use of complex prepositions in non-fiction from about 500 per million words (pmw) to about 1100 pmw in the later Gutenberg texts and 1270 pmw in the non-fiction BNC-texts, fiction texts show a gradual decrease over the centuries from about 850 pmw to 600 pmw in the BNC imaginative prose texts.

One possible reason for this phenomenon could be that the overall use of prepositions (simple and complex) has changed in the two genres over the past three centuries. I therefore had a look at the 20 most frequent prepositions in the BNC and their distribution over the Gutenberg texts.[8] The result is shown in Figure 2. As can be seen, fiction texts again show a decrease over the four periods.[9] To some extent, the same can also be said about the non-fiction texts; only the second period does not fully fit into this picture. Comparing these results to the ones in Figure 1, I conclude that the increase in the use of complex prepositions in non-fiction texts is independent of the overall use of prepositional constructions.

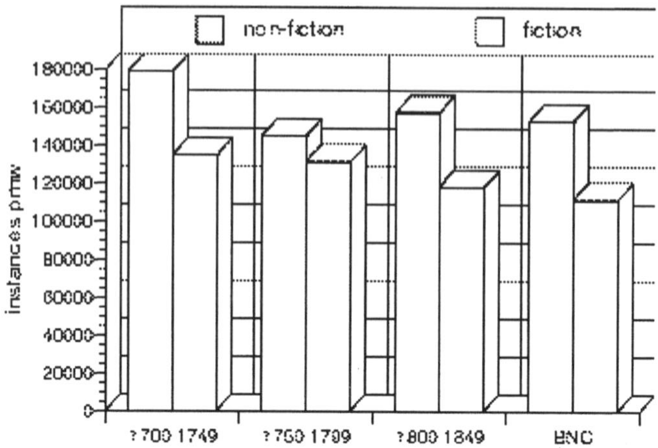


**Figure 2:** The overall frequency of the 20 most frequent prepositions (lexical search only, *to* excluded) in the Gutenberg Corpus and the BNC – instances per million words

### 4.2 Grammaticalization in progress?

The most obvious step towards an explanation of the development described in the previous section would have to be a closer analysis of the two general types of texts (fiction and non-fiction) over the time of the last three centuries. The 17th and 18th centuries mark the beginning of an immense advancement in the sciences. Imitation of the classics goes out of fashion and a clearer, more scientific style emerges that places great emphasis on clarity and precision. It seems highly probable that this could have an influence on the use of complex prepositions. Nevertheless, for the remaining part of this section, I will be concerned with a different aspect that might shed further light on the grammaticalization of complex prepositions as a whole.

Given the size of the BNC, it is bound to contain low-frequency complex prepositions which do not occur in the Gutenberg corpus at all. However, out of the 50 most common complex prepositions in the BNC, 14 do not occur at all in texts of authors who were born between 1700 and 1750. Table 1 shows these 14 prepositions and their respective frequencies in the BNC.

**Table 1:** Complex prepositions which are among the 50 most frequent types in the written part of the BNC but which do not occur in Gutenberg texts by authors who were born between 1700 and 1750.

| Complex preposition | No. of occurrences in BNC |
|---|---|
| in respect of | 2,766 |
| on behalf of | 2,466 |
| on top of | 2,263 |
| in response to | 1,969 |

| | |
|---|---|
| in charge of | 1,537 |
| in conjunction with | 1,224 |
| in line with | 1,186 |
| in contrast to | 883 |
| for use in | 699 |
| by reference to | 665 |
| in breach of | 455 |
| in control of | 455 |
| in keeping with | 445 |
| in association with | 414 |

In addition to the 14 complex prepositions shown in Table 1, a sizeable number of high-frequency combinations in today's English were only rarely found in the early Gutenberg texts (e.g. *in front of,* which will be discussed in Section 4.3 below).

Since Lehmann (1991: 503) remarked that complex prepositions first occur in specific contexts and then only gradually spread as quasi-phraseologisms into the grammar of a language, it is necessary to test whether the lower number of occurrences per million words in early non-fiction texts results from a large number of complex prepositions not being as fully grammaticalized in this particular text type as they are today. During an incipient stage of grammaticalization, variable phenomena commonly occur. Consequently, if my tentative hypothesis is correct, I would have to be able to retrieve many more instances of rival forms in early non-fiction texts than in the later ones.

In this context, the nine criteria discussed by Quirk et al. (1985) offer a useful framework. Assuming that the grammaticalization of complex prepositions would correspond to a moving up on the scale of cohesiveness, a whole range of clearly defined formal features of internal variation can be investigated for the construction in question.

In what follows, one of these criteria will be discussed in some detail: adjectival premodification of the noun in a P NP P construction. A case in point is the preposition *in pursuit of.* It occurs 332 times in the written part of the BNC. In addition to this, there are also 33 instances where the noun is premodified by one – or in one case two – adjectives. Quite clearly, *hot* is the most common adjective but a whole range of other adjectives are also used. The complete list of these adjectives is shown in Table 2:

**Table 2:** Adjectival premodification of the noun in *in pursuit of* in the written part of the BNC

| | |
|---|---|
| in *hot* pursuit of | 16 |
| in *full* pursuit of | 2 |
| in *ardent* pursuit of | 1 |
| in *breakneck* pursuit of | 1 |
| in *chaotic* pursuit of | 1 |
| in *constant* pursuit of | 1 |
| in *determined* pursuit of | 1 |

| | |
|---|---|
| in *endless* pursuit of | 1 |
| in *half-hearted* pursuit of | 1 |
| in *mad* pursuit of | 1 |
| in *personal* pursuit of | 1 |
| in *rigorous* pursuit of | 1 |
| in *silent relentless* pursuit of | 1 |
| in *self-conscious* pursuit of | 1 |
| in *steady* pursuit of | 1 |
| in *vain* pursuit of | 1 |
| in *wearying* pursuit of | 1 |
| total: | 33 |

In order to test the hypothesis that new complex prepositions initially occur with more internal fluctuation of forms than at a later, more grammaticalized stage, I divided my set of 275 prepositions into four subsets: those occurring in all three time-spans in the Gutenberg corpus and the BNC (A), those found for the first time in 1750–1799 and subsequently also in 1800–1849 and the BNC (B), those only occurring from the latest Gutenberg texts onwards (1800–1849; C) and the group of complex prepositions which are not attested in the Gutenberg corpus at all but are only found in the BNC (D). For each preposition in these four subsets, variant forms were then searched in the three time-spans of the Gutenberg corpus. Figure 3 shows the distribution of adjectival premodification across the Gutenberg corpus on the basis of these four subsets.

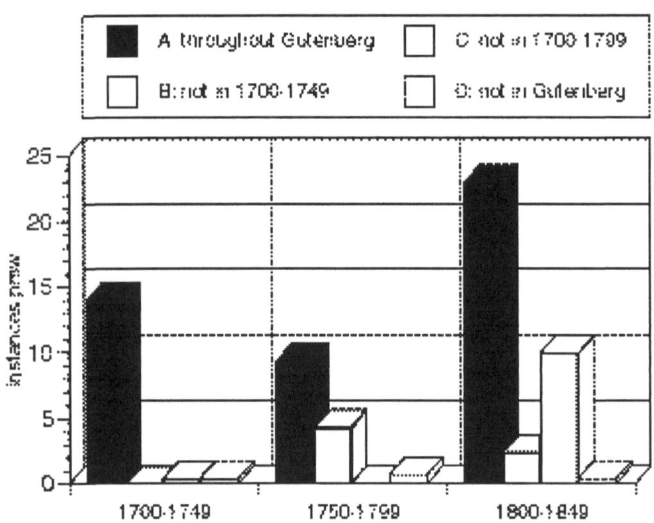


**Figure 3:** Adjectival premodification of the 275 complex prepositions in three time-spans of the Gutenberg corpus

The most noticeable result shown in Figure 3 is that complex prepositions which were part of the language before 1750 (subset A) occur with adjectival premodification in all three time-spans (between 10pwm and 23pmw). Furthermore, no trend towards less premodification – which in the present approach would correspond to an assumed increase in fixedness – can be observed; rather, the latest time-span exhibits the highest frequency of premodification per million words. The other subsets, however, show a more regular picture. Thus, with constructions that are first attested in the second time-span (subset B), this is also the period with the highest frequency of adjectival premodification. The same is true in an even more marked way for those complex prepositions which occurred for the first time in texts by authors who were born between 1800–1849 (subset C). Although it is conceivable that complex prepositions which were only found in the BNC (subset D) would – as examples of a less fixed stage – occur with adjectival premodification, such combinations are virtually absent from the Gutenberg texts (<1pmw in all three time-spans).

Figure 3 therefore invites conflicting interpretations: On the one hand, new complex prepositions exhibit most internal fluctuation in the period they enter the language. On the other hand, no general trend towards more fixedness for complex prepositions that are already part of the grammar can be attested. Quite clearly, the assumed direct connection between Quirk et al.'s scale of cohesiveness and the processes of grammaticalization needs to be investigated in more detail.[10] This is further corroborated by the fact that I found only one complex preposition with a premodified noun in the early Gutenberg texts which did not occur with adjectival premodification in the whole of the BNC: *in want of*.

(4) ... in both places the owner of the boat founds his demand on the necessity and distress of one who stands more or less <u>in absolute want of</u> his assistance, and with the urgency of these always rises in the exorbitancy of his demand ... [Fielding (1707): *Journal of a Voyage to Lisbon*]

However, with a total number of only 6 occurrences in the whole of the BNC, the complex preposition *in want of* can hardly count as a meaningful example of increased fixedness.

### 4.3 Some individual complex prepositions

In the remaining part of the paper, I am going to concentrate on three individual complex prepositions and look at their development in more detail.

#### 4.3.1 *In front of*

*In front of* is a complex preposition that is virtually absent from the early Gutenberg texts: it occurs only twice in texts written by authors born between 1700 and 1750. In contrast, with 5915 instances *in front of* is the second most frequent complex preposition in the written part of the BNC; only *in terms of* with 8712 instances occurs more frequently. Furthermore, in present-day English, *in front of* ranks very high on the scale of cohesiveness in that it allows virtually no fluctuation of forms whatsoever.

A closer look at the sharp increase in the use of *in front of* might therefore reveal tendencies that could be relevant to the grammaticalization of other prepositions, too.

Given the virtual absence of *in front of* in the early Gutenberg texts, one might first ask what writers used instead for the same semantic concept. In most cases, it was perhaps *before,* as is shown in (5) and (6):

(5) Sometimes again when I have been preaching, I have been violently assaulted with thoughts of blasphemy, and strongly tempted to speak the words with my mouth before the congregation. [Bunyan (1628): *Grace Abounding to Chief of Sinners*]

(6) 'Might not a man warmed with wine be like a bottle of beer, which is made brisker by being set before the fire' – 'Nay, (said Johnson, laughing) I cannot answer that: that is too much for me' [Boswell (1740): *Life of Johnson*]

In both sentences, *in front of* would probably be the more idiomatic choice in present-day English. The earliest combination containing the lexical item *front* in my corpus is *in the front of* as in (7):

(7) A party of them came on first, and viewed our posture, traversing the ground *in* the front of our line; and, as we found them within gunshot, our leader ordered the two wings to advance swiftly, and give them a salvo on each wing with their shot, which was done. [Defoe (1661): *The Further Adventures of Robinson Crusoe*]

The first examples of *in front of* come from Lawrence Sterne[11]:

(8) Trim! – said my uncle Toby, after he lighted his pipe, and smoak'd about a dozen whiffs. – Trim came in front of his master, and made his bow; – my uncle Toby smoak'd on, and said no more. – Corporal!
[Sterne (1713):*Tristram Shandy*]

(9) He had drawn the six field-pieces for this end, all close up together in front of my uncle Toby's sentry-box, leaving only an interval of about a yard and a half betwixt the three, on the right and left, for the convenience of charging, & c. – and the sake possibly of two batteries, which he might think double the honour of one. [Sterne (1713): *Tristram Shandy*]

Interestingly, examples (8) and (9) – as all the other very early examples of *in front of* – can be interpreted in terms of a spatial development, a movement, with *in front of* indicating the goal of the direction. Also, the collocation with *come* is highly unusual in today's context and occurs only in sentences like *Arabic negative particles come in front of the verb.*

Only in the texts of authors born in the late 18th century can the first examples of our present-day English use of *in front of* be found. This is exemplified in (10):

(10) When they stood in front of that ancient fortress, Ravenswood's emotions were of a very complicated description. [Scott (1771): *Bride of Lammermoor*]

From then onwards, the frequency of *in front of* rose steadily while *in the front of* all but disappeared from the English language. This development is shown in Figure 4:

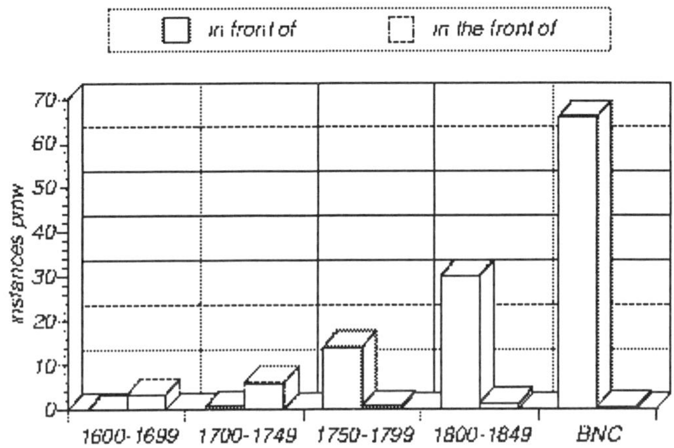


**Figure 4:** The distribution of *in front of* and *in the front of* over the Gutenberg corpus and the written part of the BNC – instances per million words

A final word on fixedness in this context: the establishment of *in front of* as a complex preposition came about with hardly any other variation than the one just described (*the* vs. ø). There are only two instances of premodification of the noun in all my corpora, one of which is found in (11):

(11) A Danton, a Robespierre, chief-products of a victorious Revolution, are now arrived in immediate front of one another; must ascertain how they will live together, rule together. [Carlyle (1795): *The French Revolution*]

The data presented in Figure 4 raises a further interesting question: *in front of* seems to have become fully grammaticalized as one of the most frequent complex prepositions within an astonishingly short period of time. Other prepositions such as *instead of* clearly took much longer to achieve a similar status (cf. Schwenter and Traugott 1995). It thus appears that for each complex preposition, individual reasons and patterns of grammaticalization need to be investigated.

### 4.3.2 *In (the) face of*

The second preposition I wish to discuss here is *in face of* or *in the face of*. *In face of* is a rare complex preposition with only 64 occurrences in the whole BNC. *In the face of* on the other hand is much more frequent, with 1439 hits in the written part of the BNC alone. Like *in front of*, *in the face of* ranks very high on the scale of cohesiveness; for example, I only found one single instance in the BNC where *face* is premodified by an adjective:

(12) In the full face of the ridicule she went to the post office evening after evening, ridicule she willed not to see or notice. (BNC; A6N:690)

In today's usage, *in the face of* has a clearly negative semantic prosody.[12] This is demonstrated in Table 3 which lists the 15 strongest noun collocates of *in the face of* in the written part of the BNC. For the calculation, a window of 1 to 3 words after the node *in the face of* was considered; the results are sorted by log-likelihood value.

**Table 3:** Noun-collocates of *in the face of* in the written part of the BNC (window +1 – +3), ordered by log-likelihood value

| No. | Word | n coll. | log-likelihood value |
|---|---|---|---|
| 1 | opposition | 70 | 762.6 |
| 2 | competition | 41 | 399.1 |
| 3 | adversity | 17 | 274.5 |
| 4 | criticism | 19 | 181.4 |
| 5 | evidence | 25 | 177.5 |
| 6 | difficulties | 19 | 167.6 |
| 7 | threat | 18 | 163.9 |
| 8 | hostility | 13 | 146.8 |
| 9 | pressures | 13 | 129.1 |
| 10 | enemy | 12 | 111.5 |
| 11 | threats | 10 | 107.6 |
| 12 | attacks | 10 | 91.5 |
| 13 | demand | 12 | 87.1 |
| 14 | pressure | 12 | 81.5 |
| 15 | odds | 8 | 80.6 |

Example (13) shows a typical use:

(13) It is to be considered, too, that as these were prisons without bars and bolts, which our common prisons are furnished with, so the people let themselves down out of their windows, even in the face of the watchman, bringing swords or pistols in their hands, and threatening the poor wretch to shoot him if he stirred or called for help. [Defoe (1661): *A Journal of the Plague Year*]

Thus, *in the face of* had a much more literal meaning then than it has now – a paraphrase could almost be *in front of*.[13]

It isn't until the 19th century that a clear example of our present-day usage occurred for the first time; *face* became metaphorically extended from a concrete face to a more abstract entity.[14] At some stage, both meanings seem to have coexisted – and could even be used in the same sentence – presumably for stylistic purposes – as shown in (14):

(14) If I am content to sit down ignorant in the face of such an impenetrable mystery as this – presented to me, day after day, every time I see a living creature come into the world or go out of it – why may I not sit down content in the face of your lady in the summer-house, and say she's altogether beyond my fathoming, and there is an end of her. [Collins (1824): *The Two Destinies*]

Figure 5 shows the distribution of the two senses of *in the face of* over the whole Gutenberg corpus.

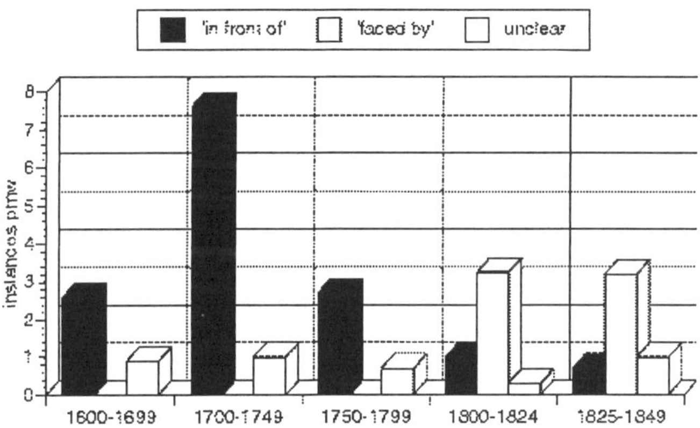


**Figure 5:** The distribution of the two senses of *in the face of* in the Gutenberg corpus – instances per million words.

While the sense 'in front of' reached its peak in works by authors who were born between 1700 and 1749 and then gradually decreased in frequency, today's preferred meaning 'faced by' only appeared after 1800. Figure 5 further shows that there is also a considerable number of instances where no clear meaning could be assigned. It is therefore conceivable that the modern sense existed before but had not yet been conventionalized to the extent that it could be used in contexts with which the older sense was incompatible.

It also has to be noted that the semantic prosody of the 19th century uses of *in the face of* was not as negative as the one found today.

(15) And though he meant to adhere to Eustacia's instructions to the letter, to deposit her where she wished and to leave her, should that be her will, the spell that she had cast over him intensified, and his heart was beating fast in the anticipated futility of such commands in the face of a mutual wish that they should throw in their lot together. [Hardy (1840): *The Return of the Native*]

In present-day English, *in the face of* and *a mutual wish* are almost irreconcilable concepts. The existence of a rather large number of 19th century examples with neutral rather than negative semantic prosody suggests that the reinterpretation of the construction in question must have happened in various stages.

### 4.3.3 *On the part of*

The final complex preposition to be briefly considered here is *on the part of*. The most interesting aspect in this context is that early newspaper texts show a completely different use from what can be found both in Gutenberg and the BNC. This is demonstrated by (16) and (17):

(16) The Count Rantzon is taking his leave here, in order to [sic] his departure through Holland for France, whither he goes to reside on the part of this King. (ZEN: foreign news, 1671)

(17) We are told of a Treaty making between this Town and the Marquis de Grana on the part of the Emperor, and that it is so far advanced, as to be ready for the Emperors Ratification. (ZEN: foreign news, 1671)

Here, as in all 30 instances of *on the part of* in ZEN before 1760, a suitable paraphrase would be *as a representative of*. This sense is not recorded in the Oxford English Dictionary and an interpretation of its development is not an easy task.[15] On the one hand this usage is possibly influenced by a metaphorically extended meaning of *part* as the 'character assigned to or sustained by an actor in a dramatic performance' (OED, *part* sense 9a). On the other hand, the recurring collocation *to reside (there) on the part of X* (where X is the ruler of the area) may suggest that another sense of *part*, 'a portion or a part of a country or territory, or of the world', could be involved, too (ibid., sense 13a), although this possible connection is called into question by the fact that all corresponding quotations contain *part* in the singular. However, a closer analysis of these subtle differences is difficult on the basis of such relatively sparse data.

The modern use, exemplified in (18), shows that a change in the thematic roles of the participants has taken place:

(18) There are no easy answers to African development, and an appropriate degree of humility on the part of donors is a necessary condition for developing a serious dialogue with recipient governments. (BNC; A6M: 981)

In (16) and (17), people act on behalf of or for another, but in (18) the humility is their own. Two possible explanations for this differing use can be offered: First, the context-specific use was restricted to newspapers alone and did not for some reason take hold in other domains of language. Second, a more archaic sense of the preposition was preserved in the newspaper language of that time while the more grammaticalized usage had already been largely adapted in most other contexts. However, only a detailed analysis of even earlier texts could shed further light on these questions.

## 5. Concluding remarks

In this paper I have tried to give a general overview of the use and distribution of complex prepositions in fiction and non-fiction over the last 300 years. After determining that complex prepositions do not follow the same pattern as simple prepositions – which were found to decrease in frequency in both genres while there was a marked increase of complex prepositions in non-fiction – I concentrated on internal fluctuation in complex prepositions as an indicator of an ongoing grammaticalization process. However, while complex prepositions do indeed exhibit a higher level of variation when they enter the language, the general picture remains inconclusive.

In the second part of the paper, I discussed three different complex prepositions in somewhat more detail. In the case of *in front of*, some variation with *in the front of* was observed in the earliest texts but on the whole, the preposition became fully fixed at an astonishing speed. With *in the face of* I described a semantic shift from the sense 'in front of' to 'faced by' and noted that the semantic prosody of earlier examples was much less negative than in present-day English usage. Finally, in the case of *on the part of* a clear difference in meaning emerged depending on whether it occurred in newspaper texts or in other contexts.

On the basis of this data, it is not an easy task to extract patterns that apply to the development of the class of complex prepositions as a whole. The overall trend, however, is completely in line with the general principles of grammaticalization, which assume a unidirectional change from denoting concrete objects towards more abstract entities. Nevertheless, the underlying discourse-pragmatic processes need to be studied in greater detail and the factors which influence the speed of grammaticalization also remain largely unknown. Even more importantly, the problem of defining the class of complex prepositions needs to be tackled. In this context, a collocation-based approach may prove to be helpful: extending the common formulae for the calculation of collocational strength from simple node–collocate pairs to constructions with two or several collocates would provide an interesting testbed for a corpus-based evaluation of Quirk et al.'s scale of cohesiveness (e.g. the node *in* followed by a noun which itself is followed by a preposition within a certain number of words, such as *in (...) pursuit (...) of*). In addition, such an approach would also make it possible to apply the same criteria for the categorization of complex prepositions within a diachronic context, since rankings of collocational strength for 17th and 20th century data are fully comparable and the common dilemma of not having access to native speaker intuition of past centuries would become much less worrying.

**Notes**

1 Cf. Table 7.2. on page 217. Total number of occurrences in the 18th century data: 214; in the 19th century data: 154.

2 ARCHER (A Representative Corpus of Historical English Registers) compiled by Douglas Biber covers a time-span from 1650 to 1990 and offers a detailed categorization into different registers; see Biber et al. (1994) for further details. However, given its overall size of less than 2 million words, the individual sections are unfortunately too small to study the development of all but the most frequent complex prepositions.

3 Further information about Project Gutenberg can be found at their official webpage at http://promo.net/pg/

4 Footnotes and other types of comments added by editors were deleted as far as they were possible to detect.

5 For example, the active progressive *the house is building* which was common in the 17th century but today is clearly ungrammatical, would conceivably have been corrected to *the house is being built.*

6 For example, adjectives and nouns ending in *-ick* which today would be spelled *-ic* are quite common in the earlier Gutenberg texts. In texts by authors who were born before the year 1800, these are the most frequent types: *publick* (157), *musick* (35), *physick* (27), *topick* (25), *critick* (24), and *domestick* (23).

7 The 20 texts from authors born in the 17th century were not classified into fiction and non-fiction because such a classification would have raised more problems than it could solve. For instance, is Swift's *A Modest Proposal* to be considered fiction or non-fiction?

8 The 20 most frequent prepositions cover almost 90 per cent of all tokens of prepositions in the BNC.

9 This search is much less reliable than that for complex prepositions because here, too, the retrieval method is strictly lexically based. Thus, instances of items such as *in* or *on* that would often be analysed as adverbs/particles will also be included in Figure 2. As an exemplification of this, consider the following sentence as tagged by ENGCG-2 in the compact representation:

> Get_Vimp away_ADV from_PREP perpetual_A need_N to_TO fill_Vinf in_ADV, fill_Vimp up_ADV, he_P wrote_Vpast. (BNC A08: 2278)

In order to minimize the impact of this retrieval methodology, the lexical item *to* was excluded due to its very high frequency as an infinitive marker (1.64 million instances in the BNC).

10 Most importantly, data for the other 8 types of internal variation need to be retrieved and interpreted in order to arrive at a more complete picture.

11 The earliest quotation for *in the front of* (*front* n., entry 10a) in the OED dates from 1698 while the first occurrence of *in front of* is taken from a work published in 1847. However, *in front of* can be found in more than 50 earlier quotations for other word entries, the earliest being for the word *rod* (n. entry 7a) from 1769:

Extending a thousand or fifteen hundred rods in front of the River. [E. Bancroft: *Guiana*]

The OED thus indirectly confirms the information on dating provided by the Gutenberg corpus for the introduction of *in front of* into the grammar of English.

12 This term was coined by John Sinclair and refers to the fact that 'words may habitually collocate with other words from a definable semantic set' (Stubbs, 1995: 25). See Stubbs (1995: 24ff.) for a more detailed discussion.

13 This observation is again given support by quotations from the OED: while the relevant entry for *face* (entry 4c(a): sense 'in front of', 'directly opposite to') gives 1879 as the earliest occurrence of this construction, several quotations from as early as 1687 containing *in the face of* meaning 'in front of' can in fact be found in the entries for other words.

14 The motivations for the emergence of such metaphorical uses are often hard to trace in detail. See Heine et al. (1991: 65ff.) for an excellent overview of the factors involved in 'context-induced reinterpretation'.

15 Entry 9b for *part (n.)* in the OED reads as follows: '*fig.* A character sustained by any one, either as a special office or function ..., or as assumed or feigned.' However, none of the illustrating quotations resembles the use found in ZEN. The specific entry for the phrase *on the part of* (*part*, entry 28) only accounts for the usage found in the Gutenberg corpus and the BNC.

**References**


Akimoto, Minoji (1999). 'Collocations and idioms in Late Modern English'. In Brinton, Laurel. J. and Minoji Akimoto (eds) *Collocational and idiomatic aspects of composite predicates in the history of English*. Amsterdam: Benjamins. 207–238.

Aston, Guy and Lou Burnard (1998). *The BNC Handbook*. Edinburgh: Edinburgh University Press.

Biber, Douglas, Edward Finegan, and Dwight Atkinson (1994). 'ARCHER and its challenges: compiling and exploring a representative corpus of historical English registers'. In Fries, Udo, Gunnel Tottie, and Peter Schneider (eds) *Creating and using English language corpora*. Amsterdam: Rodopi. 1–13.

Di Micello, Pietro, webmaster. (1992). 'History and philosophy of Project Gutenberg'. *Project Gutenberg Official Home Site*. http://promo.net/pg/history.html (accessed 15. Nov. 2000)

Heine, Bernd, Ulrike Claudi, and Friederike Hünnemeyer (1991). *Grammaticalization. A conceptual framework*. Chicago and London: The University of Chicago Press.

Hopper, Paul J. and Elisabeth C. Traugott (1993). *Grammaticalization*. Cambridge: Cambridge University Press.

Lehmann, Christian (1991). 'Grammaticalization and related changes in contemporary German'. In Traugott, Elisabeth C. and Bernd Heine (eds) *Approaches to grammaticalization*. Vol. II. Amsterdam: Benjamins. 493–535.

*OED: The Oxford English Dictionary* (1989). Oxford Clarendon Press, 2nd ed.

Quirk, Randolph, Sidney Greenbaum, Geoffrey Leech, and Jan Svartvik. (1985). *A comprehensive grammar of the English language*. London: Longman.

Schneider, Peter. This volume. 'Computer assisted spelling normalization of 18th century English'. 199–211

Schwenter, Scott A. and Elisabeth C. Traugott (1995). 'The semantic and pragmatic development of substitutive complex prepositions in English'. In Andreas H. Jucker (ed.) *Historical Pragmatics*. Amsterdam: Benjamins. 243–273.

Seppänen, Aimo, Rhonwen Bowen, and Joe Trotta (1994). 'On the so-called complex prepositions'. *Studia Anglica Posnaniensia* 29: 3–29.

Stubbs, Michael (1995). 'Collocations and semantic profiles' *Functions of Language* 2.1: 23–55.

Studer, Patrick and Peter Schneider (2000). 'The Zurich English Newspaper Corpus' *The British Library News* 27, Winter 1999/2000. 6–7.

# Pied piping and stranding from a diachronic perspective[1]

*Christine Johansson*

Uppsala University

## Abstract

*This study analyses the history of **pied piping** and **stranding**, that is, the placement of a preposition immediately before a (relative)* wh-*word (pied piping) or at the end of the sentence (stranded preposition). The study is based on the Penn-Helsinki Parsed Corpus of Middle English (Middle English prose texts from 1150–1500). In Middle English, nominal, or at least pronominal,* wh-*words occur as **relativizers** which can be preceded by prepositions. Pied piping is then used almost exclusively. Stranded prepositions are rare but the pre-stages of stranding can be discerned, such as constructions with both pied piping and stranding:* of which ... of *and preposition +* wh-*word + resumptive pronoun:* of which ... of him. *In genitive (and partitive)* of which- *constructions, only the preposition is pied piped* (of wiche the voices). *The data included in the study did not yield any instances of pied piping of preposition and the head of the* of which-*construction* (the voices of wiche).

## 1. Introduction

The aim of this paper is to discuss the history of pied piping and stranding, that is the placement of preposition and *wh*-word (in this paper relative *wh*-word) as in *The new grammar of which I heard* (pied piping) and *The new grammar which I heard about* (stranded preposition). My material is based on the Penn-Helsinki Parsed Corpus of Middle English (the UPENN corpus) and consists of the Middle English prose texts in the Helsinki Corpus from the periods M1 (1150–1250), M2 (1250–1350), M3 (1350–1420) and M4 (1420–1500) (see Kytö 1996). These texts have been tagged for type of clause and syntactic function of the clause elements. The Middle English prose texts in the UPENN corpus consist of 489,114 words (see Geisler 1998).[2]

Pied piping or the 'Pied Piping Convention' as defined by Ross (1967: 121)[3] guarantees 'that certain NPs which dominate a coreferential NP can be moved along with the coreferential NP when it is moved by relativization' (in Stockwell et al. 1973: 456). Ross's example (1967:121) is a rather complex sentence:

(1) The government prescribes the height of the lettering on the covers of the reports... (=Ross's example (2.3))

Different patterns emerge according to the placement of the preposition (*on*) and the relativizer *of which*, for example *Reports the covers of which the government prescribes the height of the lettering on* and *Reports which the government prescribes the height of the lettering on the covers of*. Some patterns are blocked, according to Ross (1967:121), for example **Reports on the covers of which the government prescribes the height of the lettering* and **Reports of which the government prescribes the height of the lettering on the covers*.

In Johansson and Geisler (1998), present-day spoken British English (formal and conversational) was found to contain more pied piping constructions than expected. The reason for this was that there are cases where pied piping is more or less obligatory, for example in adverbial expressions with *way*:

(2) We were only anxious about the way in which we would make a living
(The London-Lund Corpus of Spoken British English: 6.4 621–622)

In prepositional constructions involving the prepositions *during*, *underneath* and *beyond*, obligatory pied piping is also found in present-day English:

(3) the organ loft # which seems to # span the nave # like a great bridge # creating an archway # under i... underneath which all processions must pass #
(The London-Lund Corpus of Spoken British English: 10.6 410–441)

In (4) we see examples of Middle English pied piping constructions:

(4) of whom emonge all other of hys bokes / I purpose temprynte by the grace of god the book of the tales of cauntyrburye/ in whiche I fynde many a noble hystorye... (cmcaxpro m4 749, 752)

*Of which*-constructions, genitive and partitive, are interesting in the analysis of pied piping (cf. Ross's example above with genitive *of which*). Firstly, pied piping here involves not only a preposition but also the head of the larger NP that *of which* is part of (see Johansson 1995:138–141). Secondly, the placement of *of which* in relation to the head has changed over time: *of which the covers* (pied piping of *of*) was replaced by *the covers of which* (pied piping of the preposition *of* and the head of the larger NP) in the early 17th century (Schneider 1993:249).

The paper will first present overall frequencies of prepositional relative constructions, of pied piping and its alternatives, and of the distribution of pied piping in Middle English texts. Then an analysis of the structures of pied piping and stranding will follow. Lastly, pied piping in genitive and partitive *of which*-constructions will be discussed.

## 2. The distribution of prepositional relative constructions

Table 1 presents frequencies of relative constructions in Middle English and proportions of prepositional relative constructions (pied piping and stranding). The relative constructions included are those with *wh*-forms. Relative clauses with *that* or *zero* are not included, nor are adverbial relative clauses with *when*, *where* and *why*. Prepositional constructions are quite frequent, particularly in the first period (M1), with 21/52 or 40% (24/100,000 words) and in the third period, (M3), with 286/760 or 38% (137/100,000 words). As will be seen later in the paper, the M3 period is particularly interesting in many different respects when relativizers and pied piping are discussed.

**Table 1:** Relative constructions in Middle English

| | M1 (1150–1250) | M2 (1250–1350) | M3 (1350–1420) | M4 (1420–1500) | Total |
|---|---|---|---|---|---|
| Relative constructions | 52 | 167 | 760 | 593 | 1572 |
| Prepositional constructions | 21 | 55 | 286 | 173 | 535 |
| Normalised frequencies per 100,000 w. | 24 | 96 | 137 | 105 | 362 |
| Proportion prepositional constructions | 40% | 33% | 38% | 29% | 34% |

In Table 2, which lists pied piping and its alternatives, it is clear that pied piping constructions are frequent in the periods M1 (84%), M3 (87%) and M4 (84%) compared with other options, see examples (5)-(8). It is in the M2 period, that a lower frequency of pied piping constructions is found: 69%.

**Table 2:** Pied piping and alternatives

| | M1 | % | M2 | % | M3 | % | M4 | % | Total | % |
|---|---|---|---|---|---|---|---|---|---|---|
| Pied piping | 21 | 84% | 53 | 69% | 285 | 87% | 168 | 84% | 527 | 84% |
| Stranding | 0 | 0% | 2 | 2% | 1 | >1% | 5 | 2% | 8 | 1% |
| The adverb *whereof* | 2 | 8% | 12 | 16% | 14 | 4% | 12 | 6% | 40 | 6% |
| Other | 2 | 8% | 10 | 13% | 28 | 9% | 16 | 8% | 56 | 9% |
| Total | 25 | 100% | 77 | 100% | 328 | 100% | 201 | 100% | 631 | 100% |

(5) the sones of Israel schulden haue (thingis) aftirward, bi whiche thei schulden remembre, (cmotest m3 1352)

(6) The plate under the riet is discrived with 3 cercles, of whiche the leest is clepid the cercle of Cancre... (cmastro m3 312)

(7) dyuerse gentyl men in Oxenford two prestes bothe maystres of arte / of whome that one was quyck and coude putte hym self forth / And that other was a good symple preest. (cmcaxpro m4 669)

(8) Ah þer nis buten an godd þur hwam witerliche ha alle weren iwrahte ant of nawhit ant i þis weorlde iset us forto frourin ant to fremien. (cmkathe m1 168)

It is evident from Table 2 that stranding is, as can be expected, a very infrequent alternative. All in all there are only 8 examples in the Middle English prose texts. The first examples are from the M2 period, cf. (9) below. In the M4 period, there are five examples, one of which is (10) below. One example of stranding is found in the M3 period.

(9) Tou setted þe terme, þe which hij ne shul nougt passe ouer; (cmearlps m2 965)

(10) compleynyng to þe preste of pouerte & disese whech he was fallyn in be infortunyte... (cmkempe m4 346)

Another alternative to pied piping is the adverb *whereof*, which can replace pied piping in examples such as (11) below and in genitive and partitive expressions, as in (12)-(13). *Whereof* occurs in all the four periods, somewhat less frequently (8%) in the first period, however. The category 'Other' comprises other relative adverbs, such as *wherein*, *wherethrough* and *whereby*, which are frequent in Middle English texts (see for example Mossé 1952 and Romaine 1982).

(11) telle yowe: and y supposed that John Germyn sholde have broght to me all most x li. all this of myne awne gode; wherof cometh to me no peny. (cmpriv m4 515)
*(from which comes no penny to me)*

In example (12), *the menes wherof*, the pattern *NP of which* is represented to some extent (that is, *the means of which*) in a genitive expression. This pattern does not occur in the Middle English prose texts; we only find *of which NP* (see the discussion in the Introduction and in Section 5).

(12) speke yt with oute it be so þat þer be sume newe mocyon made to her &c.: the menes wherof I have compassid in my mynde, (cmpriv m4 1773)
*(the means of which, whose means I have compassed, of which I have compassed the means)*

(13) that y have hadde: and like to have: and yet y hadde with me xx li. and more by my trauthe; wherof of trauthe not right moche y spende yet, (cmpriv m4 509)
*(of which troth I spend not right much)*

Example (14) can be interpreted both as a genitive and a partitive *whereof*-construction:

(14) by whos sepultre is wreton on a table hongyng on a pylere his Epitaphye maad by a poete laureat wherof the copye foloweth &c. (cmcaxpro m4 242)
*(of which the copy, whose copy follows)*

## 3. Pied piping and stranding in Middle English text categories

A large number of the Middle English prose texts are religious writings, such as religious treatises (in all the four periods) sermons, homilies and the Bible. Non-religious writings include handbooks, biography, science and letters. Pied piping constructions are very frequent compared with their alternatives (see Table 2). Are pied piping constructions particularly frequent in certain text types? In Table 3, Religious writings (comprising religious treatises and sermons with 176,390 words) and Non-religious writings (consisting of handbooks, philosophy, history, biography, science and letters with 152,510 words) are compared. As is evident from the table, pied piping is slightly more frequent in Religious writings with 126/100,000 words than in Non-religious texts with 102/100,000 words.

**Table 3:** Pied piping constructions across Middle English text categories

| | Sample size | Normalised frequency |
|---|---|---|
| Religious writings | 176,390 | 126 |
| Non-religious writings | 152,510 | 102 |
| Fiction | 38,136 | 31 |
| Non-fiction | 73,271 | 121 |

Example (15) is from a sermon and (16) from philosophy.

(15) The þride askynge perteneþt to be þrid persone of þe Trynyte, þe Holygoste, to whom is apropred loue and charite, (cmroyal m34 75)
(16) whan God, that al knoweth, dooth swiche thing, of whiche thing unknowynge folk ben astonyd. (cmboeth m3 1308)

Other categories which are compared in Table 3 are Fiction (consisting of fiction and romances with 38,136 words) and Non-fiction (handbooks, letters and science, in all 73,271 words). In this case we see a clear difference: only 31 examples of pied piping/100,000 words are found in Fiction, whereas 121 occurrences/100,000 words are found in Non-fiction. Example (17) is from a romance and (18) from a letter.

(17) Than Merlyon answerde that he wold so do, and than he made the Syge Perelous in the whych Galahad sate at hys mete on Whyttsonday last past. (cmmalory m4 1289)
(18) The morun tuysday al Halwyn yeven y receyved the answeris to oure articulis at Westminster of the whiche y sende yow a true copy, (cmpriv m4 478)

It would have been rewarding if the category Drama (which is in the Helsinki Corpus) had been included in the UPENN corpus. This is a category which probably has a somewhat closer relation to the spoken language of the Middle English period. Sermons, which could be looked upon as representing more formal spoken Middle English, contain the largest number of pied piping constructions within the Religious writings (80/41,163 words, or normalised 194/100,000 words).

The category Prefaces (only in the fourth period) contains examples of pied piping in 31/6,365 words, or in normalised figures 487/100,000 words. The category consists of Caxton's *Prologues and Epilogues*, suggesting that pied piping could also be typical of one particular writer; see example (19).

(19) And accordyng to the same I dyde do enprynte a certayn nombre of them / whyche anon were sold to many and dyuerse gentyl men / of whome one gentylman cam to me / and said that this book was not accordyng in many places vnto the book that Gefferey chaucer had made / To whom I answerd that I had made it accordyng to my copye... (cmcaxpro m4 772, 774)

The eight examples of stranding are from religious treatises, sermons, the Bible and letters. These examples are all given in Section 4.3.

## 4. The history of pied piping and stranding

In the Old English period, preposition stranding was obligatory in relative clauses introduced by the relative particle *þe* (Middle English *þaet*), with zero relative clauses and in infinitival relative clauses (see Fischer 1992:388, and compare modern English relative clauses with *that* or with zero relativizer which need a stranded preposition). On the other hand, obligatory pied piping of the preposition occurred in relative clauses introduced by *se* or *se þe* (Fischer 1992:388). Lightfoot (1979:313–342 and 1991:115–125) points out that *wh*-movement has always existed in English. In Old English the *wh*-item that moved had only interrogative force (see also Campbell 1983:292). In Middle English, when the relative *wh*-forms were introduced, examples such as the following began to occur: *the bok of which that I make mencioun* with both a *wh*-word and *that*. The original or underlying structure of the sentence before *wh*-movement is *the bok that I make mencioun of which*.

Pied piping was more or less obligatory or at least customary (with *wh*-words) in the Middle English period, which is borne out by the results presented in Table 4. Pied piping occurs in 99% of the examples of prepositional relative constructions.

**Table 4:** Pied piping and stranding in the four Middle English periods (1150–1500)

| **Prepositional construction** | **N** | **%** |
|---|---|---|
| Pied piping | 527 | 99% |
| Stranding | 8 | 1% |
| **Total** | **535** | **100%** |

Lightfoot (1991:120) and Fischer (1992:390) state that sporadic occurrences of preposition stranding in relative clauses and questions can be found in the 13th century. It is not until the end of the 14th century, however, that preposition stranding becomes more common, in line with the findings of the present study. As is evident from Table 2, even in the last period, 1420–1500, there are only five examples of stranding in the Middle English prose texts. However, during this period, and also earlier, we see the beginnings of preposition stranding, the different pre-stages of the development of this construction, which will be dealt with in the following sections.

### 4.1 Pied piping

As pointed out earlier, and as is obvious from Table 4 above, in constructions with preposition and relativizer in Middle English, pied piping of the preposition occurs almost to the exclusion of preposition stranding. The underlying structure of example (20) before the preposition is pied piped with the *wh*-word is (20a):

(20) for thies bodely dedis ar tokyne and shewynge of moralle vertues, with-oute which a soule is not able forto werke gostely. (cmrolltr m24 593)

(20a) for thies bodely dedis ar tokyne and shewynge of moralle vertues, a soule is not able forto werke gostely with-oute which.

Not only can the preposition be pied piped but also parts of the noun phrase, depending on the relativizer (as pronoun or determiner) and depending on whether we are dealing with pied piping in genitive and partitive *of which*–constructions, or in other prepositional relative phrases. An important distinction to make when pied piping and stranding are analysed is whether the relative construction functions as adverbial, as in (21), or as prepositional object, as in (22). In modern English, pied piping is more frequent when the relative construction functions as adverbial (see Johansson and Geisler 1998). In Middle English, pied piping occurs regardless of the function of the relative construction. Compare, however, the discussion of the examples of stranding in Section 4.3 below.

(21) And thus the pryncipal laude / and cause of delectable and amyable thynges / in whiche mannes felycyte stondeth and resteth ought and maye wel be attributed to hystoryes... (cmcaxpro m4 324)

(22) J entende to translate this sayd book of cathon / in whiche J doubte not / and yf they wylle rede it and vnderstande they shal moche better conne rewle them self ther by. (cmcaxpro m4 632)

In Middle English, certain types of relative constructions are found which we do not use today, and it is interesting to put this fact in a theoretical framework of *wh*-movement and pied piping. We find *of/in which that* where the *wh*-item has moved but where also *that* occurs in the **complementizer** or COMP position.[4] This is the position to which a word with the <+wh> feature moves but COMP can also include *that*. In modern English the *wh*-word is deleted if *that* is used as relativizer. In Middle English, on the other hand, COMP can include both *wh*-word and *that* (see for example Lightfoot 1991: 115–125, Haegeman 1994 and Rigter and Beukema 1985). Furthermore, there are examples of *the which*: *of/in the which* and *of/in the which that*. See example (23) where the preposition is *by* in *by the wiche that*. (*The*) *which* and (*the*) *which that* are particularly frequent in periods M2, 1250–1350, and M3, 1350–1420. These constructions decrease in the last period.

(23) tis preyoure of þe Pater Noster, by þe wiche þat euery man shuld preye to God when þat þei preyed, (cmroyal m34 67)

We also find examples of a noun or a more or less complex noun phrase in COMP where *which* is the determiner: *in whiche space*, cf. example (24), *in the which solitari forme and maner of leuving* and *for the which falsnesse and disceytes*; see examples (25)-(26). In these examples not only has the preposition been pied piped with the *wh*-item but also the noun/noun phrase. There are no examples of the type: *in the which solitary form that* (with *that* in COMP as well).[5]

(24) vp on the same centre aryn but litel quantite fro the forthest forseid cercle in the lymbe in whiche space shollen ben deuyde mynutes of the lymbe / mak thanne a narwere cercle... (cmequato m3 93)

(25) half a gowne of cloth of gold, which was stolen out of here kepyng, and made here to spende vpon hym, up trust therof, xviiis. vid. and more. For the which falsnesse and disceytes, þa Mair and Aldermen, willyng þat suche shul be war be hym in tyme comyng, (cmdocu m3 1705)

(26) degre and maner of leuing, þe whiche higt Synguleer? In þe whiche solitari forme and maner of leuyng þou maist lerne to lift up þe fote of þi loue, (cmcloud m3 88)

In example (27) a *sentential relative clause* (see for example Quirk et al. 1985: 1258) is exemplified with *thing* repeated. In modern English we only have *which*. This construction with *which* as determiner in a sentential relative clause is frequent in the Middle English prose texts.

(27) the whiche prosperite men seen ofte serven to schrewes. In the whiche thing I trowe that God dispenseth. (cmboeth m3 1384)

In a sentence like (28) we would probably not pied pipe the preposition in modern English. *Make mention of something/somebody* would be regarded as an idiomatic expression, in which case we strand the preposition (as in for example *take notice of, get rid of*, see Johansson and Geisler 1998).

(28) Than leuyd stille þe modyr of þe sayd persone, of whom þis tretys specyaly makyth mencyon, (cmkempe m4 709)

It is worth noting that as many as 6 out of 13 examples of *whose* from the first period occur in pied piping constructions, as in (29). Example (29) is typical of the examples of *whose* and pied piping in the M1 period, exemplifying a type of fixed expression: *for whose name*. Here we can compare Fischer's (1992: 388) Old English example of pied piping: *þaet he us þingie wið ðone heofanlican cyning, for þaes naman he þrowode* (ÆCHom. I 29 434.33). The example translates as 'that he intercede for us with the heavenly king, for whose name he suffered'.

(29) Bihaldt me deore dohter. bihalt þin heh healent for hwas nome þu hauest al undernume þis newcin. (cmkathe m1 435)

Since the pattern *NP of which* is obligatory in constructions where genitive and partitive *of which* function as prepositional complements (**on of which the covers* versus *on the covers of which*), the only possibility is to use *whose* with any type of antecedent. See Section 5 and compare also example (12) above with *the menes whereof*, which is the closest correspondence of the pattern *NP of which* in the Middle English prose texts.

### 4.2 The beginnings of preposition stranding

During the Middle English period there is evidence of the pre-stages of stranding of the preposition. All the examples found in my material are presented in (30)-(34). One pattern is repetition of the preposition (cf. Fischer 1992: 390), that is, the preposition is both stranded and pied piped. It is worth mentioning that example (30) is from the first period, 1150–1250. In both examples (30) and (31) the preposition *of* is repeated.

(30) nim him of hwas wlite beoð awundret of; þe sunne & te mone. up-o hwas nebscheft; þe engles ne beod neauer fulle to bihalden. (cmhali m1 863)

In (31) a form of the structurally and informationally light *be* would be placed at the end of the sentence, if *of* were not repeated (cf. Johansson and Geisler 1998).

(31) Moyses seid to our Lord of þe hardnes of Pharaon in þe sones of Iacob, and grashoppes come and breses, of which no noumbre was of. (cmearlps m2 1130)

In examples (32)-(34) we find the pattern of a repeated preposition and also repetition of (parts) of the noun phrase. What is pied piped is actually repeated again in some form. In (32) we have *of whech Seynt* repeated as *of him*. The adverbial clause with *because* interrupts the sentence structure:

(32) on-to þat ordre þat was founded at Sempyngham be þe solicitude of Seynt Gilbert, of whech Seynt, be-cause I mad a special tretis on-to þe maystir of þat ordr, þerfor in þis place I touch no mor of him. (cmcapser m4 176)

In (33) *te comune seal of þe seyd hous of Bromholm* is resumed in the demonstrative *this*.

(33) te comune seal of þe seyd hous of Bromholm, which þe berare of this hath redy (cmoffice m4 508)

In (34) we have two examples of the partitive *of whiche somme* with *of hem* as a resumptive construction in the first instance.

(34) Upon this forseide plate ben compassed certeyn cercles that highten almycanteras, of whiche somme of hem semen parfit cercles and somme semen inparfit, (cmastro m3 369)

### 4.3 Stranding

As was evident in Table 4, true stranding of the preposition is a very infrequent alternative compared with pied piping in my data. Stranding of preposition is not really common until the end of the Middle English period. Eight examples of stranding occur in the Middle English prose texts, (35)–(40) and (42)–(43) below. In all cases the preposition and relativizer function as prepositional object. These findings are interesting since Fischer (1992: 390–391) states that stranding does not occur when the relative construction functions as prepositional object in Middle English. In modern English, Johansson and Geisler (1998) found that it is particularly in this function that a preposition is stranded.

(35) and þese men preise God nyte & day in holy songis & ympnis whech þei continuely be vsed too. (cmcapser m4 81)

In (36), stranding of the preposition is obligatory in modern English, since the meaning of the phrasal verb (*passe ouer*) is figurative (see for example Sopher 1974). In (37) *whech he was fallyn in* is also figurative in meaning (*whech he was fallyn in* = *which had befallen him*). (Examples (9) and (10) are repeated as (36) and (37)).

(36) Tou setted þe terme, þe which hij ne shul nougt passe ouer; (cmearlps m2 965)
(37) compleynyng to þe preste of pouerte & disese whech he was fallyn in be infortunyte... (cmkempe m4 346)

Examples (38) and (39) illustrate genitive expressions: *in proffit of her encresynge which þei haue cure of* and *whyche letter ... whyche letter Boton had the beryng off*. Cf. also example (33) above. In example (39) *off* is most probably a variant spelling of *of*. Note that the relative clause is at some distance from its antecedent in (39). Several clauses interrupt the sentence structure.

(38) tei shuld oo tyme yeven hem to besynes and worldely thyngis att resonable nede, and to the werkes of actiffe liffe in profitt of her encresynge, which þei haue cure of. (cmrolltr m24 309)

(39) in whyche letter ye myght well conceyue what I wold ye scholde do wyth þe same ryng, wyth manye other tydyngys and thyngys whyche I prayed yowe to haue doon for me; whyche letter Boton had the beryng off. (cmpriv m4 1560)

Examples (40)-(41) illustrate variation between stranding and pied piping with the prepositional verb *speak of*. The forms *the whiche* and *which* must be regarded as variants. It is worth pointing out that it is in the third period that such examples are found. As stated earlier, the period between 1350 and 1420 is in many respects the most interesting where prepositional relative constructions are concerned (see Section 2 above). There is, however, just one example of stranding from this period (example (40)).

(40) And bi þis Aaron ben vnderstonden alle þoo þe whiche I spak of abouen, (cmcloud m3 2155)
(41) We ben redi to stie to the place, of which the Lord spak, (cmotest m3 1195)

In examples (42) and (43) an adverb occurs at the end of the sentence, stranding a somewhat heavier word than a preposition (from a structural point of view). In (42) *therof* is used and in (43) *heryn*.

(42) I: ffor truly I had not so besy a weke sith I cam hedyr, exepte oone day, which sir William, and John Mathewe both can enfourme you parte þerof. (cmpriv m4 1971)

(43) owr Lord had drawyn hir thorw hys mercy & be what menys, also how meche grace he had schewyd for hir, þe whech he seyd he was vnworthy to heryn. (cmkempe m4 662)

In order to find examples of preposition-stranding, the structural patterns *which* (and variant spellings), *the which*, *the which that* and *whom* (and variant spellings) + Noun/Pronoun were checked in particular. In the Caxton text (M4), the pattern *that* + Noun/Pronoun was also checked. No further examples of stranding of the preposition were found other than the ones listed above.

## 5. Genitive and partitive *of which*–constructions and pied piping

The prepositional relative constructions in the Middle English prose texts include a number of *of which*-constructions that are genitive or partitive (partitive: also *of whom*-constructions). These constructions may involve a different type of pied piping. Genitive *of which* was introduced in the Middle English period as an alternative to *whose* to mark nonhuman antecedents. According to Schneider (1993), the origin of genitive *of which* is to be found in partitive constructions, such as the following (also quoted in Schneider 1993):

(44) that it myght come to the knowlege and vnderstondyng of suche as ben ygnoraunt. Of which the nombre is infenyte. (cmcaxpro m4 53)

As is evident from Table 5 below, however, there are more constructions with genitive *of which* than partitive *of which* in the Middle English prose texts. The first examples of genitive *of which* are from the M2 period, 1250–1350, in which we find four examples of genitive *of which* and three examples of partitive *of which*. Later on, in the M3 period, 1350–1420, genitive *of which* is more frequent (16 examples) than partitive *of which* (10 examples). We might have expected to find partitive *of which* to be more frequent than genitive *of which* if it is supposed to be the origin of the latter. In Table 5 below we see that genitive *of which*–constructions occur in 58% of the cases and partitive in 42%. The difference is small but partitive is not the dominant category.

**Table 5:** Genitive and partitive *of which*

| | M2 | M3 | M4 | Total | % |
|---|---|---|---|---|---|
| Genitive | 4 | 16 | 2 | 22 | 58% |
| Partitive | 3 | 10 | 3 | 16 | 42% |
| Total | 7 | 26 | 5 | 38 | 100% |

Pied piping in genitive and partitive constructions may involve not only the preposition, as in *of which the nombre*, but also the noun phrase, that is, the head of the *of which*–construction, as in *the nombre of which*. As was pointed out earlier, there are no examples of the latter pattern in Middle English. What are the reasons for this? Schneider (1993) states that the pattern *of which NP* occurs in Middle English because *of which* has the same position as its alternative *whose*. Another explanation why we only find the *of which NP* pattern in the Middle English period could be that pied piping of the preposition occurs in Middle English, but not the more complex pied piping of the noun phrase. In early 16th century English, the pattern *of which NP* is still the more frequent (see Rydén 1966). It is not until the early 17th century that the more complex movement of noun phrase and preposition becomes more common, which is also the more frequent pattern in modern English (see Johansson 1995 and 1997). It is worth noting that example (45) (= (38) above) illustrates a pattern which has not been found in modern spoken and written texts (see Johansson 1997).

(45) tei shuld oo tyme yeven hem to besynes and worldely thyngis att resonable nede, and to the werkes of actiffe liffe in profitt of her encresynge, which þei haue cure of. (cmrolltr m24 309)

In (45) a genitive *of which*–construction is exemplified, and the pattern is that of stranded preposition: *which þei haue (the) cure of*. The *of which*-construction functions as object and it is in this function that three patterns are available as regards the placement of *of which*. These patterns are summarised in (45a)-(45c). Note the different types of pied piping (in 45a-b) in the underlying structure *þei haue the cure of which*:

(45a) of which þei haue the cure (pied piping of *of*)
(45b) the cure of which þei haue (pied piping of *of* and the head of the *of which*–construction)
(45c) which þei haue the cure of (*wh*-movement and stranding of preposition)

There are only three examples in the Middle English prose texts of genitive and partitive constructions as objects. In all the other cases, they function as subjects of the relative clause (*of which (the) cure is*). *Of which*–constructions as prepositional complements (*in the middle of which*) are not found in the Middle English prose texts since the pattern *NP of which*, which is obligatory in such constructions, does not yet occur. Instead we find the alternative *whose*:

(46) And Moises seide to the Lord, Egipcians here not, fro whos myddil thou leddist out this puple, and the dwelleris of this loond, (cmotest m3 1109)

The pattern *of which NP* may lead to a form of *be* being placed at the end of a sentence, which is not desirable in modern English since *be* is structurally and informationally light. In example (31) above, the preposition is repeated at the end of the sentence, possibly because a form of *be* would otherwise be in final position. As pointed out above (see Section 4.2), the repetition of the preposition could also be regarded as one of the pre-stages of stranding.

Example (47) is the only one in which *that* also occurs in the COMP position (see Section 4.1), together with the moved *wh*–word and the preposition.

(47) 'Thanne mustow graunten,' quod sche, 'by semblable resoun that oon and good be o same thing; for of thinges of whiche that the effect nys nat naturely divers, nedes the substaunce moot be oo same thing.' (cmboeth m3 554)

In (48) the head (*the hole diametre*) of the genitive *of which*-construction is at some distance from *of which* since the adverbial *when* clause is inserted. This seems to be the only position for the clause, if it is to serve some explanatory function.

(48) tak ther fore a plate of metal or elles a bord þ=t= be smothe shaue / by leuel / & euene polised / of which whan it is rownd (by compas) / the hole diametre shal contene .72. large enches or elles .6. fote of mesure... (cmequato m3 44)

In (49) *which* occurs as determiner, showing that the preposition and the noun phrase (*whiche sterres*) have been moved. The same pattern is exemplified with the partitive *of whilke seuen* in (50).

(49) The names of the sterres ben writen in the margyn of the riet there as thei sitte, of whiche sterres the smale point is clepid the centre. (cmastro m3 410)

(50) Te thirde thynge of þe Sex þat I firste touchide, es þe Seuen Sacramentes þat Haly Kirke gyffes, thurghe prelates and oþer prestes þat hase þe powere. Of whilke seuen, the first fyve ilke cristen man awe lawefully to take efter his elde es; (cmgaytry m34 315)

As is obvious from the examples presented above, it is the M3 period covering the years 1350–1420 that contains the most interesting and informative examples of pied piping in genitive and partitive *of which*–constructions.

## 6. Conclusion

In the Middle English period, *wh*–words begin to be used as relativizers, and we see a change in that nominal or at least pronominal words occur as relativizers which can be preceded by prepositions. This is when pied piping is more or less the rule. The nominal form that the relativizers have in Middle English is obvious in constructions with *the which* and *the which that*. Pied piping in Middle English occurs regardless of the function of the relative construction as adverbial or prepositional object. There are also cases where we would not use a pied piping construction in present-day English, as in the following example where the relativizer is the prepositional object: *þe sayd persone, of whom þis tretys specyaly makyth mencyon.*

It is, however, important that a few examples of preposition-stranding occur in the Middle English texts examined. There we see the beginnings or the pre-stages of preposition stranding and of the variation between pied piping and stranding that we have in modern English. Firstly, both pied piping and stranding of the preposition occur, as in *grashoppes come and breses, of which no noumbre was of* (preposition + *wh* + final preposition). Secondly, we have the pattern with stranding of the preposition and a repetition of the noun phrase or parts of the noun phrase, as when *of whech Seynt* is repeated as *of him* in the following example: *Seynt Gilbert, of whech*

*Seynt, be-cause I mad a special tretis on-to þe maystir of þat ordr, þerfor in þis place I touch no mor of him* (preposition + *wh* + resumptive NP). A third pattern is stranding of a structurally heavier word than a preposition, for example the adverb *thereof* in *exepte oone day, which sir William, and John Mathewe both can enfourme you parte þerof* (*wh* + adverb).

In genitive and partitive *of which*-constructions, the preposition can be pied piped, as in *of which the noumbre*, which is the pattern found in the Middle English prose texts. Another possibility is also to pied pipe the noun phrase, that is, the head of the *of which*-construction, as in *the noumbre of which*, which is the more common pattern in modern English. This more complex movement of preposition and the head of the *of which*-construction is not represented at all in the Middle English texts studied. There is even the choice of stranding the preposition (when the *of which*-construction functions as object). One example of this pattern actually occurs in the Middle English prose texts examined: *in profitt of her encresynge, which þei haue cure of*. The period between 1350–1420, M3, is the most important and informative period to the present study. It offers the largest number of instances of prepositional relative constructions, as well as the largest variety of constructional types.

**Notes**

1 I am grateful to Christer Geisler, Uppsala University, for his help in providing the material and the statistics on the UPENN corpus and also for his valuable comments and suggestions on earlier versions of this paper. I am also grateful to Merja Kytö, Mats Rydén, Terry Walker and Donald MacQueen, Uppsala University, for their valuable comments and suggestions.

2 The Middle English texts in the Helsinki Corpus consist of 608,570 words. Certain texts have been excluded from the UPENN corpus, for example Drama and a few texts from Handbooks, Philosophy and History. Other texts have been expanded, for example certain texts from Religious Treatises and Biography.

3 The term *pied piping* first occurs in Ross (1967), in the framework of generative grammatical theory. This is also the case in Haegeman (1994) and Rigter–Beukema (1985) (the theory of government and binding). *Wh*–movement is discussed from a historical point of view by for example Fischer (1992) and Lightfoot (1979 and 1991). Schneider (1993) describes the emergence of *of which* in Middle English and also discusses the position of *of which* with regard to its head. Johansson and Geisler (1998) treat pied piping in present-day spoken British English.

4 I have exemplified only the prepositions *in* and *of*. The preposition *of* is the most common preposition, used in genitive and partitive expressions and in cases where we would use other prepositions today. The preposition *in* is also very frequent in the material.

5 There is one example of *the whos* but not in a pied piping construction: We rede of other noble men / somme lordes & somme other of lower astates reputed as goddes in dyuerse regyons / *the whos* famous actes / and excelle[{n{]t vertues only hystorye hath preseruyd fro perysshyng in eternal memorye. (cmcaxtopro m4 359)

## Primary sources

The Helsinki Corpus of English Texts: The Middle English part: 608,570 words
The UPENN corpus (the Penn-Helsinki Parsed Corpus of Middle English): 489,114 words

## References


Campbell, Alistair (1983). *Old English grammar*. Oxford: Oxford University Press.

Geisler, Christer (1998). 'Postmodifying infinitives in Middle English'. Paper presented at ICAME 18, Belfast, May 1998.

Fischer, Olga (1992). 'Syntax'. In Blake, N. (ed.). *The Cambridge history of the English language*. Volume 2. Cambridge: Cambridge University Press. 207–408.

Haegeman, Liliane (1994). *Introduction to Government and Binding theory*. Third edition. Oxford: Blackwell.

Johansson, Christine (1995). *The possessive relativizers* whose *and* of which *in Present-day English. Description and theory*. Uppsala: Acta Universitatis Upsaliensis.

Johansson, Christine (1997). 'The positional variation of the possessive relativizer *of which*'. In Fries, U., V. Müller and P. Schneider (eds). *From Ælfric to the New York Times*. Amsterdam: Rodopi. 51–64.

Johansson, Christine and Christer Geisler (1998). 'Pied piping in spoken English'. In Renouf, A. (ed.). *Explorations in corpus linguistics*. Amsterdam: Rodopi. 82–91.

Kytö, Merja (1996). *Manual to the diachronic part of the Helsinki Corpus of English Texts*. Third edition. Helsinki: Department of English, University of Helsinki.

Lightfoot, David (1979). *Principles of diachronic syntax*. Cambridge: Cambridge University Press.

Lightfoot, David (1991). *How to set parameters: arguments from language change*. Cambridge, Mass.: The MIT Press.

Mossé, Fernand (1952). *A handbook of Middle English*. (Translated by James A. Walker). Baltimore: The John Hopkins Press.

Quirk, Randolph, Sidney Greenbaum, Geoffrey Leech and Jan Svartvik (1985). *A comprehensive grammar of the English language*. London: Longman.

Rigter, Bob and Frits Beukema (1985). *A Government and Binding approach to English sentence structure*. Part 2. Apeldoorn: Van Walraven.

Romaine, Suzanne (1982). *Socio-historical linguistics*. Cambridge: Cambridge University Press.

Ross, John R (1967). 'Constraints on variables in syntax'. Ph.D. dissertation published as *Infinite syntax!* 1986. Norwood, New Jersey: Ablex Publishing Corporation.

Rydén, Mats (1966). *Relative constructions in early Sixteenth Century English. With special reference to Sir Thomas Elyot*. Uppsala: Acta Universitatis Upsaliensis.

Schneider, Edgar (1993). 'The grammaticalisation of possessive *of which* in Middle English and Early Modern English'. *Folia Linguistica Historica* XIV (1–2): 239–257.

Sopher, Haveem (1974). 'Prepositional relative clauses'. *Linguistics* 133: 63–83.

Stockwell, Robert P., Paul Schachter and Barbara Hall Partee (1973). *The major syntactic structures of English*. New York: Holt, Rinehart and Winston.

# Zero subject relative constructions in American and British English

*Hans Martin Lehmann*

University of Zürich

**Abstract**

*This large-scale corpus study documents the use of zero subject relative constructions in spoken American and British English. For this purpose, it makes extensive use of automated retrieval strategies. It shows that zero subject relatives are still present in spoken American and British English, as represented in the British National Corpus and the Longman Spoken American Corpus. Moreover, there is a sharp difference between American English with 2.5% and British English with 13% of subject relatives with zero relativizer. Although zero subject relative constructions are frequently found with existentials and* it*–clefts they are by no means limited to these constructions. The social variables of the study (most notably age) come from speaker annotation which is used to provide the apparent time dimension.*

## 1. Introduction

In this paper I will investigate the use of zero subject relatives as in (1a) and their related surface forms as in (1b) and (1c).

(1a) I have a home help Ø does my shopping. (Lodge 1992:42)
(1b) I have a home help who does my shopping.
(1c) I have a home help that does my shopping.

As Chevillet (1996: 27) points out, '[zero subject relatives] are apt to pass unnoticed to the untrained ear.' Once aware of the possibility of zero subject relativizers as in (1), I kept noticing them in direct speech situations in novels as well as in spontaneous language on the internet such as language in chat rooms or quickly typed messages. However, such constructions are not found generally acceptable (Quirk et al. 1985: 1250). This paper will document how far they are used in spoken American and British English today. In addition I will attempt to analyze zero subject relatives according to social variables, to the extent that frequency and corpus annotation allow such an undertaking.

Methodologically, I will pursue a variationist approach which will take into consideration Labov's (1969: 738) principle of accountability. In the case of this paper this means that not only zero subject relative clauses, as in (1a), but also clauses containing surface forms, as in (1b) and (1c) should be observed.

In terms of retrieval methodology, I will adapt strategies developed and described in Lehmann (1997a and 1997b) for the retrieval of object relatives, as well as in Tottie and Lehmann (1999) for adverbial relatives, to this search for subject relatives in spoken language. From here on I will use *ZSR* as an abbreviation for zero subject relative and *SSR* for surface subject relative.

## 2. Previous work

Most grammars don't mention ZSRs. Quirk et al. (1985: 1250) do, exemplifying their use in (2) to (6) below, and noting that 'Zero cannot replace the subject in a relative clause such as [2] and [3]'.

| | | |
|---|---|---|
| (2) | *The table Ø stands in the corner has a broken leg. | [2] in Quirk et al. |
| (3) | *The man Ø stands over there I know. | [3] in Quirk et al. |
| (4) | ?Anybody Ø does that ought to be locked up. | [4] in Quirk et al. |
| (5) | There's a table Ø stands in the corner. | [5] in Quirk et al. |
| (6) | It was Simon Ø did it. | [6] in Quirk et al. |

Quirk et al. find that [4] can occur only 'in very informal speech where the antecedent is an indefinite pronoun'. They state that [5] and [6] are 'more common' and point out that '[t]he obligatory nature of such portions of existential or cleft sentences would argue against our equating them with postmodifications in noun-phrase structure.' In this paper I will include the whole spectrum of ZSRs, including cleft and existential constructions as in [5] and [6]. Interestingly, [4] is marked by Quirk et al. with a question mark indicating its doubtful status.

> The reason for putting a question mark in [4] is, first, that it is of doubtful acceptability; secondly, that many speakers would condemn it as slovenly; thirdly, that it may result from the subaudibility of a relative pronoun *who* or *that* and thus not strictly be zero at all. (Quirk et al. 1985: 1250)

The fact that the phenomenon occurs in written form in novels and spontaneous internet language seems to provide evidence against subaudibility. It is also important to notice that in (2) – (4) the relative complex is sentence-initial, whereas in (5) and (6) as well as in (1) it is to be found in sentence-final position. It is thus interesting to compare the acceptability of (3) with that of (7). In an informal survey that I carried out, (7) was found more acceptable than (3) by several native speakers.

(7) I know a bloke Ø goes to the cinema every day.

The realization forms and distribution of zero relativizers in subject position have been investigated and documented by linguists working in historical linguistics. The earliest examples of zero relativizers are to be found in subject position in Old English (cf. Visser 1963). Zero relativizers in non-subject positions come into the language at a later stage. The spread of zero as a relativization strategy from subject to object position seems to follow Keenan and Comrie's (1977; 1979) noun phrase accessibility hierarchy. Dekeyser (1984: 77) shows that by Early Modern English zero relativizers had become more frequent in object position than in subject position.

Dekeyser (1984: 77), in a comparison of his data representing the period from 1600–1649 and Quirk's (1957) data for Present Day English, finds a trend towards surface relativization in subject positions with ZSRs dropping from 5.94% to 0.32%. Over the same period, Dekeyser (1984: 77) also finds a slight increase for non-subject zero relatives from 32.73% to 34.44%. These studies point towards a language change involving the loss of zero relativizers in subject position. With the present study I will attempt to document how far this change has proceeded in spoken American and British English.

Other linguists have studied ZSRs in regional or ethnic varieties of English. Their results show that ZSRs are still present in regional and ethnic varieties of English. Hackenberg (1972) investigates Appalachian English and Shnukal (1981) studies Cessnock English, the language of a small Australian community in New South Wales. Both find that more than 50% of the subject relative constructions in their data are realized by zero. They also find that older speakers as well as speakers of lower social status use more ZSRs. Orton et al. (1978) include ZSRs with human antecedents in *The Linguistic Atlas of England*. They find that a majority of informants prefer zero in the frame *I know a man ... will do it for you.* Harvie (1998: 47) studies three varieties of African American English. She finds that between 11% and 41% of the subject relatives are realized by zero, with the oldest records (1930–1945) containing the highest proportion of ZSRs. The only spoken data on ZSRs for a major standard variety of English I am aware of is provided in Sigley (1997) for New Zealand English. Sigley (1997: 282) finds that 'there are only 11 examples using Ø from 151 *there-*, *have-*, and *get-*existentials.'

## 3. Standard English and spoken data

There seems to be general agreement that ZSRs are a marker of non-standard varieties of English. Hackenberg (1972: 3) states in his study of Appalachian English:

> In our discussion of AE [Appalachian English] reference will be made to a hypothetical "norm" represented by Standard American English or SE. This is the English which has been described and codified by modern grammar books. Possible examples of speakers of this type of English might be the network newscasters and news commentators who have trained themselves to speak an English that is devoid of any regionalisms.

He contrasts Standard American English and his data collected in the Appalachian region, which he calls Appalachian English. Moreover he makes reference not to American English as a major variety, but to Standard American English, a hypothetical norm spoken by a small group and used in situations where language of the type written to be spoken dominates. He classifies ZSRs as a feature distinguishing standard from non-standard varieties of American English.

> In the case of concordance and relative pronoun deletion, all standard and nonstandard instances of the grammatical features were transcribed. The "nonstandard" instances are those which could not have been generated by SE [Standard English] rules. (Hackenberg 1972: 20)

In the title of her paper Shnukal refers to Australian English. Later she coins the term 'Cessnock English' to reflect the limitation of her data to a small community in New South Wales. All the approaches mentioned are based on spoken data acquired by elicitation and observation of informants selected to represent their regional or ethnic variety of English. They all implicitly or explicitly contrast the use of ZSRs in their data with that of standard varieties of English. However, the use of the term 'standard' is far from unproblematic. As Hackenberg (1972: 3) points out, the use of the term 'standard' implies a normative stance.

Other linguists base their definition of 'standard' on written and published forms of the language. Svartvik (1998: 22) finds that '[t]he problem is that nobody seems to know what it [Standard English] is.' For this purpose he decides that 'contemporary written, especially printed, English as regularly used by the majority media and printing houses of the inner circle' is 'as close to a standard as we can hope to find anywhere...'.

Such definitions of 'standard' are either normative and idealized and therefore not empirically identifiable, or they are based on written, published forms of the language and thus not a suitable background for studies largely based on spoken language. For these reasons I think it preferable to contrast the results from regional and ethnic varieties not with a normative, idealized mainly written standard but with the major spoken varieties of Present Day English. One of the goals of the present study is thus to provide a background for the comparison of regional and ethnic varieties with major spoken varieties.

## 4. Data and method

Such an undertaking has only recently become possible through the availability of large spoken corpora. The present study is based on the British National Corpus (*BNC*) which provides 10 million words of spoken English as well as the Longman Spoken American Corpus (*LSAC*), which contains 5 million words of spoken American English. This paper is based on LSAC and the spoken demographic part of the BNC (4.2 million words).

Another reason for the lack of data on zero relativizers is the methodological problem of finding in a corpus something that is not there. Sigley (1997: 89) states:

> ... it is impossible to use a computer to search for something which is not already in the text, and so tokens of zero must be identified and marked manually.

However, in Lehmann (1997a; 1997b) I developed strategies to cope with the problem of automatic retrieval of object zero relatives. Here I will attempt to apply a similar strategy to the retrieval of subject relatives. For a long time corpus linguistic enquiry was limited to problems which could be dealt with by searches for lexical items. This was in part due to the nature of available retrieval software. Programs like Word-Cruncher were produced with the search for lexical items in mind. Another major reason, however, was the lack of tagged corpora, which are a prerequisite for the retrieval of syntactic patterns.

While the BNC is distributed in a version annotated with CLAWS, LSAC is only available in an untagged version. Moreover, the version of CLAWS with which the BNC was tagged is not available for tagging other corpora. Tagging the two corpora with different taggers or different versions of the same tagger would have introduced unknown factors into the comparison of the two corpora. Therefore, I decided to retag both sets of data with the same tagger. I chose to use ENGCG-2 (English Constraint Grammar; cf. www.conexor.fi) for this purpose. ENGCG-2 is built on the framework described in Karlsson (1995). Being constraint-based, ENGCG-2 will apply handcrafted rules in order to eliminate ambiguity projected from the morphology and the lexicon. Remaining ambiguities appear in the output in the form of ambiguity tags also called portmanteau tags. (8) is an example of a sentence-unit in the BNC, which was retagged with ENGCG-2.

(8) If_Cs they_P 've_Vpres got_EN anything_P **that_Cs_Prel** they_P wish_Vpres to_TO say_Vinf or_Cc any_DET personal_A reminiscences_Npl ._PUN (BNC:D8Y:PS002:002)

For the corpus linguist, ambiguity tags may result in a larger amount of garbage that will have to be sorted out manually (i.e. low precision). At the same time, ambiguity tags will avoid decisions based on heuristics and thereby lower the risk of missing instances of a specific phenomenon (i.e. higher recall). Therefore constraint-based taggers are ideal for retrieval purposes in corpus linguistics, as the concern for recall is paramount. Of course, this is only true on the condition that the linguist will carry out the task of manually or computationally excluding garbage from the result set.

Using a standard tagger on spoken material without adjustments to the lexicon and rules is problematic. This is also the case with ENGCG-2, as is pointed out in the Unix manual pages:

> The present description accounts for present-day standard written English. Dialectal, colloquial or otherwise non-standard texts may receive less predictable analyses. (ENGCG-2 Unix man page)

It will therefore be necessary to test the reliability of the tagging process with an independent set of data.

## 5. Retrieval

As stated above, zero elements are not retrievable by searching for lexical items, since in current corpora they are not marked. Any space between two words would therefore be a potential candidate for a zero element. In the case of ZSRs, manual work, i.e. retrieval by reading the corpora, is not a viable option. Three attempts at retrieving ZSRs from subcorpora of 40,000 words yielded only between 0 and 2 instances of the phenomenon. Moreover, a computerized retrieval would reduce the possibility of human error. Thus the only viable option is automated retrieval based on word-class annotation. As a basis for the development of a computerised retrieval algorithm I made use of a set of 150 instances taken from Shnukal (1981), Hackenberg (1972), Harvie (1998), Tottie and Harvie (1999), Sigley (1997) and Visser (1963). In addition I included examples found in my own reading and instances generously collected by my colleagues at the University of Zurich.[1]

Considering the 150 examples at hand, I found that the most promising retrieval condition is the sequence finite verb-cluster + noun phrase + finite verb illustrated in (9):

| | | | | | |
|---|---|---|---|---|---|
| (9) | I | have | a home help | does | my shopping. |
| | | Vfin1 | NP | Vfin2 | |

As the two corpora annotated with ENGCG-2 only contain word-class annotation and no information about the phrase level, I had to translate the phrase level sequence into sequences of tags. In the case of the first verb-cluster Vfin1 I had to allow for complex predicators, as in (10):

(10) We've got a cat Ø comes to our house, a white one.
(BNC:KD8:03098:PS0LL)

The position of Vfin2 is unproblematic as it begins with a finite verb. The only variable allowed in Vfin2 is optional adverbial material in front of the finite verb as in (11).

(11) There's a girl in there Ø killed her daddy, ... (BNC:KC9:3400:PS0CR)

The intervening NP is certainly more problematic. The retrieval pattern covers non-complex noun phrases, coordination and premodification as in (12).

(12) ... so it'll be his mom, his dad, his sister and his brother-in-law and their two kids Ø will spend the night here tomorrow night. (LSAC:113401:?)

Postmodified noun phrases can take a great number of different forms, which could only have been covered with the help of a full-fledged parser. As this proved to be beyond the scope of this study, I decided to cover only postmodification by prepositional phrases as in (13).

(13) Yeah there's a lot Ø goes in apart from the chicken there's a heck of lot Ø goes in it in the. (BNC:KB7:14154:PS02G)

The pattern Vfin-NP-Vfin is by no means the only surface sequence in which ZSRs may occur in spoken language. (14)-(18) exemplify cases where my retrieval strategy may fail:

(14) "S'pose he a big boy Ø don't respect my pistol?" (Mosley: 1993: 152)
(15) The guy (that) wrote the Silent Language (LSAC:055801:?)

(14) and (15) illustrate problems specific to spoken language. Omission of a finite verb as in (14) will certainly cause problems for retrieval. This is particularly the case for AAVE, where copula deletion and the use of forms like *been* as finite verbs are frequent. As illustrated by (15), NPs postmodified by relative clauses can occur

without matrix clause in spoken language. Here, a retrieval based on the sequence of finite verb clusters is bound to fail.

Another problem is posed by inserted material between the matrix and the relative clause, as in (16). A similar problem is double embedding. Some cases, as in (17), have been retrieved; however, others may have escaped the retrieval process.

(16) To this date I still haven't seen an Epson print, including the 9000, Ø looks better than my Tektronix 440 dye-sub print. (message in internet news group: rec.photo.digital)

(17) ... I mean there's children who are grown up now at college Ø have never seen a spot of rain, ... (BNC:KC9:1312:PS0CG)

The problems outlined above certainly have to be taken into account. However, accuracy testing showed that the retrieval pattern covered 92% (138/150) of the zero relative constructions in the test set. Wrong assignment of word-class tags accounts for 6/12 errors. This is exemplified in (18).

(18) There_Ex 's_Vpres a_DET cord_N **runs_Npl** down_ADV to_PREP your_Pgen belt_N ._PUN

In (18) the verb reading for *runs* was erroneously discarded by the tagger. This is not surprising given the low frequency of ZSR constructions. The tagger obviously interpreted *a cord runs* as a noun phrase.

The other six errors were due to the problems outlined in (14)-(17). From this I conclude that such cases are rare. While the shortcomings of the retrieval patterns will prevent me from making statements about such rare types of ZSR constructions, the results based on automated retrieval will be reliable enough to describe the distribution of ZSRs in American and British English.

Running the retrieval algorithm on both corpora produced over 60,000 matches of the patterns. Of course only a few of these really were instances of ZSRs. The vast majority of results returned were other cases where two finite verb clusters follow each other. Frequent constructions producing unwanted instances were tag-questions as in (19) and verbs subcategorizing for sentences as in (20).

(19) you didn't eat all your breakfast did you? (BNC:KD1:2923:PS0JA)

(20) ... I said I will explain why later it comes into another section. (BNC:D8Y:066:D8YPS002)

By automatically excluding such obvious garbage, I was able to reduce the result set to 20,000 instances. These I then sorted out manually.

As stated above, this paper also covers SSRs (surface subject relatives). Labov's (1969: 738) principle of accountability states 'THAT ANY VARIABLE FORM (a member of a set of alternative ways of "saying the same thing") SHOULD BE REPORTED WITH THE PROPORTION OF CASES IN WHICH THE FORM DID OCCUR IN THE RELEVANT ENVIRONMENT, COMPARED TO THE TOTAL NUMBER OF CASES IN WHICH IT MIGHT HAVE OCCURRED.' There are two problems with applying this principle to ZSRs. On the one hand there may be other ways of saying the same thing than finite subject relative clauses. We might have to consider non-finite postmodification too. On the other hand there may be SSR constructions which speakers of American or British English would not realize by zero under any circumstances. In this study I will ignore the former problem. The second problem I will partially solve by limiting the observation of SSRs to those surface constructions which would have been retrieved by my retrieval patterns had the relativizer been realized by zero. For this purpose I changed the retrieval patterns developed for ZSRs in such a way that they required *who*, *that* or *which* in the position of the zero relativizer. Such a strategy is of course only a rough approximation to the Labovian principle of accountability. However, it has the advantage of imposing the same formal restrictions on the observation of SSRs as on the retrieval of ZSRs. As a consequence, I did not have to rely on native speaker intuition for the acceptability of ZSRs. In an area where linguists describe the phenomenon as being non-standard or even slovenly language this is a great advantage, as it avoids the observer's paradox inherent in the elicitation of constructions perceived as being outside the norm. However, the reader should keep the restriction imposed on the observed surface variants in mind when interpreting the results presented in this paper.

Manual sorting presented its own problems. Often it was only possible to come to a conclusive decision by going back to the co-text, and at times hesitation phenomena and false starts made a decision impossible. There were also cases of structural ambiguity as illustrated by (21), where it is impossible to tell whether the meaning is that of (21a) or (21b).

(21) No, it's just Ø the eyes Ø have grown that's all. (BNC:KDP:0740:PS0NB)
(21a) No, it's just that the eyes have grown.
(21b) No, it's just the eyes that have grown.

Such unclear and ambiguous cases were excluded from the analysis. The remaining instances can therefore be considered to be the solid core of ZSRs.

## 6. Results

The analysis left me with 94 instances of ZSRs in 5 million words in LSAC and 205 instances in 4.2 million words in the spoken demographic sample of the BNC. This certainly is a strong indication that ZSRs are about two and a half times more frequent in British English than in American English. However, as a consequence of the principle of accountability there are problems with accounting frequency per million running words. After all it could be the case that subject relative constructions allowing for a possible realization by zero are less frequent in American English overall. For this reason it is important to account for the frequency of ZSRs taking into account the overall frequency of possible occurrences including surface relativizers. The results of such an analysis are shown in Table 1.

**Table 1:** Realization forms of subject relatives in American and British English

| American English | | | | British English | | | |
|---|---|---|---|---|---|---|---|
| **surface** | | **zero** | | **surface** | | **zero** | |
| *n* | *%* | *n* | *%* | *n* | *%* | *n* | *%* |
| 3647 | *97.5%* | 94 | *2.5%* | 1376 | *87%* | 205 | *13%* |

Table 1 shows that taking into account occurrences and non-occurrences of ZSRs does not reduce the difference found above. In fact, taking into account possible occurrences results in an even greater difference between American and British English, with ZSRs being over five times more frequent in British English than in American English. Thus the results in Table 1 firmly establish a pronounced difference in the use of ZSRs between these two major varieties of English.

Table 1 also shows a striking difference in the frequency of subject relative constructions observed by the retrieval patterns. Subject relative constructions conforming to the retrieval patterns are twice as frequent in American English as in British English.

Another interesting aspect for analysis are the different matrix clauses in which ZSR complexes occur. Here I will follow Shnukal (1981), who defines four major types exemplified by (22)–(25).

(22) there's this woman Ø went out to like some Caribbean or something to have a vacation and then she met this guy (LSAC:118901:?)

(23) It was Joanne Ø said you'd go down there, so you said alright. (BNC:KDG:1795:PS000)

(24) this dog I got friendly with, they were people Ø got in there for the summer, got and just abandon it so there's all these dogs running around the coast. (LSAC:165301::2791)

(25) well I mean we had one girl Ø didn't know what she was going about, ... (BNC:KDW:6217:PS1C1)

The first type represented by (22) is characterized by existential *there* in the matrix clause. The second type features an *it*-cleft construction, as in (23). The third type has the verb *be* as a main verb, as in (24). The fourth type of matrix clause is characterized by the verb *have* as a main verb, as in (25). These are the most frequent matrix clause types discussed by Shnukal (1981). There are other less frequent verbs used in the matrix clauses in my material as in (26)–(31).

(26) … and erm thought knock on the doors and se, ask people Ø had seen it and (BNC:KD5:9674:PS0JX)

(27) knife at the back of the saw, they, it is abit dangerous, erm where's the guard Ø goes at the top. (BNC:KDM:07067:PS0RD)

(28) And I can handle any bastard Ø gets in here. (BNC:KDY:0658:PS142)

(29) and it was talking in there about one woman Ø asked the waiter to go to bed with him when she was ordering something. (LSAC:151103:2173)

(30) It's like people who eat marmalade Ø has no peel in it. (BNC:KPU:2690:PS584)

(31) either you kill each other until finally you get to one Ø gives in so one becomes the master and one becomes the slave. (LSAC:165001:2757)

(26)–(31) show that the construction is not limited to the matrix clause types exemplified in (22)–(25). Table 2 shows the distribution of the four main types and other matrix clause choices.

**Table 2:** Types of ZSRs in American and British English

| | American English | | British English | |
|---|---|---|---|---|
| **Types** | **n** | **%** | **n** | **%** |
| existential *there* | 27 | 29% | 126 | 61% |
| cleft | 24 | 26% | 25 | 12% |
| *be* | 14 | 15% | 8 | 4% |
| *have* | 9 | 10% | 15 | 7% |
| others | 20 | 21% | 31 | 15% |

Table 2 shows that the ranking of matrix clause types in American and British English is fairly similar. The only exceptions are constructions with the verb *be* and the verb *have* which are reversed in the order of their ranking. The most striking difference is found with existential *there* constructions, which cover 61% of all ZSR constructions in British English and only 29% in American English.

In the following I will try to analyze the distribution of the ZSR construction with the help of the annotation provided by the BNC and the LSAC. Both corpora are annotated with social variables for individual speakers. However, not all speakers are annotated, as it was impossible to obtain the relevant data from all interlocutors who happened to be recorded. The use of speaker annotation divides the corpora into parts of unequal size. To cope with this problem I prepared databases containing annotation and word-counts for the individual speakers. This information was then used for normalization and thus made direct comparison possible.

LSAC contains information about the ethnicity of speakers. Given the presence of ZSRs in AAVE documented in Tottie and Harvie (1999) and Harvie (1998), it is interesting to see if African Americans use ZSRs with a higher frequency than other Americans. Table 3 highlights the problem of correlating social variables with a low frequency phenomenon like ZSRs. The slightly higher frequency of ZSRs produced by African Americans is undermined by the fact that it is based on only four instances. The conclusion that can be drawn from Table 3, nevertheless, is that the majority of the occurrences are produced by European Americans and African Americans. The presence of ZSRs in spoken American English can thus not be attributed to the language use of one single ethnic group like AAVE. The absence of ZSRs from all other ethnic groups is certainly noteworthy. The high frequency of ZSRs for which speaker ethnicity is not indicated certainly raises the question of the observer's paradox. Speakers for which there is no annotation available are likely to be passers by. They may therefore be less conscious of being recorded.

**Table 3**: Distribution of ZSRs over ethnic groups in spoken American English

| **Ethnicity** | **No of Words** | **ZSR (n)** | **ZSRs per 1 million words** |
|---|---|---|---|
| White | 2,493,493 | 55 | *22* |
| Not Indicated | 800,820 | 34 | 42 |
| Black/African-American | 145,989 | 4 | 27 |
| Other | 84,474 | 1 | 12 |
| Multiple/Mixed ethnicity | 67,520 | - | - |
| Chicano/Mexican-American | 59,884 | - | - |
| AmericanIndian/NativeAmerican | 56,280 | - | - |
| Latino/OtherHispanic | 54,893 | - | - |
| Filipino/Filipino-American | 22,967 | - | - |
| Polynesian/Pacific Islander | 13,424 | - | - |
| Chinese/Chinese-American | 11,397 | - | - |
| Korean/Korean-American | 10,874 | - | - |
| Japanese/Japanese-American | 8,319 | - | - |
| Puerto Rican | 1,446 | - | - |
| Arab/Arab-American | 404 | - | - |
| Viet/Thai/Other Asian | 347 | - | - |

Another interesting variable is the age of speakers presented in Table 4.

**Table 4**: Distribution of ZSRs in the LSAC according to age of speaker

| **age of speaker** | **n** | **Number of words** | **Freq. per 1 m words** |
|---|---|---|---|
| 0–14 | 1 | 46246 | 21.6 |
| 15–24 | 11 | 852081 | 12.9 |
| 25–34 | 18 | 803259 | 22.4 |
| 35–44 | 7 | 694733 | 10.0 |
| 45–59 | 19 | 889398 | 21.4 |
| 60+ | 10 | 295592 | 33.8 |

Here again no clear picture emerges. The highest frequency for the group 60+ might suggest that ZSRs are used more frequently by older speakers. However, the data for the other age groups doesn't support such a trend. The gender of speakers using ZSRs is remarkably even: female speakers with 19 instances per million words, and male speakers with 18 instances per million words. Nor is there any support for the hypothesis that speakers using ZSRs belong to a lower social class. In terms of occupation we find professors, graduate students, lawyers, bankers as well as a cashier and a seamstress who produce instances of ZSRs.

The analysis of social variables for the British data was more successful. This is to be expected given the higher number of instances available for a breakdown according to the individual social variables, firstly on speaker age. Table 5 shows the frequency of ZSRs according to age of speakers.

**Table 5**: Distribution of ZSRs in the BNC according to age of speaker

| age of speaker | n | frequency per 1 m words |
|---|---|---|
| 0-14 | 8 | 19.2 |
| 15-24 | 9 | 21.5 |
| 25-34 | 25 | 36.3 |
| 35-44 | 36 | 51.3 |
| 45-59 | 51 | 72.3 |
| 60+ | 49 | 74.2 |
| not available | 27 | 42.9 |

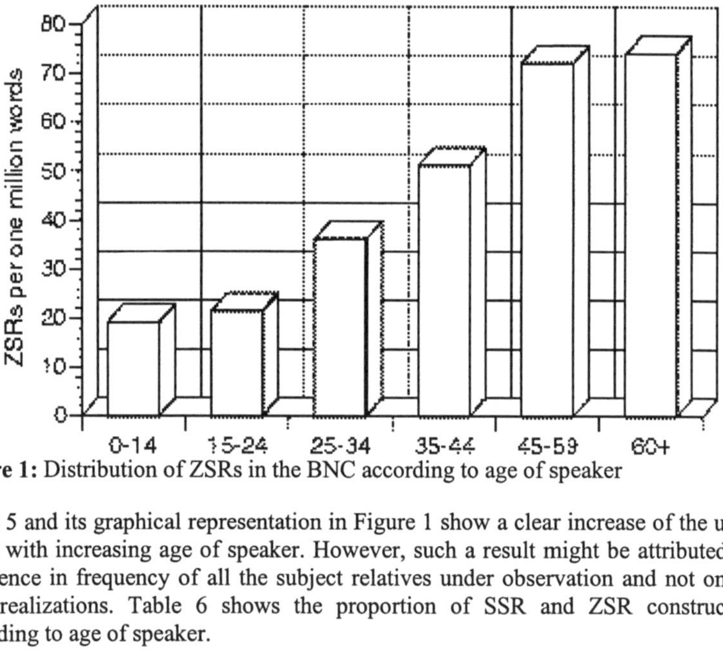


**Figure 1:** Distribution of ZSRs in the BNC according to age of speaker

Table 5 and its graphical representation in Figure 1 show a clear increase of the use of ZSRs with increasing age of speaker. However, such a result might be attributed to a difference in frequency of all the subject relatives under observation and not only to zero realizations. Table 6 shows the proportion of SSR and ZSR constructions according to age of speaker.

**Table 6**: Proportion SSRs and ZSRs according to age of speaker in the BNC

| | surface | | zero | |
|---|---|---|---|---|
| **age of speaker** | **n** | **%** | **n** | **%** |
| 0-14 | 95 | 92.2 | 8 | 7.8 |
| 15-24 | 114 | 92.7 | 9 | 7.3 |
| 25-34 | 223 | 89.9 | 25 | 10.1 |
| 35-44 | 248 | 87.3 | 36 | 12.7 |
| 45-59 | 246 | 82.8 | 51 | 17.2 |
| 60+ | 273 | 84.7 | 49 | 15.3 |

Table 6 shows that the trend observed in Table 5 and Figure 1 can't be attributed to subject relatives in general. Zero as a relativizer choice is still twice as frequent in the age group 60+ than in the age group 0–14. Figure 2 shows a graphical representation of the frequency information in Tables 4 and 5. It helps us to visualize both the distribution of subject relatives in general and the distribution of surface and zero variants.

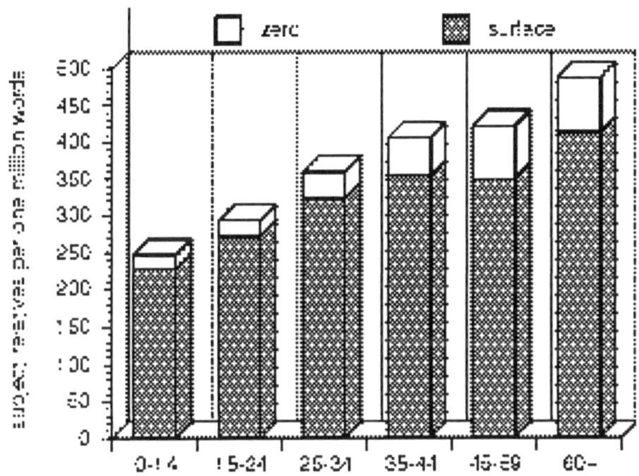


**Figure 2:** ZSRs and SSRs per one million words in the BNC

While the younger speakers certainly use fewer subject relatives, this cannot explain away the trend found in the distribution of ZSRs. This is documented by the proportion of realizations by zero, which increases with the age of speaker. Shnukal (1981: 322) comes to a similar conclusion for a dialect of Australian English.

The most important findings presented above are the difference between American English and British English and the fact that younger speakers use fewer ZSRs than older speakers. Given that, synchronically, language change is only observable as variation, a variation phenomenon like the realization form of subject relatives lends itself to speculation about an ongoing language change. On the assumption that language acquisition is completed at a certain age between 16 and 25, we may conclude that we are indeed observing an ongoing language change in British English, with an observable decrease of the use of ZSRs from the older to the younger generation. This is particularly important because variation and change do not mutually imply each other. While it is sound to extrapolate from ongoing language change to the presence of variation, the reverse does not hold. From observation of variation we may not extrapolate to the presence of language change. Variation phenomena can represent differences in registers, which may remain stable over time. Thus speaker age presents the only means of observing language change in synchronic corpora.

However, using speaker age for documenting language change is certainly not uncontroversial. Only under the assumption that language use remains stable after the phase of language acquisition can speaker age be used for documenting ongoing language change. Even if language acquisition is completed at the age of about 18, this does not necessarily mean that the frequency of use of the acquired repertoire remains stable over the course of an adult's life.

The finding that ZSRs are over five times more frequent in British English than in American English could mean that the same language change – loss of ZSRs –has progressed further in American English. This may have been caused by the large number of immigrants speaking Western European languages like German, French, Italian and Spanish, which only have overt relativizers.

## 7. Conclusion

Without a computerized algorithm it would have been virtually impossible to acquire the data presented in this study. I have shown that with a tag-based retrieval strategy it is indeed possible to locate zero elements like ZSRs in an electronic corpus. In addition, making use of the same computerized retrieval strategy for ZSRs and SSRs helped to ensure the consistency of the acquired data.

With the help of the retrieved data, I was able to show that ZSRs are still present in spoken American and British English of a fairly standard nature. Moreover, I found a sharp difference between American and British English. I also demonstrated that although ZSR constructions are frequently found with existentials and *it*-clefts, they are by no means limited to these constructions. These results as well as the distribution in terms of types can serve as a background for comparison with data found in regional dialects, sociolects and the language of ethnic groups. This is a great improvement over a situation where studies of small communities had to be compared with an idealized standard.

Together with results from historical linguistics, the data presented in this study lends support to the existence of a still ongoing language change involving the loss of ZSRs in British English. American English seems to have undergone the same language change and may indeed be ahead of British English.

## Notes

1 I am particularly grateful to Gunnel Tottie who provided material on AAVE, to Sebastian Hoffman, and to Robert Sigley, who most generously provided me with the material he found in New Zealand English in electronic form.

## References

Chevillet, François (1996). 'Relativization strategies in Early Middle English (and after)'. In Juhani Klemola, Merja Kytö and Matti Rissanen (eds) *Speech past and present*. Frankfurt am Main: Peter Lang. 321–328.

Dekeyser, Xavier (1984). 'Relativizers in early Modern English: A dynamic quantitative study'. In Jacek Fisiak (ed.) *Historical syntax. Trends in linguistics, studies and monographs* 23. Amsterdam: Mouton. 61–87.

Hackenberg, Robert H. (1972). *Appalachian English: a sociolinguistic study*. Thesis 5069. Georgetown University.
Harvie, Dawn (1998). *Tracking down old relatives: zero relatives in subject and non-subject function in Early African American English*. MA Thesis. Department of Linguistics, University of Ottawa.
Karlsson, Fred (ed.) (1995). *Constraint grammar: a language-independent system for parsing unrestricted text*. New York: Mouton de Gruyter.
Keenan, Edward and Bernard Comrie (1977). 'Noun phrase accessibility and universal grammar.' *Linguistic Inquiry* 8: 63–99.
Keenan, Edward and Bernard Comrie (1979). 'Data on the noun phrase accessibility hierarchy.' *Language* 55: 333–351.
Labov, William (1969). 'Contraction, deletion, and inherent variability of the English copula'. *Language* 45: 715–762.
Lehmann, Hans Martin (1997a). *Things nobody can see or hear: automatic retrieval of zero elements in a computerised corpus*. MA Thesis. University of Zurich.
Lehmann, Hans Martin (1997b). 'Automatic retrieval of zero elements in a computerised corpus'. In Magnus Ljung (ed.) *Corpus-based studies in English. Papers from the Seventeenth International Conference on English Language Research on Computerized Corpora*. Amsterdam: Rodopi. 179–194.
Lodge, David (1992). *Paradise news*. London: Penguin Books.
Mosley, Walter (1993). *White butterfly*. New York: Pocket Books.
Orton, Harold, Stewart Sanderson and John Widdowson (1978). *The linguistic atlas of England*. London: Croom Helm.
Quirk, Randolph (1957). 'Relative clauses in educated Spoken English'. *English Studies* 38: 97–109.
Quirk, Randolph, Sidney Greenbaum, Geoffrey Leech and Jan Svartvik (1985). *A comprehensive grammar of the English language*. London: Longman.
Shnukal, Anna (1981). 'There's a lot mightn't believe this... variable subject relative pronoun absence in Australian English'. In David Sankoff and Henrietta Cedergren (eds) *Variation omnibus*. Edmonton, Alberta: Linguistic Research Inc. 321–328.
Sigley, Robert (1997). *Choosing your relatives: relative clauses in New Zealand English*. Doctoral Thesis. Victoria University of Wellington.
Svartvik, Jan (1998). 'Varieties of English: major and minor'. In Hans Lindquist, Staffan Klintborg, Magnus Levin and Maria Estling (eds) *The major varieties of English: papers from MAVEN 97*. Växjö: Växjö University.
Tottie, Gunnel and Dawn Harvie (1999). 'It's all relative: relativization strategies in Early African American English.' In Shana Poplack (ed.) *The English history of African American English*. Oxford: Blackwell. 198–230.
Tottie, Gunnel and Hans Martin Lehmann (1999). 'The realization of relative adverbials in Present-Day British English'. In Hilde Hasselgård and Signe Oksefjell (eds) *Out of corpora: studies in honour of Stig Johansson*. 137–155
Visser, Fredericus Th. (1963). *An historical syntax of the English language*. Vol I . Leiden: E. J. Brill.

# Towards an analysis of pragmatic and stylistic features in 15th and 17th century English letters

*Manfred Markus*

University of Innsbruck

## Abstract

*A special sub-corpus of 84 letters from the* Innsbruck Letter Corpus *(1386 to 1688) was compiled with equal amounts of male and female correspondence of the 15th and 17th centuries, so that they could be analysed contrastively in terms of both gender and time. The purpose of the paper is twofold: (1) In terms of method, it attempts to prove that normalisation is indispensable for retrieval, at least in the case of Middle English and Early Modern English. (2) As a contribution to gender studies, the paper contrasts some pragmatic and stylistic features of the language of women and men, and of the language of the 15th and 17th century. Those analysed are deictic expressions, markers of emphasis, expressions of feeling, and metamessages, as expressed in formulaic* I hope, I fear, *etc., and pragmatic signals of self-expression and of appeal. The analysis reveals a few characteristic differences between the two centuries, but its main finding is that women generally show more empathy in their letters, using the channel of communication more actively, more intuitively, and more cooperatively.*

## 1. Introduction

### 1.1 State of the art in corpus-based historical English studies

One of the general deficiencies of many historical English studies is their lack of a corpus linguistic basis.[1] In spite of the keen endeavours of scholars such as Matti Rissanen and others to combine historical English studies and corpus linguistics (cf., for example, Hickey, Kytö, Lancashire and Rissanen 1997), the relationship between the two fields is hardly more than tentative, and far from being a 'happy marriage'. In particular, Middle English and Early Modern English texts have been dealt with in eclectic ways, with good examples of a point being gleaned from the material available, either with or without the help of the computer. But the potential of machine-readable texts has not yet been fully utilised.[2] For studies of the Middle and Early Modern English periods, based on the Helsinki Corpus, the Corpus of Early English Correspondence (CEEC), or the Innsbruck Letter Corpus,[3] the lack of tagged versions of the corpora concerned has caused considerable problems of retrieval.

As a result, the questions raised so far have been limited in scope and complexity; in particular, they have been restricted to formally marked units, typically words.[4] Many scholars, including the present author (2000), have taken refuge in WordCruncher index lists and in subsequent manual searches.[5] But this seems a very provisional response to the challenge of Middle and Early Modern English corpora, which consists in their idiosyncratic use of language and hence their inaccessibility.

### 1.2 The special demands of historical English corpora

English texts from 1100 to 1600, unless revised and 'improved' by a later benevolent editor, are extremely different from present-day English in their use of dialect[6], their typically unconventional spelling, the repercussions of the copying process (such as dialect mixture and inconsistency of spelling or lexis) and, finally, in their idiolectal features, all due to the lack of modern norms.

In order to enable us to use such corpus texts in a machine-readable way, they must be prepared for analysis. This preparation is no trivial matter and needs to be made explicit. It presupposes broad philological familiarity with the historical conditions of texts, for example, with medieval grammar and spelling habits[7]. Moreover, the texts have to be prepared so as to support the scholarly needs of particular research studies.

## 2. Preparation of the corpus for analysis

### 2.1 Selection

For the present purpose of investigating gender issues, a corpus of available texts first had to be selected. In order to compare the language used by men and women, the texts from the inventory of the Innsbruck Letter Corpus had to be sampled in appropriate quantities (between 8,317 and 8,972 words) and according to date, the aim being to compare the 15th century texts with those of the 17th, and the letters of women with those of men. The letters, listed in detail below in the Appendix, cover roughly the same time span.[8]

### 2.2 Normalisation

I have argued elsewhere (Markus 1997, 1999, 2000), that normalisation is necessary in order for us to render Middle English and Early Modern English texts ready for access by the machine. Obviously, the tagging procedure added to the Helsinki Corpus at Penn State University is also based on initial normalisation, namely manual normalisation. In this study I have applied the 'Trans' program introduced earlier (1997), and then proof-read the normalised lines. The procedure results in 'doubledecker' texts like these:

$I TO myn welbelovid sone. I great yow well, and avyse yow to
$N To mine wellbeloved son. I greet you well, and advise you to
(Agnes Paston 1445)
$I S=r= -- Doctor Barker has put my sister into a cours of ientell fisek
$N Sir – Doctor Barker has put my sister into a course of gentle physique
(Brilliana Harley 1625)

The advantage of this normalisation procedure is that the user always has access back to the original line. This is more than a mere question of convenience. The correspondence I dealt with turned out to be often erratic in style and line of thought, so that frequent recurrence to the original text was necessary. The normalised lines can be considered as a starting point for various other preparatory procedures imposed on the corpus texts which all run under the heading of 'tagging'.

## 2.3 Selective tagging

The various approaches to tagging and the different systems used, for example by LOB, the Lancaster tagging system, TOSCA (cf. Aarts and Oostdijk 1997), the International Corpus of English (ICE, cf. Greenbaum 1993) and the University of Penn State (Kroch and Taylor 2000), reflect the basic theoretical difficulties involved in tagging (not to mention parsing). The question is: Tagging for what?

In principle, we can distinguish the tagging of morphemes, words or parts of speech, including multi-word expressions, as well as syntactic units – i.e. phrases, clauses and sentences – and their structural features, and finally stylistic, pragmatic and/or sociolinguistic features. The tagging may be more surface-oriented (as in the case of ICE; cf. Greenbaum 1993: 16) or deep-structure oriented, as in the case of Penn State. Short corpora or shorter subsets of corpora selected for a specific analysis are preferably tagged without undue energy being invested in linguistic theory or the automatisation of the tagging process.

In the present case it therefore seemed advisable to tag only a target-oriented selection of features, namely those that were of possible interest for distinguishing the language of women from that of men. Machine-tagging is, of course, not rejected in principle, particularly on the level of word types, but it cannot be fully trusted; moreover, it is not needed in the present case.

Apart from this question of the need for tags, one has to decide on the mode of tagging. A basic problem concerning the mode is whether all the tags, no matter what linguistic level they refer to, should go into one single tagged version, or whether they should be kept apart in different versions tagged for morphological, lexical, syntactic and other features. If the tagging procedure can be reliably done automatically, one tagged version is no doubt the better option. But as long as the tags have to be proof-read, the limitation of tags according to a specific linguistic level and the production of different tagged versions seem a necessity, since a text tagged for all possible purposes is too complex and confusing a structure to be reliably proof-read. In the present case I have therefore produced two separate tagged texts, one for syntactic features[9] and the other for pragmatic and stylistic features.

Taking this particular care, both as to the number of tagged levels and their separation, may seem unnecessary from the point of view of synchronic corpus linguistics. With historical texts it is clearly appropriate – as may be illustrated by the following example, the initial address in a letter by Elizabeth Stonor (No. 49: 1476):

(1) Right reverent and worshipful and entirely best beloved Cousin.

To begin with, the word *right* is of morphological interest, Like *best* – it is a zero-marked adverb (Right_ADV0); semantically, it is an emphasiser, like *entirely* and *best*, and since emphasis can be expected to be an important feature of a semi-oral text type such as letters, it should be tagged (thus: Right_EMPRIGHT). Syntactically, *right* is of course headed by the adjective *reverent* within an adjectival phrase, so that we need the tag: (Right reverent)_ADJP. Within the wider context the ADJP is part of the noun phrase headed by the noun *Cousin*; accordingly, the whole address would have to be bracketed and marked as an NP, which, for its part, should, pragmatically, be marked as a vocative (VOC) and, stylistically, as a case of emphasis by synonyms (EMPSYN). Needless to say, the adjectival phrase *entirely best beloved* should also be marked, since it nourishes the grammarian's suspicion or knowledge that pre-nominal adjectival phrases were allowed to be more complex in the 15th century than in PD English.

Our address line, burdened with the different types of tags all in one version, looks like this:

$R ((((((((Right_ADV0_ADV_EMPRIGHT reverent_ADJ)_ADJP)_ID)_EMPALLI and_CON (worshipful_ADJ))_ADJP_EMPD and_CON ((entirely_ADV_EMPFULL best_ADV_ADV0_ADJSUP_EMPSUP beloved_ADJ))_ADJP_ID)_EMPSYN cousin_NPROP))_NP_VOC_FOR

The complexity and overlapping of the different types of tags can be disentangled by what we can call a multi-level tagging system:

$I Right Reverent and Worshipfull and enteirly best belovyd Cosyn
$N Right reverent and worshipful and entirely best beloved cousin
$M Right_ADV0 reverent and worshipful and entirely best_ADV0_ADJSUP beloved cousin
$W (Right_ADV reverent_ADJ)_ID and_CON worshipful_ADJ and_CON (entirely_ADV best_ADV beloved_ADJ)_ID cousin_NPROP
$P ((Right reverent)_ADJP and (worshipful)_ADJP and (entirely best beloved)_ADJP cousin)_NP
$S (Right reverent and worshipful and entirely best beloved cousin)_VOC
$R ((((Right_EMPRIGHT reverent)_EMPALLI and worshipful)_EMPD and entirely_EMPFULL best_EMPSUP beloved)_EMPSYN cousin)_VOC_FOR

The abbreviations stand for:

$I input text
$N normalised form
$M morphological analysis
$W words, i.e. parts of speech
$P phrases
$S syntax
$R the rest, i.e. a selection of semantics, pragmatics and stylistics

Our original line '$I' (for *input*), shows up on the screen in altogether seven different versions. With the help of a *Visual Basic* program written for the purpose[10], any of the seven lines can be fore- or backgrounded in WINWORD, depending on the user's needs, as follows (on the screen in colour):

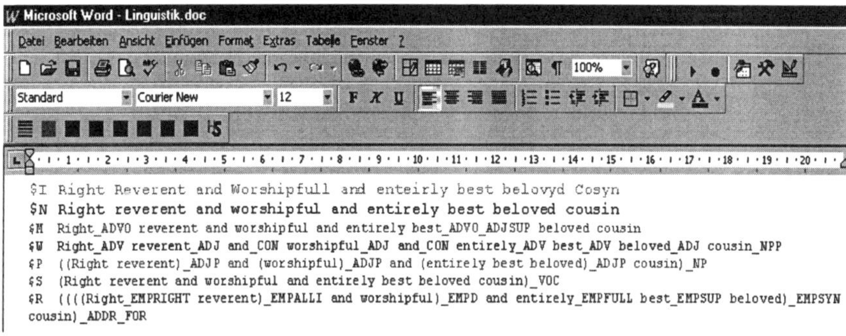


**Figure 1:** The seven correlative lines of Visual Basic

The highlighting with a button of special lines and, thus, of parameters allows the semi-automatic retrieval of special features, either for direct analysis or for the production of the tags on the other levels. The correlation of the seven lines encourages automatisation to some extent on those levels allowing it, and then well-focused, machine-supported manual work on the other levels according to need.

## 3. Pragmatics and style

On the basis of this method of analysis, a great many insights into Late ME and EModE have emerged, too many for them all to be discussed here. The features that were tagged and analysed are those that are remarkable from the point of view of present-day English. They can be seen from the following list of Table 1:

**Table 1:** Tags and frequencies of pragmatic and stylistic features

| | | | W15 | M15 | W17 | M17 | W:M | 15:17 |
|---|---|---|---|---|---|---|---|---|
| 1 | **DEI** | *deixis*: this, that, these, those, here, there, now, then, yesterday, today, tomorrow, so, thus | 180 | 161 | 277 | 219 | 457/380 | 341/496 |
| 2 | **DEIT** | *in-the-text deixis*: where, wherefore, whereby, etc. | 17 | 28 | 15 | 28 | 32/56 | 45/43 |
| 3 | **ME** | I, me, my, mine, we, us, our, ours | 413 | 471 | 613 | 478 | 1096/949 | 884/1091 |
| 4 | **YOU** | you, your, yours | 300 | 274 | 340 | 272 | 640/546 | 574/612 |
| 5 | **EMP** | *emphasis* | 188 | 149 | 155 | 85 | 343/234 | 337/240 |
| 6 | **EMPALL** | *emphasis by* all, ever, evermore | 28 | 59 | 53 | 35 | 81/94 | 87/88 |
| 7 | **EMPALLI** | *alliteration* | 1 | 3 | - | 1 | 1/4 | 4/1 |
| 8 | **EMPDP** | *emphasis by doublet* | 31 | 25 | 5 | 4 | 36/29 | 56/9 |

| | | | | | | | | |
|---|---|---|---|---|---|---|---|---|
| | | *pairs* | | | | | | |
| 9 | **EMPDO** | *periphrastic* to do *for emphasis* | 2 | - | 2 | - | 4/- | 2/2 |
| 10 | **EMPN** | *emphasis by multiple negation* | 9 | 9 | - | 1 | 9/10 | 18/1 |
| 11 | **EMPREP** | *emphasis by repetition* | 6 | 1 | 1 | 1 | 7/2 | 7/2 |
| 12 | **EMPRIGHT** | *emphasis by* right *(adv.)* | 39 | 19 | - | 1 | 39/20 | 58/1 |
| 13 | **EMPSUP** | *emphasis by superlative (incl. double superlative)* | 21 | 12 | 29 | 19 | 50/31 | 33/48 |
| 14 | **EMPVERY** | *emphasis by* very, verily, sore, full(y), entirely, truly, indeed, utterly, mightily, heartily, particularly, specially | 57 | 25 | 59 | 23 | 116/48 | 82/82 |
| 15 | **FEAR** | (I) fear, I am afraid | - | 4 | 3 | - | 3/4 | 4/3 |
| 16 | **HOPE** | (I) hope/hoped/hoping | 6 | 1 | 26 | 13 | 32/14 | 7/39 |
| 17 | **IMP** | *imperative* | 13 | 17 | 19 | 29 | 32/46 | 30/48 |
| 18 | **INT** | *interjection* | 15 | 13 | 6 | 4 | 21/17 | 28/10 |
| 19 | **KIND** | kind(er/-est), kindness | 3 | - | 9 | 3 | 12/3 | 3/12 |
| 20 | **PRAY** | (I) pray/request/ask/beg/ beseech/wish | 31 | 32 | 50 | 23 | 81/55 | 63/83 |
| 21 | **THANK** | (I) thank/thanked/thanks/ thanking | 13 | 8 | 21 | 4 | 34/12 | 21/25 |
| 22 | **VOC** | *vocative* | 52 | 11 | 32 | 33 | 84/44 | 63/65 |

As regards the evaluation of these data, I can here only give a small selection.

### 3.1 Deixis

Deictic expressions relate to the spatial, temporal and personal aspects of a given utterance situation (Reichenbach 1947). Intuitively, one would expect the women's letters in our corpus to contain more deictic markers than the men's, since a first reading of the letters suggests that women are more concerned with the topics of everyday life around them, rather than business and state affairs.

The general picture presented by the figures confirms this impression. There are 2,123 signals of deixis[11] in the women's letters from both centuries, as opposed to 1,875 in the men's. This difference is not particularly striking, because it is supported by data from the 17th century only[12].

Moreover, the 15th century figures for both sexes are considerably lower than those for the 17th century, namely 1801:2208, a ratio of roughly 4:5.

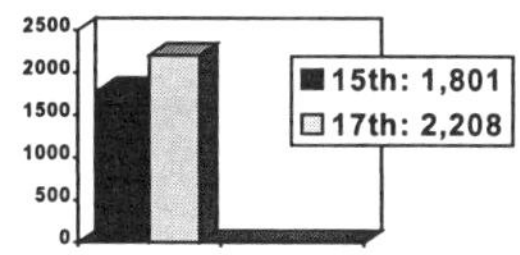


**Figure 2:** Deixis (century-specific)

How can this difference be explained? While all the letters included in our corpus are 'personal' letters, the interpretation of what 'personal' means is different in terms of the two centuries concerned. The Paston and the Stonor women were widely concerned with local politics and its impact on their or their husbands' properties, and only rarely with more personal questions such as health, relationships and gifts. In the women's letters of the 17th century, the ratio of what we could call private matters to public affairs is probably the reverse: questions of friendship and personal feelings predominate.

In splitting the figures for spatial/temporal and personal deixis, however, we come back to gender-specific results. A possible reason why the figures for deixis in the women's letters of the 15th century are about the same as those for men, is that the men are more concerned with themselves. Men's variants of the first-person pronoun, all of which I have tagged as 'ME', amount to 471 (vs. 413 with the women)[13]; see Figure 3:

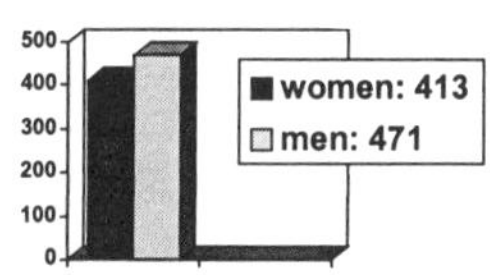


**Figure 3:** *ME* in 15th century letters

In the 17th century, however, where male self-centredness might be expected to continue, the equivalent figures prove the opposite: men refer to themselves less (478 times) than the women (613); see Figure 4:

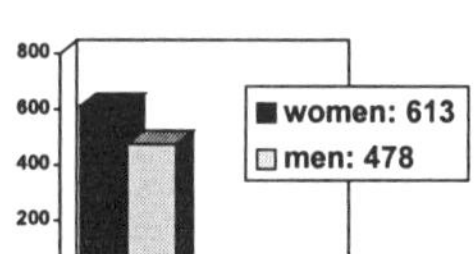


**Figure 4:** *ME* (first person) in 17th century letters

Along with these contrasting results, the letter writers' concern with their addressees, as mirrored in the use of second-person pronoun forms, is also of interest, and likewise found more often in the women's letters. The hypothesis that women 'talk to' other people more (in their letters or in general), whereas men tend to 'talk about' themselves or about things, cannot be so easily proved at the present time. But for the 15th century it can: women are more concerned about men than vice versa. Or, to put it in a less facetious way, women address their recipients (mostly men) making more use of second-person pronouns: 300 times in our letter collection of the 15th century (cf. men: 274), and 340 times in that of the 17th century (cf. men: 272); see Figures 5 and 6:

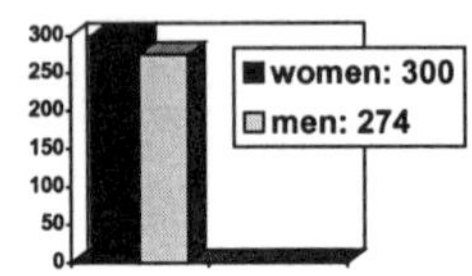


**Figure 5:** *YOU* (second person) in 15th century letters

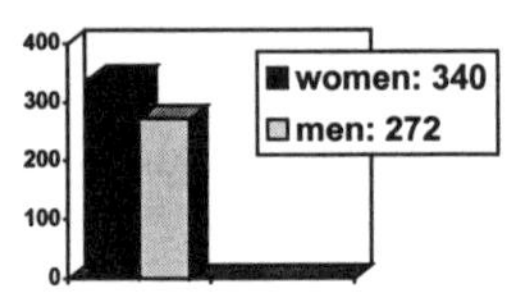


**Figure 6:** *YOU* (second person) in 17th century letters

Summing up the results of the use of ME and YOU as sememes, we can conclude that there is a clear trend towards male self-reference in the 15th century letters, but in the 17th the figures indicate that the women were more concerned both with themselves and their addressees, i.e. with personal relationships.

## 3.2 Emphasis

Emphatic forms of expression can be traced both in syntax – in the form of repetition or redundancy – and in semantics, in the form of hyperbole. They are, in any case, a stylistic feature typical of oral, above all colloquial, style, and could thus be expected in personal letters. While we may suspect that women have a particular predilection for emphatic expressions, the results on deixis show that at least the women of the 15th century were more sober and down-to-earth, perhaps due to economic necessity,[14] than later centuries would suggest.

The subtypes of emphasis that I have counted (cf. Table 1 items 5–14) and that were of relevance in the statistics[15] are the following:

(a) *all, ever, evermore* as adjectives or adverbs: *both for that matter and for* ***all*** *other*; *the best that* ***ever*** *he had*; *in my most hearty wise* ***evermore*** *thanking you*

(b) (formulaic) word pairs/doublets: *(he) will do that he can or may*

(c) multiple negation: *if he has not done, **nor will not** amend*
(d) repetition: *I understand that you somewhat amended and shall every day **better and better***
(e) *right* as a frequent, now obscured adverb: *to my **right** worshipful husband*
(f) superlatives with *most* or *-est*: *the **most despicable** wise*
(g) diverse lexical means (adverbs): *sore, very, full(y), entirely, truly, et al.*: *that I may **verily** know he does his duty*

The figures obtained show that, all in all, women were in fact more emphatic in their letters (343:234), and that writers in the 15th century were fonder of emphasis than in the 17th (337:240); see Figures 7 and 8:

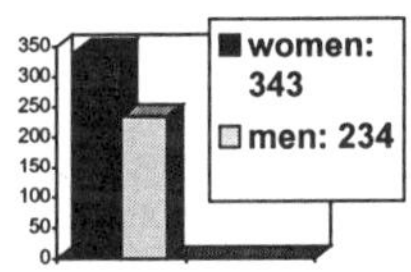


**Figure 7:** Overall expressions of emphasis used by men and women

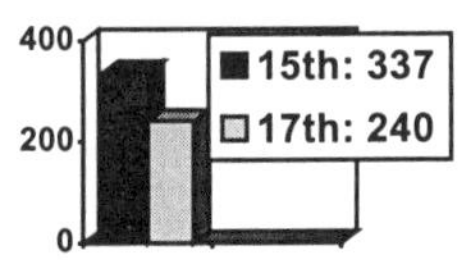


**Figure 8:** Expressions of emphasis in 15th and 17th century letters

The detailed figures for particular means of emphasis reveal both gender- and century-specific divergence. In the group of lexical emphasisers (or intensifiers; cf. Quirk et al. 1985: 583–603) *right* was the one that women were particularly fond of in the 15th century (39:19) and that had practically vanished by the 17th (1 occurrence); see Figures 9 and 10:

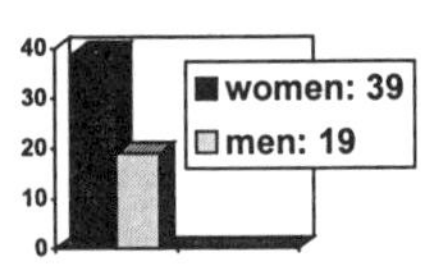


**Figure 9:** *right* (adv.): in 15th century letters

**Figure 10:** *right* (adv.): in 15th and 17th century letters

Emphasis by synonymous or formulaic doublet pairs, to which we could add the few alliterative formulae, was a stylistic feature that 15th century authors generally indulged in. The women represent the taste of the time with a few more instances (31:25); see Figure 11:

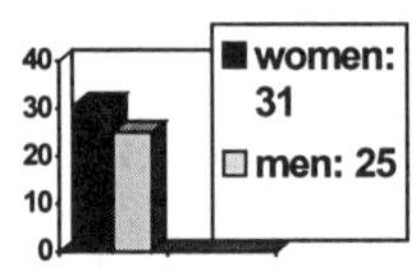


**Figure 11:** doublet pairs (15th century only)

Again, the 17th century largely did away with this habit. Category (g), listed last in the EMP category in Table 1 above, includes various lexical emphasisers from *very* to *heartily*; they are covered by the tag EMPVERY. The figures in this section confirm our general impression that women in both centuries were more fond of emphatic expressions than their male counterparts (116:48). The total figures for the two centuries, by the way, reveal the steady continuation of this feature (82:82).

Superlatives were also more frequently used by women than by men (50:31), but in this case, the 17th century shows an increase in the popularity of the category: 33 occurrences in the 15th century vs 48 in the 17th.

Finally, the syntactic category of double or multiple negation should be mentioned. As is well-known, this stylistic feature is still occasionally used in colloquial language today. However, our figures reveal that it was much more part and parcel of the language system in the 15th century, used by both sexes with the same rate of frequency (9:9). Its almost total absence in the 17th century (only one occurrence) confirms this interpretation: the logic of rationalism rejected it as a means of rhetorical emphasis, and women obviously submitted to this as much as men.

### 3.3 Fear, hope and other feelings

Guided by prejudice, I wondered if certain emotional terms and speech acts play a greater role in the women's letters than in those written by men[16]. The texts were tagged for the following semantic features (including morphological variants):

FEAR: *I/we fear*; *afraid*
HOPE: *I/we hope*; *hoping*; *hopes*
KIND: *kind(est)*, *kindness*
PRAY: *I pray*, *request*, *ask*, *beg*, *beseech*
THANK: *I thank/thanks/thanking*

After the analysis I had to stand partly corrected: hope, kindness, praying and thanking have or had a higher rank in women's writing, but fear did not. The ratios of occurrence for the two centuries are:

**Table 2:** Expression of feelings by women and men (data from 15th and 17th century letters)

| | **women** | **men** |
|---|---|---|
| HOPE | 32 | 14 |
| KIND | 12 | 3 |
| PRAY | 81 | 55 |
| THANK | 34 | 12 |
| FEAR | 3 | 4 |

I tried out other sememes of a similar kind, such as PLEASE, LOVE, WISH, but they turned out to be insignificant in number. On the basis of the output figures above, however, it seems fair to conclude that there are gender differences in the letters as regards the expression of feelings (except for FEAR) and/or the expression of 'metamessages' (Tannen 1992: 13). For it should not be forgotten that formulaic phrases such as *I hope, I pray, I am afraid* cannot always be interpreted as expressions of feeling, but are often metacommunicative signals of selective highlighting. Letters, including those of the Innsbruck Letter Corpus, deserve a more thorough analysis along sociolinguistic lines such as these.

Suffice it to say here that the expression of feelings and of metacommunicative signals both seem to have increased from the 15th to the 17th century, since the output ratio for the five sememes combined is 98 (15th century): 162 (17th century); see Figure 12:

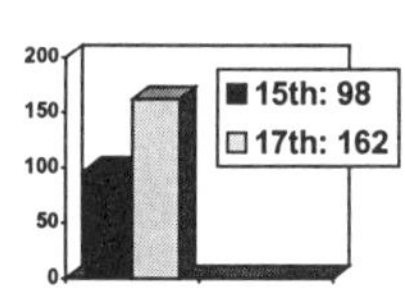


**Figure 12:** Expression of feelings in 15th and 17th century letters

### 3.4 Pragmatic signals of self-expression and of appeal

Of the three semiotic functions (Bühler 1982), the **expressive** and **appellative** play a special, text-type-specific role in letters, since the **referential** (referring to objects and states of affairs) seems to be only part of the purpose of writing letters; equally important are self-expression and appeals to the recipient. In the following, three markers of these two functions will be described: interjections, imperatives and vocatives.

Interjections are groups of words which stand outside the syntactic frame of a sentence and 'express feelings, curses, and wishes or are used to initiate conversation' (Bussman 1996). In the letters of the Innsbruck Corpus, many of the interjections refer or appeal to God, such as *God knows; God willing; God be loved*, etc. The most common is *by God's grace* or *by the grace of God*; but there are, of course, also secular interjections, such as *alas*, *I trust,* and *indeed.*

When it comes to quantifying them, slightly more occurrences of interjections can be found in the texts written by women than in those by men (21:17); however, interjections were strongly favoured in the 15th century correspondence, but less popular in the 17th. The comparative figures are 28:10; see Figures 13 and 14:

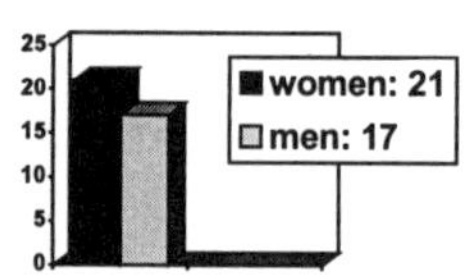


**Figure 13:** Interjections used by women and men

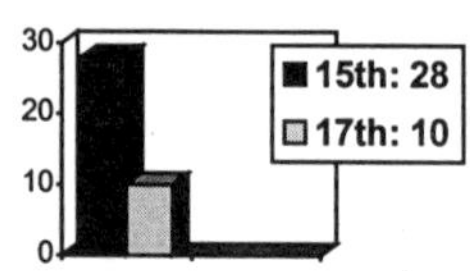


**Figure 14:** Interjections used in correspondence from the 15th and 17th centuries

In view of the strongly religious element in the interjections, this strong decrease over time could be tentatively connected with the role of Protestantism in 17th century England, though 'pious' talk in fixed phrases is certainly no Catholic prerogative.

Imperatives are not the only way of expressing how one wishes the recipient would behave, but they are the most direct. Since they are zero-marked, they must be retrieved manually. In some cases they are difficult to identify as against embedded non-finite or finite clauses. For example, in the complex sentence *I pray [that] you remember* (W17), where the conjunction *that* (added in the normalised version of the text), has been omitted. Another variant is *I pray you to bring* (W15), where *you* has been raised. But in *I pray you, Sir, send down no silk* (W17) we are undoubtedly confronted with an imperative. The borderline between the different syntactic categories seems fluid. In addition to this syntactic problem, the question may arise as to whether an imperative form introduced by *pray* is pragmatically as good or bad as one without it, or as any other. Women, we found earlier in this paper (Section 3.3. above), used formulaic *pray* more than men, particularly in the 17th century, and on closer inspection many of these forms are combined with imperatives, obviously with the aim of hedging them. Finally, the 'logic' of imperatives must be seen as depending on whether the command is contextually to the advantage of the speaker or to that of the recipient. When Dorothy Osborne writes to her husband, 'My dear, dear heart, **make** haste home, I so want thee', the imperative is, exceptionally, not an impolite or face-threatening linguistic category.

In spite of these imponderables connected with the use of imperative forms, the frequency data allow an evaluative interpretation. Which gender, then, dominates in the use of imperatives? Yes, women were more reticent in issuing commands: the overall ratio of female to male imperatives is 32:46[17]; see Figure 15:

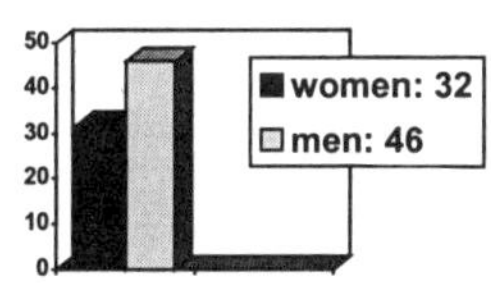


**Figure 15:** Imperatives used by men and women in their correspondence

There is an even more marked difference between the 15th and 17th century letters in the use of imperatives, with a ratio of 30:48. The low figure for the 15th century – an age of violence and with a social hierarchy as great as the 17th – could be explained in terms of the availability of other constructions as substitutes. The subjunctive was still available, as used when Agnes Paston, in the first letter of the corpus, says to her son Edmond: 'God **make** you right a good man'; and at the beginning of the same letter she avoids an imperative by giving advice: '(I) advise you to think once of the day of your father's counsel to learn the law'.

One final point of pragmatics should be discussed, which is the use of vocatives. On one occasion Margaret Paston takes sides with her son, pleading for his sake in a letter to her husband. How does she put it? 'For God's sake, **Sir**, have pity on him ...' The function of the vocative *Sir* parallels that of the interjection *For God's sake*, in that both are meant to claim the attention of the addressee. In Quirk et al.'s (1985: 773) terminology, this type of vocative is, more specifically, a 'call' rather than an 'address', with the latter subtype being used to express 'the speaker's relationship or attitude to the person or persons addressed'. But the difference does not matter much for our present purpose. In either case the speaker emphasises the appealing function of their language to gain the addressee's attention. We are again in the domain of metamessages.

The frequency figures for vocatives in the four subcorpora again confirm what feminist critics of language – from Robin Lakoff to Deborah Tannen and Deborah

Cameron[18] – have known all along: women are the more cooperative communicants (cf. Cameron 1998: 274–5). In the women's letters over the two centuries, there are 84 vocatives, as against only 44 in the men's. Taking the figures for the 15th century only, the gender difference is even more striking: 52 vs 11[19]; see Figure 16:

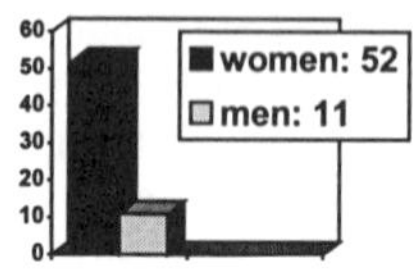


**Figure 16:** Vocatives in 15th century letters by women and men

## 4. Conclusion

This paper's interest in the gender question was partly a means to an end; my initial and second concern was to show what preparatory measures are necessary for us to render a late ME or EModE corpus accessible for machine-readable analysis. The accessibility, like the normalisation and tagging permitting it, can hardly be complete at this stage. While working with the normalised texts, I was forced to recognise repeatedly that my initial interpretation of the original text was false, or that a passage that I was first unable to make sense of was really quite simple. In synchronic linguistics the language system is ever-available as a frame of reference to corpus linguists, whereas a historical corpus, particularly one before 1600, conceals its language system to some extent. It seems therefore to be the task of corpus linguists to define the implicit linguistic system of a text hypothetically, either from the point of view of present-day English or Chaucerian English, and to test these hypotheses on a quantitative basis. Within this hermeneutical approach (to put it philosophically), the appropriate tagging procedure seems to be a multi-level tagging, allowing for later additions or revisions and, above all, for recourse to the original text when needed.

In this paper I have focussed on a few pragmatic and stylistic features. The results revealed that there are some characteristic differences between the two centuries analysed: the 15th century correspondents use emphasis to the same extent that those of the 17th century indulge in deixis. But the main result was that women in their letters generally reveal more empathy, using the channel of communication more actively, more inventively, and more cooperatively.

## Notes

1 Görlach's well-known introductions (1982 and 1991) and the papers delivered on the most recent International Conference of English Historical Linguistics in Santiago de Compostela, 7–11 September 2000 (cf. www.usc.es/ia303/11icehl/11icehl.htm) give some evidence of the validity of my statement. An MLA CD-ROM query over the last forty years on 'corpus linguistics' combined with 'historical English' provides only three hits.

2 Most of the papers presented on the topic of historical English at previous ICAME conferences or in separate publications refer either to Old English or to English after 1600.

3 See Kohnen (1997), Raumolin-Brunberg (1994), and the great number of papers based on the Helsinki Corpus and the CEEC.

4 This is particularly obvious in the case of the articles in Nevalainen and Raumolin-Brunberg (1996), based on the CEEC, e.g. Nevalainen in her otherwise exemplary paper on 'gender difference'.

5 Cf. Raumolin-Brunberg (1994: 160).

6 This is particularly true of Middle English; the standardization of the late 15th century caused dialects to be less relevant, comparatively speaking.

7 In Nevalainen's paper, mentioned above (1996: 80–82), for example, the word form *be*, which is statistically counted as a dialectal variant of *are*, can also be either the subjunctive of *to be* or a spelling variant of the preposition *by*.

8 Letters of women, 15th century: 1445–76; 17th century: 1625–98. Letters of men, 15th century: 1426–78; 17th century: 1613–88.

9 This was used for a similar gender-specific analysis but based on grammar; see Markus (2001).

10 I am obliged to Roland Mann and Christoph Praxmarer (English Department, University of Innsbruck) for writing this program.

11 I have abstained from including in-the-text deixis, as expressed in the formula *the said N* and similar phrases (*aforesaid*, etc.), because they do not give evidence of situational contextuality.

12 For the 17th century alone, the figures of frequency are 1227 (women): 981 (men). For the 15th century, the equivalent figures are 893:908.

13 The evidence of self-centredness is even more striking in a close-up analysis excluding the first-person plural and its inflected forms (*we, us, our, ours*), since these could include the addressee.

14 The toughness of business affairs in the 15th century is pointed out in Gairdner (1986), 'Introduction'.

15 I found only five cases of emphasis by alliterative formulae, e.g. in 'all imaginable **care and caution**'. Emphatic *to do* in affirmative non-interrogative clauses likewise occurs, but in only four cases altogether.

16 I counted only those cases in which the key words refer to the speaker/writer and are not part of a reporting passage about a third person.

17 Listing the centuries separately, the ratios are: 15th century: 12:17; 17th century: 19:29.

18 A good recent survey of the research on feminist critique of language is offered in the reader by Cameron (1998).

19 The fact that the figures for the 17th century are practically the same for both sexes (32:33) is likely to be influenced by the decidedly larger number of letters that I incorporated in the men's corpus of the 17th century than in the corresponding women's corpus, since the men's letters were generally shorter. As regards the number of vocatives, it can be assumed that the initial addresses, as regularly used at least once in all the letters, have an impact on the statistical output.

## References

Aarts, Jan, and Nelleke Oostdijk (1997). 'Handling discourse elements in syntax'. In Udo Fries, Viviane Müller, and Peter Schneider (eds) *From Aelfric to the New York Times. Studies in English corpus linguistics*. Amsterdam: Rodopi. 107–123.

Bussmann, Hadumod (1996). *Routledge dictionary of language and linguistics*. Gregory P. Trauth and Kerstin Kazzazi (eds). London: Routledge.

Bühler, Karl (1982) [1932]. *Semiotic foundations of language theory*. Tr. R.E. Innis. New York: Plenum Press.

Cameron, Deborah (ed.) (1998). *The feminist critique of language. A reader*. 2nd ed. London: Routledge.

Gairdner, James (ed.) (1986). *The Paston letters*. Gloucester: Alan Sutton Publishing.

Görlach, Manfred (1982). *Einführung in die englische Sprachgeschichte*. Zweite, überarbeitete Auflage. Heidelberg: Quelle & Meyer.

Görlach, Manfred (1991). *Introduction to Early Modern English*. Cambridge: Cambridge University Press.

Greenbaum, Sidney (1993). 'The tagset for the International Corpus of English'. In Clive Souter and Eric Atwell (eds) *Corpus-based computational linguistics*. Amsterdam: Rodopi. 11–24.

Hickey, Raymond, Merja Kytö, Ian Lancashire, and Matti Rissanen (eds) (1997). 'Tracing the trail of time'. *Proceedings from the Second Diachronic Corpora Workshop. New College, University of Toronto, Toronto, May 1995*. Amsterdam: Rodopi.

Kohnen, Thomas (1997). 'Text type evolution and diachronic corpora: historical writing in the history of English'. In Magnus Ljung (ed.) *Corpus-based studies in English. Papers from the Seventeenth International Conference on English Language Research on Computerized Corpora (ICAME 17). Stockholm, May 15–19, 1996*. Amsterdam/Atlanta, GA: Rodopi. 153–166.

Kroch, Anthony and Ann Taylor (2000). http://www.ling.upenn.edu/mideng/

Markus, Manfred (1997). 'Normalization of Middle English prose: Possibilities and limits'. In Magnus Ljung (ed.) *Corpus-based studies in English. Papers from the Seventeenth International Conference on English Language Research on Computerized Corpora (ICAME 17). Stockholm, May 15–19, 1996.* Amsterdam/Atlanta, GA: Rodopi. 211–226.

Markus, Manfred (1999). 'Getting to grips with chips and Middle English text variants: sampling *Ancrene Riwle* and *Hali Meidenhad*'. *ICAME Journal* 23: 35–51.

Markus, Manfred (2000). 'Normalizing the word forms in *The Ayenbite of Inwyt*'. In Irma Taavitsainen, Terttu Nevalainen, Paivi Pahta, and Matti Rissanen (eds) *Placing Middle English in context. Proceedings from the Second International Conference on Middle English in Helsinki, May 29 – June 1, 1997*. New York: Mouton de Gruyter. 181–198.

Markus, Manfred (2001). 'The development of prose in Early Modern English in view of the gender question: using grammatical idiosyncrasies of 15th and 17th century letters'. In Lilo Moessner (ed.) *Early Modern English text types*. Lisse: Swets & Zeitlinger. 181–196

Nevalainen, Terttu (1996). 'Gender Difference'. In Nevalainen, Terttu, and Helena Raumolin-Brunberg (eds) *Sociolinguistics and language history. Studies based on the Corpus of Early English Correspondence*. Amsterdam, etc.: Rodopi. 77–91.

Quirk, Randolph, Sidney Greenbaum, Geoffrey Leech, and Jan Svartvik (1985). *A comprehensive grammar of the English language*. London: Longman.

Raumolin-Brunberg, Helena (1994). 'The position of adjectival modifiers in Late Middle English noun phrases'. In Udo Fries, Gunnel Tottie and Peter Schneider (eds) *Creating and using English language corpora. Papers from the Fourteenth International Conference on English Language Research on Computerized Corpora, Zürich 1993*. Amsterdam: Rodopi. 159–167.

Reichenbach, Hans (1947). *Elements of symbolic logic*. London: Collier Macmillan Comp.

Tannen, Deborah (1991). *You just don't understand. Women and men in conversation*. London: Virago Press.

Tannen, Deborah (1992). *That's not what I meant! How conversational style makes or breaks your relations with others*. London: Virago Press.

## Appendix: Selection from the Innsbruck Letter Corpus (34,963 words)

**Letters of women: 15th century ('lettw15')**

| | | | |
|---|---|---|---|
| 32 | Agnes Paston to Edmond Paston I | (1445) | 333 |
| 33 | Agnes Paston to John Paston I | (1451) | 262 |
| 34 | Agnes Paston to John Paston I | (1451) | 369 |
| 35 | Agnes Paston, Memorandum | (1458) | 302 |
| 40 | Margaret Paston to John Paston I | (1465) | 415 |
| 41 | Margaret Paston to John Paston I | (1465) | 1,008 |
| 42 | Margaret Paston to John Paston I | (1465) | 581 |
| 43 | Margaret Paston to John Paston I | (1465) | 551 |
| 44 | Margaret Paston to John Paston I | (1465) | 693 |
| 45 | Margaret Paston to John Paston I | (1465) | 845 |
| 48 | Elizabeth Stonor to William Stonor | (1476) | 273 |
| 49 | Elizabeth Stonor to William Stonor | (1476) | 963 |
| 50 | Elizabeth Stonor to William Stonor | (1476) | 342 |
| 51 | Elizabeth Stonor to William Stonor | (1476) | 911 |
| 52 | Elizabeth Stonor to William Stonor | (1476) | 408 |
| 53 | Elizabeth Stonor to William Stonor | (1476) | 571 |
| **Total** | | | **8,827** |

**Letters of women 17th century ('lettw17')**

| | | | |
|---|---|---|---|
| 45 | Brilliana Harley to Robert Harley | (1625) | 177 |
| 46 | Brilliana Harley to Robert Harley | (1625) | 321 |
| 47 | Brilliana Harley to Robert Harley | (1627) | 412 |
| 48 | Brilliana Harley to Robert Harley | (1629) | 406 |
| 49 | Brilliana Harley to Robert Harley | (1633) | 499 |
| 50 | Brilliana Harley to Edward Harley | (1638) | 320 |
| 51 | Brilliana Harley to Edward Harley | (1638) | 779 |
| 79a | Elizabeth, Count. of Chesterf., to Count. Giffard | (1664) | 245 |
| 79b | Elizabeth, Count. of Chesterf., to Count. Giffard | (1664) | 523 |
| 79c | Elizabeth, Count. of Chesterf., to Count. Giffard | (1664) | 376 |
| 79d | Elizabeth, Count. of Chesterf., to Count. Giffard | (1664) | 167 |
| 79e | Elizabeth, Count. of Chesterf., to Count. Giffard | (1664/5) | 288 |
| 79f | Dorothy Osborne to Sir William Temple | (1664/5) | 412 |
| 79h | Dorothy Osborne to Sir William Temple | (1664/5) | 460 |
| 79l | Dorothy Osborne to Sir William Temple | (1664/5) | 155 |
| 79m | Kate Philips ('Orinda') to Sir Will. Temple's Lady | (1664) | 1,537 |
| 79n | Lady Sunderland to Lady Giffard | (1668/69) | 647 |
| 79o | Lady Sunderland to Lady Giffard | (1668/69) | 528 |
| 79p | Lady Giffard to John Osborne, her nephew | (1689) | 176 |
| 79v | Lady Giffard to Countess Portland (L. Berkeley) | (1698) | 544 |
| **Total** | | | **8,972** |
| ***Sum total lettwom*** | | | **17,799** |

**Letters of men: 15th century ('lettm15')**

| | | | |
|---|---|---|---|
| 13 | William Paston I to William Worstede | (1426) | 448 |
| 14 | William Paston I to the Abbey of Cluny | (1429) | 387 |
| 15 | Sir David Home to the Priory of Coldingham | (1438/9) | 276 |
| 16 | Sir David Home to the Priory of Coldingham | (1440) | 337 |
| 17 | Sir David Home to the Priory of Coldingham | (1442) | 1,125 |
| 36 | William, Prior of Durham, to Thomas Nessbitt | (1447) | 583 |
| 37 | William, Prior of Durham, to William Lax | (1451) | 159 |
| 38 | William, Prior of Durham, to Sir Alex. Home | (1456) | 407 |
| 39 | William, Prior of Durham, to the Priory of Dunhelme | (1456) | 398 |
| 46 | Richard Byllingham to the Priory of Dunhelme? | (1467/8) | 649 |
| 47 | Richard Byllingham to the Priory of Dunhelme? | (1472) | 860 |
| 54 | Richard Cely the elder to George Cely at Calais | (1476/7) | 335 |
| 55 | Richard Cely the elder to George Cely at Calais | (1477) | 360 |
| 56 | Richard Cely the elder to George Cely at Calais | (1477) | 149 |
| 57 | Richard Cely the elder to George Cely at Calais | (1478) | 438 |
| 58 | Richard Cely the elder at London to George Cely | (1478) | 298 |
| 59 | Richard Cely the elder at London to George Cely | (1478) | 297 |
| 60 | Richard Cely the elder to George Cely at Calais | (1478) | 316 |
| 61 | Richard Cely the elder to George Cely at Calais | (1478) | 267 |
| 62 | Richard Cely the elder at London to George Cely | (1478) | 728 |
| **Total** | | | **8,817** |

**Letters of men: 17th century ('lettm17')**

| | | | |
|---|---|---|---|
| 18 | Robert Daborne to Mr. Henslow | (1613) | 200 |
| 19 | Robert Daborne to Mr. Henslow | (1613) | 125 |
| 20 | Robert Daborne to Mr. Henslow | (1613) | 188 |
| 21 | Robert Daborne to Mr. Henslow | (1613) | 172 |
| 22 | Robert Daborne to Mr. Henslow | (1613) | 114 |
| 23 | Robert Daborne to Mr. Henslow | (1613) | 142 |
| 24 | Robert Daborne to Mr. Henslow | (1613) | 243 |
| 25 | Robert Daborne to Mr. Henslow | (1613) | 187 |
| 26 | Robert Daborne to Mr. Henslow | (1613) | 129 |
| 27 | Robert Daborne to Mr. Henslow | (1613) | 107 |
| 28 | Robert Daborne to Mr. Henslow | (1613) | 290 |
| 29 | Robert Daborne to Mr. Henslow | (1613) | 119 |
| 43 | John Chamberlain to Sir Dudley Carleton | (1625) | 653 |
| 44 | John Chamberlain to Sir Dudley Carleton | (1625) | 812 |
| 54 | Oliver Cromwell to Robert Barnard | (1642) | 232 |
| 55 | Oliver Cromwell to the inhabitants of Fen Drayton | (1642) | 252 |
| 55a | Sir Will. Godolphin to Mr. Temple and Lady Giffard | (1666) | 182 |
| 55b | Sir William Godolphin to Lady Giffard | (1666) | 173 |
| 55c | Sir William Godolphin to Lady Giffard | (1666) | 310 |
| 80 | John Wilmot, Earl of Rochester | (1670) | 532 |
| 81 | John Wilmot, Earl of Rochester | (1672) | 136 |

| | | | |
|---|---|---|---|
| 82 | John Wilmot, Earl of Rochester, to his wife | (1672) | 113 |
| 83 | John Wilmot, Earl of Rochester, to Savile | (1673) | 283 |
| 88 | Andrew Marvell to Mayor Tripp | (1670) | 392 |
| 99 | Thomas Browne to his son Edward | (1679) | 573 |
| 109 | Edward Clarke to Locke | (1688) | 751 |
| 110 | Edward Clarke to Locke | (1688) | 616 |
| 111 | Edward Clarke to Locke | (1688) | 321 |
| **Total** | | | **8,347** |
| ***Sum total lettmen*** | | | **17,164** |

# Computer assisted spelling normalization of 18th century English[1]

*Peter Schneider*

University of Zürich

## Abstract

*This paper describes the ongoing development of a software spelling normalization system named ZENSPELL. It is intended to assign normalized, present-day English spellings to 18th spelling variants with minimal user intervention while keeping the source text intact and available for comparison. The article examines the possibility of adapting 18th century English newspaper texts in order to make them comply with 20th century spelling rules. The idea is to create a hybrid text: like glossed word-for-word 'translations' of Latin texts, the target text will contain 18th century sentences, but with 20th century orthographic words. Despite somewhat doubtful linguistic qualities, the resulting 'artificial' text will be useful for two purposes: first, lexical searches can be made using one normalized search term instead of having to guess possible spelling variations of the intended term. Second, the target text can be used as input for wordclass taggers such as ENGCG[2].*

## 1. Introduction

While the primary aim of this study is to have a version of the ZEN corpus available for tagging and searching, it is conceivable that the methods could be applied to earlier English texts which are more difficult with regard to spelling variation. Dealing with 18th century spelling variants is part of the ZEN (Zurich English Newspaper) corpus project described in Fries and Schneider (2000). The corpus is in its final stages of preparation, comprising roughly 1.2 million words of text from late 17th and 18th century London newspapers. The text has been keyed in and is in the process of being annotated.

### 1.1 Previous work

A previous study (Kytö and Voutilainen 1995) has taken a different route: instead of changing the text to comply with 20th century spelling, the inner workings of the ENGCG program were adapted to suit the idiosyncrasies of the earlier English texts. This method has the advantage that the creator of the wordclass tagger has precise control over the accuracy of the process. Also, it can deal with grammatical differences, such as the use of *as* as a relative marker shown in (9) below. Unfortunately, this special version of the ENGCG tagger adapted to the Early Modern English period 1500–1710 is not publicly available. Furthermore, using a special tagger we would not get the additional benefit of having at our disposal a parallel normalized version of the ZEN text for querying and for studying spelling variation.

### 1.2 Terms and conventions

The term **source text** refers to the current, unreleased version of the ZEN corpus. The standard for determining compliance with present-day English spelling conventions is the morphological analyzer of the ENGCG Constraint Grammar Parser of English. An **unrecognized token** or **type** is any lexical item which occurs in a spelling variant flagged <?> and/or <NoBaseformNormalisation> by ENGCG. Spelling **normalization** means adapting the spelling of an unrecognized item with the intention of retaining its original sense. The **target text** is a normalized version of the source text; containing only spelling variants recognized by ENGCG[3].

## 2. An overview of spelling variation in ZEN

A typical paragraph from the ZEN corpus looks very similar to present-day English. It is for the most part easily readable and understandable by today's standards. The first thing that strikes the reader as unusual about example (1) is the capitalization of nouns. Apart from that, the place names *Hambourg* and *Burdeaux* seem slightly odd; the same goes for the hyphen in *Bridlington-Bay.*

(1) THis week arrived here Three ships from Burdeaux, laden with Wine and Prunes, and Four ships from Holland; a Vessel coming in here from Hambourg has met with ill weather at sea, but we hear not of any loss at sea: one Flyboat laden with Raffe, was with some hazard, and the loss of her Masts, driven into Bridlington-Bay. (1671 LGZ 530:3)

Contrary to my first expectations, the non-standard initial capitals did not turn out to be a problem for ENGCG. The program does not automatically annotate a capitalized word as a proper noun, as shown in Figure 1. Instead, it bases the decision between proper and other noun on its lexicon.

| | | |
|---|---|---|
| 1 | '<*t*his>' | '*t*his' <*> <?> <NoBaseformNormalisation> N NOM SG/PL @NN> |
| 2 | '<week>' | 'week' N NOM SG @SUBJ |
| 3 | '<arrived>' | 'arrive' <SV> <SVC/A> V PAST VFIN @+FMAINV |
| 4 | '<here>' | 'here' ADV @ADVL |
| 5 | '<*three>' | 'three' <*> NUM CARD @QN> |
| 6 | '<ships>' | 'ship' N NOM PL @SUBJ |
| 7 | '<from>' | 'from' PREP @<NOM @ADVL |
| 8 | '<*burdeaux>' | '*burdeaux' <*> <?> N NOM SG @<P |
| 9 | '<$\,>' | |
| 10 | '<laden>' | 'laden' A ABS @<P |
| 11 | '<with>' | 'with' PREP @<NOM @ADVL |
| 12 | '<*wine>' | 'wine' <*> <-Indef> N NOM SG @<P |
| 13 | '<and>' | 'and' CC @CC |
| 14 | '<*prunes>' | 'prune' <*> N NOM PL @<P |
| 15 | '<$\,>' | |
| 16 | '<and>' | 'and' CC @CC |

| | | |
|---|---|---|
| 17 | '<*four>' | 'four' <*> NUM CARD @QN> |
| 18 | '<ships>' | 'ship' N NOM PL @SUBJ @<P |
| 19 | '<from>' | 'from' PREP @<NOM @ADVL |
| 20 | '<*holland>' | 'holland' <*> <Proper> N NOM SG @<P |

**Figure 1:** Slightly reformatted ENGCG output[4] of the top part of (1). An asterisk * indicates a capital letter in the source text

However, the first line of Figure 1 reveals that the capitalization of the first two letters of *this* confuses the program. The <?> tag indicates that *THis* was not found in the lexicon, and the <NoBaseformNormalisation> means that, additionally, ENGCG could not find a singular noun by dropping the final *s*. Since there is no linguistic reason for keeping the double initial capitals, they will be automatically removed before spelling normalization. In line 5 and 17, ENGCG was able to recognize *three* and *four* as cardinals in spite of the non-standard initial capital. On the other hand, it didn't notice that *Burdeaux* is a place name due to the variant spelling. Spelled with an *o*, ENGCG would have described it as 'bordeaux' <*> <Proper> N NOM SG @<P., which is indeed where the wine and prunes come from.

Other idiosyncrasies of 18th century spelling are shown in examples (2) to (11) below.

## 2.1 Contractions

(2) It has been resolved … that the 7500 Danes now in Saxony, will be imploy'd in that service. (1701 EPT 00062:295)

(3) Though hard thy fate, O India's injur'd friend, Brave all the storm, it hastens to an end; (1791 PAD 17683:410)

(4) The Emperor has resolved to send further Reinforcements to Italy, which tis said will make up his Army there to 39000 Foot, (1701 LGZ 03721:21)

(5) The whole to be conducted by Mess. G. Witchell, T. Moss, &c. (1761 LCR 00667:103)

## 2.2 Two-letter consonants

(6) I have nothing to add but my thanks for the great unanimity and application with which you have hitherto carried on the publick business (1761 RWJ 08907:131)

(7) The Musick by Mr. Oswald, Chamber Composer to his Majesty (1761 LCR 00667:147)

## 2.3 Similar sounding vowels and diphthongs

(8) Observations on a Pamphlet intitled, An Answer to one Part of a late infamous Libel, (1731 DCT 09250:96)

(9) The Editor has been particularly careful to chuse such Colloquies as expose and ridicule the Absurdities of the Church of Rome (1751 GAT 05209:314)

(10) All Dogs and Cats are to be killed, as well within as without the Blockade, for a League's Distance at least; Experience having shewn, that tho' those Animals are not affected with the Distemper, they frequently communicate it.
(1721 PBY 05024:9)

(11) The Work is compleat, and will be engrav'd with all possible Expedition
(1731 DAT 00046:122)

### 2.4 Hyphenation

Hyphenation is a problematic area for ENGCG to cope with. There are many hyphenated items in ZEN which are easily understood by a human reader, but which do not seem to form part of ENGCG's lexicon. Table 1 below indicates the most frequent unrecognized hyphenated tokens, all of which are labeled <?> by ENGCG. If the item is split up into individual words where the hyphen occurs, ENGCG is able to recognize the parts.

**Table 1:** Frequent unrecognized hyphenated items

| ***Item*** | ***no. of occurrences*** |
|---|---|
| Fleet-street | 183 |
| Temple-bar | 119 |
| Covent-garden | 119 |
| Pater-noster-row | 104 |
| Contribution-money | 96 |
| Royal-exchange | 81 |
| Lombard-street | 81 |

## 3. Assessing the recognition rate of ENGCG

While it becomes clear from the examples that ZEN corpus text is readable and comprehensible, this impression has to be verified by an analysis of how many unrecognized tokens and types occur altogether. Table 2 gives an overview of the text sizes.

**Table 2:** Corpus sizes

Time Periods: A=1670–1709; B=1710–1739; C=1740–1769; D=1770–1799

| **Corpus/Section** | **Tokens** | **s-Units** | **Words/s-Unit** |
|---|---|---|---|
| Zentext A | 242758 | 7642 | 31.8 |
| Zentext B | 347825 | 12163 | 28.6 |
| Zentext C | 339362 | 14112 | 24.0 |
| Zentext D | 298249 | 11843 | 25.1 |
| **Total Zentext** | **1228194** | **45760** | **26.8** |

The corpus was split into four periods A–D in order to track potential changes in spelling conformity over time. Next, the text was prepared for input to the ENGCG program. It had to be cleaned up with respect to a few minor formatting issues, such as the problematic capitalization as in (1) and special characters like asterisks * and daggers † which frequently occur in advertisements. The resulting data was fed into ENGCG and all annotation was removed with the exception of the <?> and <NoBaseFormNormalisation> tags. Afterwards, two word lists were prepared: the first one, *badspell,* contains all unrecognized items and the second, *goodspell,* contains all other items. Frequency counts were done for each list using a simple PERL script. The lemmatization of ENGCG was left unchanged. If one lemma occurred both with and without an initial capital, it was counted as two individual items in the frequency lists. In this context, a *type* is simply an entry in the frequency list.

In the complete ZEN text consisting of 1228194 tokens and 54098 different types, there were 49043 unrecognized tokens and 20610 unrecognized types, respectively. Table 3 gives an idea of the proportions between recognized and unrecognized items in the four time periods and the complete text.

**Table 3:** Proportions of unrecognized (U) and recognized tokens and types[6]

Time Periods: A=1670–1709; B=1710–1739; C=1740–1769; D=1770–1799

| Col | 1 | 2 | 3 | 4 | 5 | 6 | 7 |
|---|---|---|---|---|---|---|---|
| **Corpus** | **Tokens** | **Types** | **U Tok.** | **U Typ.** | **% U Tok.** | **% U Typ.** | **% U Typ./ U Tok.** |
| Zentext A | 242758 | 15044 | 11303 | 5502 | 4.66% | 36.57% | 49% |
| Zentext B | 347825 | 20255 | 15692 | 7351 | 4.51% | 36.29% | 47% |
| Zentext C | 339362 | 20271 | 13537 | 6569 | 3.99% | 32.41% | 49% |
| Zentext D | 298249 | 18499 | 8511 | 4821 | 2.85% | 26.06% | 57% |
| **Zen Full** | **1228194** | 54098 | **49043** | 20610 | 3.99% | 38.02% | 42% |

Looking at column 5, the proportion of unrecognized and recognized tokens, it seems that the mere 4% unrecognized items would not really call for a large effort to normalize variants. However, the number of unrecognized types reveals a completely different picture: as many as 40% of all types were not recognized by ENGCG. If these types were annotated for word class without spelling normalization, the program would automatically assign a noun reading. This would considerably skew the proportions of the different word classes.

Table 3 also shows that the 'spelling conformity' increases in the later time periods. While in the earlier periods A and B there are more than 4.5% unrecognized tokens (column 5) and more than 36% unrecognized types (column 6), they decrease in the later periods C and D. Column 7, the proportion between unrecognized tokens and types, can be interpreted as an indicator of the 'variation' of variant spellings: the more this value increases, the fewer unrecognized types occur more than once. A value of 100% would indicate that each type occurs only once. A speculative interpretation of the higher value in period D would be that, as time progresses, there are fewer variant spellings of the same word.

## 4. Approaches to spelling normalization

The first thing that becomes obvious when looking at the number of unrecognized types is that normalizing the spelling manually would be very time consuming. Although going through a database with more than 20,000 items and finding a normalized spelling by looking at each item in context would create the ideal 18th century English corpus, it is not considered suitable for a 20th century linguistic research project. An approach must be developed which does not require inspecting *all* unrecognized types but which would still improve the operation of ENGCG compared to the unchanged source text.

An interesting aspect of the unrecognized types is the distribution of frequencies in Table 4. There is an overwhelming proportion of singletons: they make up as much as three quarters of the unrecognized types. However, they only represent one quarter of the tokens. On the other hand, slightly more than 2% of the frequent types represent one third of the unrecognized tokens. This has implications for the approach to normalization: a manageable list of around 1500 items representing half of the unrecognized tokens (those types occurring with a frequency between 5 to 10 and above) can be used to check the performance of a software program which would then deal with the rest without operator intervention. Even if the program fails on all of the other half (which is unlikely), there would be a considerable improvement on the recognition rate of ENGCG.

**Table 4:** Frequency counts with regard to the total number of unrecognized types

| | Types | % | Tokens | % |
|---|---|---|---|---|
| Types occurring only once | 14541 | 71% | 14541 | 27% |
| 2–4 times | 4529 | 22% | 11371 | 23% |
| 5–10 times | 1027 | 5% | 6749 | 14% |
| 11–1428 times | 513 | 2% | 16382 | 33% |
| **Total** | **20610** | **100%** | **49043** | **100%** |

### 4.1 Commercial spelling checkers

In Fries and Schneider (2000), we noted that there are many regularities in 18th century spelling variants which could be automatically substituted, such as the endings *-y'd* (*-ied* in present day spelling), *-our* (*-or*) and *-ick* (*-ic*). Not all substitutions can be performed unconditionally, however. Errors are likely to be introduced if there are words which genuinely possess those endings. Substitutions must always be compared with and checked against a list of correctly spelled items.

I realized that software to do this job already existed: the spelling checkers which come pre-packaged with almost any computer software that inputs or outputs text. What a spelling checker essentially does is compare each word in the source text with its internal vocabulary. When it meets an item that it cannot find there, it tries to come up with a suggestion from the vocabulary as to how this item could be spelled. The user then has to look at the list of suggestions and (hopefully) choose the item that corresponds to the misspelled word.

**Table 5:** Some suggestions made by the Microsoft Word spelling checker (version 98)

| **unrecognized item** | **suggested correction(s)** |
|---|---|
| compleat | *complete* |
| intitled | instilled intuited |
| injur'd | *injured* |
| imploy'd | *employed* |
| publick | *public* |
| chuse | chouse chase chose *choose* |
| shewn | Shawn *shown* |

Rather than re-invent the wheel, I examined the performance of existing spelling checkers on 18th century spelling variants. Table 5 gives an idea of how well the spelling checker of Microsoft Word performs with a few unrecognized items from ZEN.

Microsoft Word indeed manages to find suggestions that actually correspond to the unrecognized item in some cases, but fails in others. I did not do comprehensive testing, since a commercial spelling checker is of limited use for a research project. First, it always operates interactively, which is tedious to use with a million-word text. Second, the only kind of editable customization it offers is through the addition of user-added items to the internal lexicon. Furthermore, the method it uses to prepare the list of suggestions is a trade secret of the manufacturers and therefore intentionally opaque. The ENGCG corpus normalization project, however, needs customizability and transparency: the solution lies in a combination of a newly developed framework program which makes use of already implemented and available software.

## 4.2 Open source spellcheckers

Thanks to the popularity of freely distributable operating systems, there are also a number of readily available software packages for spellchecking. The one that proved to be most suitable for the task of normalizing 18th century English is called *aspell*, an open source project coordinated by Kevin Atkinson[7]. It is still under development, and it is constantly being improved, but nevertheless very useful in its present state. The main advantage for me and the ZEN project is that it is completely customizable *without* having to understand, change and recompile the source text of the program. It offers very good facilities for customization and adaptation. While there are many word lists and suggestion rules available on installation, their use is not mandatory. Any list of words can be used as its lexicon, and its phonetic rules for suggesting alternative spellings, while not heavily documented, can be adapted for 18th century idiosyncrasies. Furthermore, the program has multiple levels for how far-fetched a suggested term may be, and since the phonetic algorithms are no trade secret, there is a built-in command for showing how a word was transformed.

### 4.3 Developing a specialized lexicon

Using the huge modern American or British lexicon which is pre-packaged with *aspell* would be problematic for ZEN. The present-day dictionaries contain so many items that it is highly likely that 18th century spelling variants might be misidentified as correctly spelled Modern English words. In addition to this problem, the program is also prone to coming up with suggestions which have no correspondence with the source term. Table 6 presents some suggestions made by *aspell* without any customization or alteration. The leftmost word is the one considered most suitable by the program. The list of suggestions has been truncated at the point where it matched (in my opinion) the unrecognized item. Ideally, the leftmost suggested word should always match, since in that case, the normalization could be performed unsupervised.

**Table 6:** Suggestions made by the *aspell* spelling checker (version 0.32-6 alpha) Standard wordlist

| **unrecognized item** | **suggested correction(s)** |
|---|---|
| compleat | *complete* |
| intitled | *entitled* |
| injur'd | *injured* |
| imploy'd | implode, *employed* |
| publick | *public* |
| chuse | Chase, chase, chose, chaise, chaser, cheese, *choose* |
| shewn | Shawn, sheen, *shown* |

*Aspell* performs about the same as Microsoft Word (see Table 5). On the positive side, it correctly suggests *entitled* for *intitled* where Word failed to come up with the right suggestion. On the negative side, it gave more superfluous suggestions than Word in the case of *imploy'd, chuse* and *shewn*. It must be noted, however, that the capitalized suggestions will be ignored by ENGCG since there is no necessity to change case.

In order to improve the suggestion performance, a lexicon was created on the basis of *goodspell*, the list of all recognized types. This is the basis of the ENGCG lexicon. Using this list, *aspell* cannot come up with suggestions which ENGCG would be unable to recognize. However, the downside is that it also cannot provide suggestions that might be compatible with ENGCG but which do not occur anywhere in the ZEN text. Therefore, in the process of checking the high-frequency types, those suggestions will be gradually added to the lexicon. Table 7 shows some improvements with the ZEN-based lexicon.

**Table 7:** Improved suggestions made by the *aspell* spelling checker Lexicon based on list of items recognized by ENGCG

| **unrecognized item** | **suggested correction(s)** |
|---|---|
| imploy'd | *employed* |
| shewn | Sheen, *shown* |

With the special lexicon configured, *aspell* is now able to come up with *employed* in first place simply because *implode* doesn't occur in ZEN. Similarly, *shewn* is now suggested to be replaced by *shown* in second place after the capitalized *Sheen*.

### 4.4 Adding pseudo-phonetic replacement rules

In order to make suggestions for misspelled words, the spelling checker makes use of phonetic replacement rules. In addition to an orthographic representation, the lexicon O is also stored in a database P containing phonetic equivalents. The equivalents are created by applying a set of phonetic replacement rules O -> P designed to capture the 'sound' of a word. (Strictly speaking, the rules should be called 'pseudo-phonetic' since the sound of a word has to be guessed from its graphic representation.) In the case of English, this process is not robust: there is no way for a program to correctly guess the pronunciation of an orthographic word. In order to simplify the guessing, the phonetic equivalence algorithms for English leave all vowels out of consideration. This accounts for some of the problematic suggestions in Tables 5–7.

In order to find a suggestion for a misspelled word $O^*_m$ (i.e. when an item is not a member of O), the spelling checker performs the same transformation on the word as it did to prepare the P database: $O^*_m$ -> $P?_m$. It then tries to match items in P, allowing a given amount of error (the degree of proximity between two items is called *edit distance*). The matching item(s) $P_m$ are reconverted to orthographic items $O_m$, almost invariably resulting in more items because there are only a few phonetic equivalents which represent only one orthographic word. Table 8 shows a small excerpt of *aspell*'s English phonetic replacement table. Unfortunately, the phonetic replacement driver is neither well documented nor self-explanatory or easily guessed. There are about a hundred rules altogether which reduce the orthographic words into pseudo-phonetic equivalents consisting only of the symbols *@BFHKLMNPRSTWYX_, where * represents an initial vowel, @ the dental fricatives (as in *think* and *rather*), and X the palatal affricates (as in *hitch* and *edge*). Except for B and P, there is no differentiation between voiced and voiceless sounds. (-^ and $ are used for ordering character sets and rules).[8]

**Table 8:** Phonetic simplification rules for English (excerpt)

| | | |
|---|---|---|
| AH(AEIOUY)-^ | -> | *H |
| CIA | -> | X |
| CK | -> | K |
| COUGH^ | -> | KF |
| GNED$ | -> | N |
| KN^ | -> | N |
| LAUGH^ | -> | LF |
| TH | -> | @ |

The problem with this pseudo-phonetic replacement process is that the spelling checker usually creates far too many suggestions, and in suboptimal order.[9] If all the suggested orthographic words stem from the same phonetic equivalent, the results are simply listed alphabetically, with no indication as to which suggestion could be the best guess.

(12) antient intent, *ancient*, anoint, anting, entente, indent, intend, sentient, Antoine, Antoinette, Antone, Anton, Internet, anted, antenna, inpatient, intents, penitent, Antony, ancienter, andante, ardent, attend, content, incident, indigent, intoned…

In example (12), it appears odd that *intent* should stand in front of the ideal suggestion *ancient*. This is easily explained: in the standard phonetic tables, *antient* is transformed to *NTNT which 'perfectly' matches *intent* *NTNT, but seems to differ from *ancient* *NSNT by one letter. There is obviously a rule missing. In order to improve the situation, I have added TIEN -> SN to the phonetic table. Together with the ZEN lexicon, this improves the suggestion list as shown in example (12a):

(12a) antient Ancient, *ancient*, Ancients, Intent, intent, anciently, Assent, Incident, assent, incident

Examples (13) and (13a) also show the effect of an added phonetic transformation rule by improving the rank of the preferred suggestion:

(13) burthen bur then, bur-then, Burton, berthing, birthing, *burden*, berthed, birthed, earthen, Bethune, burn, then, Barth, Bethe, bathe, berth, birth, butane, Bertha, Bethany, bather, bathing, bother, burgeon, burner, Barton, Bergen, Borden, barren, bathed, bathes, batten, beaten, berths, births, bitten, button, northern

To get the result in (13a) (which is actually 'perfect' since the first two items *bur then* and *bur-then* are the result of the buggy run-together word function in *aspell*), a rule RTHEN-- -> T was added. This avoids treating all *th* letter combinations as dental fricatives.

(13a) burthen bur then, bur-then, Burden, Burton, *burden*, Buren, Barton, Borden, Burdon, Button, beaten

It is imaginable that the performance of the suggestion mechanism can be further improved by introducing a system with more distinctions.

### 4.5 Problems

In spite of the potential of improving the performance of the spelling checker by customizing the lexicon and improving the phonetic rule set, there are a few areas of concern. There is still no fail-safe ranking system for determining which of the suggested items is actually the normalized form. In an upcoming version of *aspell* which will be tested soon, there is the new possibility of disallowing suggestions whose phonetic equivalent does not completely match the unrecognized item (i.e. requiring an edit distance of zero). This could shorten the lists of suggestions.

There is also the problem of the great number of unrecognized hyphenated types. *Aspell* currently refuses to recognize hyphenated items even if individual parts are recognized: *State-lottery* returns zero suggestions although *state lottery* is considered correct. To make matters more complicated, *aspell* automatically splits up *Fleetstreet* into *Fleet street*, but also suggests *Fleet-street* as a valid suggestion even though the program will not accept the hyphenated version it suggested! However, ENGCG can provide a workaround for this problem by dealing with hyphenation itself.

The basic problem of the slightly circular approach of extracting the spell checker's lexicon from the text itself is that the automatic normalization of items *not* occurring in standard orthography is impossible. While for a word processor it may be desirable to compile lexicons of ever-increasing size from all possible sources, this is not an option for ENGCG. It is more desirable to let ENGCG handle an un-normalizable item than to risk changing the text for the worse. There are partial solutions for the normalization of unrecognized proper names including place names which do not occur in recognized form in the corpus: such items can be normalized if necessary and will be added manually to the lexicon. Since going through the complete list of uppercase items is not an option, a heuristic is used: capitalized items following known titles and first names are a good source for potential proper names. Furthermore, a list of roughly 300 place names is available in ZEN from report headings such as *Milan, August 14, 1761* which have been annotated throughout the corpus.

Then, there is the possibility that a 'perfectly spelled' word is simply unknown to ENGCG. In the worst case, ENGCG would try to come up with a normalized item that is accepted by ENGCG but which no longer corresponds to the source word. Care will be taken to locate and add such items to the lexicon even though ENGCG won't be able to identify them. 'Improving' ENGCG is not a goal of this project, it is making ENGCG more available to texts with a slight proportion of non-standard spelling.

## 5. Conclusion

It is a long way from a decent interactive spelling checker to automatic spelling normalization. Experimentation with a customizable open source program has so far proven to be an effective route towards more automation, since more time can be invested in linguistically oriented performance testing rather than computer programming. Improvements can be made both by carefully limiting as well expanding the lexicon. The addition of more precise phonetic replacement rules which more closely reflect 'actual' pronunciation further helps the success rate of the spelling checker.

While a 90% or higher success rate is unlikely to be achieved without context sensitivity or sense disambiguation, pseudo-phonetic transformation aided by a ranking of generated suggestions should considerably improve ENGCG's recognition rate of 18th century texts.

## Notes

1 The author gratefully acknowledges the support of the Swiss National Science Foundation.

2 For a description of ENGCG, see Voutilainen and Heikkilä (1994).

3 Strictly speaking, it is TWOL, the two-level lexical analyzer program which handles the ENGTWOL lexicon. I am using the name ENGCG here since this is the actual program the user is dealing with. Because TWOL is invoked by ENGCG, the lexical analyzer has no available user interface.

4 For a description of ENGCG tags, please see http://www.lingsoft.fi/doc/engcg/intro/mtags.html.

5 Corpus references consist of the year of publication followed by the three-letter title code and five digits which usually refer to the issue number of the newspaper. LGZ: *The London Gazette*; EPT: *The English Post*; PAD: *The Public Advertiser*; LCR: *The London Chronicle*; RWJ: *Read's Weekly Journal*; DCT: *The Daily Courant*; GAT: *The General Advertiser*; PBY: *The Post Boy*; DAT: *The Daily Advertiser*.

6 Please note that only columns 1 and 3 add up. Type counts prepared for individual time periods cannot be simply added together since there are overlapping items.

7 For more information about *aspell*, please see http://aspell.sourceforge.net

8 Please note that pseudo-phonetic replacement was originally developed for practical use in US-American genealogy, not as a scientific method to derive a true phonetic representation. It is intended to simplify while retaining essential differences. For instance, in many dialects, written word-medial or word-final *d, dd, t* and *tt* are all pronounced /d/, which is why it is practical to drop the distinction between D and T. However, since this is not the case for *b*, *p* and /b/, B and P are kept as distinct items.

9 The pseudo-phonetic replacement algorithm operates without case sensitivity: items are capitalized in the list of suggestions because they are also capitalized in the vocabulary.

## References

Fries, Udo, and Peter Schneider (2000). 'ZEN: preparing the Zurich English Newspaper Corpus'. In Friedrich Ungerer (ed.) *English media texts - past and present. Langage and textual structure*. Amsterdam/Philadelphia: John Benjamins. 3–24.

Kytö, Merja, and Atro Voutilainen (1995). 'Applying the constraint grammar parser of English to the Helsinki Corpus'. *ICAME Journal* 19: 23–48.

Voutilainen, Atro, and Juha Heikkilä (1994). 'An English constraint grammar (ENGCG): a surface-syntactic parser of English'. In Udo Fries, Gunnel Tottie and Peter Schneider (eds) *Creating and using English language corpora. Papers from the Fourteenth International Conference on English Language Research on Computerized Corpora, Zürich 1993*. Amsterdam: Rodopi. 189–199.

Corpus-based language description

# *Whom* is not dead?

*Pieter de Haan*

University of Nijmegen

**Abstract**

*This article reviews some of the recent literature on the ongoing discussion about the use of* whom *in spoken and written English. Some linguists claim that* whom *is artificially kept alive by prescriptive grammarians, and that it has virtually disappeared from the spoken language. Investigations of the occurrence of* whom *in a number of recent English corpora show its continuing use in various text categories, especially the more formal types of writing, although it is by no means confined to writing. Its chief syntactic function is that of complement to a preposition, most notably in the construction* of whom *when postmodifying an NP headed by a numeral or a quantifier. Almost one fifth of all occurrences of* whom *are of this type.*

## 1. Introduction: the questions

This study was occasioned by a discussion on the Corpora Distribution List[1] in the summer of 1999, initiated by Carsten Breul, who invited comments on the occurrence of *who* complementing a preposition.

> I am writing a paper on relative 'who'/'whom' as complement of a preposition (e.g. 'the man to whom you spoke'; 'the man who you spoke to'). I am especially interested in the case where the preposition precedes the relative pronoun. The grammars ('normative', 'didactic', 'descriptive') seem to be unanimous in judging Prep+whom correct and Prep+who incorrect. The sentences listed below, which are from the British National Corpus, do not conform to this rule. All but (8) are from written sources.
>
> (1) A passionate lover of the Savoy Operas, she was a founder member of the Bradford Gilbert and Sullivan Society, with who she had a long association. (C8G: 418)
>
> (2) It's almost impossible to put him down in the tackle, and there are few players about who you an [sic; probably 'can' is intended] say that. (CB2: 396)
>
> (3) They need to keep their bankers happy by reducing a £3 million-plus debt in the next few months, and Robson, in who Leeds are already showing an interest, will become their most disposable asset. (CBG: 305)
>
> (4) It has one senior bishop, two suffragans, one dean, four archdeacons, and 21 rural deans of who one is a woman. (ED9: 3029)
>
> (5) They must be treated as adequate because they reflect the statutory provisions in regard to appeals by persons upon who intervention notices are served by S.I.B. in the exercise of the intervention powers

delegated to it by the Secretary of State (as to which see section 97 of the Act). (FD1: 413)

(6) Instead, the sites are used by local residents, of who some 25 per or so come by foot and use the sites like an urban park, primarily to take a walk (Harrison, 1981). (FR2: 453)

(7) Through its founder Molly Braithwaite, for who we held a heartfelt admiration, we feel an affectionate living bond with all those in positions of responsibility within the MEDAU SOCIETY. (HU8: 57)

(8) I would also I think put in a word for the work of the joint [...] policy panel [...] which is shared between this committee and the social services committee because it seems to me that it is not [unclear] for us to be thinking that there is a group of children for who nursery education is necessary [...] or desirable and a different group of children for whom something else [...] is necessary and desirable, largely because of their parents' position. (JWA: 149)

What I would like to have your opinion on is this:

Do native-speakers of English actually use Prep+relative who?
In other words: Do you think that the sentences may very well be correct representations of the text-producers' usage?
Or would you consider it likely that there are printing/typing (or transcription) errors involved here (omission of 'm' in 'who'), which distort the picture? (I think my question points to a, perhaps seldom relevant, but nevertheless interesting problem for corpus linguistics if low frequency features are concerned: How sure can we be that the corpus represents text-production authentically?) (Breul 1999)

## 2. Initial reactions

This gave rise to a number of reactions from native and non-native subscribers, generally pointing to the conclusion that to many native speakers of English (including speakers of different varieties) the use of a preposition immediately followed by *whom* was felt to be awkward, obsolete, bookish, and that many would avoid this construction at all possible cost, preferring the so-called stranded preposition instead. This is how it was worded by James Fidelholtz.

> Now that I actually see the data, I have to say that I wouldn't use those forms, but *they almost sound better to me than the forms with 'whom'*, which I obviously don't use either, since *I just postpose the preposition.* I strongly suspect that this sort of construction is similar to *what we find in cases of real language death*: the grammar just goes all to hell, especially the morphology, and *I think this construction is in an advanced state of near-death*, and so perhaps the analogy holds (people with access to megacorpora could check this out for frequency, which I bet is very low). Of course, another possibility is that *the construction has already died* (read: changed to the postposed version), *and is just being artificially kept 'alive' by the (pseudo-) 'grammarians'* who rail at 'ending sentences with prepositions', etc., in much the same way that the change of various verb forms to 'ain't' has been kept by the grammarians from going to completion for over 400 years already. (Fidelholz 1999 – italics mine)

However, it would be an exaggeration to say that *whom* is 'in an advanced state of near-death', for in a word rank list drawn up on the basis of the Brown, LOB, Frown and FLOB corpora (well over 4 million words in all) *whom* is on rank 583, with 704 occurrences, out of a total of 86,705 different types. Another reaction came from Dan Slobin:

> I'm quite confident that the examples with PREP+who are genuine, and not transcription errors. *At least in American English, "whom" seems to be non-existent in spoken registers* – probably entirely absent for speakers younger than middle-age, and marginal in older speakers. I don't think my students know the difference between "who" and "whom." And there are strange overcorrections – for example, a formal academic letter from a colleague in his 50s, using "whom" as sentence subject (probably because it sounds archaic). In Sapir's famous discussion of "whom" in 1921 (his chapter on drift, in *Language*), he said: "We may venture to surmise that...*whom* will ultimately disappear from English speech." He predicted: "It is safe to prophesy that within a couple of hundred years from to-day not even the most learned jurist will be saying 'Whom did you see?'" *It took less than a half-century for that form to disappear, and the PREP+**whom** form seems to be on its way out too.* (Slobin 1999 – italics mine)

An opposing view was expressed by Keith J. Miller:

> Just on a personal, anecdotal level from one person who has taught foreign language to another who is currently teaching... I am a native (American) English speaker, and not a stickler for grammar, but I don't think I've ever caught myself using the PREP+who construction that everyone on the list seems to think is so prevalent. In fact, *the examples really sound awful to me*. I would be inclined to either 1) use whom or 2) rework the sentence to avoid the construction altogether. But if I find *I've talked myself into a corner and a preposition followed by some form of WHO is looming in the distance, I definitely choose **whom** rather than **who**.* (Miller 1999 – italics mine)

Interestingly, hardly any of those who commented made any reference to corpus research, but they provided their intuitive reactions, which considering the name of the list was remarkable. One contributor, Douglas McCarthy, noticed this, too, saying:

> Given that the name of this list is 'corpora', I'm a little surprised at the amount of introspective speculation which we've seen in this thread.
> Perhaps we ought to bear two things in mind here:
>
> 1.differentiation of language varieties (a virtually endless task)
> 2.design of neutral elicitation of people's attitudes to language use.
>
> In answer to the original question: yes, the forms quoted are highly possible today. That is about as far as I would like to go in the context of a list devoted to corpora.
> (McCarthy 1999)

As I am a grammarian but also a non-native speaker of English and an EFL teacher I joined in the discussion, asking how to present this problem to my students, and what I should teach them. I also drew (de Haan, 1999) the list readers' attention to the construction in Breul's sixth example above:

> Instead, the sites are used by local residents, *of who* some 25 per or so come by foot and use the sites like an urban park, primarily to take a walk.

Here the alternative construction with the postposed preposition does not exist – which must have something to do with the fact that in these cases the PP in which the relative pronoun functions is itself part of an NP, rather than an adverbial on the level of the relative clause.

## 3. Intuitions, intuitions...

I myself have become extremely cautious about making statements about my native language based on my own intuitive feelings. I often see and hear many of my fellow native Dutch speakers write and say things which

- the native speaker in me understands and relates to
- the linguist in me is able to analyse in terms of the language system
- the prescriptivist in me downright abhors

So my own intuitive judgement of what is proper or acceptable may be quite different from many of my fellow speakers and precisely for that reason I have come to distrust my own intuitions. I have no reason to assume that it will be very different in the case of many of my fellow linguists. So naturally I was interested to find out how the commentators' reactions fitted in with what grammarians have stated about this phenomenon. A look at the well-established *Comprehensive Grammar* (Quirk *et al.* 1985: 1249) tells us that:

> When the governing preposition precedes its complement, as in the rather formal 'the person ***to whom*** he spoke', the choice of *whom* is obligatory. When it does not, as in 'the person ***who(m)*** he spoke <u>*to*</u>' or when the relative pronoun is the object of the verb, as in 'the person ***who(m)*** he met', there is some choice between *who* and *whom*.

The latter is preferred in formal English, the former is preferred in informal use, where however the zero form is by far the most common. So for Quirk *et al.* the use of *whom* is definitely something that belongs to formal language, and moreover, the use of *whom* is obligatory when it is immediately preceded by a governing preposition.

The recent *Longman Grammar of Spoken and Written English* (Biber *et al.* 1999), surprisingly, has very little to say about the occurrence of *whom*. Based as it is on the Longman corpus of English, it provides all kinds of statistical information, especially frequency of occurrence and register variation. *Whom* is discussed as an alternative to *who*, together with *that* and *zero*. It is said that *whom* only occurs in non-subject position, and that in non-restrictive clauses it is the only relativizer available for non-subject position, in contrast to restrictive clauses, where *that* and *zero* are alternatives. No comment at all is made about the specific occurrence of *whom* as a prepositional complement.

## 4. Grammarians' views on *who* and *whom*

The use of *whom* has been studied and commented on by grammarians from the 18th century. Aarts (1994) presents a survey of what the most important grammarians of the eighteenth and nineteenth centuries have had to say about the use and misuse of *whom*. On the basis of the evidence presented by spoken English data he shows that 'there is obviously a clash in this area of English grammar between what people actually say and what prescriptivists believe they ought to say' (1994: 71). Aarts also cites Sapir (cf. Slobin's citation above) and Gowers (1962), who thinks that getting rid of *whom* might be a good idea, but predicts that '*whom* will take some killing' (1962: 206).

What the prescriptivists used to say about the use of *who* and *whom* is basically that *who* should be used as subject only, and *whom* in all other cases. Much of their discussions are about the incorrect use of *whom*, particularly in cases such as *he interviewed a girl whom he thinks will be excellent*, in what generative grammarians call 'long movement', and what in Quirk *et al.* (1985) is referred to as 'pushdown' relative clauses.

Aarts claims that prescriptivist teaching in the past two centuries has ensured that most educated speakers are aware of the existence of rules for the use of relative *who* and *whom* in specific syntactic contexts, but that they are not always sure what these contexts are. This leads to insecurity and in some cases errors, or hypercorrection (Quirk *et al.* ascribe the use of *whom* in pushdown relative clauses to hypercorrection).

Schneider (1992) has studied the use of *whom* in British and American English, in an attempt to shed more light on any possible differences between two well-established national varieties of English in an area of diachronic change. Schneider argues that 'diachronically, the replacement of *whom* by the uninflected form *who* is in line with the proposed development of English from a largely synthetic to a predominantly analytic language (Sapir 1921). Synchronically, the result of this process is a relatively unstable situation, a modern usage problem under the impact of prescriptivism (1992: 231)'.

Schneider has looked into the use of *who* and *whom* in non-subject positions in the Brown and LOB corpora, and concludes that there are but a few subtle differences between the two varieties, with a slight preference for British English to use the form *whom*.

Both Aarts and Schneider suggest that the use of *whom* is largely teaching-induced. If this is what Fidelholz (see above) means by 'being kept artificially alive by grammarians' he may be right. The point remains, however, that language users apparently incorporate the use of *whom* into their language system.

## 5. Corpus research

On the one hand, as we have seen, there is a discrepancy between what native speakers/linguists feel about this issue, and what the descriptive and prescriptive grammars have to say about it (if anything is said at all). On the other hand, there is the question as to what native speakers actually do (for whatever reason). I decided that it was time for another look at corpus data to find independent evidence for the use of *whom* in actual language use data. From the discussions on the Corpora list I had distilled the following two questions:

- Does *who* as a complement of a preposition[2] occur at all?
- Is *whom* indeed obsolescent?

The obvious choice in my case was to start by doing a count of the occurrences of *whom* in the standard corpora (Brown and LOB) and the later Frown and FLOB corpora, and see whether a closer look at what I found there would shed any new light on what was discussed on the Corpora list. I also included the recent part of the BNC (1975–1993) in my study. Not that I did not trust Carsten Breul, but I wanted independent confirmation of any tendency or tendencies that the comparison between Brown and Frown or between LOB and FLOB might show.

It should be borne in mind that the BNC material contains both spoken and written material. In 75 million written words I found 10,710 occurrences of *whom*, and in 10 million spoken words a mere 269 occurrences. So the contribution by the spoken material to the total number of observations in the BNC material is almost negligible. At the same time, these numbers alone would seem to refute the claim that *whom* is obsolescent, coming, as they do, from recent British language use data. I will come back to this below.

The first question, whether *who* is found at all as a complement of a preposition, must be answered affirmatively. In the written corpora, I found *who* complementing a preposition once, in the Frown corpus, in an interrogative utterance: 'One of who?' (Frown K09 11). In the spoken BNC material Carsten Breul had found one example (his example # 8, cited above). Of course, Breul had also found seven other examples of *who* complementing a preposition, so I assume that they were found in the earlier written part of the BNC. It is obvious that the construction does not occur very frequently.

The second question, whether *whom* is becoming obsolete, is far more interesting, for if it is, and at the speed that some of the commentators mentioned above were suggesting, it might show up in a comparison of 1960's language use with 1990's language use. Figure 1 sums up a number of my findings. It may be a bit naive to expect great differences between Brown/LOB (1960s) and Frown/FLOB (1990s), but Figure 1 at least suggests that the situation is rather more complex than might have been expected. Disregarding the BNC material, it would seem that while for British English the native speakers' assumption is confirmed (i.e. a decrease in the occurrence of *whom* across the two broad varieties), for American English the situation seems to be the opposite. What complicates matters is that in the far larger BNC corpus the figures for imaginative and informative writing are comparable to what is found in Frown.

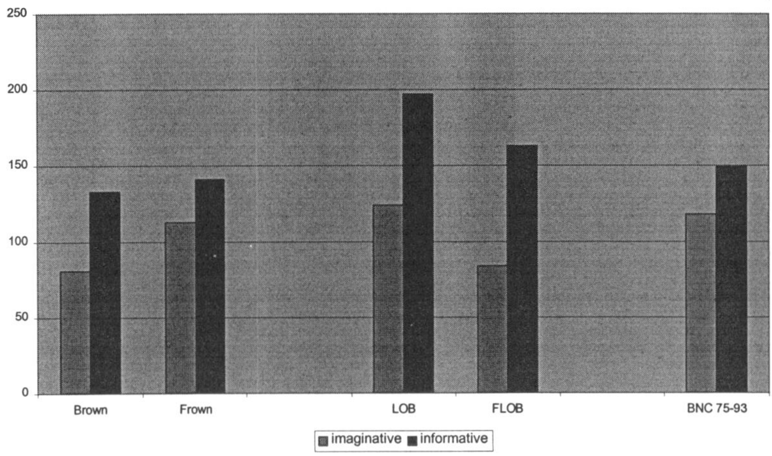


**Figure 1:** Occurrences of *whom* per 1 M words in imaginative and informative writing

It was Douglas McCarthy (see citation above) who suggested looking at differentiation according to varieties of language, which I did first for the BNC material. Figure 2 clearly shows great differences between the varieties, where imaginative writing has by no means the fewest occurrences; the fewest occurrences per million words are found in applied and social sciences, while the category of 'belief & thought' has the most. Figure 2 also shows that *whom* occurs far less often in spoken English, especially in dialogue, than in any variety of written English. A tentative conclusion might therefore be that *whom* is typically an element of formal written English.

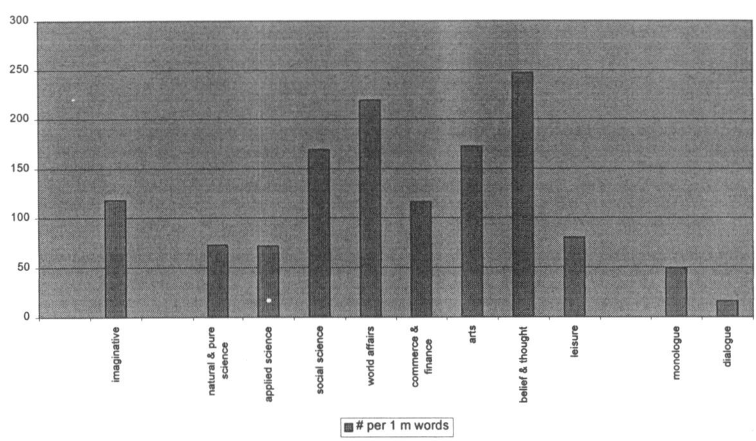


**Figure 2:** Occurrences of *whom* in various text types of the BNC

## 6. More detailed questions

So much for basic statistics. I was naturally interested in finding out more, especially the following:

(i) In what varieties is the increase in the use of *whom* in American English and the decrease in British English most noticeable?
(ii) In what sentence/clause types does *whom* occur?
(iii) What syntactic function or functions does *whom* have?
(iv) What is the proportion of *whom* complementing a preposition?
(v) Which prepositions are typically complemented by *whom*?
(vi) Does *whom* always immediately follow the preposition it complements?

Let me start with the first question. Figure 3 shows how the occurrences of *whom* are distributed over the various text categories in Brown and Frown.

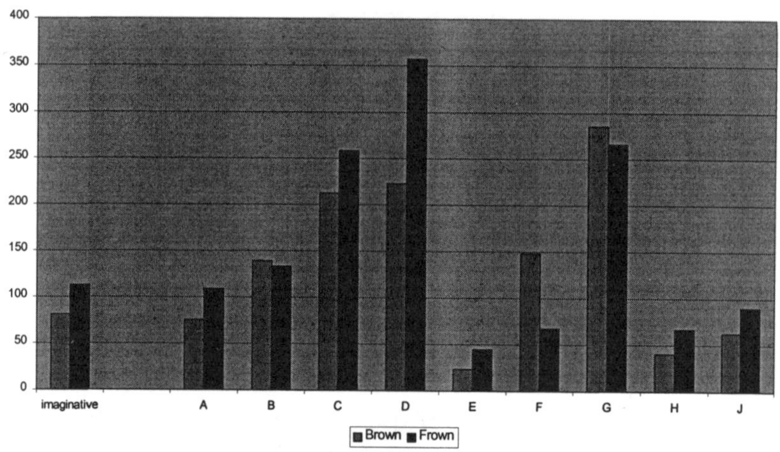


**Figure 3:** Occurrences of *whom* in Brown and Frown

It is clear that category D especially shows a considerable increase in the occurrence of *whom*. This category more or less covers the BNC category, 'belief & thought', where we also saw a very high occurrence of *whom*. Bearing in mind Quirk's comments, we might conclude that American formal writing remains formal, if the occurrence of *whom* is anything to go by.

A similar comparison for the British material is shown in Figure 4.

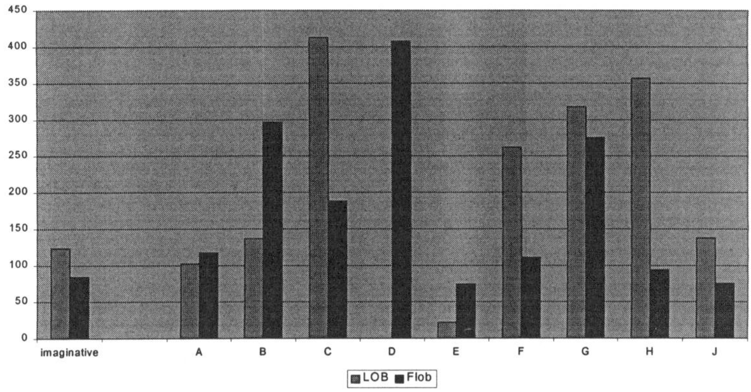


**Figure 4:** Occurrences of *whom* in LOB and Flob

Curiously, given the fact that overall the occurrence of *whom* has decreased in the British material, there are two very noticeable exceptions, viz. category B (press editorial) and D (religion). As to B, the question is raised whether British editorials have become more formal over the last 30 years, again on the assumption that the level of formality is signalled by the occurrence of *whom*.

Even more curious is the finding that whereas *whom* does not occur at all in category D in LOB, this category has one of the highest scores in FLOB. There is no straightforward explanation. It is not a case of a single text being responsible. A dispersion plot shows that *whom* is found throughout the sample, which covers various texts. Again, the question is whether religious writing in British English is becoming more formal. It should be borne in mind that in the BNC material the category 'belief & thought' scored highest as well. A comparison of these figures with the figures for religious writing in the Brown and Frown corpora suggests that religious writing has become more formal on both sides of the Atlantic and that British English has 'caught up' with American, in this respect.

The next question I set out to answer is what the prevalent clause type is in which *whom* occurs. Note that Figure 5 and the following figures show the comparison between Brown, LOB, Frown, FLOB and the spoken part of the BNC. The older material is represented on the left, while the more recent material is represented on the right.

There do not seem to be large differences across the five corpora I studied. The majority of *whom*s are found in relative clauses (as everybody always rightly assumes). There are individual differences, but it would be fair to say that overall it is found more often in non-restrictive clauses, and that that may be a trend that is developing. After all, most contributors on the Corpora list seemed to indicate that they would prefer a postposed preposition, which in restrictive clauses could also be used with the alternative relativizers *that* and *zero*, whereas the non-restrictive clause does not offer this possibility.[3] Note also that spoken English does not differ greatly from written English in this respect.

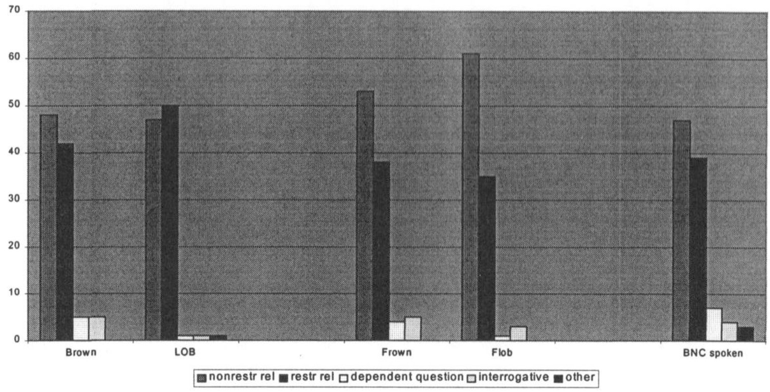


**Figure 5:** Clause types in which *whom* occurs

As to the function of *whom*, consider Figure 6, which shows how *whom* functions syntactically in the sentences in which it occurs.

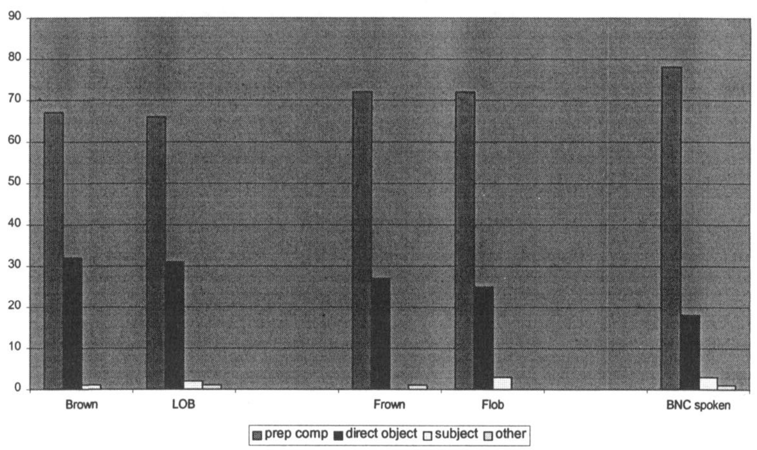


**Figure 6:** Functions of *whom*

Figure 6 shows that in 60 to 80 per cent of all the cases *whom* indeed functions as prepositional complement, with possibly a tendency to increase, whereas the direct object function seems to be decreasing. This especially begs the question why in the Longman grammar (Biber et al. 1999) no example of prep+*whom* is given at all, but only one or two of *whom* functioning as direct object.

Given the fact that it is especially prepositions that are complemented by *whom*, it might be interesting to look at which prepositions precisely are complemented by *whom* across the various corpora. This is shown in Figure 7.

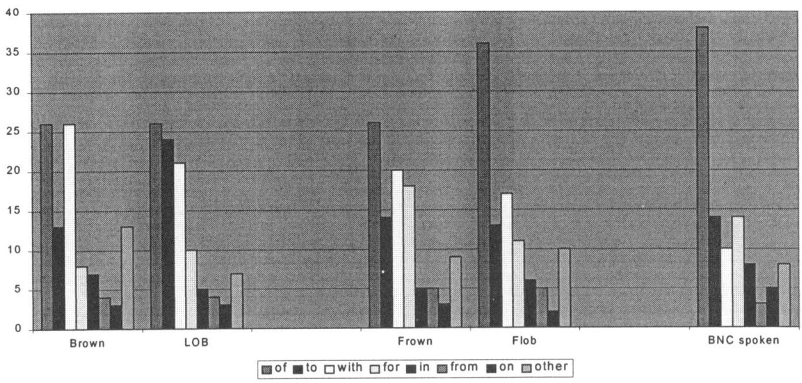


**Figure 7:** Prepositions complemented by *whom*

They are actually the same prepositions you would find in a top ten list of prepositions used overall (cf. de Haan 1992), although there are slight differences between the rank orders. What is striking is the difference between *of* and the other prepositions in the recent British material. This can be accounted for precisely by the occurrence of the *of* + *whom* as postmodifier in an NP, as in:

> … Joan Collins, Madonna and Clive James, <u>*all of whom*</u> may soon be reaching out to Russia. (FLOB B07 24)

A closer look at the occurrences of *of* followed by *whom* shows that no fewer than 90 per cent of those are postmodifiers in NPs. The heads of these NPs are typically quantifiers and numerals, like *all, both, most, some, many, one.*

The last of the questions raised above is whether *whom* is always immediately preceded by the preposition that it complements. This is shown in Figure 8.

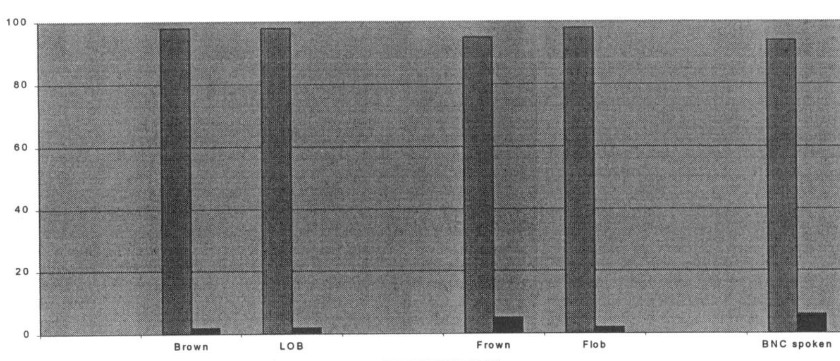


**Figure 8:** Position of the preposition relative to *whom*

The p1 position in Figure 8 means the first position immediately to the left of *whom*. It is clear that in well over 95 per cent of all the cases where *whom* complements a preposition, in all the corpora studied here, the preposition immediately precedes *whom*.

## 7. Summary and conclusion

In the sections above I have reported a number of findings made in this study of the occurrence of the word *whom*. These lead to the following (tentative) conclusions.

- *Whom* is certainly not dead; it is not even dying.
- There is a certain amount of variation across text categories: on the whole it is especially the more formal text types where *whom* occurs relatively frequently, but it is by no means limited to writing.
- Its chief function is that of complement to a preposition.
- It is definitely the form to use when it is immediately preceded by the preposition it complements.
- A prominent role is played by *of whom* functioning as postmodifier in an NP headed by a numeral or a quantifier. These make up almost one fifth of the total number of occurrences of *whom*.

The more general conclusion that I wish to draw from this study is that native speakers' intuition (or should I say native linguists' intuition?) has failed to predict language use in the case of *whom*. The corpus data in general confirm what is said in the standard grammars, and if *whom* 'is just being artificially kept "alive" by the (pseudo-) "grammarians"' (Fidelholz 1999), then they are apparently very successful at it.

At this point I am tempted to make a few predictions, however dangerous this may be, but on the basis of what this study has shown I would expect that

- *whom* will probably gradually disappear as an object relative pronoun, first in restrictive clauses, but ultimately also in non-restrictive clauses;
- *whom* is here to stay as a prepositional complement of a non-stranded preposition, particularly in non-restrictive clauses, where the relativizers *that* and *zero* are not available;
- the construction *X of whom*, where X stands for a numeral or a quantifier, will become the single most frequent syntactic structure involving *whom*.[4]

In this study I set out to find out whether there is any corpus proof for the assumption that '*whom* is in a state of near-death' (Fidelholz 1999). Obviously this is not so. What remains to be studied in any case is:

- how the figures for *whom* compare with those for the other relativizers in non-subject position, and if any shift is observable in recent years (cf. Aarts, 1993, who has studied the occurrence of *who/whom/that/Ø* in two corpora of spoken English, and has shown that for non-subject functions *that/Ø* is preferred);

- the role played by *whom* in various text categories, in more detail than has been done so far;
- the way in which the terms 'formal' and 'informal' can be related to 1 and 2.

**Acknowledgement**

I am grateful to Nelleke Oostdijk for reading my paper for me at the ICAME 2000 Conference, which I was unable to attend, due to circumstances beyond my control.

**Notes**

1 The entire discussion can be found in the Corpora Distribution List Archives at http://helmer.hit.uib.no/corpora/1999-3/.

2 It should be borne in mind that what we are interested in is any occurrence of a PP in which the complement is realised by the form *who*. There a fair number of cases where a preposition is followed by *who*, but where the two do not make up a single constituent, as in the following:

The number depends on who is talking at the moment (Brown E32 1290).

3 In de Haan (1989) I found no examples of *whom* as a complement of a stranded proposition at all.

4 During a recent seminar I conducted at the University of Stockholm, David Minugh (personal communication) handed me a KWIC concordance of *whom* from *USA Today* 1990 to June 1992. About one third of slightly under 2000 cases occurred in precisely this structure. Likewise, in a KWIC concord of *whom* from the *Online Student College Newspapers*, about a third of nearly three hundred occurrences were found to function in this structure. For an interesting discussion on how to form a genitive construction on this structure, see Olofsson (2001).

**References**

Aarts, Flor (1993). '*Who*, *whom*, *that* and *Ø* in two corpora of spoken English'. In *English Today*, 9: 19–21.

Aarts, Flor (1994). 'Relative *who* and *whom*: prescriptive rules and linguistic reality'. In *American Speech*, 69: 71–79.

Biber, Douglas, Stig Johansson, Geoffrey Leech, Susan Conrad and Edward Finegan (1999). *Longman grammar of spoken and written English*. Harlow: Pearson Education Ltd.

Breul, Carsten (1999). Contribution to the *Corpora discussion list* on 1 July 1999.

Fidelholz, James (1999). Contribution to the *Corpora discussion list* on 1 July 1999.
Gowers, Sir Ernest (1962). *The complete plain words*. Harmondsworth: Penguin.
de Haan, Pieter (1989). *Postmodifying clauses in the English noun phrase*. Amsterdam: Rodopi.
de Haan, Pieter (1992). 'The optimum corpus sample size?'. In Leitner, G. (ed.) *New directions in English language corpora*. Berlin & New York: Mouton de Gruyter. 3–19.
de Haan, Pieter (1999). Contribution to the *Corpora discussion list* on 2 July 1999.
McCarthy, Douglas (1999). Contribution to the *Corpora discussion list* on 5 July 1999.
Miller, Keith (1999). Contribution to the *Corpora discussion list* on 2 July 1999.
Olofsson, Arne (2001). 'The genitive of *one of whom*. A gap in the morphology and syntax of present-day English'. In Aijmer, K (ed.) *A wealth of English*. Gothenburg: Acta Universitatis Gothoburgensis. 13–22.
Quirk, Randolph, Sidney Greenbaum, Geoffrey Leech and Jan Svartvik (1985). *A comprehensive grammar of the English language*. London & New York: Longman.
Sapir, Edward (1921). *Language*. New York: Harcourt.
Schneider, Edgar (1992). '*Who(m)*? Case marking of *wh*-pronouns in written British and American English. In Leitner, G. (ed.) *New directions in English language corpora*. Berlin & New York: Mouton de Gruyter. 231–245.
Slobin, Dan (1999). Contribution to the *Corpora discussion list* on 1 July 1999.

# *Can* and *could* in contemporary British English: a study of the ICE-GB corpus

*Roberta Facchinetti*

University of Verona

> *Lady Macbeth, which I never could, and cannot, and never shall can act.*
> F. A. Kemble (Mrs. Butler) (1882) III. 165 (quoted in Oxford English Dictionary, on-line version 2000)

## Abstract

*The aim of the present study is to chart the distribution and semantic/pragmatic values of* can *and* could *in Present-day British English. To do so, I have analysed the* British Component *of the* International Corpus of English *(ICE-GB), covering 1,000,000 words distributed across a variety of textual categories. The quantitative figures of the two modals have been drawn from the whole corpus, while a 10% random sample has been selected for semantic analysis. The data confirm that in contemporary British English* can *and* could *exhibit a spectrum of quantitative distributions and semantic values. This is particularly true of the overall higher frequency of* can *as opposed to* could, *and the discrepancy between the two modals recorded in their epistemic and dynamic uses. Special attention has been given to instances of 'dynamic implication', which are superficially similar to the occurrences of dynamic ability, but need a broader pragmatic framework to be interpreted correctly.*

## 1. Aim and scope of the study

Over the past few decades, scholars have written extensively on English modality and on modal verbs in particular. A quick mention of only a few studies carried out and/or published over the last two years shows how research has thrived particularly in the field of Present-day English modal verbs (Papafragou 2000a, 2000b; Winford 2000; Palmer 2001) and of their historical development (Krug 2000, Vihla 2000, Facchinetti forthcoming). *Can* and its past-tentative form *could* are among the most targeted modals, due to the dramatic semantic changes they have undergone through the centuries, and their wide-ranging uses in present-day English.

Faithful to this long-lasting research tradition, and in the hope of contributing to enlightening some still shaded tessellas in the mosaic of present-day *can* and *could*, I have carried out a corpus-based study of these two modals, with the aim of charting their distribution and semantic/pragmatic values.

The preliminary results of this analysis, based on the *British Component* of the *International Corpus of English* (ICE-GB), are illustrated in the present paper, showing the quantitative distribution of the two modals within all the textual categories covered in the corpus, and the semantic analysis of a 10% sample of ICE-GB.

## 2. The corpus

ICE-GB exhibits a great variety of texts, involving a number of sociolinguistic variables. Like the other ICE corpora[1], it covers about 1 million running words, for a total of 500 samples, 300 spoken and 200 written, each reaching c. 2,000 words. All texts date from 1990 to 1993, and embody the English used by 'adult', 'educated', 'British' people, that is, the English used by people aged 18 or over, formally educated through the medium of English to at least the completion of the secondary school, and born in England, Scotland, or Wales, or living there since their early age. The following textual categories are represented in the corpus[2]:

**Spoken** (300)
- *Dialogue* (180)
  - Private (100)
    - Face-to-face conversations (90)
    - Phonecalls (10)
  - Public (80)
    - Classroom lessons (20)
    - Broadcast discussions (20)
    - Broadcast interviews (20)
    - Parliamentary debates (10)
    - Legal cross-examinations (10)
    - Business transactions (10)
- *Monologue* (100)
  - Unscripted (70)
    - Spontaneous commentaries (20)
    - Unscripted speeches (30)
    - Demonstrations (10)
    - Legal presentations (10)
  - Scripted (30)
    - Broadcast talks (20)
    - Non-broadcast speeches (10)
- *Mixed* (20)
  - Broadcast news (20)

**Written** (200)
- *Non-Printed* (50)
  - Non-professional writing (20)
    - Student essays (10)
    - Student examination scripts (10)
  - Correspondence (30)
    - Social letters (15)
    - Business letters (15)
- *Printed* (150)
  - Academic writing (40)
    - Humanities (10)
    - Social sciences (10)
    - Natural sciences (10)
    - Technology (10)
  - Non-academic writing (40)
    - Humanities (10)
    - Social sciences (10)
    - Natural sciences (10)
    - Technology (10)
  - Reportage (20)
    - Press news reports (20)
  - Instructional writing (20)
    - Administrative/regulatory (10)
    - Skills/hobbies (10)
  - Persuasive writing (10): press editorials
  - Creative writing (20): novels/stories

Although the written and the spoken components are categorised separately, the typological diversification of each medium allows the researcher to view a linguistic feature within a continuum of language variation, rather than as separate poles. For example, since monological scripted texts are read from a prepared, written script, they provide an overlap between the written and the spoken medium; similarly, private correspondence, despite being written, exhibits features which are also typical of informal spoken language. This textual diversification can be expected to provide interesting insights into the distribution of the modals under scrutiny, as well as specific aspects of the different text types.

In the corpus, repetitions, self-corrections, hesitations, misspellings, and items deleted by the author in hand-written texts were transcribed by the compilers and categorised as 'ignored material'. The software retrieval program ICECUP can include or exclude these data, according to the aim of the research. Since they would skew my quantitative results, such non-fluencies will be excluded from the study of the corpus under scrutiny.

## 3. Distribution of *can* and *could* in ICE-GB

The data yielded by ICE-GB are close to those recorded by Biber et al. (1999), whose study is based on a 40-million-word corpus and includes representative samples from a number of registers, broadly identifiable under the labels 'conversation', 'fiction', 'news', and 'academic prose'. These macro-categories are paralleled in ICE-GB respectively by 'spoken dialogue', 'written creative writing – novels/stories', 'written reportage – news reports', and 'academic writing', thus allowing a direct comparison between the results from the two corpora.

Both Biber et al.'s data and those from ICE-GB show the general tendency of the two modals to occur more frequently in spoken dialogue than in the written medium. Similarly, both show that *can* is used much more heavily than *could*, independently of the text category; indeed, ICE-GB exhibits an overall frequency of 3.4 per thousand words for *can* and 1.5 for *could*, as shown in Table 1[3]:

**Table 1:** Positive and negative *can* and *could* in ICE-GB (percentages and overall frequency per 1,000 words)

| TEXT CATEGORY | CAN | | | COULD | | |
|---|---|---|---|---|---|---|
| | + | - | Freq. per 1000w | + | - | Freq. per 1000w |
| | % | % | Total | % | % | total |
| 1. SPOKEN | 74 | 26 | 3.6 | 82 *** | 18 | 1.6 |
| 1.a Dialogue | 70 | 30 | 4.0 | 79 *** | 21 | 1.8 |
| 1.a.a Private | 66 | 34 | 4.4 | 76 *** | 24 | 1.8 |
| Direct conversations | 66 | 34 | 4.6 | 76 | 24 | 1.8 |
| Telephone calls | 65 | 35 | 3.2 | 70 | 30 | 2.0 |
| 1.a.b Public | 75 | 25 | 3.5 | 83 ** | 17 | 1.9 |
| Classroom lessons | 78 | 22 | 5.0 | 81 | 19 | 2.4 |
| Broadcast discussions | 69 | 31 | 2.5 | 83 | 17 | 1.2 |
| Broadcast interviews | 73 | 27 | 2.8 | 85 | 15 | 2.1 |
| Parliamentary debates | 85 | 15 | 2.5 | 83 | 17 | 1.4 |
| Legal cross-examinations | 65 | 35 | 3.1 | 78 | 22 | 2.4 |
| Business transactions | 81 | 19 | 4.9 | 94 | 6 | 1.7 |
| 1.b Monologue | 84 | 16 | 3.1 | 86 n.s. | 14 | 1.2 |
| 1.b.a Unscripted | 85 | 15 | 3.4 | 85 n.s. | 15 | 1.0 |
| Spontaneous commentaries | 81 | 19 | 1.9 | 65 | 35 | 0.5 |
| Unscripted speeches | 85 | 15 | 3.6 | 90 | 10 | 1.1 |
| Demonstrations | 88 | 12 | 7.4 | 91 | 9 | 1.0 |
| Legal presentations | 75 | 25 | 1.5 | 84 | 16 | 1.4 |
| 1.b.b Scripted | 82 | 18 | 2.5 | 88 n.s. | 13 | 1.6 |
| Broadcast talks | 80 | 20 | 2.5 | 90 | 10 | 1.8 |
| Non-broadcast speeches | 85 | 15 | 2.5 | 81 | 19 | 1.3 |
| 1.c Mixed - broadcast news | 84 | 16 | 1.7 | 95 * | 5 | 1.7 |
| | | | | | | |

| | | | | | | |
|---|---|---|---|---|---|---|
| **2. WRITTEN** | 82 | 18 | 3.1 | 85 n.s. | 15 | 1.5 |
| **2.a Non printed** | 75 | 25 | 3.6 | 86 ** | 14 | 1.3 |
| **2.a.a Non-professional writing** | 82 | 18 | 3.7 | 86 n.s. | 14 | 0.7 |
| **Untimed student essays** | 88 | 12 | 3.4 | 76 | 24 | 0.8 |
| **Student examination scripts** | 76 | 24 | 4.0 | 100 | - | 0.5 |
| **2.a.b Correspondence** | 70 | 30 | 3.6 | 86 *** | 14 | 1.8 |
| **Social letters** | 63 | 37 | 4.3 | 77 | 23 | 1.4 |
| **Business letters** | 82 | 18 | 2.8 | 93 | 7 | 2.2 |
| **2.b Printed** | 85 | 15 | 2.9 | 84 n.s. | 16 | 1.5 |
| **2.b.a Academic writing** | 94 | 6 | 2.6 | 89 n.s. | 11 | 1.0 |
| **Humanities** | 73 | 27 | 1.0 | 83 | 17 | 1.1 |
| **Social sciences** | 100 | - | 2.8 | 88 | 12 | 1.6 |
| **Natural sciences** | 100 | - | 2.3 | 100 | - | 0.2 |
| **Technology** | 92 | 8 | 4.2 | 93 | 7 | 1.3 |
| **2.b.b Non-academic writing** | 86 | 14 | 3.5 | 85 n.s. | 15 | 1.4 |
| **Humanities** | 82 | 18 | 0.9 | 80 | 20 | 1.1 |
| **Social sciences** | 71 | 29 | 2.3 | 79 | 21 | 2.0 |
| **Natural sciences** | 87 | 13 | 4.7 | 100 | - | 1.1 |
| **Technology** | 91 | 9 | 6.5 | 88 | 12 | 1.6 |
| **2.b.c Reportage - news reports** | 80 | 20 | 1.2 | 89 n.s. | 11 | 1.8 |
| **2.b.d Instructional writing** | 86 | 14 | 5.2 | 93 n.s. | 7 | 0.3 |
| **Administrative/regulatory** | 78 | 22 | 5.5 | 100 | - | 0.2 |
| **Skills and hobbies** | 93 | 7 | 5.0 | 89 | 11 | 0.4 |
| **2.b.e Persuasive wr. - editorials** | 72 | 28 | 2.6 | 90 * | 10 | 2.0 |
| **2.b.f Creative wr. - novels/stories** | 70 | 30 | 1.7 | 74 n.s. | 26 | 3.3 |
| TOTAL | 77 | 23 | 3.4 | 83 *** | 17 | 1.5 |

*** p = <0.001 ** p = <0.01 * p = <0.05
n.s. not statistically significant

The discrepancy between the two modals is stable in both the spoken and the written component, particularly in 'demonstrations' (7.4 for *can* vs 1 for *could*) and in written 'non-academic technological' texts (6.5 vs 1.6). Only a handful of written textual categories exhibit a counter-tendency, with *could* occurring slightly more frequently than *can*; this is true of humanistic writing[4] – both academic (1.0 vs 1.1) and non-academic (0.9 vs 1.1), news reports (1.2 vs 1.8), and novels/stories (1.7 vs 3.3). Undoubtedly, in novels/stories (and to some extent in news reports), the discrepancy in favour of *could* is largely due to their narrative/reporting feature, which privileges the past form of the modal. Hence, overall, these results largely confirm Biber et al.'s findings:

| | CONVERSATION | FICTION | NEWS | ACADEMIC |
|---|---|---|---|---|
| **Biber et al. (1999) ~ ICE-GB** | can>could | can<could | can<could | can>could |

Table 1 also exhibits the breakdown into percentages of positive and negative *can* and *could*; for the purpose of the quantitative analysis, it was decided to rule out wider discussion involving the polarity of the whole sentence where the modals occur. Hence, I classified as 'negative' only the instances of the two modals accompanied by *not* as a marker of negation, while I counted as 'positive' all occurrences of *can* and *could* in any other negative polarity context, that is, for example, in co-occurrence with negative or semi-negative particles like *only*, *just*, and *no longer*, as follows[5]:

(1) Privately I think that the majority of the European leaders and the diplomats believe that the Gulf crisis has shown that the Community can no longer afford not to have the authority to decide uh to act and speak with one voice in an area like this <ICE-GB:S2B-013 #16:1:C>

The data show firstly the preference of both modals to occur with their positive form in every single text category, secondly the tendency for *could* to outdo *can* in this respect (overall 83% of *could* as opposed to 77% of *can*). The difference between *could* and *can* is statistically significant in dialogic spoken sections; in contrast, in monological samples and in the written component, *could* still keeps ahead of *can*, although in a non-statistically significant way (85% vs 82%). Interestingly, in the written medium, 'correspondence' texts show that positive *could* occurs significantly more than positive *can*. Indeed, despite belonging to the written component, these texts exhibit informal features which are typical of the dialogic sections as well, where positive *could* is particularly frequent. Hence, I can conclude that in contexts implying interaction between two or more interlocutors, positive *could* occurs significantly more frequently than positive *can*.

Interesting results concerning the negative variants of the two modals can also be gathered from Table 2, showing the percentages of distribution with reference to each modal, while the raw figures are given in the Appendix (Table 2a). The data exhibit all the negative variants of the two modals, including two columns featuring *can/could not*, either in adjacent position or separated by one or more words, as in 'can/could you not':

**Table 2:** Distribution of negative variants of *can* and *could* (percentages)

| TEXT CATEGORY | CAN | | | COULD | |
|---|---|---|---|---|---|
| | can't % | cannot % | can (*) not % | couldn't % | could (*) not % |
| 1.SPOKEN | 89 | 9 | 2 | 85 | 15 |
| 1.aDialogue | 95 | 3 | 2 | 92 | 8 |
| 1.a.a Private | 97 | 1 | 2 | 96 | 4 |
| Direct conversations | 97 | 1 | 2 | 95 | 5 |
| Telephone calls | 100 | - | - | 100 | - |
| 1.a.b Public | 89 | 8 | 3 | 85 | 15 |
| Classroom lessons | 91 | 4 | 5 | 89 | - |
| Broadcast discussions | 88 | 12 | - | 89 | 11 |
| Broadcast interviews | 94 | 6 | - | 100 | - |
| Parliamentary debates | 38 | 50 | 12 | 20 | 80 |
| Legal cross-examinations | 96 | 4 | - | 91 | 9 |
| Business transactions | 95 | - | 5 | 100 | - |
| 1.b Monologue | 68 | 29 | 3 | 60 | 40 |
| 1.b.a Unscripted | 80 | 18 | 2 | 64 | 36 |
| Spontaneous commentaries | 100 | - | - | 100 | - |
| Unscripted speeches | 69 | 29 | 2 | 29 | 71 |
| Demonstrations | 95 | - | 5 | 100 | - |
| Legal presentations | 50 | 50 | - | 40 | 60 |
| 1.b.b Scripted | 37 | 60 | 3 | 54 | 46 |
| Broadcast talks | 36 | 64 | - | 88 | 12 |
| Non-broadcast speeches | 38 | 50 | 12 | - | 100 |
| 1.c Mixed - broadcast news | 75 | 25 | - | 50 | 50 |
| | | | | | |

| | | | | | |
|---|---|---|---|---|---|
| **2.WRITTEN** | 41 | 58 | 1 | 44 | 56 |
| **2.a Non printed** | 61 | 37 | 2 | 58 | 42 |
| **2.a.a Non-professional writing** | 21 | 76 | 3 | - | 100 |
| **Untimed student essays** | 22 | 78 | - | - | |
| **Student examination scripts** | 20 | 75 | 5 | - | - |
| **2.a.b Correspondence** | 78 | 20 | 2 | 73 | 27 |
| **Social letters** | 96 | 4 | - | 90 | 10 |
| **Business letters** | 20 | 73 | 7 | 40 | 60 |
| **2.b Printed** | 27 | 73 | - | 40 | 60 |
| **2.b.a Academic writing** | 8 | 92 | - | - | 100 |
| **Humanities** | - | 100 | - | - | 100 |
| **Social sciences** | - | - | - | - | 100 |
| **Natural sciences** | - | - | - | - | - |
| **Technology** | 14 | 86 | - | - | 100 |
| **2.b.b Non-academic writing** | 27 | 73 | - | - | 100 |
| **Humanities** | - | 100 | - | - | 100 |
| **Social sciences** | 43 | 57 | - | - | 100 |
| **Natural sciences** | 15 | 85 | - | - | - |
| **Technology** | 31 | 69 | - | - | 100 |
| **2.b.c Reportage - news reports** | 10 | 90 | - | 25 | 75 |
| **2.b.d Instructional writing** | 9 | 91 | - | - | 100 |
| **Administrative/regulatory** | 4 | 96 | - | - | - |
| **Skills and hobbies** | 29 | 71 | - | - | 100 |
| **2.b.e Persuasive wr. - editorials** | 20 | 80 | - | - | 100 |
| **2.b.f Creative wr. - novels/stories** | 77 | 23 | - | 81 | 19 |
| TOTAL | 76 | 23 | 1 | 71 | 29 |

For *can*, the contracted form *can't* is used far more often than *cannot* (76% vs 23%), but different data emerge from the two mediums. Unsurprisingly, *can't* is considerably more frequent in spoken than in written data, particularly in dialogue. In the written samples, however, the difference between the two variants is smaller, with *cannot* occurring slightly more frequently than its contracted counterpart (58% as opposed to 41%). Interestingly, a counter-tendency shows up in the spoken subsection of the monologic scripted data (broadcast talks and non-broadcast speeches), with a higher incidence of *cannot*[6]; and in the written subsection of the non-printed data, in social letters (96% of *can't* as opposed to 4% of *cannot*). Creative writing also appears to have a high incidence of *can't*, but a closer look at the data shows that 14 out of its 17 instances occur in dialogic sections of the novels. All these figures confirm that the language related to unofficial contexts, including dialogue and nonprofessional texts, favours the contracted form, while official language, including the scripted monologues of broadcast talks and non-broadcast speeches, tends to privilege uncontracted forms.

As for the variant *can not*, generally it involves either main verb negation or special emphasis on the negation itself. In the corpus, only 1% of all instances of negative *can* have been detected, for a total of 7 recordings, 5 of which are transcriptions of spoken extracts, while 2 are from the written unscripted section, respectively a student examination script and a business letter. The paucity of these occurrences, on the one hand, and the fact that their occurrence might very well be ascribed to the subjective choice of the transcribers, on the other, precludes us from drawing any objective conclusions concerning this form.

Finally, like *can't*, the contracted form of *could* occurs more frequently in the spoken data, while written samples have an overwhelming majority of *could not*. Since *could* is not as frequent as *can*, the difference between the contracted and the uncontracted figures is even more evident, with scores of 100% in the written and in the spoken component. Once again, it is the peculiarity of the single category, rather than the fact that it belongs to one medium or the other, which governs the frequency of negative variants. All categories appear to obey the same superordinate criterion; specifically, samples relating to official or public texts tend to exhibit a higher number of uncontracted forms. Hence, parliamentary debate is the only category in the dialogic section that exhibits a higher incidence of the uncontracted variant; similarly, in the written medium nonprinted texts yield 58% *couldn't* vs 42% *could not*, while the opposite occurs with printed data (40% vs 60%).

## 4. Semantic analysis

### 4.1 Preliminary terminological remarks

Both *can* and *could* embody a variety of meanings which can be qualified within the spectrum of epistemic, deontic and dynamic modality. For *can*, epistemic values are the least represented and generally limited to interrogative and negative polarity contexts, where the modal is the negative counterpart of either epistemic possibility *may* or epistemic necessity *must*[7]:

It must/may be John → It can't be John
=It is not possible that it is John

This restricted use of *can* has been recently questioned by Coates, at least with reference to American English, where she has recorded the following epistemic occurrence in an assertive context: 'We hope this coding system can be useful' (Coates 1995: 153). Judging from the data yielded by ICE-GB, this might be true of British English as well, since a few instances of epistemic *can* have been recorded in positive polarity contexts:

(2) We have displayed your posters in our college careers offices and hope that we can attract some good London students to the event. <ICE-GB:W1B-026 #6:1>

While this epistemic value of *can* is still debated, deontic permission and dynamic ability are undoubtedly the meanings the modal conveys to a very large extent. With reference to the former, deontic *can* expresses the speaker's/writer's request for/granting of permission:

(3) Can I can I read it just a little bit so people get the idea <ICE-GB:S1B-026 #128:1:A>
(4) If you're not in one of the three groups shown above, you can't have an NHS voucher. <ICE-GB:W2D-001 #102:1>

Here *can* is used as the less formal counterpart of *may* and tends to be more frequent in spoken than in written English; indeed, in ICE-GB it occurs twice as often in speech as writing (6 vs 3 per thousand words). The scope of the negation is generally considered to cover the modal rather than the proposition, and this is confirmed by all deontic instances of *can't/cannot* recorded in ICE-GB. Palmer (1987: 111) remarks that negation of the proposition is also possible, generally when the context makes it clear and when *not* is emphasised.

The most prevalent type of modality with *can* is dynamic, broadly classified along the two discrete poles of 'physical or mental ability' and 'possibility'. The former has *can* in co-occurrence with verbs of ***sensation*** (*see, hear, smell*...), with private verbs (*remember, understand, believe*...) or with verbs denoting action/activity. In such contexts the modal normally requires an animate subject, with agentive function, as in (5); yet inanimate subjects can also be found with ability values, as in (6):

(5) I 'd like to but, I 'm just not sure about a i what how I could, how I c how how I can dance what I can do <ICE-GB:S1A-001 #65:1:B>
(6) And I think one of the excitements of the next ten years is going to be to see whether the regional theatres can take on board the discoveries that have been made by by the small-scale touring companies <ICE-GB:S1B-050 #90:1:B>

When the action depends not on inherent properties of the subject, but on external circumstances, it is dynamic possibility that is expressed:

(7) I mean, there 're certain things that you can get cheaper out there <ICE-GB:S1A-048 #340:1:B>

In such contexts, the author has no authority or ability to shape the events according to his/her will; it is merely 'possible for' him/her to carry out an action or to find himself/herself in a situation. Because of this, unlike deontic permission and dynamic ability, the possibility value of *can* is not necessarily associated with agentivity nor is it restricted to either polarity.

Within dynamic modality, a few more peculiar uses of *can* should be mentioned, which need a broader pragmatic framework to be interpreted correctly; this is the case with suggestions, offers, and requests, as in (8) and (9):

(8) Well I mean we you know we can have a chat on the twentieth when we see each other anyway <ICE-GB:S1A-096 #227:1:B>
(9) Can you wash those few cups up uhm Rich Stuart please <ICE-GB:S1A-019 #337:1:A>

In (8) the modal expresses the subject's willingness to perform an action, while (9) is an instance of 'whimperative', whereby the speaker makes implicitly clear his desire for the addressee to act. In ICE-GB I have recorded instances of the modal followed by a private verb, as in (10), and with 3rd person subjects, expressing surprise/disagreement, as in (11):

(10) and you can also see that the the caricature quite early on in England tends to divide itself, uh quite naturally between on the one hand uh political caricature caricature addressing specific political issues uhm and then caricatures that're attacking taste <ICE-GB:S2A-057 #22:1:A>
(11) I mean, he can't just send me a bill like that <ICE-GB:S1A-078 #160:3:B>

In (10) the speaker is not merely remarking on a physical capability of his interlocutor, but rather is implicitly inviting him to view and consider the situation as he suggests, so that the utterance might be paraphrased by 'please notice that…'. Similarly, in (11) the speaker is not directly imposing an action, but rather referring to a third person, judging his behaviour and implicitly providing his own point of view as to how action should be or should have been taken.

The semantic label of 'dynamic ability' which might be applied to all such uses would not qualify them properly, since they belong only superficially to this category. So, following Palmer's categorization (1990: 86), they have been subsumed under the separate heading 'dynamic implication', since their literal semantic meaning is dynamic and their correct interpretation depends on their illocutionary force.

*Could* also embodies dynamic implication values; in this context, it is used as a polite form of *can* and as a marker of politeness and tact both when expressing a 'whimperative', as in (12) and when suggesting a course of action, as in (13):

(12) Please could the college give consideration to offering me financial support in my study for a Master's degree <ICE-GB:W1B-022 #167:14>
(13) Cos I was going to suggest uh that we could go to your humble abode <ICE-GB:S1A-098 #247:3:A>

*Could* is formally the past of *can* and as such it is employed with all types of modality in narration/reported speech:

(14) [Deontic possibility] I thought that also was because the Levites were so upset that they weren't allowed to do what the Aaronites could do <ICE-GB:S1B-001 #23:1:B>
(15) [Epistemic possibility] A useful review by Barrett and Hill (1984) argued that not all policy emerged from the top, but could develop in response to a frontline problem. <ICE-GB:W2A-014 #44:1>
(16) [Dynamic ability] A spokesman for Trilion said yesterday that neither of the company's two directors who could comment on the issue were available <ICE-GB:W2C-017 #52:3>
(17) [Dynamic possibility] And he described i in uhm uh, uh detail, uhm how he had been uhm endeavouring to or indeed had picked up this uh lintel, uhm which was one of the hundred and sixty-eight pound lintels or thereabouts, himself, uh in order to get it up the slope uh i in order to get it into a position where it could be uhm uh put back o on to the fork lift truck <ICE-GB:S2A-067 #67:1:A>

When no narration or reporting speech is involved, only dynamic modality is acceptable with *could*, be it 'possibility' or 'physical/mental ability', in collocation with verbs of sensation or with private verbs. With the dynamic ability value of past-time reference *could*, scholars have been attempting to draw a semantic line between the catenative *was/were able to* and the modal. Specifically, *was/were able to* is generally used to refer to a single action in semantically assertive contexts, while *could* lacks an implication of actuality and is preferred in non-assertive contexts:

(18) I couldn't get it started on the Saturday night because I was going to come back on Sunday <ICE-GB:S1A-038 #66:1:C>

This main qualification has been confirmed not only by the ICE-GB data, but also by a previous study (Facchinetti 2000) based on the *Lancaster-Oslo/Bergen* corpus, the *Freiburg-LOB* corpus, and the *British National Corpus*, respectively exhibiting data from 1961, 1991, and 1975 to 1993. According to the results of this study, aimed at assessing any change in the quantitative and qualitative distribution of *be able to* over a period of 30 years, *could* has maintained its semantic values virtually unaltered, and confirmed its strong one-to-one relationship with potentiality and non-assertivity, as opposed to *was/were able*, which appears to be encroaching into some of the semantic and syntactic fields generally agreed to be typical of *could*.

Past tense uses of *could* are found in 44% of its occurrences in ICE-GB, while 56% of them refer to a present or future situation, be it hypothetical or counterfactual. This use is called 'modal-past' by Palmer (2001: 14) and is used for all three types of modality, including the epistemic one in affirmative contexts:

(19) And it could cover all sort of aspects couldn't it I mean travel and uh background human interest and things like that <ICE-GB:S1A-066 #191:1:A>

Yet according to Palmer this epistemic use of affirmative *could* is not equal to *might*, which merely represents the thoughts of the speaker, while *could* 'is based on knowing facts' (Palmer 2001: 32).

Deontic and dynamic modality are also expressed by *could*, though dynamic is far more frequent (48% vs 2% of deontic modality in ICE-GB):

(20) [Deontic modality] I'm sorry could I hear Kendall again <ICE-GB:S1B-070 #135:1:B>
(21) [Dynamic ability] I couldn't tell you what it's called <ICE-GB:S1A-016 #145:1:E>
(22) [Dynamic possibility] Single- and three-phase electrical supplies are generally available in a milking parlour where they are commonly used to power the milking vacuum pumps, and could be used to power a robot. <ICE-GB:W2A-033 #53:1>

Undoubtedly, the above-mentioned uses of *can* and *could* do not cover all their semantic/pragmatic realizations, since ever-changing contextual situations foster a whole range of indeterminate occurrences. In order to give account of the indeterminate uses recorded in ICE-GB, a separate category of 'borderline' values has been created. In these occurrences of *can* and *could*, two or even all three types of modality merge to the point that it is difficult to discriminate which is prominent. This is the case with (23) and (24):

(23) If you paid and/or were credited with Class 1 contributions at the full rate in the tax years on which your claim is based, you can get Unemployment Benefit if you satisfy both the contribution conditions on page 9.
<ICE-GB:W2D-002 #24:1>
[Dynamic possibility: 'it is possible for you to get ...']
[Deontic possibility: 'You are allowed to get ...']

(24) I feel that if only he had a home, secure and fulfilling job, close friends, he could bounce back easily. <ICE-GB:W1B-015 #105:5>
[Dynamic ability: 'he would be able to bounce back...']
[Dynamic possibility: 'it would be possible for him to bounce back...']
[Epistemic possibility: 'it is possible that he would bounce back...']

## 4.2 Results

The 10% subcorpus selected to chart the semantic values of the two modals under scrutiny covers a total of 517 occurrences, 350 for *can* and 167 for *could*. Undoubtedly the sample data hamper a thorough, exhaustive analysis in every single textual category, since, particularly with reference to *could*, a few sub-categories are covered by a lower number of texts than others in the whole corpus. Hence, in these data, they exhibit even lower figures. Still, this corpus can yield an overall view of the semantic values conveyed by *can* and *could*, as shown in Figure 1:

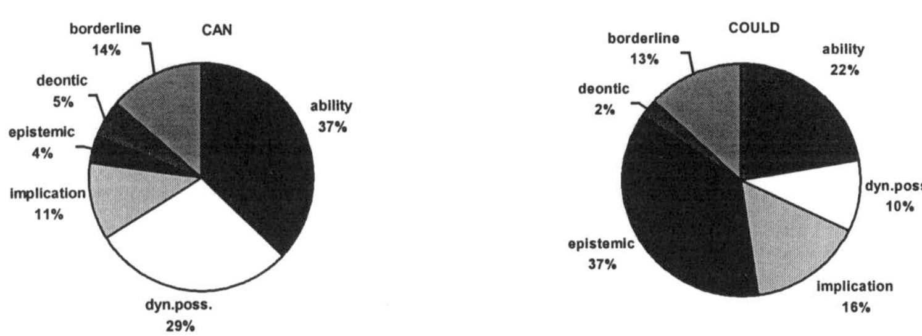


**Figure 1:** Overall semantic values of *can* and *could* in the 10% sample of ICE-GB

*Can* and *could* appear to behave differently with reference to the types of modality they favour. Indeed, while epistemic modality is by far the least represented in *can* (4%), it is the most common in *could* (37%); in contrast, dynamic ability and dynamic possibility values together account for almost two thirds of the total occurrences of *can*, while they are expressed to a far lower extent in *could*. Only deontic values, instances of dynamic implication, and borderline cases maintain a relatively similar frequency in the two modals.

The breakdown of data into a few textual macro-categories allows me both to identify the specific areas where the difference between the two modals is particularly manifest, and to compare my results with those produced by Biber et al. (1999). Tables 3a and 3b show in detail the raw figures of each semantic value:

**Table 3a:** Semantic values of *can* in the 10% sample of ICE-GB with reference to the main textual categories (percentages of each semantic meaning within one category are given in brackets)

| TEXT CATEGORY | DYNAMIC | | | EPISTEMIC | DEONTIC | BORDERLINE | TOTAL |
|---|---|---|---|---|---|---|---|
| | ability | possibility | implication | possibility | possibility | | |
| **1. SPOKEN** | 102 (44) | 44 (19) | 35 (15) | 9 (4) | 14 (6) | 26 (11) | 230 |
| **1.a Dialogue** | 68 (43) | 29 (18) | 27 (17) | 8 (5) | 10 (6) | 16 (10) | 158 |
| **1.a.a Private** | 44 (44) | 16 (16) | 19 (19) | 5 (5) | 7 (7) | 10 (10) | 101 |
| **1.a.b Public** | 24 (42) | 13 (23) | 8 (14) | 3 (5) | 3 (5) | 6 (11) | 57 |
| **1.b Monologue** | 27 (45) | 12 (20) | 7 (12) | 1 (2) | 4 (7) | 9 (15) | 60 |
| **1.b.a Unscripted** | 18 (41) | 10 (23) | 5 (11) | - | 4 (9) | 7 (16) | 44 |
| **1.b.b Scripted** | 9 (56) | 2 (13) | 2 (13) | 1 (6) | - | 2 (13) | 16 |
| **1.c Mixed - broadcast news** | 7 (58) | 3 (25) | 1 (8) | - | - | 1 (8) | 12 |
| | | | | | | | |
| **2. WRITTEN** | 28 (23) | 57 (48) | 4 (3) | 5 (4) | 4 (3) | 22 (18) | 120 |
| **2.a Non printed** | 9 (28) | 13 (41) | 2 (6) | 3 (9) | 1 (3) | 4 (13) | 32 |
| **2.a.a Non-professional wr.** | 4 (22) | 9 (50) | - | 2 (11) | - | 3 (17) | 18 |
| **2.a.b Correspondence** | 5 (36) | 4 (29) | 2 (14) | 1 (7) | 1 (7) | 1 (7) | 14 |
| **2.b Printed** | 19 (22) | 44 (50) | 2 (2) | 2 (2) | 3 (3) | 18 (20) | 88 |
| **2.b.a Academic writing** | 5 (24) | 15 (71) | - | - | - | 1 (5) | 21 |
| **2.b.b Non-academic writing** | 2 (8) | 16 (64) | - | 1 (4) | 1 (4) | 5 (20) | 25 |
| **2.b.c Reportage - news reports** | 3 (50) | 1 (17) | 1 (17) | - | - | 1 (17) | 6 |
| **2.b.d Instructional writing** | 3 (14) | 11 (50) | - | - | 2 (9) | 6 (27) | 22 |
| **2.b.e Persuasive writing- editorials** | 1 (17) | - | - | 1 (17) | - | 4 (67) | 6 |
| **2.b.f Creative writing - novels/stories** | 5 (63) | 1 (13) | 1 (13) | - | - | 1 (13) | 8 |
| TOTAL | **130 (37)** | **101 (29)** | **39 (11)** | **14 (4)** | **18 (5)** | **48 (14)** | **350** |

**Table 3b:** Semantic values of *could* in the 10% sample of ICE-GB with reference to he main textual categories (percentages of each semantic meaning within one category are given in brackets)

| TEXT CATEGORY | DYNAMIC | | | EPISTEMIC | DEONTIC | BORDERLINE | TOTAL |
|---|---|---|---|---|---|---|---|
| | ability | possibility | implication | possibility | possibility | | |
| **1. SPOKEN** | 25 (23) | 10 (9) | 19 (18) | 40 (37) | 4 (4) | 10 (9) | **108** |
| **1.a Dialogue** | 17 (23) | 3 (4) | 18 (25) | 27 (37) | 2 (3) | 6 (8) | **73** |
| **1.a.a Private** | 9 (21) | 3 (7) | 11 (26) | 16 (38) | - | 3 (7) | **42** |
| **1.a.b Public** | 8 (26) | - | 7 (23) | 11 (35) | 2 (6) | 3 (10) | **31** |
| **1.b Monologue** | 6 (21) | 7 (24) | - | 11 (38) | 2 (7) | 3 (10) | **29** |
| **1.b.a Unscripted** | 5 (26) | 3 (16) | - | 8 (42) | - | 3 (16) | **19** |
| **1.b.b Scripted** | 1 (10) | 4 (40) | - | 3 (30) | 2 (20) | - | **10** |
| **1.c Mixed - broadcast news** | 2 (33) | - | 1 (17) | 2 (33) | | 1 (17) | **6** |
| | | | | | | | |
| **2. WRITTEN** | 12 (20) | 7 (12) | 7 (12) | 21 (36) | - | 12 (20) | **59** |
| **2.a Non printed** | 2 (14) | 3 (21) | 5 (36) | 2 (14) | - | 2 )14) | **14** |
| **2.a.a Non-professional wr.** | 1 (20) | 1 (20) | - | 2 (40) | - | 1 (20) | **5** |
| **2.a.b Correspondence** | 1 (11) | 2 (22) | 5 (56) | - | - | 1 (11) | **9** |
| **2.b Printed** | 10 (22) | 4 (9) | 2 (4) | 19 (42) | - | 10 (22) | **45** |
| **2.b.a Academic writing** | - | 2 (29) | - | 3 (43) | - | 2 (29) | **7** |
| **2.b.b Non-academic writing** | 1 (17) | 1 (17) | - | 2 (33) | - | 2 (33) | **6** |

| | | | | | | | |
|---|---|---|---|---|---|---|---|
| **2.b.c Reportage - news reports** | 1 (9) | 1 (9) | - | 7 (64) | - | 2 (18) | **11** |
| **2.b.d Instructional writing** | - | - | - | 1 (50) | - | 1 (50) | **2** |
| **2.b.e Persuasive writing - editorials** | - | - | - | 2 (100) | - | - | **2** |
| **2.b.f Creative writing - novels/stories** | 8 (47) | - | 2 (12) | 4 (24) | - | 3 (18) | **17** |
| **TOTAL** | **37 (22)** | **17 (10)** | **26 (16)** | **61 (37)** | **4 (2)** | **22 (13)** | **167** |

Undoubtedly, the peculiarities of the different textual varieties affect the incidence of the modal meanings; hence, for example, the intrinsically interactive features of spoken data partly justify the high incidence of deontic and dynamic implication values for both *can* and *could* in this medium, as opposed to the corresponding results for the written data.

Overall, my results match those recorded by Biber et al. (1999), the most striking similarities being the following:

(i) dynamic ability:
- higher frequency of *can* in conversation than in academic writing;
- low frequency of *could* in academic writing;
- high frequency of *could* in fiction;

(ii) dynamic possibility (Biber et al.'s 'extrinsic possibility'): high frequency of *can* in academic writing;

(iii) epistemic possibility (Biber et al.'s 'logical possibility'): high frequency of *could* in academic writing;

(iv) deontic possibility: rare use of *can* and *could* in academic writing.

More specifically, in my sample corpus, the vast majority of the 130 occurrences of *can* with dynamic ability values are concentrated in the spoken medium, be it dialogue or monologue; whereas, of the total 120 occurrences in the written sample, only 28 were recorded with dynamic ability values. This appears to be a constant feature of all written data, with the exception of news reports and narrative texts; however, the raw figures exhibiting this counter-tendency are too low to lead to statistically conclusive results.

Similarly, dynamic ability *could* is slightly more frequent in spoken than in written contexts, although in the latter its high frequency depends on creative writing. In the quantitative analysis, *could* proved to have a high incidence in creative writing, which seems to be largely accounted for by ability values.

Interestingly, with dynamic possibility, there is no substantial difference between written and spoken medium for *could*, nor is there any prevailing textual type; whereas for *can*, dynamic possibility values are featured to a limited extent in spoken contexts (19%), and written data show high figures (48%), both in non-printed and in printed texts, with the highest incidence (71%) in academic writing. The breakdown of textual categories, however, shows that within non-printed data, in 'correspondence' texts, dynamic possibility *can* tends to behave in the same way as in spoken texts, with a relatively low frequency. Once again, the peculiar features of 'correspondence' are like those of the spoken medium. Finally, printed news reports and narrative samples show an extremely low frequency of dynamic possibility *can*, with only one occurrence. Undoubtedly, the figures are too low to produce statistically significant results, yet the data recorded confirm the preference in narrative texts for *could* rather than for *can*.

For *could* even more than *can,* a larger number of occurrences is needed to reach conclusive results, particularly when it comes to the breakdown into textual categories and subcategories. The lack of deontic occurrences can only confirm the very limited frequency of this type of modality with *could* recorded by Biber et al. as well, but at the same time can give us no insights into textual differentiation.

In contrast, epistemic modality is by far the most common use of *could* and is present both in spoken and in written contexts. While in the spoken data it is equally frequent in dialogic, monologic and in mixed data, the written samples show greater diversity. Once again, this might be mainly due to the limited number of occurrences analysed semantically; and undoubtedly call for further study.

Finally, 'implication' is strongly connected to the pragmatic context and intrinsically conveys the illocutionary force of requests, suggests, and proposals. This is why both *can* and *could* are frequent in dialogue, while in monologue *could* does not occur at all; in written data it occurs more frequently in non-printed written texts and in correspondence.

## 5. Conclusion

Provisional as it may be, this study has confirmed that in contemporary British English *can* and *could* exhibit a spectrum of quantitative distributions and semantic/pragmatic values. This is particularly true for the overall higher frequency of *can* as opposed to *could*, and to the discrepancy between the two modals in their epistemic and dynamic uses.

ICE-GB has proved of great use in the description of such a variety of uses, thanks to the wide range of text categories of the corpus. Indeed, this diversification has shown that there is a strong relationship between the peculiarities of text type and the quantitative/qualitative distribution of a linguistic variant.

Finally, the present study has also drawn attention to **dynamic implication** modality, which has been shown to be superficially similar to, but inherently different from **dynamic ability**. Indeed, like a villager living on the border between two countries and having the right of citizenship in both, dynamic implication exhibits values which can be traced in the semantic field of ability, but whose discourse implications require them to be interpreted pragmatically as suggestions, proposals or requests.

The 10% sample of ICE-GB which has been analysed semantically has been an interesting resource for the analysis of these and other meanings of the two modals under scrutiny; yet more data will certainly prove indispensable in providing a clearer picture of them and of their distribution in British English.

## Notes

1 The project of the *International Corpus of English*, first launched by Sidney Greenbaum in 1988, is envisaged to assemble a database comprising samples of written and spoken English in countries where English is a medium for intranational communication between natives. In order to provide adequate means of variationist linguistic analysis, all core corpora are intended to share the same design and methods of processing. To date, 4 component corpora – Great Britain, New Zealand, East Africa, and Hong Kong – have been released. An in-depth analysis of the major features of ICE is provided in Greenbaum (1996).

2 The figures in parentheses indicate the number of 2,000-word texts in each category.

3 For the purpose of this discussion, the figures show the percentages over the total numbers, while the raw data are given in the Appendix (Table 1a). In the textual macro-categories (1, 1.a, 1.a.a, 1.a.b, 1.b, 1.b.a, 1.b.b, 1.c, 2, 2.a, 2.a.a, 2.a.b, 2.b, 2.b.a, 2.b.b, 2.b.c, 2.b.d, 2.b.e, 2.b.f, total), the asterisks and the symbol n.s. (= non significant) in the column of the percentages of positive could refer to the degree of statistical significance of these figures as compared to the corresponding ones of positive can.

4 The category of 'Humanities' includes published books, journals, magazines, leaflets, and newspapers.

5 In all the examples the modal has been underlined.

6 Parliamentary debates belonging to the dialogical section also exhibit 4 occurrences of *cannot* as opposed to the 3 of *can't*, but the number of data are not significantly relevant; in contrast, parliamentary debates show a higher level of formality, which leads the speaker to employ linguistic forms typical of the written medium.

7 With reference to the negation of epistemic *must*, the use of *can not* is mostly typical of British English, since in American English *must not* is also exploited (Tottie 1985, Palmer 1990, and De Haan 1997, among others).

## References

Aarts, Bas and Charles F. Meyer (eds) (1995). *The verb in contemporary English*. Cambridge: Cambridge University Press.

Biber, Douglas, Stig Johansson, Geoffrey Leech, Susan Conrad and Edward Finegan (1999). *Longman grammar of spoken and written English*. London: Longman.

Coates, Jenifer (1995). 'The expression of Root and Epistemic possibility in English'. In B. Aarts and C.F. Meyer (eds), 145–156.
De Haan, Ferdinand (1997). *The interaction of modality and negation. A typological study*. New York: Garland Publishing.
Facchinetti, Roberta (2000). 'Be able to in Present-day British English'. In C. Mair and M. Hundt (eds), 117–130.
Facchinetti, Roberta (forthcoming). 'A corpus-based study of *can* in Early Modern English'. In J. Fisiak (ed.).
Fisiak, Jacek (ed.) (forthcoming). *Festschrift to celebrate Akiro Oizumi*. Berlin: Mouton de Gruyter.
Greenbaum, Sidney (ed.) (1996). *Comparing English worldwide: the International Corpus of English*. Oxford: Clarendon Press.
Kirk, John (ed.) (2000). *Corpora Galore. Analyses and techniques in describing English. Papers from the 19th International Conference on English Language Research on Computerized Corpora (ICAME 1998)*. Amsterdam: Rodopi.
Krug, Manfred (2000). *Emerging English modals: a corpus-based study of grammaticalization*. [Topics in English Linguistics]. Berlin: Mouton de Gruyter.
Mair, Christian and Marianne Hundt (eds) (2000). *Corpus linguistics and linguistic theory. Papers from the Twentieth International Conference on English Language research on Computerized Corpora (ICAME 20)*. Amsterdam: Rodopi.
Palmer, Frank Robert (1965/1987). *The English verb*. London: Longman
Palmer, Frank Robert (1990). *Modality and the English modals*. London: Longman.
Palmer, Frank Robert (2001). *Mood and modality*. (2nd ed.) Cambridge: Cambridge University Press.
Papafragou, Anna (2000a). *Modality: issues in the semantics-pragmatics interface*. Amsterdam: Elsevier.
Papafragou, Anna (2000b). 'On speech-act modality'. *Journal of Pragmatics* 32: 519–538.
Tottie, Gunnel (1985). 'The negation of epistemic necessity in present-day British and American English'. *English World-Wide* 6.1: 87–116.
Vihla, Minna (2000). 'Epistemic possibility: a study based on a medical corpus'. In J. Kirk (ed.), 209–224.
Winford, Donald (2000). 'Irrealis in Sranan: mood and modality in a radical creole'. *Journal of Pidgin and Creole Languages* 15.1: 63–126.

## Appendix

**Table 1a**: Positive and negative *can* and *could* (raw data)

| TEXT CATEGORY | CAN | | | COULD | | | TOTAL |
|---|---|---|---|---|---|---|---|
| | + | - | total | + | - | total | |
| 1. SPOKEN | 1687 | 579 | 2266 | 833 | 182 | 1015 | **3281** |
| 1.a Dialogue | 1052 | 458 | 1510 | 545 | 143 | 688 | **2198** |
| 1.a.a Private | 601 | 311 | 912 | 280 | 90 | 370 | **1282** |
| Direct conversations | 558 | 288 | 846 | 252 | 78 | 330 | **1176** |
| Telephone calls | 43 | 23 | 66 | 28 | 12 | 40 | **106** |
| 1.a.b Public | 451 | 147 | 598 | 265 | 53 | 318 | **916** |
| Classroom lessons | 163 | 46 | 209 | 83 | 19 | 102 | **311** |
| Broadcast discussions | 75 | 34 | 109 | 45 | 9 | 54 | **163** |
| Broadcast interviews | 45 | 17 | 62 | 40 | 7 | 47 | **109** |
| Parliamentary debates | 45 | 8 | 53 | 24 | 5 | 29 | **82** |
| Legal cross-examinations | 42 | 23 | 65 | 40 | 11 | 51 | **116** |
| Business transactions | 81 | 19 | 100 | 33 | 2 | 35 | **135** |
| 1.b Monologue | 573 | 109 | 682 | 217 | 35 | 252 | **934** |
| 1.b.a Unscripted | 439 | 79 | 518 | 126 | 22 | 148 | **666** |
| Spontaneous commentaries | 65 | 15 | 80 | 15 | 8 | 23 | **103** |
| Unscripted speeches | 203 | 35 | 238 | 64 | 7 | 71 | **309** |
| Demonstrations | 147 | 21 | 168 | 21 | 2 | 23 | **191** |
| Legal presentations | 24 | 8 | 32 | 26 | 5 | 31 | **63** |
| 1.b.b Scripted | 134 | 30 | 164 | 91 | 13 | 104 | **268** |
| Broadcast talks | 88 | 22 | 110 | 69 | 8 | 77 | **187** |
| Non-broadcast speeches | 46 | 8 | 54 | 22 | 5 | 27 | **81** |
| 1.c Mixed - broadcast news | 62 | 12 | 74 | 71 | 4 | 75 | **149** |
| | | | | | | | |
| 2. WRITTEN | 1072 | 230 | 1302 | 524 | 96 | 620 | **1922** |
| 2.a Non printed | 283 | 94 | 377 | 120 | 19 | 139 | **516** |
| 2.a.a Non-professional writing | 128 | 29 | 157 | 24 | 4 | 28 | **185** |
| Untimed student essays | 64 | 9 | 73 | 13 | 4 | 17 | **90** |
| Student examination scripts | 64 | 20 | 84 | 11 | 0 | 11 | **95** |
| 2.a.b Correspondence | 155 | 65 | 220 | 96 | 15 | 111 | **331** |
| Social letters | 85 | 50 | 135 | 34 | 10 | 44 | **179** |
| Business letters | 70 | 15 | 85 | 62 | 5 | 67 | **152** |
| 2.b Printed | 789 | 136 | 925 | 404 | 77 | 481 | **1406** |
| 2.b.a Academic writing | 208 | 13 | 221 | 78 | 10 | 88 | **309** |
| Humanities | 16 | 6 | 22 | 19 | 4 | 23 | **45** |
| Social sciences | 60 | 0 | 60 | 30 | 4 | 34 | **94** |
| Natural sciences | 49 | 0 | 49 | 4 | 0 | 4 | **53** |
| Technology | 83 | 7 | 90 | 25 | 2 | 27 | **117** |
| 2.b.b Non-academic writing | 261 | 44 | 305 | 105 | 18 | 123 | **428** |
| Humanities | 18 | 4 | 22 | 20 | 5 | 25 | **47** |
| Social sciences | 34 | 14 | 48 | 33 | 9 | 42 | **90** |
| Natural sciences | 84 | 13 | 97 | 22 | 0 | 22 | **119** |
| Technology | 125 | 13 | 138 | 30 | 4 | 34 | **172** |
| 2.b.c Reportage - news reports | 41 | 10 | 51 | 67 | 8 | 75 | **126** |
| 2.b.d Instructional writing | 189 | 32 | 221 | 13 | 1 | 14 | **235** |
| Administrative/regulatory | 91 | 25 | 116 | 5 | 0 | 5 | **121** |
| Skills and hobbies | 98 | 7 | 105 | 8 | 1 | 9 | **114** |
| 2.b.e Persuasive wr. - editorials | 38 | 15 | 53 | 38 | 4 | 42 | **95** |
| 2.b.f Creative wr. - novels/stories | 52 | 22 | 74 | 103 | 36 | 139 | **213** |
| TOTAL | **2759** | **809** | **3568** | **1357** | **278** | **1635** | **5203** |

**Table 2a:** Distribution of the negative variants of *can* and *could* (raw data)

| TEXT CATEGORY | can't | cannot | can * not | can not | Total | couldn't | could not | could * not | total |
|---|---|---|---|---|---|---|---|---|---|
| 1.SPOKEN | 517 | 51 | 6 | 5 | 579 | 154 | 23 | 5 | **182** |
| 1.a Dialogue | 434 | 16 | 6 | 2 | 458 | 131 | 8 | 4 | **143** |
| 1.a.a Private | 303 | 4 | 2 | 2 | 311 | 86 | 2 | 2 | **90** |
| Direct conversations | 280 | 4 | 2 | 2 | 288 | 74 | 2 | 2 | **78** |
| Telephone calls | 23 | - | - | - | 23 | 12 | - | - | **12** |
| 1.a.b Public | 131 | 12 | 4 | - | 147 | 45 | 6 | 2 | **53** |
| Classroom lessons | 42 | 2 | 2 | - | 46 | 17 | - | 2 | **19** |
| Broadcast discussions | 30 | 4 | - | - | 34 | 8 | 1 | - | **9** |
| Broadcast interviews | 16 | 1 | - | - | 17 | 7 | - | - | **7** |
| Parliamentary debates | 3 | 4 | 1 | - | 8 | 1 | 4 | - | **5** |
| Legal cross-examinations | 22 | 1 | - | - | 23 | 10 | 1 | - | **11** |
| Business transactions | 18 | - | 1 | - | 19 | 2 | - | - | **2** |
| 1.b Monologue | 74 | 32 | - | 3 | 109 | 21 | 13 | 1 | **35** |
| 1.b.a Unscripted | 63 | 14 | - | 2 | 79 | 14 | 8 | - | **22** |
| Spontaneous commentaries | 15 | - | - | - | 15 | 8 | - | - | **8** |
| Unscripted speeches | 24 | 10 | - | 1 | 35 | 2 | 5 | - | **7** |
| Demonstrations | 20 | - | - | 1 | 21 | 2 | - | - | **2** |
| Legal presentations | 4 | 4 | - | - | 8 | 2 | 3 | | **5** |
| 1.b.b Scripted | 11 | 18 | - | 1 | 30 | 7 | 5 | 1 | **13** |
| Broadcast talks | 8 | 14 | - | - | 22 | 7 | 1 | - | **8** |
| Non-broadcast speeches | 3 | 4 | - | 1 | 8 | - | 4 | 1 | **5** |
| 1.c Mixed - broadcast news | 9 | 3 | - | - | 12 | 2 | 2 | - | **4** |
| | | | | | | | | | |
| 2.WRITTEN | 94 | 134 | - | 2 | 230 | 42 | 54 | - | **96** |
| 2.a Non printed | 57 | 35 | - | 2 | 94 | 11 | 8 | - | **19** |
| 2.a.a Non-professional writing | 6 | 22 | - | 1 | 29 | - | 4 | - | **4** |
| Untimed student essays | 2 | 7 | - | - | 9 | - | 4 | - | **4** |
| Student examination scripts | 4 | 15 | - | 1 | 20 | - | - | - | **0** |
| 2.a.b Correspondence | 51 | 13 | - | 1 | 65 | 11 | 4 | - | **15** |
| Social letters | 48 | 2 | - | - | 50 | 9 | 1 | - | **10** |
| Business letters | 3 | 11 | - | 1 | 15 | 2 | 3 | - | **5** |
| 2.b Printed | 37 | 99 | - | - | 136 | 31 | 46 | - | **77** |
| 2.b.a Academic writing | 1 | 12 | - | - | 13 | - | 10 | - | **10** |
| Humanities | | 6 | - | - | 6 | - | 4 | - | **4** |
| Social sciences | | - | - | - | - | - | 4 | - | **4** |
| Natural sciences | | - | - | - | - | - | - | - | |
| Technology | 1 | 6 | - | - | 7 | - | 2 | - | **2** |
| 2.b.b Non-academic writing | 12 | 32 | - | - | 44 | - | 18 | - | **18** |
| Humanities | | 4 | - | - | 4 | - | 5 | - | **5** |
| Social sciences | 6 | 8 | - | - | 14 | - | 9 | - | **9** |
| Natural sciences | 2 | 11 | - | - | 13 | - | - | - | |
| Technology | 4 | 9 | - | - | 13 | - | 4 | - | **4** |
| 2.b.c Reportage - news reports | 1 | 9 | - | - | 10 | 2 | 6 | - | **8** |
| 2.b.d Instructional writing | 3 | 29 | - | - | 32 | - | 1 | - | **1** |
| Administrative/regulatory | 1 | 24 | - | - | 25 | - | - | - | |
| Skills and hobbies | 2 | 5 | - | - | 7 | - | 1 | - | **1** |
| 2.b.e Persuasive wr. - editorials | 3 | 12 | - | - | 15 | - | 4 | - | **4** |
| 2.b.f Creative wr. - novels/stories | 17 | 5 | - | - | 22 | 29 | 7 | - | **36** |
| TOTAL | **611** | **185** | **6** | **7** | **809** | **196** | **77** | **5** | **278** |

# What's a word like *girl* doing in a place like this? Occupational labels, sexist usages and corpus research[1]

*Janet Holmes and Robert Sigley*

Victoria University of Wellington

**Abstract**

*In this paper, we use corpus data to track social change in patterns of gender-marking between 1961 and 1991. Focussing initially on frequency data for general terms such as* woman *and* man, *the analysis identifies differences between patterns found in the Brown and LOB corpora, compared to the Frown, FLOB and Wellington corpora of written English, and considers several alternative social interpretations of the data. The distributional patterns for occupational terms in the LOB, FLOB and Wellington corpora are then examined in more detail, with attention paid both to the use of gender pre-modification and post-modification. The results suggest that women continue to be the linguistically marked gender. However, there is some evidence to support a positive interpretation, since the relevant marked contexts reflect the entry of women into occupational domains previously considered exclusively male.*

## 1. Introduction

Sexist language is one means by which a culture or society can perpetuate sexist attitudes, and for this reason it has attracted much attention from feminists. Analyses of sexist usages in a number of varieties of English have identified many ways in which sexist attitudes are encoded, maintained and systematically re-created or constructed in everyday interaction (Holmes 1999). Areas which have been examined include the use of pseudo-generic terms, such as *-man* and *he;* gender-neutral terms such as *chairperson;* sexist suffixes such as *-ess* and *-ette*; metaphorical reference terms such as *bitch* and *stud;* and terms of address such as *Ms* and *dear* (Holmes 1993a, 1993b, 1993c, 1997, in press, Pauwels 1998, Wolfson and Manes 1980). Such analyses indicate that women are often assigned subordinate status by virtue of their gender alone, and that they are treated linguistically as subordinate, regardless of their actual power or social status in a particular context. The English language appears to collude in the subordination of women, in that females are 'marked' compared to males. However, what counts as 'marked' is often socially rather than linguistically determined (as shown by the fact that different types of behaviour in lifestyle and occupation are 'marked' for each gender): marked behaviour is that which bucks conservative social expectations. Corpus analysis of such differences in markedness can therefore provide interesting insights into social change.

Feminists long ago identified the linguistic markedness of women as a particular cause for concern in the battle for equal treatment of the sexes. Moreover, according to at least one recent analysis (Romaine 1999: 130), there is little reason to believe that feminist initiatives have brought about any radical change in the situation in the last few decades. Romaine cites evidence of the linguistic markedness of women from the 100 million word British National Corpus. She points to disparities in patterns such as *lady doctor* (125 instances) vs *gentleman doctor* (0). Clearly, women are still the marked gender in the area of occupational labels, as in so many other semantic areas. However, it is not immediately clear whether such discrepancies extend much beyond the particular well-known examples cited – which could be considered almost stereotypical. A more detailed search of a wider range of tokens in a range of contexts thus seems worthwhile.

This paper pursues such issues a little further by examining data from corpora constructed on similar principles at different points in time, in order to identify linguistic evidence of social change in progress. After examining the patterns revealed by frequency data alone, we focus on the area of occupational labels, comparing the relative frequencies of forms used for referring to men and women. The distributional patterns for occupational terms in the LOB, FLOB and Wellington Written corpora are examined in some detail, with attention paid both to the use of gender pre-modification and post-modification.

Our data (raw frequencies, and more detailed consideration of use in context) are drawn from 5 parallel million-word corpora of edited written English, as listed in Table 1. Each contains 500 2000-word texts, following the text category composition established for the Brown Corpus of American English (Francis 1964) and its British equivalent, the Lancaster-Oslo-Bergen (LOB) Corpus (Johansson 1978). Time depth is provided by comparing these corpora (based on texts published in 1961) with parallel samples from 1991 (known respectively as the Frown and FLOB corpora), and with the Wellington Corpus of Written New Zealand English (WWC) based on texts from 1986–90 (described in Bauer 1993).

**Table 1:** Parallel million-word corpora of edited written English

| Name: | National variety | Texts published in | Completed |
|---|---|---|---|
| Brown | American | 1961 | 1964 |
| LOB | British | 1961 | 1978 |
| Frown | American | 1991 | 1999 |
| FLOB | British | 1990–91 | 1999 |
| WWC | New Zealand | 1986–90 | 1994 |

## 2. *Women, men* and social salience

Even using the grossest level of analysis, there are indications that the position of women in society has changed over the last forty years. An earlier analysis of the relative frequency of tokens of *woman/women* vs *lady/ladies*, for instance, indicated that in British, American and New Zealand usage, instances of *woman/women* had increased dramatically over the last thirty years, while by comparison, *lady/ladies* had decreased (Holmes 1999).

**Table 2:** Overall corpus frequencies of *woman/women, man/men, female(s)* and *male(s)*

| | Brown | LOB | Frown | FLOB | WWC |
|---|---|---|---|---|---|
| | (1961 AmE) | (1961 BrE) | (1991 AmE) | (1991 BrE) | (1986–90 NZE) |
| | | | | | |
| *woman* | 248 | 267 | 478 | 267 | 426 |
| *women* | 223 | 223 | 851 | 461 | 743 |
| | | | | | |
| *man* | 1354 | 1194 | 840 | 738 | 757 |
| *men* | 788 | 641 | 556 | 454 | 510 |
| | | | | | |
| *female* | 54 | 38 | 144 | 86 | 111 |
| *females* | 17 | 7 | 24 | 17 | 51 |
| | | | | | |
| *male* | 37 | 40 | 177 | 89 | 161 |
| *males* | 19 | 8 | 47 | 22 | 59 |

Table 2 provides information on the frequency with which the terms *woman/women* and *man/men* appeared in written material over a thirty-year period; this data is graphed as Figure 1.

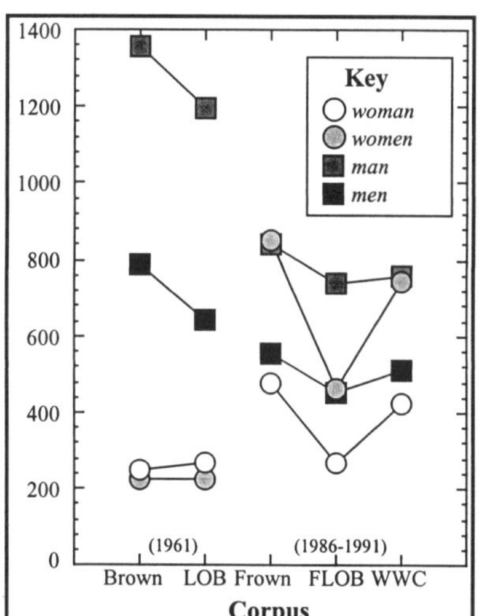


**Figure 1:** Overall frequencies of *woman/women* and *man/men*

It is clear from these figures that, overall, references to women have more than doubled between 1961 and 1991 – a pattern confirmed in the British National Corpus by Romaine (1999: 139). The WWC and Frown figures are particularly high, with FLOB lagging somewhat. At first sight, this might suggest that women have taken unusually prominent roles in New Zealand and the United States; and indeed, New Zealand in 1986 had, for the first time, a Ministry of Women's Affairs, and a sizeable minority of female Cabinet members. (At the time of writing, women comprise 11 of 26 Cabinet members, and have been appointed to all of New Zealand's top 5 political and judicial posts – Prime Minister, Leader of the Opposition, Chief Justice, Attorney-General, and Governor-General.)

But it is important to note that the increase is disproportionately in reference to *women* in the plural, rather than to the singular *woman*. Indeed, while *men* is more frequent in Brown and LOB, *women* is more frequent than *men* in all three of the more recent corpora. The plural form tends to be used in discussing women as a group, so this increase in *women* indicates that proportionately more texts now have women as a topic. This is at least partly due to inclusion of texts promoting, or at least discussing, feminist viewpoints on a variety of issues. The increasing text frequency of *women* in these corpora can thus be regarded, in part, as a sign of ongoing consciousness-raising, as shown by examples (1)–(4).

(1) the feminist view that prostitution is a form of exploitation of women, [...] (WWC G52 024)[2]
(2) Women are not objects there for men to use and are under no obligation to have sex with a man, even if he is their husband. (WWC J22 039)
(3) [M]en's control of women's sexuality places additional constraints on women's lives. (Frown F25 091)
(4) [...] there is much evidence that women in general enjoy lower status than men, both at home and at work [...] (FLOB J22 042)

Some examples, though, point towards contributions from other, less positive social trends. For example, increases in reported violence against women could indicate, not just increasing awareness or condemnation, but also a real increase in such behaviour.

(5) In recent years there has been a marked increase in the amount of violent crime committed in urban centres, especially involving rape and sexual assault. [...] As a result, urban parks have become increasingly dangerous to women and unaccompanied children. (WWC F41 002-007)
(6) [...] headlines began to scream all over the country with a renewed, shall we say, outbreak of visible incidents involving the victimization of women. (Frown H03 057)

Still other examples display a more reactionary stance:

(7) After all women are only what their husbands are. (WWC L20 159)

By contrast, the frequency of the singular *woman* (to the extent that it makes reference to women as individuals) is probably a closer index of real social progress towards gender equality, at least in terms of whose stories are judged important enough or interesting enough to write and publish. The raw frequency of such references seems to have increased in New Zealand and the United States, though not in Britain; but despite this evidence of progress, it is still true that far fewer individual women than men are singled out as topics of discussion in these corpora, so that equality remains a legitimate feminist goal.

Beyond this, it is necessary to move beyond raw frequencies to examine in more detail whether this increase in frequency is accompanied by changes in attitudes and usage. Even if more individual women are mentioned in texts, this is not necessarily a positive step if they continue to be mentioned in sexist ways. For example, while FLOB contains several references to female Prime Ministers, these are less than complimentary:

(8) Nehru also harboured a protectionist obsession even more paranoically than does the troubling new woman prime minister of France. (FLOB B12 040-042)

(9) She believes that "the so-called womanly qualities – like listening and supporting – make for ideal MP's." Those are qualities that she feels Margaret Thatcher lacks: "I think it's an absolute tragedy that she was the first woman Prime Minister. She's done nothing for women and is so unwomanly, so uncaring. She's a role model for politics that young women *shouldn't* follow." (FLOB F13 155-161)

The fact that comparable figures for the terms *man/men* have declined rather than increased throws the increase in *woman/women* into even starker contrast. Figures for *man/men* are complicated by its (pseudo-)generic usage, though that does appear to be decreasing.[3] The consistent decrease in frequency of *man/men* between Brown/LOB and Frown/FLOB/WWC seen in Table 2 may be due partly to this change in usage; however, this cannot account for all of the observed shift (since (pseudo)generics accounted for at most 1/3 of *man/men* tokens even in the older corpora).

One further related possibility is that *man/men* may increasingly be replaced by *male(s)*, to clarify that male-only reference is intended instead of a generic: and indeed, there has been a marked increase in frequency of *male(s)*, as plotted in Figure 2. On the other hand, there has also been an almost exactly parallel increase in *female(s)*, so it is more likely that these terms indicate an increase in explicit gender comparisons.

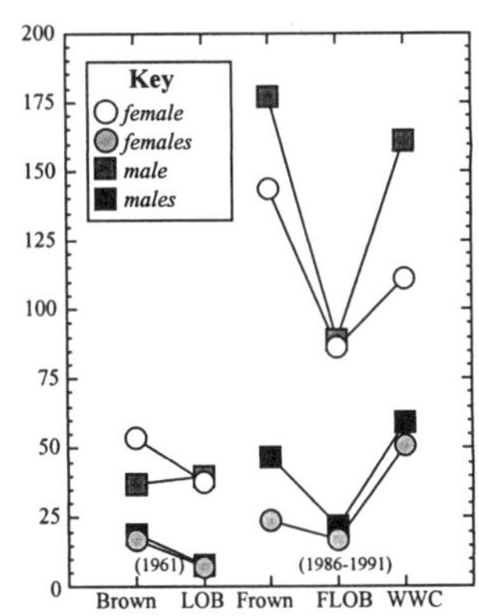


**Figure 2:** Overall corpus frequencies of *female(s)* and *male(s)*

We turn now to examine the trends in the occupational labels in the corpora and then proceed to explore some of the socio-semantic implications of the contexts in which items appear in different texts.

## 3. Occupational terms

The increase in references to women gives us evidence of increased interest in and description of women as a group. But it is also important to examine what perspective this description takes. One extremely important arena of social change over the last 40 years has been the workplace, where older divisions of labour and differences in salary by gender have come under scrutiny. For this reason, occupational terms are potentially an important area where language can provide some indication of social change in progress.

Gendered occupational terms are of special interest because linguistically unmarked items tend to follow traditionally expected behaviour, while marked items signal a dangerous transgression of established boundaries, threatening the status quo. For example, Romaine (1999: 130) draws attention to the lack of gender parallelism in the occurrence of terms such as *family man* but not *family woman* (what else would she be after all?), and *career woman* or even *career girl* (but rarely *career man*). As she puts it,

> Expressions such as *career woman/lady/girl* count as two strikes against women. On the one hand, they suggest that as women, females can't be real professionals, and on the other, they suggest that as professionals, females can't be real women. (Romaine 1999: 131)

So is there any evidence that such sexist patterns are changing? To answer this question, we examined the distribution of items which designated an occupation, and which were accompanied by a gender marker in LOB, FLOB and WWC. Occupational labels associated with the suffixes *-person* and *-people* were also included as possible equivalents in post-head position (e.g. *spokesperson, business person*). The term 'occupation' was interpreted in a relatively wide sense, to include terms such as *chairperson, professional man* and *women slaves*. In particular, the terms *chairman* and *spokesperson*, while strictly roles rather than occupations, nevertheless designate positions of some authority, and so are retained. Terms relating to sports, hobbies, and military roles (e.g. *batsman*; *horsewoman*; *seaman*; *swordsman*; *infantryman*) are excluded.

The following search patterns were used:

(i) words containing *-man*, *-woman*, etc. as a bound suffix, e.g. *spokesman, chairwoman, frontperson*;
(ii) gendered heads preceded by an occupational indicator (including hyphenated tokens): e.g. *cleaning woman, maintenance man, call-girl*;
(iii) gendered phrasal premodifiers followed by an occupational indicator, e.g. *woman doctor, male nurse, lady teacher.*

Classes (i) and (ii) can be usefully grouped together as consisting of occupational descriptors followed by gendered heads. These categories show much the same trends between corpora, so it is of lesser importance (except perhaps as a rough indication of how recent a given formation is) whether the gendered head is represented orthographically as within the word or as a separate word. The overall distribution of these gendered heads is shown in Table 3.

**Table 3:** Gendered heads following occupational descriptors (including bound morphs, hyphenated forms, and phrases)

| Head: | LOB | FLOB | WWC |
|---|---|---|---|
| *man/men* | 434 | 408 | 342 |
| *woman/women* | 8 | 13 | 22 |
| *lady/ ladies* | 12 | 11 | 6 |
| *person(s)/ people* | 18 | 23 | 40 |
| *boy(s)* | 11 | 10 | 6 |
| *girl(s)* | 11 | 9 | 2 |

While LOB and FLOB provide only slight evidence of any decrease in use of *-man* terms in BrE, such terms are significantly less frequent in WWC ($X^2(2df)=11.39$, $p=0.003$). Occupational terms headed by *lady/ladies, boy(s)* and *girl(s)* also show little difference between LOB and FLOB, but appear to be dispreferred in NZ writings. However, the numbers of tokens for these three heads are very small.

By contrast, terms in *-woman* and *-people* both show a slight increase between LOB and FLOB, and though comparably rare even in WWC, are almost twice as common there as in FLOB.

These figures reflect the decrease in *man/men*, the increase in *woman/women*, and the decrease in *girl(s)*, seen in the overall figures in the preceding section.

**Table 4:** Occupational terms with gender premodification

| Premodifier: | LOB | FLOB | WWC |
|---|---|---|---|
| *man/men* | 1 | 0 | 0 |
| *male* | 2 | 7 | 17 |
| *woman/women* | 7 | 22 | 14 |
| *female* | 4 | 11 | 11 |
| *lady* | 1 | 2 | 2 |
| *boy* | 1 | 1 | 2 |
| *girl* | 5 | 0 | 0 |

Occupational terms premodified by gender (Table 4) are also largely consistent with the overall frequency trends already noted.

One linguistic asymmetry is immediately evident: the productive use of *woman/women*, but not *man/men*, as an occupation premodifier (the sole example *men servants* from LOB is no more than an historical relic), so that it may be possible to talk of a *woman doctor*, but impossible to remark on a **man doctor*. This is consistent with men having a continuing unmarked status in relation to most occupations, while women continue to be marked. Moreover, the same interpretation might be given to the pattern in Table 3 whereby occupational terms in *-man* apparently decrease in WWC, while *-woman* terms increase.

However, it is worth considering the implications of this data in a little more detail. Firstly, gender marking using *male* is increasing alongside forms with *female* and *woman/women*, suggesting a more general trend towards marking of both genders where appropriate. At the same time, unmarked terms (using *-person*) are increasing alongside *-woman* terms, which could indicate a trend towards avoidance of gender marking where it would be inappropriate. Overall, then, we may expect that choice of whether or not to mark gender in occupational contexts is now determined by (prescriptive) societal, rather than linguistic, rules. One sign that the changes in marking gender of occupational terms are conscious – or even externally imposed – is that they are occasionally overtly parodied, as in (10).

(10) [Noddy] turned the corner and was waved down by WPC Plod. "Where's Policeman Plod?" he asked. "He was sent down for racially harassing Golliwog," the woman policeperson told him. "Golly!" Noddy exclaimed. "Right. You're nicked as well." (FLOB R05 216-221)

Meanwhile, the trivialising or pseudo-polite post-modifer *lady* seems to be disappearing; this also suggests a conscious change in attitudes.[4]

In this light, the apparent shift from post-modifiers (mainly of the form *-man*), to pre-modifers (mainly of the form *woman*) could be interpreted as encouraging evidence that women are increasingly gaining attention when they break into professional areas they have not previously occupied. We would predict that for any given profession in which women are gaining access, the first few individuals will be 'marked', because they are (at that time) unusual.

(11) The media love women candidates – we're newsworthy (FLOB F13 179)

But while women are thus 'marked', they are at least not ignored, and these usages document their inroads into professional areas which have been considered male bastions in the past. If women go on to become a sizeable minority of a profession, then they will not attract automatic marking, and other reference possibilities will open up.[5]

This process of initial marking has sometimes been delayed by pseudo-generic usage where occupations were previously designated by terms in *-man* – an example of the 'invisible women' syndrome (e.g. Pauwels 1998: 43f), whereby women's gains go unnoticed because they are absorbed by labels associated with men. When women first began to deliver mail and work as fire officers, their presence was generally subsumed under the pseudo-generic labels *postman* and *fireman*. But with the steady decline in the generic use of (-)*man* (Holmes 1993c), it has become more common to use either gender-neutral alternatives such as *postie*, *firefighter*, or *-person* forms, or else explicit gender-marking (using *woman* as suffix or pre-modifier).

### 3.1 Contextual considerations

The analysis of occupational terms raises some interesting issues which require greater attention to the context of use. Firstly, it is worth considering the general underlying assumption that marking gender in relation to occupations is unwarranted, and thus provides evidence of sexist attitudes. In fact, there are only a few instances where the gender marking is clearly superfluous to the text, as in (12):

(12) A woman journalist insisted that unemployment was our major difficulty in Britain. She simply smiled disbelievingly at the statement that, in fact, there were more situations vacant than people looking for jobs. (LOB B21 118)

though it is true that 'sexist attitudes' may surface even where the gender-marking itself is justified. For example, the marking in (13) is unexceptionable, as it makes an explicit comparison between women and men – albeit one founded on sexist stereotypes.

(13) 'Though there are not many women registrars yet, I think we can give men registrars a lead in some ways,' she told me with a smile. 'Men may be more efficient and businesslike, but on the personal side of Births, Deaths and Marriages women have a more sympathetic approach.' (LOB F18 027-031)

In practice, most examples of premodification by *woman/women* in the later corpora can be attributed to consciousness-raising and explicit contrast between genders. This supports our interpretation of the increased frequency of *woman/women* in these corpora.

(14) The Labour Research survey shows there are only 20 women judges out of the 527 surveyed, a miserable 4% and an increase of only three over the last five years. There is only one woman judge in the Court of Appeal and one in the High Court. (FLOB G72 130)

(15) Proving herself as capable as any man on the job has been Hawke's Bay's only woman lead-light maker's most difficult task in her first year of business (WWC A41 047)

(16) Despite their success, women police were, until 1946, employed only as temporary constables. (WWC F30 114)

There are only a handful of occupational *woman* tokens in FLOB and WWC which cannot be explained in this way; and these occur in fiction, or in discussion of historical periods, where we may expect presentation of unreconstructed viewpoints without authors necessarily agreeing with them. We can safely assume that the writer of (17), for example, is being sarcastic.

(17) [After WWII] the life of the nation, freed of the necessary wartime aberrations such as women tram conductors, could resume its rightful, natural pattern: Dad at work, Mum at home with the kids. (WWC G40 048)

A second important concern is the kinds of occupations which are associated with different heads. To some extent, these may merely reflect (with greater or lesser accuracy) real-world differences in employment. For example, on examining the kinds of occupations associated with the head *-man*, we can note a general decrease over time in the range of terms designating occupation using this form. Table 5 provides exemplification of this trend for items with 5 or more tokens in LOB vs FLOB vs WWC.

**Table 5:** Occupational terms headed by *man* in LOB, FLOB and WWC

| **LOB** | | **FLOB** | | **WWC** | |
|---|---|---|---|---|---|
| chairman | 119 | chairman | 111 | chairman | 109 |
| craftsman | 29 | spokesman | 50 | spokesman | 35 |
| alderman | 25 | policeman | 39 | fisherman | 26 |
| spokesman | 22 | fisherman | 31 | policeman | 24 |
| statesman | 16 | businessman | 23 | businessman | 19 |
| fisherman | 16 | fireman | 12 | ombudsman | 14 |
| policeman | 15 | salesman | 10 | headman | 13 |
| business(-)man | 14 | clergyman | 10 | tradesman | 8 |
| clergyman | 11 | watchman | 9 | foreman | 6 |
| workman | 10 | craftsman | 8 | craftsman | 5 |
| barman | 10 | churchman | 6 | barman | 5 |
| ombudsman | 9 | tradesman | 5 | | |
| salesman | 8 | statesman | 5 | | |
| cattleman | 7 | doorman | 5 | | |
| tradesman | 6 | | | | |
| foreman | 5 | | | | |

At the lower-frequency end, many of the *-man* items in LOB constitute conservative or old-fashioned labels for occupations, some of which are now relatively rare, or have no exact modern equivalents: e.g. *crossbowman, liveryman, herdsman, cowman, coachman.* An important contribution to the overall decrease in occupational *-man* items between LOB and FLOB is a predictable decrease in reference to such occupational classes. (One other contribution to decreasing frequency of some items is the adoption of non-gender-marking alternatives specific to one occupation: e.g. *firefighter*, which occurs in Frown and FLOB, but not in the earlier corpora.)

But there are still several areas where the choice of label makes a difference to meaning. One of these is the use of *lady*. As Lakoff (1975) suggested, the head and premodifier *lady* is used as a politeness device to add or attribute status to the referent, and not surprisingly, this is most necessary in relation to 'demeaning' jobs, such as *cleaning lady* and *tea lady*. (The only occupational term in LOB, FLOB and WWC is *landlady*, but the American corpora do contain a *saleslady* (Brown) and an *Elevator Lady* (Frown), as well as *professional ladies*, or *ladies of the night*!) Hence, in current usage, serious occupations such as *judge* and *doctor* tend to be modified by the terms *woman/women*, rather than *lady* (see Holmes 1999). As a premodifier, *lady* is used for a curiously limited set of occupations in these corpora, mainly concerned with writing:

we find references to a *lady singer* (LOB), *lady novelists* and a *lady writer* (FLOB), and a *lady editor* and *lady poet* (WWC). These closely parallel suffixed forms such as *poetess* or *editress*, which tend to suggest dilettantish scribblers rather than serious scribes (Holmes 1993b: 360).

Conversely, alternative meanings are also available for some labels. The persistence of the use of *-man* as a (pseudo-)generic means we cannot always be sure of the extent to which *-man/men* terms are restricted to male referents. Most of the tokens in the corpora have specifically male referents, reflecting the reality of a working world still dominated by men. Nevertheless, there are also several instances of occupational terms ending in *-man* which are used to refer to women. *Chairman* is the easiest case to identify, as it is generally used to refer to named individuals.

(18) He is, he adds: 'A very great supporter of chairman Mrs Miscampbell.'
(FLOB A42 024)

It has been suggested (e.g. Salter-Duke 1983: 18; Ehrlich and King 1994; Romaine 1999) that terms such as *chairperson* might in practice be used to refer mainly to women (and so mask women's presence). In fact, as Table 6 illustrates, *-person* terms are still comparatively rare in writing, and there is little evidence for any gender preference in their use. *Chairperson* is not found in Brown, LOB or FLOB, and there are only 6 tokens in WWC – of which one refers to a man, one to a woman, and the remainder do not refer to specific individuals. (Meanwhile, Frown contains two tokens: one referring to a woman, and the other unspecified.) Nevertheless, many other occupational terms cannot straightforwardly be assigned a gender in context (*spokesman* and *spokesperson* in particular are almost always used without naming or even pronominalising the referent), and so it is possible that there is a level of concealed sexist usage in the corpora, where terms such as *postman* or *spokesperson* are used to refer to a woman, without this being evident from the context.

Some more positive, though less direct, evidence for increasing avoidance of *chairman* is provided by an increased use of *chair* in several alternative constructions: as a verb (19); as a noun referring to the position (20); and as the title of the occupant (21).

(19) He will also chair a conference session on sheepmeats. (WWC A26 178)
(20) LABOUR OUTVOTED — SO A TORY GETS THE CHAIR (LOB A28 089)
(21) Now he was off [...] to see the chair of Parliament's Foreign Affairs and Defence Committee, Helen Clark (WWC A14 034)

The data available suggests the verb is favoured in NZ, while *chair* is used in the US as a direct equivalent of *chairperson*; but the frequencies are low, so these findings cannot be conclusive.

**Table 6:** Chairman, chairperson, chairwoman, and chair

| | Brown | LOB | Frown | FLOB | WWC |
|---|---|---|---|---|---|
| ***chairman/ men*** | 79 | 119 | 69 | 111 | 106 |
| male individual | 50 | 85 | 59 | 68 | 76 |
| female individual[6] | 19 | 3 | 3 | 5 | 7 |
| no information | 9 | 31 | 7 | 38 | 23 |
| ***chairperson*** | 0 | 0 | 2 | 0 | 6 |
| male individual | | | 0 | | 1 |
| female individual | | | 1 | | 1 |
| no information | | | 1 | | 4 |
| ***chairwoman*** | 0 | 0 | 0 | 1 | 2 |
| ***chair*** (verb) | 0 | 1 | 5 | 7 | 11 |
| male subject | | 1 | 3 | 5 | 7 |
| female subject | | 0 | 1 | 0 | 1 |
| general/collective | | 0 | 1 | 2 | 3 |
| ***chair*** (=position)[7] | 3 | 8 | 3 | 5 | 3 |
| ***chair*** (=person) | 0 | 1 | 10 | 3 | 1 |
| male individual | | 0 | 6 | 2 | 0 |
| female individual | | 0 | 4 | 0 | 1 |
| general/collective | | 1 | 0 | 1 | 0 |

Overall, this survey of occupational terms reveals a consistent (if quantitatively small) series of shifts in British English. There is a slight decrease between LOB and FLOB in *-man*, which appears to be partly driven by a decrease in reference to more traditional rural or historical roles, and partly a result of more contemporary terms (where women are competing in the real world) being replaced by alternatives (including terms headed by *-person*, as well as more idiosyncratic items such as *chair* or *firefighter*) which, within the limits of our data, seem to be used as true epicenes rather than covertly marking female gender. At the same time, there has been an increase in marking women's presence in the workplace (whether by specific labels headed by *-woman*, or by premodification), which may be attributed both to increased real-world participation, and continued attention to equal opportunity issues.

The New Zealand data emerges as more progressive than FLOB for all of these changes. It would be nice to think that this reflects a real and considerable social progress; however, it may simply reflect a higher proportion of female authors in WWC (which would itself indicate some positive progress towards equality).[8]

## 4. *Girls* in the workplace

In the workplace, a context where status is important, there is little doubt that referring to female adults as 'girls' can be regarded as a putdown, denying their competence and independence, and relegating them to subordinate status, as illustrated in (22).

(22) Looking at Nell's endless CV, Emilia had tried to crack the ice: 'Well, you seem to be quite a bright girl, don't you?' She had seen the younger woman's face

harden ever so slightly, and realized with a certain sudden pleasure that she was feeling patronized. (FLOB N21 095-100)

One might reasonably expect decreasing use of *girl* in contexts such as this, where competence and status should be more relevant than age and appearance. Table 7 lists the total frequencies of *girl(s)* and *boy(s)* used in workplace contexts (excluding address terms and idioms not directly related to the setting, but including occupation titles headed or modified by *girl* or *boy*). Comparing LOB/Brown with the more recent corpora, we see evidence of a general decrease in all 4 items.

**Table 7:** *Girl(s)* and *boy(s)* in workplace contexts

| | **Brown** | **LOB** | **Frown** | **FLOB** | **WWC** |
|---|---|---|---|---|---|
| *girl* | 12 (5 adult) | 16 (6 adult) | 6 (1 adult) | 6 (1 adult) | 10 (3 adult) |
| *girls* | 14 (13 adult) | 15 (6 adult) | 8 (3 adult) | 10 (3 adult) | 4 (4 adult) |
| *boy* | 18 (2 adult) | 16 (0 adult) | 7 (0 adult) | 10 (0 adult) | 4 (0 adult) |
| *boys* | 15 (7 adult) | 8 (7 adult) | 7 (0 adult) | 2 (1 adult) | 5 (4 adult) |

However, we must be cautious in interpreting this shift, as it may in part reflect other social trends, e.g. a longer average education, resulting in a higher average age on entering the workforce. Certainly, the use of the singular *girl* in the workplace has not yet totally vanished, even in the most recent corpora, and even for positions of some responsibility – as when hiring staff:

(23) 'Have you library qualifications?' asked the girl at the reference desk. (WWC K97 063)

By emphasising (lack of) age, the term *girl* also makes reference to appearance rather than capability – and again, this is often especially inappropriate in a work setting. (24) is a particularly blatant example; the term *girls* is used alongside a number of sexist adjectives to describe the appearance of women working in a massage parlour.

(24) the unclaimed gaggle of salady, dishy, peachy and camera girls sat around formica tables like seedy narcissists (WWC K35 056)

*Girl* is more than three times more likely than *boy* to refer to an adult (Sigley and Holmes, forthcoming), and this asymmetric age behaviour spills over into workplace contexts. *Boy* is almost entirely avoided in reference to adults, resulting in such imbalances as:

(25) there are no more skilful operatives than the girls and men who make the popular Society shirts (LOB H30 150)

Virtually all use of *boy* in workplace contexts is reserved for low-status, entry-level occupations which are in fact usually occupied by individuals of school age, and which are in consequence not entirely equivalent to similar terms using *man*. For example, a *delivery boy* might well become a *delivery man*, but probably only by upgrading his responsibilities from pizza to furniture, while a *newsboy* would have to change professions entirely to become a *newsman*. *Girl* is similarly used for women in occupations of subordinate status – but with far less regard to the age of the incumbent, so that, for example, one woman in her seventies can describe herself as 'Wapping's oldest office girl' (WWC L13 060). Such girls are not allowed to 'grow up' to take on more adult responsibilities (office woman? shop woman?), and so these labels provide a linguistic version of the 'glass ceiling'.

Plurals appear to function somewhat differently, rather as if the impoliteness that attaches to using a juvenile term for an adult individual gets diluted over a larger group. In contrast to the infrequent occurrence of *boy* referring to adults in the workplace, groups of adults in various professions are readily referred to as *the boys*. References to *the girls* or *the boys* in a workplace setting may even serve to mark in-group solidarity, in much the same way that a country's armed forces become 'our boys' during wartime (e.g., WWC G40 045).

(26) If any of the girls at work sniggered behind her back and she found out, she'd punch them in the face. (WWC K60 194)
(27) I want you to spend time with the girls in Reception. Get them to show you how the whole system works – they're a nice bunch of girls, I'm sure you'll get along well with them (FLOB P15 081-083)
(28) I could drag you down to police headquarters and the boys could stand you under the lights (LOB N22 212)
(29) I guess I'd better go and break it to the boys in the lab (LOB P09 042)

However, the reference tends to be more belittling where the group is viewed by an outsider.

(30) FASHION-CONSCIOUS policewomen in Nottingham have been told [...] to stop shortening their skirts. The girls thought their skirts were too old fashioned [...] (LOB A24 094-097)

Interestingly enough, *boys* often refers to groups of particularly successful or powerful males (*the big boys; the four-figure boys*), in a mirror image of the singular form's subordinate status. This could be interpreted as an expression of envy, or the 'tall-poppy syndrome', whereby such groups must be brought down to size to be made bearable.

(31) Obviously the Aussie television boys decided it was a bit wordy, so they cut that segment. (WWC B20 056)
(32) The security services, Tony old chap. Those nice boys with the OBEs who take people like you out to lunch and invite you to do a little something for Queen and country. (FLOB N07 045)

Overall, then, there is as yet only slight evidence that the asymmetries in use of *girl* versus *boy* in the workplace are decreasing: this is probably because, unlike occupational titles, they are not often explicitly proscribed, and tend to occur in contexts not governed by institutional prescription.

## 5. Conclusions

Raw frequencies of terms for male and female humans show significant differences: references to women have more than doubled between 1961 and 1991, while references to men have decreased over the same period (partly through avoidance of (pseudo-) generic *man*). Meanwhile, frequencies of *female(s)* and *male(s)* have increased dramatically, suggesting more frequent explicit comparison of gender groups.

Comparison of occupational terms in LOB, FLOB and WWC tends to confirm these trends of increased reference to women, and increased discussion of gender issues. Our data provides clear evidence of an increase in gender premodification, and in the use of forms suffixed by *-woman*, between 1961 and 1986/1991. In the occupational domain, then, women continue to be linguistically marked compared to men. However, it seems that such usages should not be regarded negatively. Almost all examples from the more recent corpora can be attributed to consciousness-raising and explicit contrast between genders; the marking increase thus reflects both increased real-world participation, and continued attention to equal opportunity issues. To a large extent, the marking of women serves as an affirmation. In other words, while women are only just beginning to gain entry to more powerful positions, it can be argued that it helps to note, rather than to ignore, the existence of 'women judges'.

At the same time, there is a slight decrease between LOB and FLOB in *-man*, which appears to be partly driven by a decrease in reference to more traditional rural or historical roles, and partly a result of more contemporary terms (where women are competing in the real world) being replaced by alternatives (including terms headed by *-person*, as well as more idiosyncratic items such as *firefighter*) which, within the limits of our data, seem to be used as true epicenes rather than covertly marking female gender. Where prescriptions are not applied, it is possible that less politically correct usages may surface, as with the continued occurrence of *girl* in the workplace. However, we have reason to believe that the attention focussed on pseudo-generics and similar sexist terminology in the workplace has had some real effect. The New Zealand data emerges as more progressive than FLOB for all of these changes, indicating a higher awareness of feminist issues, at least among the New Zealand writing population.

In conclusion, then, while women continue to be the linguistically marked gender, there is some evidence to support a positive interpretation of many of the patterns identified in the most recent corpora, since the relevant marked contexts reflect inroads made by women into occupational domains previously considered as exclusively male.

## Notes

1 We would like to thank Rowan Shoemark for her assistance in extracting some of the collocational data, and Laurie Bauer, Tom Lavelle and Jan Svartvik for their insightful comments on drafts and presentations of this material.

2 Corpus markup has been removed from all cited examples. Example references are in the format (Corpus Text Line): e.g. WWC G52 024 is from line 24 of text 52 in category G (Belles Lettres) from WWC.

3 An analysis of the relative frequency of pseudo-generic vs non-generic instances of man in the New Zealand press found that by 1986 no more than 16% of instances were (pseudo-) generic, a decline of about 50% over the last thirty years if comparison with the 1961 LOB Corpus is used as an indication of earlier usage patterns (see Holmes 1994, in press).

4 See Holmes (1999) for a discussion of the socio-semantics of *lady* in current usage.

5 As women are still just beginning to gain access to certain professions, overall corpus frequencies for gender-marked occupational terms may remain static, or even continue to increase: but over time there should be a turnover in the types present, reflecting the progress of the cutting edge.

6 Of the Brown tokens with female reference, 11 come from one text (A18) describing a gala committee.

7 These figures exclude references to academic chairs at universities.

8 The precise gender distribution of authors is something we are not able to determine, as information is lacking for many sections of the corpora.

## References

Bauer, Laurie (1993). *Manual of information to accompany the Wellington Corpus of Written New Zealand English.* Wellington: Department of Linguistics, Victoria University of Wellington.

Ehrlich, Susan and Ruth King (1994). 'Feminist meanings and the (de)politicization of the lexicon'. *Language in Society* 23: 59–76.

Francis, W. Nelson (1964). *Manual of information to accompany a standard sample of present-day edited American English, for use with digital computers.* Providence, R.I.: Department of Linguistics, Brown University.

Holmes, Janet (1993a). 'Charpersons, chairpersons and goddesses: sexist usages in New Zealand English'. *Te Reo* 36: 99–113.

Holmes, Janet (1993b). 'Sex-marking suffixes in written New Zealand English'. *American Speech* 68.4: 357–370.

Holmes, Janet (1993c). 'He-man beings, poetesses, and tramps: sexist language in New Zealand'. In Laurie Bauer and Christine Franzen (eds) *Of pavlova, poetry and paradigms: essays in honour of Harry Orsman*. Wellington: Victoria University Press. 34–49.

Holmes, Janet (1994). 'Inferring language change from computer corpora: some methodological problems'. *ICAME Journal* 18: 27–40.

Holmes, Janet (1997). 'Generic pronouns in the Wellington Corpus of Spoken New Zealand English'. *Kotare* 1: 32–40.

Holmes, Janet (1999). 'Ladies and gentlemen: corpus analysis and linguistic sexism'. *Proceedings of the 20th annual meeting of the International Computer Archive of Modern/Medieval English*. Freiburg: University of Freiburg. 141–155

Holmes, Janet (in press). 'Gender identity in New Zealand English'. In Marlis Hellinger and Hadumod Bussman (eds) *Gender across languages. The linguistic representation of women and men*. Vol 1. Amsterdam: Benjamins.

Johansson, Stig (1978). *Manual of information to accompany the Lancaster-Oslo/Bergen Corpus of English English, for use with digital computers*. Oslo: Department of English, University of Oslo.

Pauwels, Anne (1998). *Women changing language*. London: Longman.

Romaine, Suzanne (1999). *Communicating gender*. Mahwah, New Jersey: Lawrence Erlbaum.

Salter-Duke, Linden (1983). *Woman-machine interaction: a computational investigation into the disparity between feminine and masculine pronouns in the LOB Corpus*. MA thesis, Lancaster University.

Sigley, Robert and Janet Holmes (forthcoming). 'Looking at *girls* in English corpora'. *Journal of English Linguistics*.

Wolfson, Nessa and Joan Manes. 1980. 'Don't 'dear' me!' In Sally McConnell-Ginet, Ruth Borker and Nelly Furman (eds) *Women and language in literature and society*. New York: Praeger. 79–92.

# On polysemy and interpretation. The case of *eventual*[1]

*Göran Kjellmer*

University of Gothenburg

## Abstract

*Some semantic changes are quite drastic and clear for all to see, while others are more insidious and more difficult to pinpoint. This paper attempts to show that corpora can be of great help in charting the semantic development of words belonging to the latter variety. One such word is* eventual.*The normal meaning of English* eventual, *'final, ultimate', differs from that of its Continental and Scandinavian cognates, which all mean 'possible, potential'. English* eventual *was formerly used in this sense, too, but it is now marked as 'archaic' in modern dictionaries. However, with the help of a battery of criteria, an analysis of corpus material indicates that, alongside its normal sense, the Continental sense is current in the English word, particularly in spoken British English, which in this respect is close to American English. American English may have preserved the older, European Continental usage, which is now being strengthened or reintroduced in spoken British English under American influence.*

## 1. Introduction

Work in corpus linguistics has been devoted to problems in various linguistic fields, but perhaps it could be said that semantics is not a field that has attracted the attention of corpus linguists in a particularly high degree. It is against this background that I hope to show in the present paper how corpora can help in illustrating the process by which a semantic change takes place. Some such changes are quite drastic and result in salient new verbal entities, as when *gay* acquires the sense 'homosexual', or when *crane* 'kind of large bird' comes to be used figuratively to mean 'kind of lifting implement'. Other changes are more inconspicuous, slow and less easy to trace. The relevant verbal material of this second type is often characterised by semantic vagueness, and as large language corpora can supply a great variety of relevant examples, they can frequently throw light on the semantic processes involved. A case in point here is *eventual.*

When it is viewed from many Continental languages, and also from the Scandinavian languages, English *eventual* is a so-called 'false friend'. Its normal sense is 'resulting in, final, ultimate', as defined for instance in LDOCE[3] (1995): 'happening or achieving something at the end of a process'. [The full titles of LDOCE[3] and other dictionaries referred to are listed with the references.] This is a typical example from the Cobuild Corpus:

(1) After ten years in the Tower of London, his second expedition ... ended in failure and his eventual beheading. (Corpus: UKephem/02. Text: E0000001502.)

In all the other languages, however,[2] the corresponding words (*éventuel, eventual(e), eventuel(l), eventueel*) mean approximately 'contingent upon (unspecified) circumstances, possible, potential' ('qui peut ou non se produire'[3], 'che può accadere come non accadere'[4]). Here is an example from a Swedish newspaper:

(2) [Several Swedish companies are planning to move their headquarters abroad.] Andra – bland dem Astra och SCA – diskuterar eventuell flytt mer informellt. (GP (1998) (Others – such as Astra and SCA – are discussing a possible move more informally [i.e. if the occasion should arise].)

and here is a French example (from André Gide):

(3) Il n'y a guère que le choix entre un mal certain et un mal éventuel ['a certain evil and a possible evil']. (Quoted by Rey and Rey-Debove (1983.)

It is obvious that cross-linguistic misunderstandings are very likely to occur here.

## 2. Dictionary evidence

In a historical perspective, it is clear that the Continental and Scandinavian usage is the older one.[5] It has also existed in English. The OED$^2$ records first two obsolete senses dating from the 17th and 18th centuries,[6] and then, as its third sense, 'That will arise or take place in a particular contingency'. This third sense is in fact the French (etc.) sense, which I will henceforth refer to as the 'potentiality sense', as is shown by the OED$^2$ examples, e.g. one from 1767:

(4) William aspired to secure to himself the eventual succession to the crown of that kingdom [France], in case that Louis ... should die before his father.

The examples that the OED$^2$ gives under sense 3 date from 1767 to 1874.

It is under sense 5 that we find the modern English sense of *eventual*: 'Ultimately resulting', which then represents a later development of the chronologically primary senses. (The first example in the OED$^2$ is from 1823.) This sense will henceforth be referred to as the 'finality sense'.

Although terms like *false friend* and *misunderstandings* suggest that the use of *eventual* with the potentiality meaning would be inappropriate in present-day English, this is not necessarily so. At the very least, it seems to have existed until recently in English, making *eventual* a case of polysemy. Unlike senses 1 and 2, OED$^2$ sense 3 (above) is not marked 'obsolete', and RHD (1987) defines *eventual* as '1. happening at some indefinite future time or after a series of occurrences; ultimate [the finality sense] 2. depending upon uncertain events; contingent [the potentiality sense].' But there is a strong tendency in modern dictionaries to regard the potentiality sense of *eventual* as a thing of the past. They either say so openly ('archaic'), or else imply it by including the sense in early editions and omitting it from later ones. The following dictionaries call the sense 'archaic' (the dotted line indicates the potentiality sense):

W[3] (1961) 1a *obs:...* b *obs:* ...1c *archaic: dependent or contingent upon certain conditions:* CONDITIONAL. 2: taking place, arising, or becoming something at an unspecified later time: ultimately resulting: ULTIMATE, FINAL

Collins (1979) 1. (*prenominal*) happening in due course of time; ultimate. 2. *Archaic.* contingent or possible

AHD[3] (1992) 1. Occurring at an unspecified time in the future; ultimate 2. *Archaic.* Dependent on circumstance; contingent.

And the following imply the same thing:

COD[1-7] (1914–82) That will happen under certain circumstances; ultimately resulting
COD[8-9] (1990–95 Occurring or existing in due course or at last; ultimate

OALDCE[1] (1963) likely to happen under certain circumstances; coming at last as a result
OALDCE[3] (1974) coming at last as a result; ultimate

LDOCE[1-3] (1978–95), Cobuild[1-2] (1987–95) and CIDE (1995) do not even mention the potentiality sense. Lexicographers working in the 1970s and 1980s must have come to consider that sense as no longer current in *eventual.*

## 3. Corpus aspects

However, we may wonder whether the potentiality sense of *eventual* is indeed as archaic or obsolete as these dictionaries are suggesting. Even a quick look at the relevant material in our large corpora will actually bring to light instances of *eventual* that could be interpreted as 'possible' or 'potential'. Here are some from the British National Corpus (BNC):

(5) Sir Peter Imbert and the Yard reformers have important allies in the regional forces: Geoffrey Dear, the West Midlands chief constable, whose boldness at disbanding his serious crimes squad cannot be discounted, whatever his eventual career ambitions; and Paul Condon, the new Kent chief, formerly in charge of Met training and personnel. (A7Y 548)
(6) When American troops were first sent to the Gulf Region after the Iraqi occupation of Kuwait, the reason given by the US for this deployment of troops was the protection of Saudi Arabia from an 'eventual invasion by Iraq'. (ARW 455)
(7) Yet as he went on to say, the procedure, whatever its eventual remedial consequences, had 'punitive consequences'. (AN5 302)

In sentences such as these the potentiality interpretation seems at least as likely as the finality one. At the same time, it is plain that the finality sense has come to be the predominant one. While the semantic intricacies of *eventual* seem worth looking into, it should be noted that the adverb *eventually* does not seem to have the same semantic indeterminacy.

## 4. An opinion poll

As a preliminary pilot study, a limited number of informants were asked to give their views of the meanings of 10 sentences containing the adjective *eventual*, which was assumed to have either the finality or the potentiality sense. The informants were seven middle-aged native speakers of English, and the sentences they were invited to pronounce on were all genuine 1990s ones from the British National Corpus and the Cobuild Corpus. It turned out that all the sentences except one allowed of both interpretations according to the informants regarded as a group. Individually, the informants mostly gave just one alternative for each sentence. (The questionnaire and the answers are shown in the Appendix.) The outcome of the poll thus indicates that things in this area are by no means as straightforward as lexicographers would seem to suggest.

## 5. Speech and writing

*Eventual* is a word that occurs much more frequently in writing than in speech. In the Cobuild Corpus it is distributed over the different text categories as follows:

**Table 1:** Distribution of *eventual* over text categories

| Corpus | Total Number of Occurrences | Average Number per Million Words |
|---|---|---|
| BBC | 55 | 21.1/million |
| Times | 62 | 10. 8/million |
| OZnews | 51 | 9.6/million |
| UKbooks | 50 | 9.3/million |
| USbooks | 47 | 8.4/million |
| UKmags | 37 | 7.5/million |
| Today | 37 | 7.0/million |
| NPR | 19 | 6.1/million |
| Sunnow | 31 | 5.3/million |
| UKephem | 13 | 4.2/million |
| USephem | 2 | 1.6/million |
| UKspok | 10 | 1.1/million |

As we can see, *eventual* has the lowest frequency of all in the spoken British module, UKspok, where it occurs only 1.1 times per one million words. (The BBC material can be assumed to derive from written sources read out aloud.) The spoken London-Lund Corpus does not have a single occurrence of it. To study it, we thus have to turn to written sources. In the large English corpora BNC (100 million words) and Cobuild Direct (57 million words), both based on predominantly written material, there are 1035 and 414 occurrences, respectively.[7] The Cobuild material, and to some extent the BNC material, have here been looked at a little more closely. In the Cobuild examples, the references follow the text, in examples from the BNC, they precede them.

## 6. Semantic criteria

If we assume that *eventual* is being used in two different senses even in present-day English, one potentiality sense and one finality sense, the question arises how we can distinguish between them – what are the linguistic cues that determine the interpretation of the word? How can they be kept apart? A further question is, how do the senses interact in the language? To try to answer such questions we shall look for evidence that will suggest which of the two senses is the intended one in each individual case. Such evidence is often many-sided, where different elements in the context contribute to the final judgement of the reader (or listener). Often overlapping, the evidential elements as presented here, particularly those for the potentiality sense, are therefore to be seen as suggestive rather than conclusive. We shall call the potentiality sense A, and the finality sense B and start with the criteria for A.

### 6.1 Criteria for the potentiality sense

**A1.** The NP in which *eventual* occurs is introduced by Ø or the indefinite article. The potentiality sense appears to be closer to hand than the finality one when a phenomenon or an event is presented as indefinite rather than definite. Cf. 'to prepare for an eventual ground attack' and 'to prepare for the eventual ground attack', where the former suggests A ('possible') and the latter B ('final'). Examples are:

(8) Speak with lenders for specific details concerning PMI costs, the length of coverage provided, and the possibility of refunds. <p> The ability to obtain an eventual refund may seem enticing, but a better deal may be lump-sum PMI without a refund. (Corpus: USbooks/09. Text: B9000000515.)

(9) Mr Watson confirmed that ADI had received in principle approval from the Australian Government for the possible sale of Steyr infantry rifles, saying such approval was routinely sought for a range of products in case of an eventual sale. (Corpus: OZnews/01. Text: N5000950118.)

(10) Walt Boomer, the senior Marine commander, also worried about Kibrit; he had gambled by putting the logistics base so far forward in anticipation of an eventual allied ground attack. (Corpus: USbooks/09. Text: B9000001151.)

**A2.** The event or phenomenon to which the NP featuring *eventual* refers is represented as not yet having taken place at the time of speaking or at the time of the action. The future is less certain than the present or the past. Cf. 'the incident threatened their eventual agreement' and 'he recorded their eventual agreement', where *threatened* places the agreement at a point in time later than the threat and rather suggests it may not take place at all, whereas *recorded* shows that the agreement is already a thing of the past and thus not in doubt. Reference to future time can be expressed by means of future-tense verb forms and of words like *prepare, preparation, propose, create basis for, threaten, anticipate, delay, jeopardise, point to, (not) accept.* The reference to future time must not be dependent on an act of will, a prescription or a plan, see B4, below.

(11) Road improvements will be inevitable, with eventual connection to the new autoroute planned from Bordeaux (Corpus: Today/11. Text: N6000941210.)
(12) Before any eventual takeover of the Pearl is completed by AMP, their voice should be heard. (A1S 160)
(13) The worry here is that the protocol will reduce the ability of the EC's poorer members – including eventual newcomers from Eastern Europe – to compete in the great market. (CR7 2097)

**A3.** The context expresses uncertainty or vagueness about the event, phenomenon or result. This can be indicated by the use of verbs like *discuss, talk of, think about, wonder, ask, be interested in, may, might.*

(14) At the moment, Asahi Shinwa is officially only affiliated to AA International, but there are no obvious barriers to an eventual merger and the two firms are already thought to be holding discussions. (CBU 515)
(15) Guy Rakotondravahatra, Bishop of Ihosy, Madagascar, summed up the reasons for optimism: We have had a chance, for the first time ever, to talk about our problems, our desires, our hopes and our eventual disagreements. (Corpus: UKbooks/08. Text: B0000001257.)
(16) Few AFLers mused about an eventual harmony of interests with capital; but neither did they indulge in the emotional attacks on 'robber barons' and 'plutocrats' that had been so popular in the 1880s and early 1890s. (Corpus: USbooks/09. Text: B9000001351.)

**A4.** The context expresses contingency, potentiality, hypothesis. The means of expression can for instance be *could, would, in case of, possibility, perhaps, if any.*

(17) Mr Howard would dearly love the position of Chancellor as a platform from which to launch an eventual bid for ultimate power. (Corpus: Today/11. Text: N6000920918.)
(18) Surely $10 million would have provided a new Government House or presidential mansion Australia's eventual republic would be proud of. (Corpus: OZnews/01. Text: N5000951022.)
(19) If the two moderates fail to develop their message, then Pat Buchanan will be a force in this election for longer than many suspect. Even in eventual failure, he could succeed in moving the Republican agenda towards a fatal outcome for the final standard-bearer. (Corpus: Times/10. Text: N2000960222)

**A5.** *Eventual* is part of the last member of a rising series of related notions. This is an uncertain criterion, as the last member of the series can be viewed as the logical and definitive outcome of the events referred to by the first members of the series, or as a thing of the past, as in the following example from BNC (which is thus seen as a (B) case):

(20) This book is about Britain's Defence policy in her post-imperial era, and is the sequel to my Withdrawal from Empire, published in 1986, in which I looked through military eyes at the creation, development and eventual transformation of the Empire into the loosely-knit British Commonwealth. (ABA 5)

Nevertheless, there are a number of such series where *eventual* as the last member could rather suggest the meaning '(and) perhaps even':

(21) The greatest loss of love comes when a loved person dies. Many accounts of this trauma have been written, detailing the phases of numbness, pain, anger and eventual integration of the loss. (Corpus: UKbooks/08. Text: B0000001312.)
(22) Counselling can often deal with the personal anger, frustration and eventual depression caused by the losses such illness brings. (CE1 1630)
(23) Searle (1987) has found evidence linking insecure attachments, significant delays in developmental mastery, and eventual primary child abuse to maternal PPD. (Corpus: USbooks/09. Text: B9000001357.)

**A6.** Several outcomes are envisaged. In such cases there is obviously a measure of uncertainty with regard to the realisation of the event, phenomenon or result.

(24) All relationships are predicated on the existential dilemma of choosing intimacy in the face of eventual separation or loss, and life-threatening illness heightens this universal form of anticipatory loss.
(Corpus: USbooks/09. Text: B9000001387.)
(25) The procedures cover each stage from initial identification of a possible change, through the approval procedure, to eventual rejection or implementation. (EAM 35)
(26) Yet as he went on to say, the procedure, whatever its eventual remedial consequences, had 'punitive consequences'. (AN5 302)

### 6.2 Criteria for the finality sense

**B1.** The event or phenomenon to which the NP featuring *eventual* refers is represented as having taken place at the time of speaking or at the time of the action. The means of representing this is often the past tense of the verb.[8]

(27) LORD HOFFMANN said that the charges alleged errors in Dr McCandless's diagnoses of three patients and failure to refer them to hospital. Two subsequently died and the other was found on her eventual admission to hospital to be seriously ill. (Corpus: Times/10. Text: N2000951212.)

(28) Haig ridiculed the Sirdar's desire for a 'triumphal entry into Berber – a sort of Roman triumph with Mahmoud tied to his horse's tail'. The eventual ceremony was even more vulgar than he had expected.
(Corpus: UKbooks/08. Text: B0000000551.)

(29) The eventual release of the hostages took place on January 20th 1981 – less than an hour after Mr. Reagan had been sworn in as President.
(Corpus: BBC/06. Text: S1000910801.)

**B2.** The context contains specification of result. If details of the *eventual* result are given which are only ascertainable after it has materialised, this is a clear indication of the finality sense. But even here there is some room for doubt, as in the following case:

(30) But Miss Venezuela, the eventual winner, will be in for a year of travelling charity works and meeting people. <p> Everything, in fact, that she has always wanted to do. (Corpus: Times/10. Text: N2000951216.)

Is Miss Venezuela only assumed to become a winner, so that whatever the outcome of the competition she will travel and meet people, or has the competition already taken place? The limited context does not give enough guidance. Other cases are clearer, particularly where there is added support from criterion B1.

(31) A perfect example is The Chocolate Watch Band, a Californian outfit who achieved retrospective cult acclaim after their eventual split in 1970.
(Corpus: UKmags/03. Text: N0000000692.)

(32) Early indications were that together they would raise between £200m and £230m and some financial analysts expressed surprise at the eventual £172m sale tag.
(Corpus: Times/10. Text: N2000951104.)

(33) Butler did a better second lap, taking 1–17 out of Illingworth to finish an eventual fourth. (Corpus: UKmags/03. Text: N0000000901.)

**B3.** The context expresses confidence in, certainty about or the necessity of the event, phenomenon or result referred to by the NP containing *eventual.*

(34) But with the eventual outcome never in any doubt, the sending off of Stewart deepened the gloom on an ill-tempered night.
(Corpus: Today/11. Text: N6000920930.)

(35) '... The proposal looks likely to go ahead and we hope it will be in place in time for the eventual inevitable turnaround when the drought ends,' he said.
(Corpus: OZnews/01. Text: N5000951022.)

(36) The realisation that reckless exploitation of the earth's resources can lead only to eventual global disaster is unlikely to be a passing enthusiasm;
(Corpus: UKephem/02. Text: E0000002490.)

Note that the question of confidence, etc., refers only to the head of the NP where *eventual* is found. The following instance of *eventual* does not belong here:

(37) But the guerrillas want to keep the camp population as a captive constituency inside Cambodia, guaranteeing them votes in an eventual national election ...

because what is guaranteed is not the election but the votes.

**B4.** The event (etc.) is presented as the result of an act of will, a commitment, a prescription, a plan. Here the relevant verbs are for instance *demand, call for, plan, advocate, propose, argue for.*

(38) The Czechoslovak authorities are committed to their eventual departure because with unemployment rising they want all jobs to be available for Czechs and Slovaks. (Corpus: BBC/06. Text: S1000900927.)
(39) While advocating the eventual removal of nuclear weapons from the Middle East, Noumkan said he thinks Israel should not be forced to destroy all its nuclear weapons immediately. (Corpus: NPR/07. Text: S2000911026.)
(40) In talks in September the rebels demanded the eventual disappearance of military forces on both sides. (Corpus: BBC/06. Text: S1000901102.)

**B5.** The existence of the head noun is taken for granted, cannot be doubted, or follows as a matter of course.

(41) it is during the second part of a child's second year when a major step is made in transforming primary narcissism into a more adult state. Difficulties or traumas at that time mean that the eventual adult retains narcissism in an unhealthy way (Corpus: UKbooks/08. Text: B0000000649.)
(42) If there isn't any snow, I can go out and find a cluster of tight rosettes waiting for the first warm day to shed their purple hue and start lengthening out into leafy blue-green stalks. The eventual height of the stalk is about two and a half feet, and ... (Corpus: USbooks/09. Text: B9000000523.)
(43) Although the house is simple in concept, meticulous attention has been paid to its eventual appearance. (Corpus: UKmags/03. Text: N0000000084.)

## 7. Comments on analysis

Information in the immediate linguistic context is often insufficient to distinguish between the two meanings. For example, in

(44) Hurst hauled 21-year-old Justin up on to tiptoe until he went blue in the face. <p> Sandy Morrison, defending at Plymouth, Devon, denied the event at HMS Illustrious had any bearing on Justin's eventual suicide six months later. (Corpus: Today/11. Text: N6000940618.)

we cannot conclude from the text whether Justin actually committed suicide six months later (the finality sense), or whether it is being suggested that his death could have been due to other circumstances (the potentiality sense) – in other words that it was not a suicide at all. The decision therefore frequently depends on textual information outside the sentence in which *eventual* occurs, as in

(45) Okay, it might have been different if Roy Keane's pulverising drive had been there all season and Giggs hadn't occasionally been hamstrung. But they are only parts of the equation of eventual failure. The bottom-line truth is this was a United team that switched off for Europe – and could not switch back on. It was a disaster waiting to happen – except for Arsenal.
(Corpus: Sunnow/17. Text: N9119980420)

It is only in the two sentences following the *eventual* one that we are told that the failure has already occurred.

The decision on whether or not an example meets a given criterion can also be dependent on the reader's knowledge of extralinguistic factors. For instance, in the following sentence

(46) This is McGinnis's very personal speculation about the Kennedy family's private life and the rise and eventual failure of Senator Ted Kennedy.
(Corpus: OZnews/01. Text: N5000950823)

the reader who knows that Ted Kennedy did fail will interpret *eventual* here as meaning 'final, ultimate', while the sentence may be ambiguous to one who does not know. Similarly, if we do not know whether Bolton's opponents in the following passage were actually to become their 'companions in distress' or if this was just a possibility at the time, we are in no position to decide between the two meanings:

(47) Because it is the goal that never was – undetected by the match officials at the Reebok Stadium last September, when Bolton fought a scoreless draw with their eventual companions in distress. Oh, it was picked up by television's magic eye for all to see, but the evidence was ignored, never used as any basis of an appeal.
(Corpus: Sunnow/17. Text: N9119980513.)

In many cases the criteria overlap. For instance, if an event is seen as occurring in the future, it is natural that a degree of uncertainty should be associated with it. Similarly, an event whose actualisation is seen as conditional upon something else will normally be thought of as possibly occurring in future time. These cases illustrate the co-occurrence of different A criteria, and in the same way there is often co-occurrence of B criteria, as in

(48) The search for the latest Man In Black, the sixth in the series, was a bit like the hunt for the next James Bond. <p> The eventual choice was Mark Keller ...
(Corpus: Today/11. Text: N600094121)

where the past-time reference and the specification of the result cooperate to suggest a B interpretation. In such cases, then, an interpretation suggested by one criterion receives support from another.

In other cases, conflicting A and B criteria can co-occur. In the following example,

(49) The petition was made very much in anticipation of the eventual establishment in eighteen-thirty-eight of a representative town council.
(Corpus: UKspok/04. Text: S0000000090.)

'in anticipation of' suggests that the event has not taken place at the time of the action (criterion A2), and 'in eighteen-thirty-eight' specifies the event and thus indicates that it has already taken place (criterion B2). How will such cases be interpreted?

Let us consider the two senses of *eventual* again. Sense A is 'possible, potential, possibly resulting in or occurring', and sense B is 'final, ultimate, finally occurring'. In other words, (A) presents an open choice between (α) realisation and (β) non-realisation of the event/phenomenon. The meaning of *eventual* (B) is thus included as one of the options of *eventual* (A), viz. option (α). If there are (B) indications in the text, i.e. indications of the realisation of the event/phenomenon, any uncertainty as to its occurrence mediated by the A criterion consequently disappears. In other words, if there are indicators both of uncertainty (A) and of certainty (B) in the same context, the certainty indicators will prevail.

In theory, then, the problem of distinguishing between senses (A) and (B) is simple: no (A) interpretation is possible if there are (B) indicators present. In actual practice, it is not so simple. For one thing, it is often difficult to decide if a (B) indicator is present. For example, in

(50) Yet for a child of loving parents with no shortage of money, there was no need to grow up fast. Young Anthea had plenty of distractions to keep thoughts of her eventual career at bay. (Corpus: Today/11. Text: N6000950904.)

can one see the existence of *her eventual career* as something that is 'taken for granted, cannot be doubted or follows as a matter of course' (B5)? That is, can a career of any kind be taken for granted? Also, if speaker/writer and listener/reader have access to different types of evidence, the same statement involving *eventual* could receive different interpretations; the speaker/writer may intend (A), but the listener/reader, who knows that the potentiality implied by the speaker/writer has been implemented, interprets the statement as (B). And for another thing, even if there is no (B) indicator, the context is often of little help in deciding whether the speaker/writer does, in fact, intend the potentiality sense. For instance, in the following sentence from BNC,

(51) He allowed this to continue in expectation of eventual compensation, but in April 1962 issued proceedings against the company. (CDD 110)

*eventual compensation* could mean both 'possible compensation' and 'ultimate compensation'.

## 8. Results of analysis

All the 414 occurrences of *eventual* in the Cobuild Corpus were analysed in accordance with the criteria set out above. All of them could be accommodated in one or several of the criterial classes. If we want to see how the (A) and (B) criteria are distributed, we get the following picture, with due reservations for borderline cases and fuzzy examples:

**Table 2:** Distribution of *eventual* over criteria

| A1 | A2 | A3 | A4 | A5 | A6 | B1 | B2 | B3 | B4 | B5 |
|---|---|---|---|---|---|---|---|---|---|---|
| 156 | 99 | 26 | 45 | 8 | 4 | 65 | 78 | 70 | 59 | 40 |

The total, 650, exceeds 414, since there are many cases of co-occurring criteria. The examples are distributed over the criteria and their sources in the following way:

**Table 3:** Distribution of *eventual* over sources and semantic types

| | (A) only | (B) only | (A) + (B) | Total |
|---|---|---|---|---|
| **UK spoken** | 26 (40%) | 26 (40%) | 13 (20%) | 65 (100%) |
| BBC[9] | 24 | 20 | 11 | 55 |
| UKspok | 2 | 6 | 2 | 10 |
| **UK written** | 63 (27%) | 98 (43%) | 69 (30%) | 230 (100%) |
| Sunnow | 5 | 11 | 15 | 31 |
| Times | 19 | 28 | 15 | 62 |
| Today | 10 | 15 | 12 | 37 |
| UKbooks | 15 | 25 | 10 | 50 |
| UKephem | 8 | 4 | 1 | 13 |
| UKmags | 6 | 15 | 16 | 37 |
| **US spoken** | 7 (37%) | 9 (47%) | 3 (16%) | 19 (100%) |
| NPR[10] | 7 | 9 | 3 | 19 |
| **US written** | 23 (47%) | 21 (43%) | 5 (10%) | 49 (100%) |
| USbooks | 21 | 21 | 5 | 47 |
| USephem | 2 | 0 | 0 | 2 |
| **Australian** | 15 (29%) | 20 (39%) | 16 (31%) | 51 (100%) |
| OZnews | 15 | 20 | 16 | 51 |
| **Total** | 134 (32%) | 174 (42%) | 106 (26%) | 414 (100%) |

In most of the textual categories the '(A) only' and the '(B) only' types are roughly equal in size, but in the category that supplies the major part of the material, UK written, there is a clear preponderance of the '(B) only' type, a preponderance that also shows up in the overall results. This group with (B) indicators will normally be intended and interpreted as having the finality meaning. And, as was argued above, so will the fairly large group with both (A) and (B) indicators, in most cases.

There remains the third of the material that is provided with (A) indicators only. In many of these examples there is an element of uncertainty, where *eventual* can be assumed to receive different interpretations by different readers or listeners. Consider, for instance, the following BNC example about the sales of records:

(52) The cost of this is covered by increased singles sales and the eventual high sales of the album. (A6A 1018)

Some would regard the high sales of the album in this context as a possibility that may materialise (the (A) meaning), while others would see it as the undoubted final outcome of the present state of affairs (the (B) meaning). Changing from one interpretation to the other will not affect the understanding of the passage materially. (Compare the expression *if or when*, as in 'if or when the album sells well'.) This kind of situation is the seedbed of a particular type of semantic change, the type that Stern calls 'permutation', where 'the *meaning* of the phrase changes, but the changed meaning is equally applicable to the referent'.[11] In describing the semantic transition from *beads* 'prayers' to *beads* 'balls of a rosary', he says that 'it was often quite immaterial whether the phrase was understood in the one way or the other; it remained, nevertheless, an adequate designation for its total (phrase) referent.'[12] The case of *eventual* is interesting in this perspective. On the one hand, it is clear that the change from 'possible' to 'final' is widespread, as is shown by the number of examples with (B) indicators and by the testimony of (very) modern dictionaries. The change is clearly an example of Stern's permutation. On the other hand, while this change is well attested and affects perhaps the major part of the *eventual* material, the corpus material suggests that the process is not yet completed and that the historically primary meaning lives on as a possibility in the word. Indeed, it is even showing signs of reestablishing itself in the language as a vital alternative of the finality sense. Definitions such as those quoted from the $OED^2$ and RHD (above) as well as examples like the following (from BNC), where a possibility/potentiality reading seems more inviting, at least to my mind, than a finality one, indicate that the semantics are here in a state of flux, offering ideal conditions for semantic change of the permutation type.

(53) But the early experience of monarchy had its advantages, at least from the viewpoint of those trying to impose a more central control; the 'ealdermen', or earls, eventual successors to the 'kings', were expected to collect quite considerable taxes at the behest of their overlords. [Neither ealdormenn nor earls could count on becoming successors to the 'kings'. GK] (CB6 37)

(54) This also enables any eventual profit to be kept in the long term, avoiding the problem that if it is retained, any eventual surplus would have to go back to the borrower. (CBT 2659)

## 9. Conclusion

If a comparison of the figures for the American and British usage of *eventual* show anything – and as was been pointed out above, the criteria on which they are based are brittle at times – it is that UK spoken usage is more or less in line with US usage in general, showing a considerable incidence of potentiality cases, whereas UK written usage differs substantially from it in tending more to favour the finality sense. One interpretation of this is that American English could have preserved the older, European Continental usage as a viable option and that this is now being strengthened or reintroduced in spoken British under American influence. One additional reason why the Continental sense of *eventual* is now apparent in British English may be that English speakers are in closer contact with Continental ones than they have been for centuries. Improved communications, a booming tourist trade, better education and, not least, a stream of information from Brussels officials working for the European Union have all contributed to making the average English speaker aware of other European languages than his or her own. As for influence from Brussels, it is not unlikely that translators and interpreters occasionally happen to use *eventual* as an English translation of French *éventuel* or German *eventuell*, thus underpinning the traditional use of the English word.

When a semantic process is taking place under our very noses, corpora can help us to observe details of the process by which a semantic change takes place. In the case of *eventual*, then, the movement has been from a potentiality sense, identical to that in Continental and Scandinavian languages, to fairly clear open-choice instances with either potentiality or finality interpretations, to clearly constrained finality instances by the addition of 'certainty indicators'. As the corpora indicate, we now seem to be coming back to an open-choice situation. From the point of view of Continental speakers, it is quite clear that *eventual* will continue to be a false friend.

## Notes

1 I am greatly indebted to David Wright for his comments on an earlier version and for his help with the questionnaire.

2 French, Italian, Spanish, Portuguese, German, Dutch, Danish, Norwegian, Swedish.

3 Rey and Rey-Debove (1983).

4 D'Anna (1986).

5 In Swedish it has remained practically unchanged since the 16th century, according to the SAOB.

6 'Of or pertaining to events or occurrences; consisting in events; of the nature of an event' and 'That happens to exist' (OED s.v. eventual 1 and 2).

7 Unfortunately, there are no occurrences at all of the word in the historical corpora the Helsinki Corpus and the Corpus of Late Modern English Prose.

8 But note that a past-tense form of the verb is no guarantee that the event has already taken place: 'They considered his eventual success very unlikely.' – 'At a news conference before leaving Rwanda, the president said he is looking for a peaceful solution and that he did not rule out eventual talks with the rebels themselves.' (Corpus: bbc/06. Text: S1000901015.)

9 Material from the radio stations BBC and National Public Radio has here been regarded as spoken despite the fact that large parts of it can be assumed to be written material read out aloud.

10 See Note 9.

11 Stern (1931: 351).

12 Stern (1931: 168).

13 One informant abstained.

**References**

AHD[1] = Morris, William (ed.) (1970). *The American heritage dictionary of the English language*. Boston: American Heritage & Houghton Mifflin.

AHD[3] = Soukhanov, Anne H. (ed.) (1992). *The American heritage dictionary*, 3rd ed. Boston and New York: Houghton Mifflin.

Aston, Guy, and Lou Burnard (1998). *The BNC handbook*. Edinburgh: Edinburgh University Press.

BNC = British National Corpus, see Aston and Burnard (1998).

CIDE = Procter, Paul (ed.) (1995). *Cambridge international dictionary of English*. Cambridge University Press.

Cobuild = Cobuild Corpus, cf. Sinclair (1987).

Cobuild[1] = Sinclair, John McH. (ed.) (1987). *Collins* COBUILD *English language dictionary*. London & Glasgow: Collins

Cobuild[2] = Sinclair, John McH. (ed.) (1995). *Collins* COBUILD *English dictionary*. New ed. London: Harper Collins.

COD[1] = Fowler, H. W., and F. G. Fowler (eds) (1914). *The concise Oxford dictionary of current English*. Oxford: Clarendon.

COD[4] = Fowler, H. W., and F. G. Fowler (eds) (1951). *The concise Oxford Dictionary of current English*, 4th ed. Revised by E. McIntosh. Oxford: Clarendon.

COD[5] = Fowler, H. W., and F. G. Fowler (eds) (1964). *The concise Oxford Dictionary of current English*, 5th ed. Revised by E. McIntosh. Oxford: Clarendon.

COD$^{6}$ = Sykes, J. B. (ed.) (1976). *The concise Oxford dictionary*, 6th ed. Oxford: Clarendon,

COD$^{8}$ = Allen, R. E. (ed.) (1990). *The concise Oxford dictionary of the English language*, 8th ed. Oxford: Clarendon.

COD$^{9}$ = Thompson, Della (ed.) (1995). *The concise Oxford dictionary of current English*, 9th ed. Oxford: Clarendon.

Collins = Hanks, Patrick, Thomas Hill Long and Laurence Urdang (1979). *Collins dictionary of the English language*. London & Glasgow: Collins.

D'Anna, Giacomo (ed.) (1986). *Dizionario italiano ragionato*. Firenze: Sintesi.

LDOCE$^{1}$ = Procter, Paul (ed.) (1978). *Longman dictionary of contemporary English*. Harlow & London: Longman.

LDOCE$^{2}$ = Summers, Della (ed.) (1987). *Longman dictionary of contemporary English*, 2nd ed. Harlow & London: Longman.

LDOCE$^{3}$ = Summers, Della (ed.) (1995). *Longman dictionary of contemporary English*, 3rd ed. Harlow, Essex: Longman.

OALDCE$^{1}$ = Hornby, A. S., E. V. Gatenby and H. Wakefield (eds) (1963). *The advanced learner's dictionary of current English*. London: Oxford University Press.

OALDCE$^{3}$ = Hornby, A. S. (ed.) (1974). *Oxford advanced learner's dictionary of current English*, 3rd ed. London: Oxford University Press.

OED$^{2}$ = Simpson, J. A., and Weiner, E. S. C. (eds) (1989). *The Oxford English dictionary*, 2nd ed. Oxford: Clarendon.

Rey, A., and J. Rey-Debove (1983). *Le petit Robert. Dictionnaire alphabétique et analogique de la langue française*. Paris: Le Robert.

RHD = Flexner, Stuart Berg (ed.) (1987). *The Random House dictionary of the English language*, 2nd ed. New York: Random House.

SAOB = *Ordbok över svenska språket utgiven av Svenska Akademien*. 1– . Lund (1898– ).

Sinclair, J. McH. (ed.) (1987). *Looking up. An account of the COBUILD project in lexical computing*. London and Glasgow: Collins.

Stern, Gustaf (1964) [1931]. *Meaning and change of meaning*. Bloomington: Indiana University Press. Originally published as *Göteborgs högskolas årsskrift* (1932:1).

W$^{3}$ = Gove, Philip Babcock (ed.) (1961). *Webster's third new international dictionary of the English language*. Springfield, Mass.: Merriam.

## Appendix: the pilot study

A request for your 'eventual' assistance

The adverb *eventually* means 'in the end' (e.g. 'Eventually Arsenal scored.') The adjective *eventual* normally has a similar 'finality' sense (e.g. 'The eventual score was 2-0.'). Sometimes, though, it seems that *eventual* is being used to convey the meaning 'possible' (e.g. 'Any eventual doubt about the result will be rapidly dispelled by Arsenal's new aggressive tactics.')

Please mark (by putting a cross in the relevant boxes below) which, if any, of the 10 sentences can be given the 'finality' interpretation, and which, if any, can be given the 'possibility, potentiality' interpretation.

Note: You may think that both interpretations are conceivable, but that one seems more likely than the other. In that case, put a cross in both columns and then put a ring round one of the crosses to show your preference.

Any comments will be welcome – but don't feel obliged.

(1) The worry here is that the protocol will reduce the ability of the EC's poorer members – including eventual newcomers from Eastern Europe – to compete in the great market.

(2) Or might the turmoil of schemes and unemployment be preparing youth more thoroughly (as has long been the case in the USA) for better adaptation to eventual permanent employment?

(3) Progress within bondage had to take precedence over liberation to secure the safety of any eventual freedom.

(4) This is bound to be seen as further evidence that Britain risks cutting itself off from the mainstream of European integration because of hostility both to economic and monetary union and to eventual political union.

(5) When American troops were first sent to the Gulf Region after the Iraqi occupation of Kuwait, the reason given by the US for this deployment of troops was the protection of Saudi Arabia from an 'eventual invasion by Iraq'.

(6) Rescues are sometimes dangerous and often frustrating because these wild mammals, although weakened, struggle to avoid capture. But a successful rescue begins a chain of events designed to bring an animal on the verge of death back to health and an eventual return to the ocean.

(7) Guy Rakotondravahatra, Bishop of Ihosy, Madagascar, summed up the reasons for optimism: We have had a chance, for the first time ever, to talk about our problems, our desires, our hopes and our eventual disagreements.

(8) But the guerrillas want to keep the camp population as a captive constituency inside Cambodia, guaranteeing them votes in an eventual national election ...

(9) He allowed this to continue in expectation of eventual compensation, but in April 1962 issued proceedings against the company.

(10) This also enables any eventual profit to be kept in the long term, avoiding the problem that if it is retained, any eventual surplus would have to go back to the borrower.

| | Answers: | |
|---|---|---|
| Sentence | Preferred interpretation | Conceivable interpretation |
| (1) | Finality: 2, potentiality: 5 | Finality: 4, potentiality: 5 |
| (2) | Finality: 6, potentiality: 1 | Finality: 6, potentiality: 3 |
| (3) | Finality: 4, potentiality: 3 | Finality: 5, potentiality: 4 |
| (4) | Finality: 5,5, potentiality: 1,5 | Finality: 6, potentiality: 4 |
| (5) | Finality: 1, potentiality: 6 | Finality: 1, potentiality: 6 |
| (6) | Finality: 7, potentiality: 0 | Finality: 7, potentiality: 0 |
| (7) | Finality: 2, potentiality: 5 | Finality: 3, potentiality: 5 |
| (8) | Finality: 5, potentiality: 2 | Finality: 6, potentiality: 2 |
| (9) | Finality: 5, potentiality: 2 | Finality: 5, potentiality: 3 |
| (10) | Finality: 1, potentiality: 5[13] | Finality: 1, potentiality: 6 |

# Functions of intonation in sentences and texts

*Ilka Mindt*

University of Würzburg

## Abstract

*The data analysed are taken from the Lancaster/IBM Spoken English Corpus. Based on an acoustic analysis of the fundamental frequency of falling tones, the function of falls is investigated in two units: major tone groups (roughly equivalent to sentences) and complete texts. Starting points and end points of falls show a clear correlation between the location within the speaker's range and their position within the major tone group. The emerging pattern is termed 'the gradient of falls', which can be analysed as indicating declination. Across texts, the configuration of starting points and endpoints shows great variation. A downward direction of starting points and endpoints as well as an upward direction can be found. The downward trend is analysed as being normal and unmarked, whereas an upward trend of starting points and endpoints across a text is interpreted as conveying paralinguistic meaning. Thus the analysis of the same intonation contour at two different units shows two discrete functions: the function of declination at the local level of the major tone group and the function of paralinguistic meaning at the global level across a complete text.*

## 1. Introduction

The focus of this paper is on one type of intonation contour, the falling tone. I will examine the distribution of falling tones according to their occurrence in certain positions within a tone group. I shall also consider their location within the speaker's range and the succession of starting points and endpoints of falls. After a short description of the corpus which has been used for this analysis, falling tones will be described at two levels: at major tone groups and across texts. Possible explanations for the observed direction of starting points and endpoints of falls at the two levels will be given. Finally, I will illustrate the relationship between the patterns of falls found at these two levels.

## 2. Corpus

A total of 21 texts from the Lancaster/IBM Spoken English Corpus (SEC) have been analysed. The texts are taken from 4 different categories as can be seen in Table 1: commentary, news broadcasts, magazine-style reporting and dialogue.

**Table 1:** Analysed text categories

| Text category | Number of texts | Speakers |
|---|---|---|
| A: commentary | 11 | 11 |
| B: news broadcasts | 4 | 15 |
| F: magazine-style reporting | 4 | 14 |
| J: dialogue | 2 | 5 |
| Total | 21 | 45<br>Without double listings: 40 |

Eleven texts are from the category labelled 'commentary', which includes broadcasts by BBC reporters on events happening around the world. All the texts from categories B and F are BBC radio broadcasts. One text from category J, ('dialogue'), is a BBC report as well, the other, a dialogue between two MA students about working abroad. For each category the number of texts and speakers are listed. The 21 different texts of this study involve 40 different speakers altogether. Five speakers take part in more than one text, which accounts for the actual numbers of speakers listed in Table 1.

The texts in the SEC have been divided into chunks of different sizes. Longer chunks which roughly correspond to sentences are termed 'major tone groups'. Smaller chunks which can be associated with phrases or clauses are referred to as 'minor tone groups'.

**Text 1:** Major tone group 2 from text A01

> ↑`more ·news about the ¯Reverend _Sun ·Myung `Moon | _founder of the Unifi`cation ·Church | who's ˇcurrently in ·jail | for `tax evasion ||

Text 1 shows the prosodic annotation of the second major tone group from text A01. A major tone group is indicated by the double bars at the end. This major tone group corresponds to a sentence. Four minor tone groups can be identified, each delimited by a single bar.

The SEC has been annotated prosodically by two transcribers. The different tones in the prosodic transcription are falls, rises, levels, fall-rises and rise-falls. The most frequent intonation contour in all 21 texts analysed is the fall.

**Table 2**: Frequency of intonation contours in the texts analysed

| tone | | fall | level | fall-rise | rise | rise-fall | total |
|---|---|---|---|---|---|---|---|
| frequency in texts | absolute | 3,545 | 3,129 | 1,536 | 938 | 8 | 9,156 |
| | relative | 38.72% | 34.17% | 16.78% | 10.24% | 0.09% | 100% |

Falls account for 38.72% of all intonation contours. The second most frequent contour is the level tone, followed by fall-rises, rises and rise-falls.

For this study, all falls which were annotated as such in the transcriptions of the 21 texts have been analysed. The fundamental frequency of the falls was measured using the Loughborough Sound Images speech workstation; and all measured frequencies in Hertz were normalised using a scale from zero to one hundred percent, to allow for comparisons between speakers. The figures presented here will refer to the normalised frequencies in percent.

In this study the focus will be on falls only. The aim is to describe the location of falls within the speaker's range in major tone groups and across complete texts.

## 3. Falls in major tone groups

First of all, the distribution of falls within the major tone group will be described. Then the discussion will focus on where the falls are located within the speaker's range. In addition, the succession of starting points and endpoints of all falls within the speaker's range will be discussed.

Altogether, more than 3,000 falls occurred (3,545; 3,243 of these could be measured). The function of falls is described by Cruttenden in the following way:

> Both falling tones [high and low (I.M.)] involve a sense of finality, of completeness, definiteness, and separateness when used with declaratives; hence both tones are more common on sentence final intonation-groups than on sentence non-final intonation-groups. (Cruttenden 1997: 91)

The term 'intonation-group' is equivalent to a major tone group. Cruttenden expects to find most falls at the end of sentences/major tone groups. He only takes into account falls which are considered to be the nucleus of a major tone group. In the prosodic annotation of the SEC, no distinction is made between nuclear and non-nuclear tones. However, Williams (1996: 52) points out that in the prosodic annotation of the SEC, a nucleus can be assumed to be the final accented syllable within a tone group.

### 3.1 Distribution of falls

In the following, the distribution of falling tones will be discussed in two ways: first without any theory of nuclear tones in mind, and second in terms of the internal structure of tone groups as described by Cruttenden. The distribution of falls in the tone group is given in Table 3.

**Table 3**: Distribution of falls

| | before a major tone group boundary | before a minor tone group boundary | inside a tone group | total |
|---|---|---|---|---|
| falls | 1,169 (32.98%) | 881 (24.85%) | 1,495 (42.17%) | 3,545 (100%) |

Three positions for falls within a tone group have been distinguished: (1) at the end of a sentence, i.e. occurring before a major tone group boundary; (2) at the end of a phrase or clause, i.e. occurring before a minor tone group boundary and (3) inside a tone group, i.e. not immediately preceding a boundary. In fact most falls occur inside a tone group. The second most frequent place of occurrence is before major tone group boundaries, accounting for almost 33%. In about 25% of all cases, the falls were found before a minor tone group boundary.

In Cruttenden's analysis, only falls before major tone group boundaries and those before minor tone group boundaries could be considered to be functioning as nuclei of intonation-groups. The fact that a majority of falls occur at major tone group boundaries and at minor tone group boundaries (33% + 25% = 58%) supports his approach. Falls occurring inside a tone group would normally be considered to be non-nuclear and could function as heads or pre-heads, but they are rarely mentioned in intonational theory. Since so many of the falls in this study occur inside a tone group (42%), they clearly need to be included in a theory of intonation. The distribution presented in Table 3 supports the conclusion that the function and meaning of falls has to be reconsidered.

### 3.2 Falls in a speaker's range

I will now consider where falls are located within a speaker's range. The speaker's range is presented as the normalised Hertz frequency on a scale from 0 to 100 percent. The falls will be considered according to their distribution in the tone group. Figure 1 shows the calculated means of all measured falls within a speaker's range.

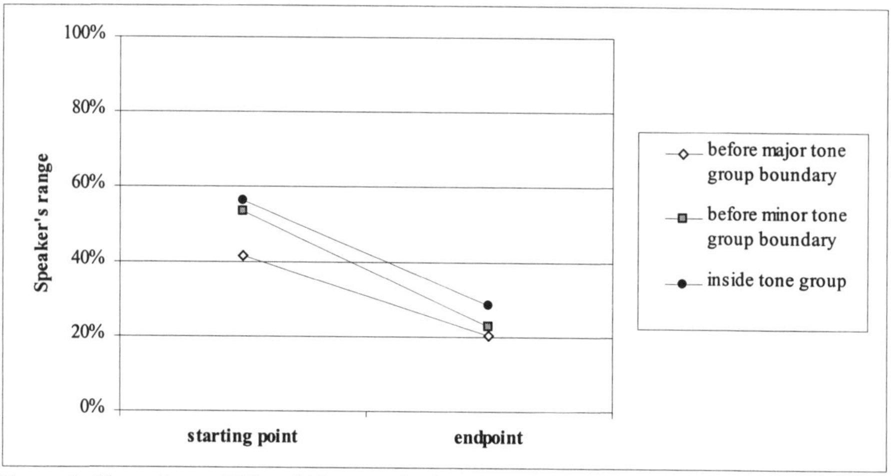


**Figure 1:** The pattern of falls within a speaker's range

The y-axis represents normalised pitches as percentages from 0% to 100%. On the x-axis the starting points of falls and the endpoints are indicated. It can be seen that falls which occur before major tone group boundaries begin lowest in the speaker's range and end lowest on average. Falls before minor tone group boundaries begin higher and end higher, whereas falls inside a tone group begin highest and end highest.

Figure 1 shows that there is a correlation between the position of falls in a tone group and their height within a speaker's range. Falls before major tone groups are lowest in the speaker's range, falls inside a tone group highest. I will refer to this correlation between the position and the height within a speaker's range as the 'gradient' of falls.

### 3.3 The gradient of falls in two texts

The gradient of falls given in Figure 1 is based on averages. In individual tone groups this gradient can be observed more or less clearly. Two examples will be discussed, the first of which is taken from text B01, a news report. Major tone group 51 has been selected as an example.

**Text 2:** Major tone group 51 from text B01

> the ˏcongressmen | and ˏMr ·Raison | can ˋalso (79.10%-15.82%) expect to be ¯lobbied for ·help in the _search for ˋlong-·term (66.10%-11.30%) soˋlutions (37.29%-9.04%) to ¯Ethiopia's _food ˋcrisis (30.51%-3.95%) | and in parˇticular | in reˋsettling (79.10%-3.39%) | ·two-and-a-half ˇmillion ·people | from the ˇdrought-·prone areas | to more ˇfertile ·land | ·over the next ten ˋyears (27.68%-0.00%) ||

The figures given in brackets after each annotated fall show the normalised fundamental frequencies as percentages. As can be seen in this example, the fall at the end of the major tone group begins and ends lowest of all falls in this major tone group. The two falls occurring before minor tone group boundaries end higher, and the falls inside the tone groups end highest in the speaker's range. The average gradient of all six falls in this major tone group is shown in Figure 2.

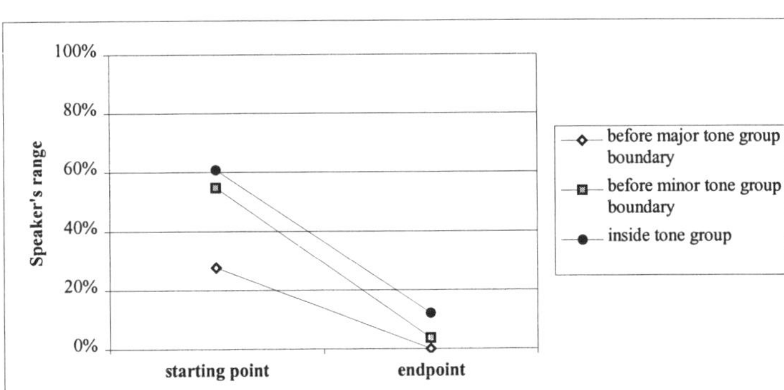


**Figure 2:** Falls in the speaker's range (in major tone group 51, text B01)

The fall before the major tone group is lowest in the speaker's range; the falls before minor tone group boundaries are higher and falls inside a tone group average highest.

In Figure 3 the falls are given in the order of their occurrence in this major tone group. The graph presents the direction of the topline (all starting points of falls), and the direction of the baseline (all endpoints of falls).

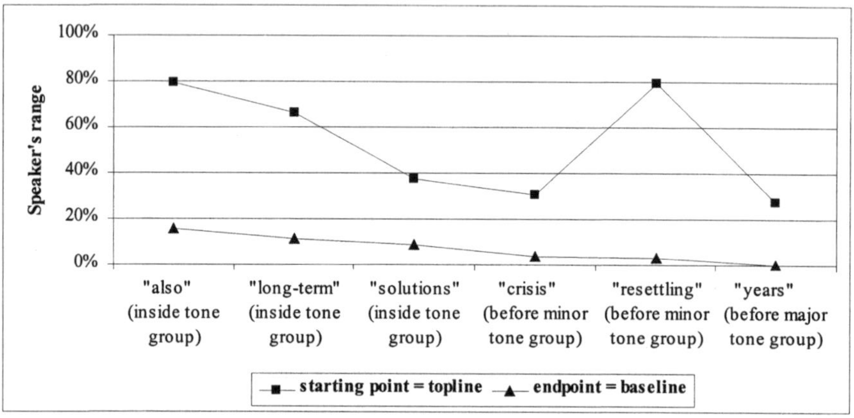


**Figure 3:** Topline and baseline (major tone group 51, text B01)

The baseline of all falls declines across the major tone group as a whole. The topline declines until the fourth fall, which indicates the endpoint of the first part of the sentence before the coordinating conjunction. The topline is reset on the fifth fall and then declines again.

The second example is taken from text A01, a commentary.

**Text 3:** Major tone group 2 from text A01

> ↑`more (100%-17.78%) ·news about the ¯Reverend _Sun ·Myung `Moon (28.15%-5.93%) | _founder of the Unifi`cation (47.41%-34.07%) ·Church | who's ˅currently in ·jail | for `tax (24.07%-11.11%) evasion ||

In major tone group 2 the endpoint of the last fall is low in the speaker's range (at 11%), but it is not the lowest endpoint inside that major tone group. The fall on *Moon* ends lowest, at about 6% of the speaker's range. The gradient of the falls at the three different positions is given in Figure 4.

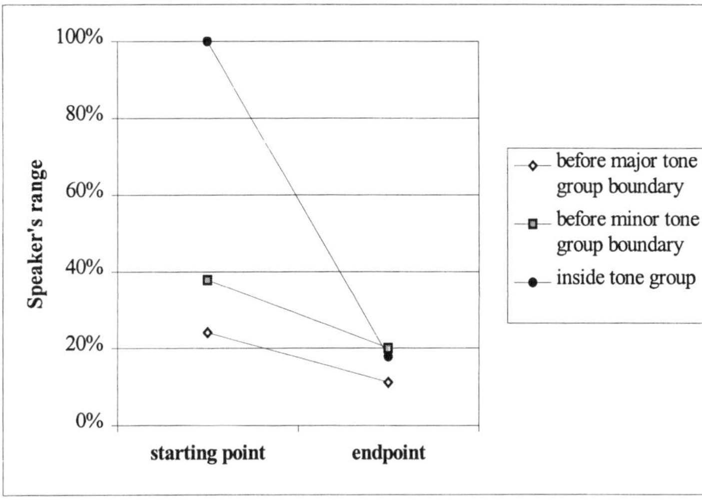


**Figure 4:** Falls in the speaker's range (in major tone group 2, text A01)

In this example the fall before the major tone group boundary is on average lowest within the speaker's range. The starting point of the falls before minor tone group boundaries is higher; falls inside a tone group begin highest. It can be seen that the endpoint of falls occurring inside a tone group is on average slightly lower within the speaker's range than the endpoint of falls before a minor tone group boundary. The falls in this major tone group differ from the average gradient of falls as shown in Figure 1, where falls inside tone groups end higher than falls before a minor tone group, though the deviation is only small.

The graphic presentation of the direction of the topline and the baseline appears in Figure 5.

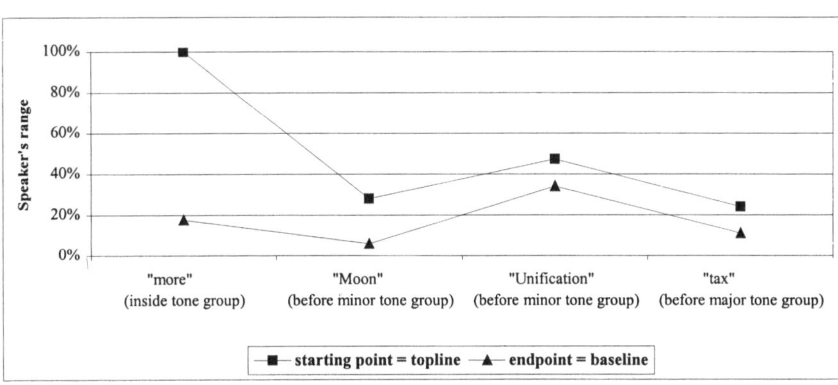


**Figure 5:** Topline and baseline (Text A01)

Both the topline and the baseline show a decline from the first to the second, and the third to the fourth fall. The starting point of the last fall is lowest in the speaker's range; all other starting points are higher. The first fall begins highest in the speaker's range.

### 3.4 The gradients of falls across all texts

The general pattern of gradients already mentioned – falls before major tone groups being lowest within the speaker's range, those before minor tone groups higher, and falls inside tone groups highest – can be observed in two thirds of all analysed texts. In all texts, falls before a major tone group boundary begin lower in the speaker's range than the falls in any other position.

The gradient of falls inside major tone groups can be analysed as indicating the phenomenon of declination. Declination refers to the lowering of the fundamental frequency in this unit of speech (cf. Cruttenden 1997: 121, Ladd 1984: 53, Laver 1994: 459).

## 4. Falls across individual texts

The unit in which declination takes place is a topic of considerable debate. Since falls are the most frequent intonation contour, I have studied their location in the speaker's range not only in major tone groups but also across the whole text. For this purpose, the text was divided into two halves. More precisely, the number of falls occurring in a text was taken as the basis and divided into two halves. The average mean was calculated for all falls in the first half, and the same was done for the falls in the second half. The means were compared. No distinction was made as to the position of the falls inside tone groups.

In text B01 there are 203 falls, with 101 falls making up the first half, and 101 the second. The 102nd fall was counted as belonging to both text halves.

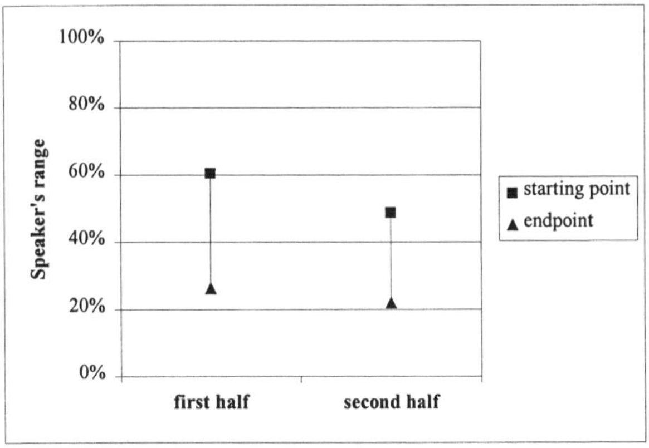


**Figure 6:** Average means of falls in text B01

The falls in the first half begin on average at 60.39% and end at 26.14% of the speaker's range. Those in the second begin at 48.78% and end at 21.91%. The direction of the falls in text B01 is downward. The falls begin and end higher in the first half than in the second.

A different configuration of the topline and the baseline can be observed in text A01.

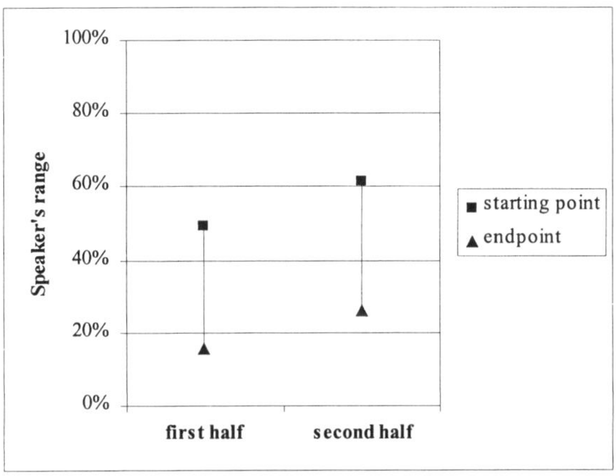


**Figure 7:** Average means of falls in text A01

The falls in the first half begin at 49.32% and end at 15.52%. In the second half they reach from 61.39% to 25.78%. The falls show an upward direction.

The direction of the falls of all 21 texts which were analysed is presented in Figure 8.

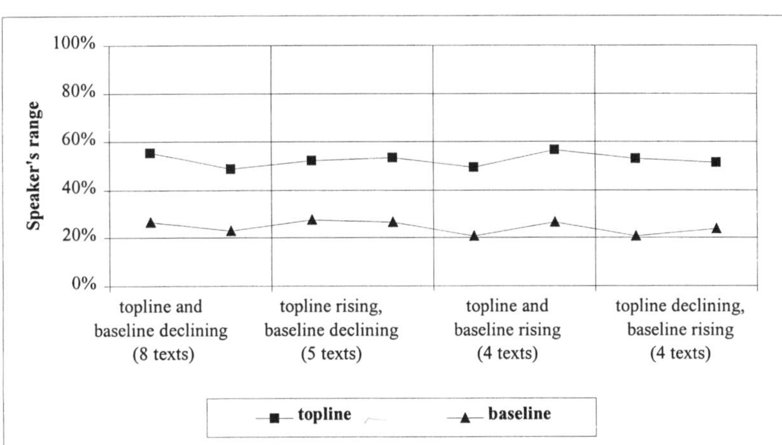


**Figure 8:** Direction of toplines and baselines (all analysed texts)

In eight texts the topline and the baseline are declining. In five texts the topline is inclining slightly, whereas the baseline declines. In 4 texts baseline and topline rise, and in four other texts the topline declines whereas the baseline rises. No clear preference for either direction can be observed across texts.

## 5. Possible explanations

What explanations can be given for the various directions of toplines and baselines? The upward direction of text A01 has already been mentioned. The climax of this text can be found at the end, so the incline supports the text structure. Text A01 is a commentary and deals with miracles and religion. Two different viewpoints are presented in text A01. A general one is contrasted with a scientific point of view. The upward direction of the normalised fundamental frequency could thus be explained as an increase in the paralinguistic range of the speaker. By raising her paralinguistic range, the speaker can point towards the climax of the text, as well as using such indicators as text structure and lexical-semantic information.

On the other hand, a downward direction can be described as being normal, most usually expected, and unmarked. Functions such as finality, completeness etc. could be associated with that direction.

As for cases of diverging directions between the toplines and the baselines, it is unclear how they can be interpreted in a paralinguistic framework.

## 6. Summary of findings

Two functions of the fundamental frequency of falls have been described: one for falls in major tone groups showing a gradient, and the other for falls across individual texts in terms of directions of topline and baseline.

Falls inside major tone groups generally show a clear declining gradient. Falls at the beginning of a major tone group are always higher in the speaker's range than falls at the end of a major tone group. A clear correlation between the position of falls within the tone group and their height in the speaker's range was observed. This observation calls for a reformulation of the function of falls within major tone groups.

Falls across individual texts display a different pattern. The normal, unmarked direction is for starting points and endpoints of falls to decline across the text. Yet in some texts the baseline and/or the topline of the falls rises, whereas in others the topline and baseline show diverging directions. The incline in topline and/or baseline was explained as being marked, and can be used to convey paralinguistic meaning.

Declination is used to divide texts into smaller chunks: tone groups. Across individual texts the direction of the fundamental frequency of the starting points and endpoints of falls can be declining or rising or both. A paralinguistic interpretation – that the direction of the fundamental frequency expresses the choice of the speaker – has been proposed. The global direction across texts operates independently of the local gradient at the tone group level. Yet no matter which direction of topline and baseline occurs across the text, the gradient of major tone groups is on average always declining.

**References:**

Cruttenden, A. (2nd ed.) (1997). *Intonation*. Cambridge: CUP

Ladd, D. Robert (1984). 'Declination: a review and some hypotheses.' In *Phonology Yearbook* 1, 53–74

Laver, J. (1994). *Principles of phonetics*. Cambridge:CUP

Williams, B. (1996). 'The formulation of an intonation transcription system for British English'. In Knowles, G., Wichmann, A., Alderson, P. (eds) *Working with speech: perspectives on research into the Lancaster/IBM Spoken English Corpus*. London: Longman. 38–57

# Grammatical word class variation within the British National Corpus Sampler

*Paul Rayson, Andrew Wilson and Geoffrey Leech*

UCREL, Lancaster University

## Abstract

*This paper examines the relationship between part-of-speech frequencies and text typology in the British National Corpus Sampler. Four pairwise comparisons of part-of-speech frequencies were made: written language vs. spoken language; informative writing vs. imaginative writing; conversational speech vs. 'task-oriented' speech; and imaginative writing vs. 'task-oriented' speech. The following variation gradient was hypothesized: conversation – task-oriented speech – imaginative writing – informative writing; however, the actual progression was: conversation – imaginative writing – task-oriented speech – informative writing. It thus seems that genre and medium interact in a more complex way than originally hypothesized. However, this conclusion has been made on the basis of broad, pre-existing text types within the BNC, and, in future, the internal structure of these text types may need to be addressed.*

## 1. Introduction

In this paper, we present some of the findings that have emerged from our frequency study of the British National Corpus (BNC). Over the past year or so, we have been engaged in a substantial analysis of both lexical items and part-of-speech categories in the corpus. Our results have recently been published in the form of a frequency dictionary – *Word frequencies in written and spoken English: based on the British National Corpus* (Leech, Rayson and Wilson, 2001) – which also includes brief discussions of selected word groups as well as reproducing the frequency lists themselves.

Chapter 6 of Leech, Rayson and Wilson (2001) presents frequency lists of part-of-speech categories in a subsample of the British National Corpus known as the BNC Sampler. These lists show to what extent the two different mediums (speech and writing) and four different genres (conversation, task-oriented speech, imaginative writing, and informative writing) that are represented in the corpus vary according to their preferences for employing different parts of speech. This paper provides a study and interpretation of those lists.

## 2. The tagged BNC Sampler

The BNC as a whole contains approximately one hundred million words of running text (both written and spoken), which has also undergone part-of-speech tagging using the CLAWS suite of programs (see, e.g., Leech, Garside and Bryant 1994). Despite advances in tagging technology, including the use of a Template Tagger to correct common errors (Fligelstone, Rayson and Smith 1996), the tagging still has an error rate in the region of 2% and therefore, in order to reach 100% accuracy, texts still need to be manually postedited. However, for reasons of scale, it has not been possible to hand-correct the entire tagged BNC. Hence, in order to provide users with a fully accurate tagged corpus, a 2% sample of the entire BNC has been manually postedited. This smaller corpus is known as the BNC Sampler.

In order to achieve maximal accuracy without hand editing, the entire tagged BNC makes use of a set of part-of-speech categories – the C5 tagset – which contains fewer detailed distinctions than previous tagsets that have been used by CLAWS. Also, preferring ambiguity to inaccuracy, it makes use of so-called 'portmanteau tags': these are assigned where there is a very small difference in the likelihood of two possible tags being correct, and in such cases both possible tags are assigned together – for example, past tense *and* past participle of a verb. In contrast to the entire tagged BNC, the tagged BNC Sampler makes use of the most detailed part-of-speech tagset used by CLAWS – the C7 tagset – and does not need to make use of portmanteau tags, since it has been manually edited for full accuracy.

The BNC Sampler, therefore, makes a more reliable data set for an analysis of variation in part-of-speech usage than does the BNC as a whole. Although it is substantially smaller than the entire BNC, this does not necessarily mean that it is less representative for the task in hand. As shown by Biber (1993), the size of corpus needed to be representative is closely linked to the frequency of the item(s) under examination. Since part-of-speech categories are much more frequent than lexical items (as each contains many lexical items) it is possible to work reliably with a much smaller corpus.

## 3. Methodology

Given two subcorpora of the BNC sampler we wished to compare, we produced a part-of-speech (POS) frequency list for each subcorpus. For each tag in the two frequency lists we calculated the log-likelihood (LL) statistic recommended by Dunning (1993). This was performed by constructing a contingency table as in Table 1.

**Table 1:** Contingency table for tag frequencies

| | SUBCORPUS ONE | SUBCORPUS TWO | TOTAL |
|---|---|---|---|
| Frequency of tag | a | b | a+b |
| Frequency of other tags | c-a | d-b | c+d-a-b |
| TOTAL | c | d | c+d |

Note that the value 'c' corresponds to the number of tags (or words) in subcorpus one, and 'd' corresponds to the number of tags (or words) in subcorpus two (N values). The values 'a' and 'b' are called the observed values (O). We then calculated the expected values (E) according to the following formula:

$$E_i = \frac{N_i \sum_i O_i}{\sum_i N_i}$$

In our case N1 = c, and N2 = d. So, for this tag, E1 = c*(a+b) / (c+d) and E2 = d*(a+b) / (c+d). The calculation for the expected values took account of the size of the two subcorpora, so we did not need to normalise the figures before applying the formula. We then calculated the log-likehood value according to this formula:

$$-2\ln\lambda = 2\sum_i O_i \ln\left(\frac{O_i}{E_i}\right)$$

This equated to calculating LL as follows: LL = 2*((a*ln (a/E1)) + (b*ln (b/E2)))

The tag frequency list was then sorted by the resulting LL values. This gave the effect of placing the largest LL value at the top of the list, representing the tag which had the most significant relative frequency difference between the two subcorpora. In this way, we can see the tags most indicative (or characteristic) of one subcorpus, as compared to the other subcorpus, at the top of the list. The tags which appeared with roughly similar relative frequencies in the two subcorpora appear lower down the list. Given the non-random nature of tags in a text, we are always likely to find frequencies of tags which differ across any two texts, and the higher the frequencies, the more information the statistical test has to work with. For a 2x2 contingency table, the minimum significant LL value is 3.8 (for $p<0.05$ and 1 d.f.).

An example of the result from this technique can be seen in Table 2 which shows the top 20 tags with the highest LL value for the comparison of the spoken subcorpus with the written subcorpus of the BNC sampler.

The frequencies shown are per million words and rounded to the nearest whole number. It is possible that a tag has a high frequency not because it is widely represented in the language as a whole but because it is 'overused' in a much smaller number of texts, or parts of texts, within the subcorpora. Moreover, this 'overuse' may be due to some factor which was not controlled during the selection of samples for the corpus: for example, the selection of a leisure book about fly-fishing rather than hang-gliding. Important additional information, range and dispersion, was therefore calculated for occurrences in each subcorpus. These showed how widely spread the occurrence of a tag is: whether it is frequent because it occurs in a lot of text samples in the corpus or whether it is frequent because of a very high usage in only a few samples. Frequent tags with high dispersion values may be considered to have high currency in the language as a whole; high frequencies associated with low dispersion values should, in contrast, be treated with caution.

**Table 2:** LL comparison of spoken and written sampler subcorpora

| | Spoken Sampler | | | | | Written Sampler | | |
|---|---|---|---|---|---|---|---|---|
| **POS** | **Freq** | **Ra** | **Disp** | **O/U** | **LL** | **Freq** | **Ra** | **Disp** |
| UH | 31705 | 50 | 0.92 | + | 35177 | 1210 | 37 | 0.74 |
| FU | 23010 | 50 | 0.93 | + | 29404 | 252 | 26 | 0.67 |
| NP1 | 14469 | 50 | 0.94 | - | 19819 | 49089 | 50 | 0.92 |
| PPIS1 | 31379 | 50 | 0.95 | + | 17304 | 6701 | 48 | 0.82 |

| | Spoken Sampler | | | | | Written Sampler | | |
|---|---|---|---|---|---|---|---|---|
| POS | Freq | Ra | Disp | O/U | LL | Freq | Ra | Disp |
| PPY | 26531 | 50 | 0.96 | + | 16894 | 4656 | 48 | 0.81 |
| NN1 | 89193 | 50 | 0.96 | - | 16762 | 152639 | 50 | 0.98 |
| JJ | 36979 | 50 | 0.97 | - | 13395 | 75496 | 50 | 0.97 |
| NN2 | 25432 | 50 | 0.94 | - | 12373 | 57048 | 50 | 0.96 |
| PPH1 | 25899 | 50 | 0.96 | + | 9462 | 8308 | 50 | 0.94 |
| VV0 | 28729 | 50 | 0.97 | + | 8037 | 11113 | 50 | 0.91 |
| AT | 39031 | 50 | 0.95 | - | 7997 | 68200 | 50 | 0.98 |
| IO | 13406 | 50 | 0.93 | - | 7156 | 31039 | 50 | 0.95 |
| VBZ | 26524 | 50 | 0.97 | + | 6472 | 11117 | 50 | 0.95 |
| DD1 | 20945 | 50 | 0.98 | + | 6215 | 7802 | 50 | 0.96 |
| II | 44809 | 50 | 0.97 | - | 6200 | 71619 | 50 | 0.98 |
| XX | 18067 | 50 | 0.95 | + | 6127 | 6135 | 50 | 0.91 |
| VD0 | 7395 | 50 | 0.94 | + | 4875 | 1230 | 50 | 0.83 |
| PPIS2 | 10880 | 50 | 0.93 | + | 4292 | 3277 | 49 | 0.84 |
| VH0 | 9180 | 50 | 0.97 | + | 3356 | 2944 | 50 | 0.94 |
| RR | 42555 | 50 | 0.98 | + | 2928 | 28183 | 50 | 0.97 |

Each subcorpus was divided into 50 roughly equal sized segments, each of about 20,000 words. Sometimes text files were split across two segments. The range and dispersion statistics reflect occurrences of tags in these segments.

Range (Ra) is a simple count of how many segments include the tag in question. Dispersion (Disp) is a statistical coefficient (Juilland's D) of how evenly distributed a tag is across successive segments of the corpus. This is useful, because many segments and texts are made up of a number of smaller, relatively independent units – for example, sectors and stories in newspapers. It may be that, even *within* a text, certain word classes are overused in a given part – e.g. the football-reporting sector of a newspaper. Juilland's D is more sensitive to this degree of variation. It was calculated as follows:

$$D = 1 - \frac{V}{\sqrt{n-1}}$$

where $n$ is the number of segments in the subcorpus. The variation coefficient $V$ is given by:

$$V = \frac{s}{x}$$

where $x$ is the mean sub-frequency of the tag in the subcorpus (i.e. its frequency in each segment averaged) and $s$ is the standard deviation of these sub-frequencies. We selected Juilland's D as it has been shown by Lyne (1985) to be the most reliable of the various dispersion coefficients that are available. It varies between 0 and 1, where values closer to 0 show that occurrences are focussed in a small number of segments, and values closer to 1 show a more even distribution across all segments.

The other column in the table (O/U) shows overuse (+) or underuse (-) of a tag in the spoken subcorpus relative to the written subcorpus.

The figures for range and dispersion are not quoted in the paper but are taken into account in our studies of variation.

## 4. Results

We made four pairwise comparisons of part-of-speech frequencies in the tagged BNC Sampler:

- written language vs. spoken language
- informative writing vs. imaginative writing
- conversational speech vs. 'task-oriented' speech
- imaginative writing vs. 'task-oriented' speech

As a result of previous studies on both English and other languages, we had strong hypotheses in regard to the first two comparisons.

Hoffmann (1985: 137), for example, presented analyses of various genres of Russian writing, including a sample of imaginative prose and several scientific genres. His figures showed that the proportion of nouns, adjectives and prepositions tended to be higher in the scientific genres, whereas verbs, adverbs and pronouns were more frequent in imaginative prose.

Working on English, Nakamura (1991) used Hayashi's Quantification Method Type III (a procedure somewhat similar to factor analysis) to analyse the tag frequencies in the LOB corpus according to the 15 genre categories within it. The first, and major, axis of his results can be interpreted as a dimension distinguishing the imaginative from the informative genres, with informative genres such as newspaper discourse located closer to the mid-point of that axis than learned and scientific writing. Some of the most characteristic major parts of speech were again nouns, adjectives and prepositions (for the informative genres) and verbs, adverbs and pronouns (for the imaginative genres).

To Nakamura's study can also be added the detailed corpus-based study by Biber et al. (1999). Working with a larger corpus of more recent English, Biber et al.'s findings again mirrored studies such as Nakamura's: nouns, adjectives and prepositions were shown to be more frequent in informative genres, and verbs, pronouns, and adverbs more frequent in imaginative genres. Moreover, Biber et al. also found a similar gradient to Nakamura, with news writing taking an intermediate position between scientific writing and fiction on the informative-imaginative scale. However, an important advance of Biber et al.'s study, made possible by the composition of their corpus, was the inclusion of conversational speech. Compared with informative writing, this showed a part-of-speech frequency profile somewhat similar to that of imaginative writing, but, when compared with imaginative writing, the trends were magnified: for instance, pronouns were yet more frequent in conversation than in fiction.

On the basis of these previous studies, therefore, we might hypothesise that there exists a part-of-speech variation gradient showing a gradual progression from informal, conversational speech at one extreme through more formal speech towards increasingly formal written genres at the other extreme:

CONVERSATION FICTION NEWS SCIENCE
[imaginative] [informative]
[speech] [writing]

One comparison that has not yet been made concerns what the BNC compilers termed context-governed speech. (We have chosen in our work to call this task-oriented speech.) This is speech which is closely tied to particular activity types: for example, medical consultations, committee meetings, sermons, lectures, court proceedings, etc. On the whole, we might characterise such speech as more public, and hence, probably, more formal, although in many instances it will still involve substantial amounts of relatively spontaneous speaking as well as prepared reading.

If our hypothesis about a single variation gradient is correct, we would expect task-oriented speech to be positioned somewhere between conversational speech and imaginative writing. We therefore made two comparisons using task-oriented speech. Firstly, we compared it with conversational speech, to ascertain whether task-oriented speech appeared to differ from conversation in a similar direction to that in which writing differs from speech overall; and, secondly, we compared it with imaginative writing, to see whether it differed from that genre in the same direction as speech when compared with writing. Our detailed findings on the major part-of-speech categories for each of our four comparisons are discussed in the following paragraphs. Table 3 summarises these findings by showing overused POS categories in each of the four comparisons.

**Table 3:** Overused POS categories within four comparisons

| | **Wri.** | **Spoken** | **Inf.** | **Imag** | **Conv** | **Task O.** | **Imag.** | **Task O.** |
|---|---|---|---|---|---|---|---|---|
| **Conj.** | CC | CS<br>but | CC | CS<br>but | CS<br>but | CC | as<br>than | CC<br>CS |
| **Noun** | N* | | N* | | NP | N*<br>NPM* | NN1 | NN2 |
| **Verb** | VV* | VM<br>aux V<br>VVGK | VVN | VM<br>VV* | V* | | VVD | V*<br>VVN |
| **Pron.** | PNQ*<br>PNX1 | P* | PNX1 | P* | P* | we<br>us | he/she<br>him/her | they |
| **Adverb** | RRR<br>RRT | R* | RRR<br>RRT<br>REX | R* | RR<br>RL<br>RT | R* | RL | R* |
| **Adject.** | J* | | J* | | | J* | J* | |
| **Prep.** | I* | | I* | | | I* | I*<br>IW | IF<br>IO |
| **Article Determ.** | A* | DA1<br>DB* | A* | DA1<br>DB* | DA1<br>DB* | A* | A* | DA* |

### 4.1 Conjunctions

In terms of the 'basic' categories of coordinating conjunction (mainly representing *and*) and subordinating conjunction, the significant differences between spoken and written language were in the opposite direction to that predicted by early studies on medium variation (e.g. Blankenship 1962 and Kroll 1977): spoken language contained significantly more subordinating conjunctions than written language (with the exception of *that*), and written language contained significantly more coordinating conjunctions than speech. This, however, corroborated the more recent findings of Biber et al. (1999: 81). Biber et al. also found that *but*, in contrast to *and*, was favoured by speech more than writing, and this was again corroborated by our study (*but* being a special category of coordinating conjunction in the C7 tagset). Furthermore, again as found by Biber et al., coordinating conjunctions were more frequent in informative (as opposed to imaginative) writing, with the exception of *but*, which was more common in imaginative writing. A reverse trend in the case of subordinators was again evident. In comparing conversational and task-oriented speech, the pattern was similar to that between speech and writing: conversation tended to have more subordinators and task-oriented speech tended to have more coordinators (again apart from *but*). However, a different pattern emerged in comparing task-oriented speech with imaginative writing: most conjunctions (both coordinating *and* subordinating) showed a preference for task-oriented speech, with the exception of the subordinators *as* and *than*. The coordinator *but* did not show a statistically significant difference.

### 4.2 Nouns

As found by previous studies, nouns tended, on the whole, to be more frequent in writing (as opposed to speech) and informative (as opposed to imaginative) writing. Our study also found them to be more common in task-oriented (as opposed to conversational) speech, although, within the class of nouns, conversation had more proper nouns than task-oriented speech (the exception being the names of months). The comparison between imaginative writing and task-oriented speech was, however, more ambivalent. Around half of the noun tags showing significant differences (i.e., 9 out of 16) showed a preference for task-oriented speech and the other half a preference for imaginative writing. This included a clear split within the class of common nouns: singular common nouns were preferred in imaginative writing and plural common nouns in task-oriented speech.

### 4.3 Verbs

Our findings on verbs again broadly supported previous studies. In the comparison of imaginative and informative writing, the modal verbs, and most forms of lexical verbs, were more common in imaginative writing. The exception here in the case of lexical verbs was the past participle (VVN), which was commoner in informative writing. This finding almost certainly reflects a greater use of the passive in informative genres (cf. Biber et al. 1999: 477; Svartvik 1966). Other verb forms preferred by informative writing were: *being*, *be* (as infinitive), *been* (again a past participle), *are*, and *has*. The comparison of conversation and task-oriented speech presented a very similar picture, with the majority of verbal forms showing a preference for conversation. The exceptions list was likewise similar to the previous one: it contained the past participle of lexical verbs, together with *were*, *being*, *be* (infinitive), *been*, and *are*. The overall comparison of speech and writing was rather more complicated. The modal verbs, and most of the auxiliary verbs (though not necessarily in an auxiliary function), were preferred in speech, the exceptions being *had* (past tense), *having*; *be* (finite base form), *were*, *was*, *being*, *be* (infinitive), and *been*. Speech also preferred the base and infinitive forms of lexical verbs, as well as the catenative *-ing* participle (e.g. *going to*). Other forms of lexical verb, however, tended to be more frequent in writing. The comparison of task-oriented speech and imaginative writing was again complex. Most of the verb forms listed above were frequent in task-oriented speech. However, there were a number of exceptions, which included the simple past-tense forms of both lexical verbs and auxiliaries as well as the present and past participles of *be*, the present participle of lexical verbs, and the third person singular of lexical verbs. Interestingly, the past participle of lexical verbs, which was preferred in writing, was, in this comparison, preferred in the spoken text type.

### 4.4 Pronouns

Again confirming the findings of previous studies, pronouns were generally more common in speech, conversational (as opposed to task-oriented) speech, and imaginative writing (when contrasted with informative writing). There were, however, some exceptions to this general trend. In the comparison of speech and writing, the WH (i.e. relative and interrogative) pronouns were more common in writing, as were the reflexives. The same exceptions applied in the comparison of conversational versus task-oriented speech, where, additionally, the first-person plural pronouns (*we/us*) were more common in task-oriented speech than in conversation, probably reflecting more speech on behalf of groups and organisations rather than on behalf of the individual speaker. In the comparison of imaginative and informative writing, the only exception was the reflexive indefinite pronoun (*oneself*). But the comparison of task-oriented speech and imaginative writing once again introduced a more mixed picture, and, as with nouns, there was an approximately 50:50 split in the direction of preference for those pronouns showing a significant difference. For example, *he* and *she* were preferred by imaginative writing, whereas *they* was preferred in task-oriented speech. However, although *him* and *her* were also strongly preferred in imaginative writing, *them* was not equally preferred in task-oriented speech (the preference was in the direction of imaginative writing, but fell just short of statistical significance).

### 4.5 Adverbs

Confirming once again the previous studies cited above, in the comparison of spoken and written language, most adverbs showing a significant difference were more frequent in the spoken language. The exceptions were the comparative and superlative forms, which were all significantly more frequent in written language, as well as those introducing appositive constructions (such as *e.g.* or *namely*). The picture was broadly similar in the comparison of imaginative and informative writing (the adverbs being more common in imaginative writing); the comparatives, superlatives and appositives were again exceptions, although the comparative general adverb was preferred in imaginative writing. In the comparison of conversation and task-oriented speech, the trend was towards task-oriented speech. The exceptions in this case were the base form general adverb, the locative and temporal adverbs, and the particle: this suggests a greater use of spatial and temporal deixis in conversation, as well as more phrasal verbs, both hypotheses being supported by Biber et al.'s (1999) detailed grammatical analysis. In the comparison of task-oriented speech and imaginative writing, most adverbs were preferred in the spoken genre, apart from locative adverbs, particles, superlative degree adverbs, catenative prepositional adverbs, and comparative general adverbs. In this case, then, the appositives, preferred in written language and informative writing, were preferred in task-oriented speech.

### 4.6 Adjectives

In all comparisons, adjectives showed straightforward and expected preferences. All types of adjective were significantly more common in, respectively, writing, informative (as opposed to imaginative) writing, and task-oriented (as opposed to conversational) speech. The only exception was a slight preference for the catenative adjective (e.g. *able to/willing to*) in speech as opposed to writing, which, however, was not significant at the $p < 0.05$ level ($LL = 1.2$). For once, the comparison of task-oriented speech and imaginative writing straightforwardly followed the hypothesised direction: all adjectives (again with the exception of catenative) were preferred in the written genre.

### 4.7 Prepositions

In three of the comparisons, the usage patterns of prepositions supported previous findings: they were more frequent in writing, task-oriented speech (as opposed to conversation), and informative (as opposed to imaginative) writing. However, there was again a 50:50 split in the comparison of imaginative writing (which showed a greater use of *with/without* and general prepositions) and task-oriented speech (which showed a greater use of *of* and *for*). The preference for *of* in task-oriented speech is suggestive of more complex, postmodified noun phrases.

### 4.8 Articles and determiners.

As expected, articles showed a preference for writing, informative (as opposed to imaginative) writing, and task-oriented (as opposed to conversational) speech: this is obviously tied to the higher frequency of nouns in these genres. Determiners were somewhat harder to interpret, as in CLAWS tagging many are ambiguous between pronominal and determiner functions. However, the singular determiner and the pre-determiner certainly showed preferences in the same direction as pronouns (i.e. towards speech, imaginative writing, and conversation). In the comparison of task-oriented speech and imaginative writing, the singular article and pre-determiner did not show significant differences. The general article showed a preference for imaginative writing, and the singular and plural determiners both showed a preference for task-oriented speech. In this case, therefore, the trends were approximately as hypothesised, with the written genre behaving like writing and the spoken genre behaving like speech.

To summarise, then, these findings, like those of Biber et al. (1999), show a close correlation between the preferences on three of the dimensions of variation. Thus, the parts of speech that are more common in spoken language are also more common in conversation and in imaginative writing, whereas those parts of speech that are more common in writing are also more common in task-oriented speech and in informative writing. However, the findings also clearly refute the hypothesis that both genre variation (e.g., imaginative vs. informative) and medium variation (i.e., speech vs. writing) can be represented on a single gradient going from conversational speech to informative writing. This is because task-oriented speech, when compared with imaginative writing, has an unstable pattern of preferences: sometimes it shows more similarity to written language and informative writing than it does to spoken language and conversation, and sometimes the reverse is the case. For example, with adjectives, we get the following gradient:

| LEAST ADJECTIVES | | | MOST ADJECTIVES |
|---|---|---|---|
| ◄ | ——— | ——— | ► |
| conversation | task-oriented | imaginative | informative |
| SPEECH | | | WRITING |

but with certain key part-of-speech subcategories (e.g. past participles) we get a gradient like the following:

| LEAST PAST PARTICIPLES | | | MOST PAST PARTICIPLES |
|---|---|---|---|
| ◄ | ——— | ——— | ► |
| conversation | imaginative | task-oriented | informative |
| [SPEECH] | [WRITING] | [SPEECH] | [WRITING] |

and, in several cases (such as with prepositions), no overall direction of preference can be ascertained.

## 5. Conclusion

Our results suggest that genre and medium may interact in a much more complex way than hypothesised, and particularly that certain spoken genres may show a greater trend towards the overall norms of written language than do some of the actual written genres.

However, it has to be emphasised that this conclusion has been made on the basis of rather broad, pre-existing genre categories within the BNC, and it is possible that we need, in future studies, to re-think the way in which some text categories are made up and used in medium and genre variation studies. For instance, one reason why imaginative writing turns out to be more speech-like than other written genres is almost certainly that it contains a higher proportion of direct speech quotation. Arguably, therefore, we are not strictly comparing speech and writing, but, at least in part, speech and speech (albeit invented speech). Nevertheless, dialogue is an integral part of fictional prose and its inclusion is therefore valid.

In contrast, some text categories may involve artificial inconsistencies. In particular, it may be that the category of task-oriented (or context-governed) speech, which showed such an ambiguous position when compared with conversation and imaginative writing, is ill-defined. For example, it contains rather formal, and frequently prepared, monologues (such as sermons) as well as less formal, more spontaneous, and interactive discourse (such as meetings). It is thus quite probable that, strictly speaking, this category contains examples of written informative language that are simply, or largely, read out, as well as spontaneous discourse that is genuinely spoken language. In the same context, it is worth noting that Biber's (1988) first dimension of variation – which Lee (2000), for example, found to be the only stable and replicable dimension – is **involved** versus **informative**, not speech versus writing: even thinking introspectively, we have both primarily involved (e.g. dialogue) and primarily informative (e.g. monologue) texts represented within the task-oriented category of the BNC. Thus, if we were to separate out, for instance, the dialogue and monologue components of the category, it is conceivable that our initial hypothesis of a single gradient of variation could still hold.

## References

Biber, Douglas (1988). *Variation across speech and writing*. Cambridge: Cambridge University Press

Biber, Douglas (1993). 'Representativeness in corpus design'. *Literary and Linguistic Computing* 8: 243–57.

Biber, Douglas, Stig Johansson, Geoffrey Leech, Susan Conrad, Edward Finegan (1999). *Longman grammar of spoken and written English*. London: Longman.

Blankenship, Jane (1962). 'A linguistic analysis of oral and written style'. *The Quarterly Journal of Speech* 48: 419–422.

Dunning, Ted. (1993). 'Accurate methods for the statistics of surprise and coincidence'. *Computational Linguistics*, 19.1, March 1993: 61–74.

Fligelstone, Steven, Paul Rayson and Nicholas Smith (1996). 'Template analysis: bridging the gap between grammar and the lexicon'. In Jenny Thomas and Mick Short (eds), *Using corpora for language research*. London: Longman. 181–207

Hoffmann, Lothar (1985). *Kommunikationsmittel Fachsprache: eine Einführung*. 2nd ed. Tübingen: Günter Narr.

Kroll, Barbara (1977). 'Ways communicators encode propositions in written and spoken English. A look at subordination and coordination'. In Elinor Keenan and Tina Bennett (eds) *Discourse across time and space*. Southern California Occasional Papers in Linguistics, No. 5. Los Angeles, CA: University of Southern California. 69–108.

Lee, Yong Wey David (2000). *Modelling variation in spoken and written language: the multi-dimensional approach revisited.* Ph.D. thesis, Lancaster University.

Leech, Geoffrey, Roger Garside and Michael Bryant (1994). 'The large-scale grammatical tagging of text: Experience with the British National Corpus'. In Nelleke Oostdijk and Pieter de Haan (eds) *Corpus-based research into language.* Amsterdam: Rodopi. 47–64.

Leech, Geoffrey, Paul Rayson and Andrew Wilson (2001). *Word frequencies in written and spoken English: based on the British National Corpus*. London: Longman.

Lyne, Anthony (1985). *The vocabulary of French business correspondence.* Geneva: Slatkine.

Nakamura, Junsaku (1991). 'The relationship among genres in the LOB corpus based upon the distribution of grammatical tags'. *JACET Bulletin* 22: 44–74.

Svartvik, Jan (1966). *On voice in the English verb.* The Hague: Mouton.

# Temporal specification of the present perfect: a corpus-based study

*Norbert Schlüter*

Free University of Berlin

## Abstract

*Temporal relations in English are expressed by both verbal patterns and non-verbal elements, such as temporal adverbials. Most grammatical descriptions referring to temporal adverbials in this function, however, are not derived from empirical investigations but from intuitive impressions. The aim of this paper is to present results of a corpus-based study on the temporal specification of the present perfect. The paper investigates the degree of temporally specified utterances with the present perfect and distinguishes the temporal adverbials according to their syntactic realisations. In the final part, the paper lists the 10 most frequent temporal adverbials co-occurring with the present perfect in British and American English and compares both lists to each other. The analysis presented here is part of a more comprehensive empirical study of the present perfect in British and American English and in ELT.*

## 1. Introduction

If we look up verb patterns like the present perfect or the preterite in grammar books we find not only a description of the forms and the functions of the particular verb patterns but in the majority of cases also some hints as to which temporal adverbials co-occur with the verb pattern. A typical entry looks like this:

> Adverbial phrases like the following are used with the present perfect because they clearly connect the past with the present moment: *before (now), It's the first time ..., so far, so far this morning, up till now, up to the present.* (Alexander 1988: 72).

These kind of lists raise a number of questions:

(a) Are the quoted adverbials indeed the most frequent temporal adverbials co-occurring with the present perfect?
(b) How many utterances with the present perfect co-occur with a temporal adverbial at all? and
(c) Does the temporal specification vary with regard to discourse functions, meanings of the perfect, registers and regional varieties (British and American English)?

The following sections will answer most of these questions.[1] The structure of this paper is as follows. Part two describes the corpora used in this investigation and defines the type of utterances the present study is based on. Part three gives examples of temporally specified and unspecified utterances. Part four looks at the degree of temporal specification found with the present perfect in British and American English taking into account the registers spoken conversation, fictional texts and expository prose. Part five is concerned with the syntactic subclasses of temporal adverbials which are most frequently used with the present perfect. The final part presents the ten most frequent temporal adverbials co-occurring with the present perfect in British and American English and compares them to the adverbials quoted above by Alexander (1988).

## 2. The data

The results of this investigation are based on the analysis of machine-readable corpora of contemporary English. In order to investigate differences as well as similarities between the temporal specification of the present perfect in British and American English the *Lancaster-Oslo/Bergen Corpus* (LOB) and the *Brown-University Corpus* (BROWN) were used. In addition the *Corpus of English Conversation* (CEC) which forms part of the *London-Lund Corpus* was analysed to include data from the register of spoken conversation in British English.[2] Taking into account pedagogical criteria five sub-corpora were extracted from these corpora.[3] Each sub-corpus contains approximately 600 utterances of the present perfect. These sub-corpora were named: CONV (British spoken conversation), LOB EP (British expository prose), LOB FT (British fictional texts), BROWN EP (American expository prose) and BROWN FT (American fictional texts). The following table shows the origin and size of these sub-corpora.

**Table 1**: Corpora used in the investigation

| **British English** | | | **American English** | |
|---|---|---|---|---|
| Spoken | Written | | Written | |
| London-Lund Corpus | LOB Corpus | | BROWN Corpus | |
| CEC<br>204,608 words | LOB A – J<br>756,323 words | LOB K – R<br>257,445 words | BROWN A – J<br>759,696 words | BROWN K – R<br>253,948 words |
| ↓ | ↓ | ↓ | ↓ | ↓ |
| **CONV**<br>113,023 words<br>(Spoken Conversation) | **LOB EP**<br>133,495 words<br>(Expository Prose) | **LOB FT**<br>239,242 words<br>(Fictional Texts) | **BROWN EP**<br>133,769 words<br>(Expository Prose) | **BROWN FT**<br>235,671 words<br>(Fictional Texts) |

Excluded from the analysis are instances of the modal perfect: 'You *must have been* good at history at school' as well as utterances containing a form of the perfect infinitive: 'One might pretend never *to have seen* one before, or, to more purpose, that there would never be another like it'. All examples presented in this paper are authentic and taken from the corpora mentioned above.

## 3. What is temporal specification?

Utterances containing a verb phrase of the present perfect can occur with or without temporal adverbials. Examples (1) and (2) are utterances specified by one or more temporal adverbials.

(1) Over the last few days the character of the radiation has changed.
(2) I have warned the country again and again of this since I became Chancellor.

In contrast the following examples (3) and (4) lack temporal specification by means of adverbials.

(3) I've solved the mystery of the little bag.
(4) We have taught him a lesson.

In this paper the term *adverbial* is used to cover single word adverbs as well as other syntactic structures with adverbial functions such as prepositional phrases or finite clauses. In some cases an utterance contains more than one temporal adverbial, but multiple temporal specification is rare. Less than 10 per cent of all temporally specified utterances contain more than one temporal adverbial. A detailed description of multiple occurrences of temporal adverbials cannot be given within the limits of this paper.

## 4. Frequency of temporal specification with the present perfect

Figure 1 displays the percentages of utterances which are specified by at least one temporal adverbial in each of the five sub-corpora. The degree of temporal specification is very stable, covering around one third of all cases in each sub-corpus.[4]

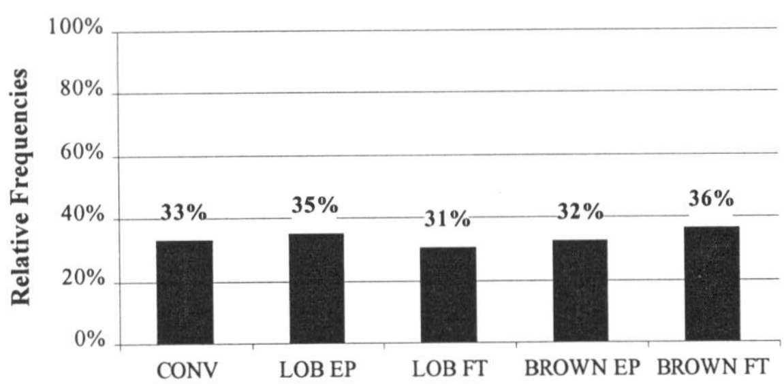


**Figure 1:** Frequency of temporal specification with the present perfect in British and American English taking into account different registers

The differences between the sub-corpora are statistically not significant. The analysis shows that the degree of temporal specification does not differ with regard to register and geographical variety. Two thirds of all utterances are unspecified, which means that the majority of all utterances with the present perfect do not depend on additional temporal specification apart from the verbal structure itself.

## 5. Subclasses of temporal adverbials used with the present perfect

Adverbials occur in the form of different syntactic structures. In order to determine which subclasses of temporal adverbials co-occur most often with the present perfect the following six subclasses were distinguished:[5]

| | |
|---|---|
| (a) Single adverbs: | *always, just, already, etc.* |
| (b) Adverb phrases: | *so far, long enough, all along, etc.* |
| (c) Noun phrases: | *all the time, a few hours, the whole afternoon, etc.* |
| (d) Prepositional phrases: | *at the moment, for a long time, since the election, etc.* |
| (e) Finite clauses: | *which began about 6 years ago, since I met you, etc.* |
| (f) Non-finite clauses: | *after spending a few days at the Palace Hotel, etc.* |

Figure 2 displays the distribution of these six subclasses for all five sub-corpora. The order of the bars from left to right is the same for all six subclasses: CONV, LOB EP, LOB FT, BROWN EP and BROWN FT.

The first conclusion to be drawn from the chart is that the present perfect is on aggregate most frequently specified by single adverbs. Second in frequency are prepositional phrases followed by noun phrases. The other three subclasses are considerably less frequent.

The chart also shows that the distribution is not the same for the different registers. Clearly, two different groups can be distinguished. The first group consists of the three corpora CONV, LOB FT and BROWN FT representing the more informal registers of spoken conversation and fictional texts, which have a very similar distribution of adverbial subclasses. The second group consists of the EP categories from LOB and BROWN representing the more formal register of expository prose. The distribution of adverbial subclasses within this group is also similar.

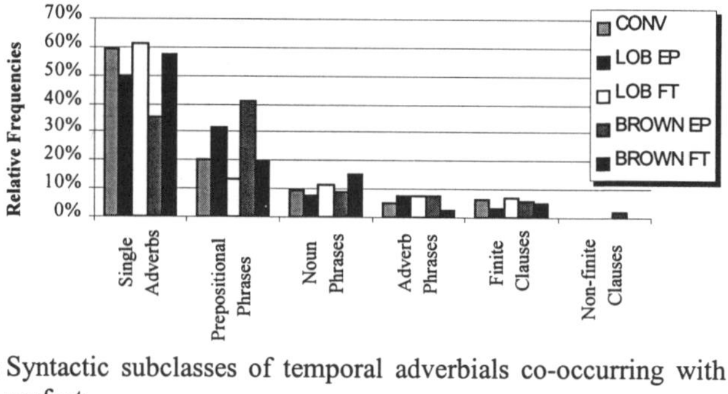


**Figure 2:** Syntactic subclasses of temporal adverbials co-occurring with the present perfect

The difference between the two groups is that in informal registers the present perfect is specified mainly by single adverbs, whereas in formal registers more prepositional phrases are used and significantly fewer single adverbs. Although the overall degree of temporal specification is the same for all sub-corpora (cf. Figure 1), differences can be detected between the different sub-categories in terms of register (cf. Figure 2). There is however no indication of geographical variation.

## 6. The ten most frequent temporal adverbials used with the present perfect in British and American English

The final part of this paper is concerned with two questions: (a) What are the most frequent temporal adverbials co-occurring with the present perfect? and (b) Does the type of specification vary with regard to geographical variety? In order to compare the use of temporal adverbials in British and American English a separate list of individual adverbials was compiled for each variety. Since in American English so far no corpus of spoken conversation is available which resembles in size and content the *Corpus of Spoken Conversation* in British English, the data from CONV were excluded from this part of the investigation.

In many cases temporal adverbials, especially prepositional phrases and noun phrases, differ semantically in the time span they specify, although they belong to the same syntactic sub-class. Consider, for example, the prepositional phrases *for a month, for two years* and *for a long time.* In order to arrive at intelligible results, groups of syntactically and semantically similar adverbials were established. The three prepositional phrases mentioned above and all similar phrases (except cases like *for the first time*) were subsumed under the label *for + tmp NP* (tmp NP = temporal noun phrase). Comparable groups are *in + tmp NP* (*in the past year, in the last 18 months*) and (*ever*) *since* (+ *tmp NP/CL*)[6], which contains temporal adverbials like the following: *since, ever since, since last May, since then, since you left, ever since you were a girl.* The following tables list the ten most frequent temporal adverbials/groups of adverbials co-occurring with the present perfect in British English (Table 2) and American English (Table 3).

**Table 2:** The 10 most frequent adverbials co-occurring with the present perfect in British English (LOB EP and LOB FT)

| Rank | Absolute Frequency | Relative Frequency | Cumulative Frequency | Temporal Adverbial |
|---|---|---|---|---|
| 1 | 51 | 12.5 % | 12.5 % | *(ever) since (+ tmp NP / CL)* |
| 2 | 41 | 10.0 % | 22.5 % | *never* |
| 3 | 39 | 9.5 % | 32.0 % | *for + tmp NP* |
| 4 | 31 | 7.6 % | 39.6 % | *now* |
| 5 | 21 | 5.1 % | 44.7 % | *in + tmp NP* |
| 6 | 19 | 4.6 % | 49.3 % | *already* |
| 7 | 17 | 4.2 % | 53.5 % | *before* |
| 8 | 17 | 4.2 % | 57.7 % | *always* |
| 9 | 16 | 3.9 % | 61.6 % | *just* |
| 10 | 14 | 3.4 % | 65.0 % | *ever* |

**Table 3:** The 10 most frequent adverbials co-occurring with the present perfect in American English (BROWN EP and BROWN FT)

| Rank | Absolute Frequency | Relative Frequency | Cumulative Frequency | Temporal Adverbial |
|---|---|---|---|---|
| 1 | 49 | 14.2 % | 14.2 % | *(ever) since (+ tmp NP / CL)* |
| 2 | 41 | 11.8 % | 26.0 % | *in + tmp NP* |
| 3 | 30 | 8.7 % | 34.7 % | *for + tmp NP* |
| 4 | 27 | 7.8 % | 42.5 % | *never* |
| 5 | 18 | 5.2 % | 47.7 % | *now* |
| 6 | 14 | 4.0 % | 51.7 % | *before* |
| 7 | 14 | 4.0 % | 55.7 % | *always* |
| 8 | 13 | 3.8 % | 59.5 % | *ever* |
| 9 | 12 | 3.5 % | 63.0 % | *already* |
| 10 | 10 | 2.9 % | 65.9 % | *just* |

The two tables show that the ten most frequent temporal adverbials co-occurring with the present perfect in British English are identical to the ten most frequent temporal adverbials co-occurring with the present perfect in American English, even if their order differs slightly. In both regional varieties utterances with the present perfect are most often specified by adverbials containing the word *since.* In British English these adverbials cover 12.5 % of all temporal adverbials used with the present perfect, whereas in American English this group of adverbials shows a relative frequency of 14.2 %.

In British English *(ever) since* (+ *tmp NP/CL*) is followed by *never* (10.0 %), *for* + *tmp NP* (9.5 %), *now* (7.6 %) and *in* + *tmp NP* (5.1 %). In American English the second most frequent adverbials or group of adverbials is *in* + *tmp NP* (11.8 %) followed by *for* + *tmp NP* (8.7 %), *never* (7.8 %) and *now* (5.2 %). These first five adverbials / group of adverbials in British and American English all display a relative frequency of more than 5 per cent, whereas the adverbials occupying rank six to ten have a relative frequency between 4.6 % and 2.9 %. In both geographical varieties this second group of adverbials is made up of single adverbs only.

The application of the Chi-square test shows that the observed differences in the distribution of the first ten adverbials are statistically not significant.[7] Further agreement between the two tables can be seen by calculating their cumulative frequencies. In both British and American English the first ten adverbials cover around 65 per cent of all temporally specified utterances. These findings contradict the view that assumes substantial differences between the temporal specification of the present perfect in British and American English.

Finally, if we compare the list of temporal adverbials mentioned by Alexander (1988: 172): *before (now), It's the first time ..., so far, so far this morning, up till now, up to the present* with the lists in this study, we find that he does not include the adverbials that most frequently co-occur with the present perfect. From his list only *before* appears among the ten most frequent adverbials. *Before* occupies rank 7 in British English and rank 6 in American English. However, out of 31 total occurrences (17 in British English and 14 in American English) only one utterance occurred with the combination *before now. So far* is fairly common both in British and American

English, appearing on rank 12 in British English and rank 11 in American English. *It's the first time ...* appeared twice in British English but *up till now* and *up to the present* did not occur in the investigation at all.

This comparison shows that future grammars will have to take into account to a much greater extent the results of corpus-based investigations in order to provide linguists, teachers and learners with reliable information on the real use of the English language.

## 7. Conclusion

In this paper I have dealt with a number of questions concerning the temporal specification of the present perfect. In particular, the following results were obtained:

- On average, only one out of three utterances with the present perfect co-occurs with a temporal adverbial.
- The degree of temporal specification is the same across the registers of conversation, expository prose and fictional texts in British as well as in American English.
- The present perfect is most frequently specified by single adverbs and secondly by prepositional phrases.
- The distribution of syntactic sub-classes of temporal adverbials varies across different registers.
- The ten most frequent temporal adverbials co-occurring with the present perfect in British and American English are identical.
- The most frequent temporal adverbial/group of adverbials co-occurring with the present perfect both in British and American English is (*ever*) *since* (+ *tmp NP/CL*).

Further research will take into account different discourse functions (affirmative statements, negative statements, etc.) as well as investigating the position of temporal adverbials within the sentence.

## Notes

1 Substantial differences in the degree of temporal specification taking into account different meanings of the present perfect have already been described in Schlüter (2000).

2 At the time of the investigation two corpora of spoken American English were available: The Santa Barbara Corpus of Spoken American English and the Corpus of Spoken Professional American-English. These two corpora differ considerably not only in size but also with regard to the discourse structure and spontaneity of the conversation if compared to the CEC. Since there is no common ground for a valid comparison, the two American corpora of spoken conversation were not included in the investigation.

3 The sub-corpora have been compiled considering the learning objectives of foreign language learners. Thus LOB EP (British expository prose) contains selected texts from the following categories (in parentheses are the code numbers of the samples): A *Press: Reportage* (A01-A24), B *Press: Editorial* (B01-B11), C *Press: Reviews* (C01-C07), F *Popular Lore* (F01-F12) and G *Belles Lettres, Biography, etc.* (G01-G12). The selection of text samples for BROWN EP (American expository prose) was made along the same lines. LOB FT (British fictional texts) contains all text samples from the imaginative part of the LOB Corpus: K *General fiction,* L *Mystery and detective fiction,* M *Science fiction,* N *Adventure and western fiction,* P *Romance and love story* with the exception of category R *Humour*. The same applies to the sub-corpus BROWN FT (American fictional texts).

4 These results are in line with similar findings by Elsness (1997), who also observed temporal specification in 33 per cent of all utterances with the present perfect. However, he does not distinguish between different registers and different regional varieties.

5 This categorisation follows Biber et al. (1999: 767f.).

6 This group of adverbials comprises all temporal adverbials which contain the word *since. Since* appears in four different syntactic sub-classes: (a) single adverb (*since*), (b) part of adverb phrase (*ever since*), (c) prepositional phrase (*since last Sunday*) and (d) finite clause (*since I started work*), which are covered by the notation (*ever*) *since* (+ *tmp NP/CL* = temporal noun phrase or clause). The appearance in the different sub-classes corresponds to three different functions of *since*: adverb, preposition and conjunction. Quirk et al. report the following distribution of *since*: 'In the Survey of English Usage corpus, instances as conjunction (excluding casual use) and as preposition are roughly equal in number, but adverbial use accounts for only about 15 per cent of occurrences.' (Quirk et al. 1985: 536).

These findings differ from the results of the present analysis. In British English (LOB EP and LOB FT) the following distribution was found: adverb (or part of adverb phrase) 29.4 %, preposition 45.1 % and conjunction 25.5 %. In American English (BROWN EP and BROWN FT) *since* is distributed as follows: adverb (or part of adverb phrase) 12.2 %, preposition 55.1 % and conjunction 32.7 %. This shows that both in British and American English *since* in combination with the present perfect is used in the majority of all cases as a preposition. The distribution of the two remaining functions varies slightly. In British English the number of utterances in which *since* appears as an adverb are almost identical to the number of utterances in which *since* appears as a conjunctions, whereas American English seems to prefer the use as a conjunction to the adverbial use. Statistically, however, these differences are not significant.

7 Taking into account the absolute frequencies of the adverbials in both tables the Chi-square test returns a value of 14.74, which is below the critical value of 16.92 (level of significance: 0.05).

## References

Alexander, L. G. (1988). *Longman English grammar*. London: Longman.

Biber, D., S. Johansson, G. Leech, S. Conrad and E. Finegan (1999). *Longman grammar of spoken and written English.* Harlow: Pearson Education.

Elsness, J. (1997). *The perfect and the preterite in contemporary and earlier English.* Berlin, New York: Mouton de Gruyter.

Quirk, R., S. Greenbaum, G. Leech and J. Svartvik (1985). *A comprehensive grammar of the English language.* London: Longman.

Schlüter, N. (2000). 'The present perfect in British and American English: selected results of an empirical analysis.' In Mair, C. and M. Hundt (eds) *Corpus linguistics and linguistic theory. Papers from the Twentieth International Conference on English Language Research on Computerised Corpora* (ICAME 20). Amsterdam: Rodopi. 313–320.

# Ever moving on? The progressive in recent British English.

*Nicholas Smith*

Lancaster University

## Abstract

*There is a fair degree of consensus that progressive aspect has undergone a substantial growth in use in late modern English, but so far few studies have systematically exploited corpus data to reveal the extent to which changes are still going on. The availability of 'matching' one-million word corpora of recent written English, namely the British LOB and FLOB corpora dating from 1961 and 1991 respectively, and their American counterparts Brown and Frown, allows some redressing of the balance: Mair and Hundt (1995) have found that in the newspaper sections of these corpora some functions of the progressive already existing in the 1960s become more common in the 1990s. This paper aims to extend the analysis by exploring the full versions of the British corpora, looking at a wider range of variables. The most striking rise in the progressive occurs in the present tense, where it is realised by a wider range of verb types (increasingly with a contracted auxiliary verb), and appears increasingly far more in main clauses than in subordinate clauses. However, as cautioned by Mair and Hundt, the impression of 'pure' grammatical change is somewhat clouded by evidence in the written corpora of stylistic change, in particular a drift towards more colloquial speech habits.*

## 1. Introduction

One might wonder whether in the latter part of the twentieth century the grammatical and functional extension of the English progressive had already 'run its course'. All the major known aspectual and non-aspectual developments in progressive meaning, for example its use in habitual and not just ongoing situations, its combination with verbs that typically express states, its adoption as a means of talking about the future, or expressing certain kinds of subjective attitude, were well established long before the first computer corpora appeared on the scene. (See for example, Jespersen 1931, Mossé 1938 and Visser 1973 for early examples of these uses.) Moreover, some syntactic constraints, such as the difficulty of accepting the progressive passive well into the late nineteenth century (Denison 1998: 155–158), would surely no longer apply.

The availability of matching one million word corpora of written British English (LOB and FLOB) and American English (Brown and Frown) from 1961 and 1991–92 provides an excellent opportunity to see what changes, if any, have occurred in recent use of the construction. Mair and Hundt (1995) have already revealed that, at least in the press sections of these corpora, the progressive showed a significant rise in frequency over the short sampling period. They explore a range of variables, and conclude that the two most likely explanations are either (a) grammatical, namely that some 'filling out' of the grammatical functions of the progressive is still going on, or (b) stylistic, in that texts written for publication are being influenced more and more by colloquial speech; the progressive, which is purportedly far more common in speech, will increasingly find its way into written language.

In this study I aim to build on Mair and Hundt's investigation to see whether the patterns observed in press genres hold for other genres of the twin British corpora. Any conclusions drawn from these corpora will have to be treated with caution: even with a million words, the progressive examples can become quite sparse once they are broken down into different tenses and text categories. Secondly, we do not know how reliable a picture LOB and FLOB provide of what was happening in English at the end of the twentieth century: we have only two sampling points 30 years apart, and nothing very closely comparable from before, in between or since. More importantly, parallel corpus data from spoken language still need to be investigated, as this is the most likely locus of innovation in progressive use.

## 2. Distribution of progressive forms

Table 1 below presents distributions of the progressive in the two corpora according to tense, modality and voice. A rise or fall in frequency is expressed as a percentage of the LOB count. The significance of the change, and most other changes reported in this paper, is measured using the log likelihood statistic, which has been claimed to have greater reliability than the chi-square statistic at some frequency levels (Dunning 1993).[1] Although all errors in the retrieved cases, due to POS-tagging mistakes and under-specification in the retrieval algorithm, have been manually corrected, a small number of additional examples in each category should be expected, in cases where a less common adverbial or noun phrase pattern separates the *BE* from the *–ing* form, or where the *–ing* form has been ellipted. The counts exclude the semi-auxiliary *be going to*, which interestingly exhibits no noticeable rise in frequency in the LOB and FLOB data (see section 3.4).[2]

The advancement of the progressive in written British English appears most significant ($p < 0.01$) in the present tense, both in active and passive voice. While progressives in the present perfect, in the past tense with passive voice, and in combination with modal verbs, have increased also, the totals involved are somewhat smaller than for the present forms, and the significance levels far lower. The same could be said for the declining numbers in the modal perfect active and modal passive. More noteworthy is the 9% drop in the past active, with a probability between $p < 0.05$ and $p < 0.01$, which is not matched by its passive variant. Why has there been such a rise in the present progressive, and is the growth of the passive form a result of the same process(es) of change as the active, or more connected with a rise of progressive passives generally? Why has the past progressive declined? My investigations so far have concentrated on the present progressive active, as the growth is clear and there are more plentiful data with which to attempt an explanation. The areas addressed here are text type distribution, different kinds of meaning, syntactic environment, and the possibility of colloquialization of the written language. Where possible I provide data also for progressives outside of quotation; most quotations are of direct speech, and they contain a higher proportion of progressives than the non-quoted material.[3]

**Table 1:** Distribution of progressives in LOB and FLOB

**Active forms**

| | LOB | FLOB | overall change % | Log likelihood |
|---|---|---|---|---|
| Present | 985 | 1273 | +29.2% | 36.83 |
| Past | 1299 | 1182 | -9.0% | 5.52 |
| Present Perfect | 129 | 139 | +7.8% | 0.37 |
| Past Perfect | 110 | 99 | -10.0% | 0.58 |
| Modal | 149 | 194 | +30.2% | 5.92 |
| Modal Perfect | 17 | 13 | -23.5% | 0.53 |
| *to*-infin | 59 | 70 | +18.6% | 0.94 |
| Perfect *to*-infin | 0 | 0 | 0.0% | 0.00 |
| **Total** | **2748** | **2970** | **+8.1%** | **8.62** |

**Passive forms**

| | LOB | FLOB | overall change% | Log likelihood |
|---|---|---|---|---|
| Present | 123 | 179 | +45.5% | 10.44 |
| Past | 73 | 80 | +9.6% | 0.32 |
| Present Perfect | 0 | 0 | 0.0% | 0.00 |
| Past Perfect | 0 | 0 | 0.0% | 0.00 |
| Modal | 2 | 1 | -50.0% | 0.34 |
| Modal Perfect | 0 | 0 | 0.0% | 0.00 |
| *to*-infinitive | 0 | 0 | 0.0% | 0.00 |
| Perfect *to*-infin | 0 | 0 | 0.0% | 0.00 |
| **Total** | **198** | **260** | **+31.3%** | **8.42** |

**All forms**

| | LOB | FLOB | overall change% | Log likelihood |
|---|---|---|---|---|
| Present | 1108 | 1452 | +31.0% | 46.37 |
| Past | 1372 | 1262 | -8.0% | 4.60 |
| Present Perfect | 129 | 139 | +7.8% | 0.37 |
| Past Perfect | 110 | 99 | -10.0% | 0.58 |
| Modal | 151 | 195 | +29.1% | 5.61 |
| Modal Perfect | 17 | 13 | -23.5% | 0.53 |
| *to*-infinitive | 59 | 70 | +18.6% | 0.94 |
| Perfect *to*-infin | 0 | 0 | 0.0% | 0.00 |
| **Total** | **2946** | **3230** | **+9.6%** | **13.06** |

## 3. Analysis of the present progressive

### 3.1 Text category distribution

The frequency of the present progressive across the fifteen text categories of the two corpora is shown in Table 2, together with the ratio to the simple present. Note that counts for the simple present are estimates, based on corrected samples of the automatically POS-tagged corpora.[4] There appears to be considerable variation between the genres, with the highest concentrations in press reportage (section A), and in FLOB only, government documents and industrial reports (H). At this stage of investigation, it is difficult to tell whether the relative proportions of speech content, in the form of parliamentary debates, in LOB and FLOB section H is a factor. Learned and scientific articles (J) have the lowest ratio, at around 1%. The simple present remains high in academic texts presumably because it is the norm for describing abstract relationships, although there are signs that the progressive is gaining ground. It is interesting to compare these data with Ota's (1963: 37) ratios obtained from spoken American English, recorded around the same time as LOB. In unrehearsed conversation on the radio, present progressives averaged at 6.4% , and in scripted television drama 9.5%. Since even Ota's written material averages at 4.5%, higher than FLOB, it is tempting to regard American English as leading the way, perhaps influencing British English, in progressive development. However, a close analysis of American corpora of similar design to LOB and FLOB, namely the parallel Brown and Frown, would be necessary to substantiate this.

**Table 2:** Ratio of present progressive to simple present (active forms only)

| | LOB | | | FLOB | | | |
|---|---|---|---|---|---|---|---|
| **Corpus Text category** | **Pres Prog** | **Simple Pres (est.)** | **Proportion in Pres Prog** | **Pres Prog** | **Simple Pres (est.)** | **Proportion in Pres Prog** | **Change in proportion** |
| A : press reportage | 150 | 2233 | 6.3% | 189 | 2506 | 7.0% | +0.7% |
| B : press editorial | 101 | 2038 | 4.7% | 114 | 2039 | 5.3% | +0.6% |
| C : press reviews | 28 | 1467 | 1.9% | 36 | 1621 | 2.2% | +0.3% |
| D : religion | 32 | 1523 | 2.1% | 49 | 1212 | 3.9% | +1.8% |
| E : skills, hobbies | 84 | 2914 | 2.8% | 120 | 3016 | 3.8% | +1.0% |
| F : popular lore | 97 | 2792 | 3.4% | 147 | 3083 | 4.6% | +1.2% |
| G : belles lettres, essays, biographies | 86 | 3860 | 2.2% | 73 | 3572 | 2.0% | -0.2% |
| H : govt documents, industrial reports | 53 | 1553 | 3.3% | 102 | 1707 | 5.6% | +2.3% |
| J: learned & science | 51 | 5097 | 1.0% | 77 | 5872 | 1.3% | +0.3% |
| K : general fiction | 62 | 1227 | 4.8% | 91 | 1540 | 5.6% | +0.8% |
| L : mystery | 36 | 923 | 3.8% | 71 | 1291 | 5.2% | +1.5% |
| M : science fiction | 12 | 332 | 3.5% | 4 | 299 | 1.3% | -2.2% |
| N : adventure | 82 | 1371 | 5.6% | 101 | 1503 | 6.3% | +0.7% |
| P : romance | 87 | 1407 | 5.8% | 70 | 1437 | 4.6% | -1.2% |
| R : humour | 24 | 556 | 4.1% | 29 | 561 | 4.9% | +0.8% |
| **Total** | **985** | **29293** | **3.3%** | **1273** | **31232** | **3.9%** | **+0.7%** |
| **Average** | | | **3.7%** | | | **4.2%** | |

Part of the explanation for the increase in present progressives may relate to reference time. Across the corpora the estimated number of simple present forms also rises, and, while it may be a coincidence, it is interesting that in three of the four text categories in which use of the present simple falls (G, M and P), the present progressive falls too. Although present tense in English does not directly correlate with present reference time, where occurrences of simple present are more abundant, presumably there will be more opportunities for present progressive to compete with it. The only categories where the present progressive falls in relation to the non-progressive are those in which the latter numerically declines, that is categories G, M and P. [5]

### 3.2 Meaning and the progressive

The numerous different ways in which the progressive has been investigated with regard to meaning can roughly be grouped as follows:

(a) situation type and aspectual meaning
(b) semantic classes of verbs
(c) pragmatic meanings
(d) other uses, such as future time reference

With (a) the focus is on the complex interaction between the progressive and the inherent meaning of a verb representing different ontological situations, for example, states, processes and achievements (as in e.g. Vendler 1957). The meanings are typically decomposed into the notions of durativity, telicity and agentivity. The use of a telic verb in the present progressive (e.g., *John is cooking the dinner*) denotes an event with an inherent endpoint that is not yet reached, while a non-durative verb entails a repeated or habitual event (e.g., *Mary was coughing all night*). The semantic classes of verb in (b) may incorporate aspectual notions, for example the 'status' verbs and 'process' verbs of Joos 1964, or they may relate to more specific domains such as physical activity, mental processing, communication and relationship (Dixon 1991, Biber et al. 1999). Pragmatic meanings (c) of the progressive include its use by speakers to express a subjective attitude in, for example, hyperbolic expressions of irritation (*You're* always *moaning!*) and interpretations of situations (Buyssens 1968, Ljung 1980). In this example from FLOB the author seems to use the progressive to foreground his interpretation of what Gascoigne says.

> [...] when Paul Gascoigne says he will not be happy until he stops playing football, he is talking rot (FLOB A09)

Future-referring uses (d) can be see in examples such as:

> And now comes the new that Frankie Taylor is turning pro shortly. (LOB E17)

Few corpus-based studies have attempted to quantify cases of the progressive by meaning types other than (b), largely because the status of the categories involved is not clear-cut. Regarding the (a) type, one of the many difficulties is distinguishing a single event from an episodic one, as in

> REFUGEES are pouring out of East Germany into West Berlin faster than ever. (LOB A06).

With regard to (c) only Buyssens 1968, Wright 1995 and Mindt 2000, so far as I am aware, have attempted to quantify interpretative uses, but since they operate on very different criteria for identifying such cases, their counts differ greatly. For the present study I have limited my quantitative analysis to the semantic domains of verbs and the expression of future meaning.[6]

### 3.2.1 Verb Classes

The simple taxonomy of verb domains that has been applied comes from Biber et al. 1999: 360f. Verbs are grouped according to the following categories: **activity** (denoting actions and events controlled by a volitional agent, e.g. *run, draw, take*), **communication** (e.g. *speak, advise*), **mental processing** (e.g. *consider, hear, regret*), **causation** (e.g. *enable, make, force*), **occurrence** (reporting events of non-volitional activity, e.g. *happen, become*), **existence and relationship** (e.g. copulas such as *be, seem* and *appear*) and **aspectual verbs** (e.g. *begin, continue*). In applying this scheme to present progressives in the two corpora (Table 3), it is difficult to be objective. Cases which in context seem to belong to more than one domain are tallied under each relevant one, and so the frequencies in each domain add up to more than the total.[7]

**Table 3:** Distribution of present progressive (active) by semantic domain

| | **LOB** | | **FLOB** | | **Proportional change** | | **Overall change** | |
|---|---|---|---|---|---|---|---|---|
| **Semantic domain** | ***Freq*** | **%** | **Freq** | **%** | **%** | **LL** | **%** | **LL** |
| Activity | 602 | 61.1% | 705 | 55.4% | -5.7% | 3.14 | +17.1% | 8.13 |
| Communication | 112 | 11.4% | 170 | 13.4% | +2.0% | 1.76 | +51.8% | 12.01 |
| Mental | 238 | 24.2% | 337 | 26.5% | +2.3% | 1.17 | +41.6% | 17.13 |
| Causative | 23 | 2.3% | 35 | 2.7% | +0.4% | 0.37 | +52.2% | 2.50 |
| Simple occurrence | 185 | 18.8% | 251 | 19.7% | +0.9% | 0.25 | +35.7% | 10.03 |
| Existence/ Relationship | 54 | 5.5% | 59 | 4.6% | -0.8% | 0.79 | +9.3% | 0.22 |
| Aspectual | 21 | 2.1% | 27 | 2.1% | 0.0% | 0.00 | +28.6% | 0.75 |
| **Total** | **985** | | **1273** | | | | | |

It seems that while each semantic category has increased overall, the proportion of activity verbs in the total has declined, while communication and mental verbs have increased. Significance tests using log likelihood are far from conclusive, although we find general support for the trend when we break the basic domains down further. Among the mental verbs, for example, verbs of perception (e.g. *see, ignore, experience*) occur in an approximate ratio of 30:50 in LOB and FLOB; verbs of cognition (e.g. *think, suppose, contemplate*) 32:50; decision (e.g. *accept, choose, opt*) 5:11, emotion (e.g. *bug, regret, worry*) 12:22, and mental effort or intent (e.g. *aim, expect, try*) 107:93. In all except the last of these sub-groups, the newer corpus contains both more types and tokens than the older one, although there are differences at the level of individual verbs. *Think*, for instance, appears 16 times in LOB, 9 in FLOB. In terms of text distribution, the fifteen individual categories from A to R contain few examples, but an approximate grouping into four broader categories (as in Hofland and Johansson 1982) – press (sections A-C), general prose (D-H), learned and scientific (J) and fiction (K-R) – again supports a general rise of mental verbs. In press genres, the proportion of LOB to FLOB cases is 76:101 (a 2.6% proportional rise), general prose 81:134 (a 4.3% rise), learned 9:23 (29.9% rise). Fiction bucks the trend with a decline of 2.2%, which drops to 1.6% when all quotations are removed. If the overall trend *is* significant, several possible explanations may be put forward:

- The progressive could be (still) going through a process of extension from its prototypical domain of use with overt activity verbs. For instance, the dynamicity in activity verbs can be extended by analogy to mental processing of various kinds, and perhaps also to communication. Here we can include many so-called 'inert' cognition verbs, such as *think (of)* and *suppose*, which in the progressive have dynamic and agentive meaning.

  > It is at this time when the public are thinking of planning their forthcoming annual holiday. (LOB E35)

  > 'How far does the help extend?' asked Owen. The Prince smiled. 'Not as far as you are evidently supposing', he said. (FLOB L09)

- There may be a general trend towards relaxing the constraints on certain verb classes that previously were highly resistant to the progressive, notably the stative types. As well as the mental domain we find just a few examples of verbs expressing existence or relationship: *average* (no examples in LOB, but 1 in FLOB), *cost* (2:1), *have to* (1:4), *require* (0:1); and sensory copulas: *look* (4:4), *sound* (0:1). They generally refer to temporary states:

  > And fast bowler Malcolm Marshall ... is having to rest after falling down the steps at the team's hotel. (FLOB A22.)

  > In this respect, things are looking good for the identity-theorist. (FLOB J51)

  Progressive use of such verbs is widely held (e.g. Allen 1955: 78) to be more common in speech. While this may point towards colloquialization in the later corpus, we would probably expect more examples of other verbs which are common in the progressive in British conversation today, such as *want* and *mean*, to occur too. In fact, *want* does not appear in the present progressive in FLOB, but twice in LOB (once in Scots dialect).

- Increasing numbers of mental and communication verbs may reflect a rise in subjective (interpretative) uses of the progressive. According to Ljung (1980: 80f.) and Wright (1995: 159), subjective uses co-occur naturally with private verbs expressing non-observable phenomena, because they allow a means of interpreting what cannot be seen, e.g.:

  > '...It's almost like psychoanalysis. I'll do no work for weeks and then write solidly for 12 hours. I think what I'm really seeking all the time is the source of Original Sin in myself...'. (LOB A19)

Wright adds (p.158) that subjective uses of the progressive are more common (and 'unmarked') in dialogue than in literary prose, thus again raising the possibility of colloquialization.

### 3.2.2 Future meanings

Mair and Hundt (1995: 116) suggest that reference to future events with the progressive is a promising source of increase in the construction, but that there are many problems in distinguishing clear future meaning. Unless there are clear contextual clues, the future often seems to merge with the present:

> However, for the present, this first Canadian Eskimo magazine is a wonderful accomplishment. To the continuing of it, the Department of Northern Affairs is sparing no effort or expense. (LOB F36)

While the consistency in rating cannot be guaranteed, the figures I obtained suggest future uses are not a major factor in the rise of the present progressive in LOB and FLOB. I identified just 51 clear future-referring examples in LOB, and 29 in FLOB. Of these, 41 cases and 21 cases respectively were within dialogue, leaving only a handful of written examples. When ambiguous cases (such as the example above) were included, the frequencies rose to 134 in LOB and 128 in FLOB, and approximately 79 and 62 respectively when speech is excluded.

## 3.3 Grammatical environment

### 3.3.1 Person of subject; clause negation

Third person subjects seem at first sight to be a major source of increase, although the proportional rise of these subjects is not significantly high, and in fact disappears when we discard examples from quoted speech. Similarly, clause negation in present progressive has risen slightly, but not significantly, because the frequencies involved are quite low.

**Table 4:** Person of subject in present progressive in LOB and FLOB

(a) All present progressives (active)

| | LOB | | FLOB | | Proportional change | | Overall change | |
|---|---|---|---|---|---|---|---|---|
| | Freq | % | Freq | % | % | LL | % | LL |
| 1st person | 170 | 17.3% | 231 | 18.1% | +0.9% | 0.25 | +35.9% | 9.32 |
| 2nd person | 112 | 11.4% | 108 | 8.5% | -2.9% | 4.71 | -3.6% | 0.07 |
| 3rd person | 703 | 71.4% | 934 | 73.4% | +2.0% | 0.31 | +32.9% | 32.71 |

(b) Excluding spoken quotations

| | LOB | | FLOB | | Proportional change | | Overall change | |
|---|---|---|---|---|---|---|---|---|
| | Freq | % | Freq | % | % | LL | % | LL |
| 1st person | 62 | *10.0%* | 79 | 9.4% | -0.6% | 0.13 | +27.4% | 2.05 |
| 2nd person | 20 | 3.2% | 35 | 4.2% | +0.9% | 0.86 | +75.0% | 4.14 |
| 3rd person | 540 | 86.8% | 728 | 86.5% | -0.4% | 0.01 | +34.8% | 27.98 |

**Table 5:** Clause negation in present progressives

| | LOB | | FLOB | | Proportional change | | Overall change | |
|---|---|---|---|---|---|---|---|---|
| | **Freq** | **%** | **Freq** | **%** | **%** | **LL** | **%** | **LL** |
| all data | 43 | 4.4% | 51 | 4.0% | -0.4% | 0.17 | +18.6% | 0.68 |
| excluding quotation | 22 | 3.5% | 27 | 3.2% | -0.3% | 0.12 | +22.7% | 0.51 |
| quoted speech only (estimated) | 21 | 6.1% | 24 | 5.8% | -0.2% | 0.32 | +14.3% | 0.20 |

### 3.3.2 Clause Type

**Table 6:** Clause types in which present progressives appear

(a) All present progressives (active)

| | LOB | | FLOB | | Proportional change | | Overall change | |
|---|---|---|---|---|---|---|---|---|
| | **Freq** | **%** | **Freq** | **%** | **%** | **LL** | **%** | **LL** |
| Main clause | 555 | 56.3% | 758 | 59.5% | +3.2% | 0.98 | +36.6% | 31.51 |
| Subord clause | 430 | 43.7% | 515 | 40.5% | -3.2% | 1.35 | +19.8% | 7.66 |
| Adverbial clause | 119 | 12.1% | 136 | 10.7% | -1.4% | 0.96 | +14.3% | 1.13 |
| Relative clause | 143 | 14.5% | 145 | 11.4% | -3.1% | 4.22 | +1.4% | 0.01 |
| *that*-clause | 121 | 12.3% | 143 | 11.2% | -1.1% | 0.52 | +18.2% | 1.84 |
| *wh*-clause | 38 | 3.9% | 84 | 6.6% | +2.7% | 7.98 | +121.1% | 17.78 |
| **Total** | **985** | | **1273** | | | | | |

(b) Excluding examples in quotations

| | LOB | | FLOB | | Proportional change | | Overall change | |
|---|---|---|---|---|---|---|---|---|
| | **Freq** | **%** | **Freq** | **%** | **%** | **LL** | **%** | **LL** |
| Main clause | 299 | 48.1% | 483 | 57.4% | +9.3% | 5.84 | +61.5% | 43.70 |
| Subord clause | 323 | 51.9% | 359 | 42.6% | -9.3% | 6.58 | +11.1% | 1.90 |
| Adverbial clause | 91 | 14.6% | 105 | 12.5% | -2.2% | 1.24 | +15.4% | 1.00 |
| Relative clause | 106 | 17.0% | 101 | 12.0% | -5.0% | 6.36 | -4.7% | 0.12 |
| *that*-clause | 91 | 14.6% | 103 | 12.2% | -2.4% | 1.54 | +13.2% | 0.74 |
| *wh*-clause | 29 | 4.7% | 46 | 5.5% | +0.8% | 0.45 | +58.6% | 3.89 |
| **Total** | **622** | | **842** | | | | | |

Both tables indicate that main (or independent) clause progressives have increased somewhat, both overall and in proportion to the present progressive total. Excluding quotations – most of which are quoted speech – accentuates this trend, with a 9.3% proportional rise; it also seems to highlight the fact that it is relative clauses which contribute most to the decline in subordination. Using the same broad genre categories as in section 3.2.1, we find that only in fiction is the rising use of main clause present progressive not repeated. Strang (1982) has shown that in the eighteenth and nineteenth centuries there was a strong preference in written (especially literary) narrative for locating a progressive within a subordinate clause, a tendency which relaxed as time went on. Smitterberg (2000) confirms this trend in the nineteenth century, but across a wider range of genres, and suggests that rising use of the subjective/interpretative progressive could be responsible, since it commonly occurs in main clauses as a foregrounding device (see also Wright 1995). This trend may have continued into the late twentieth century and the rise of 'private' (mental and communication) verbs discussed earlier may be part of the same process.[8] Alternatively – or additionally – main clause increase could be a further example of written language imitating speech habits. In quoted speech in LOB and FLOB approximately two-thirds of progressives are in main clauses. However, in the past tense, main clause use in progressives does not rise at all but remains stable at around 53%. An investigation of clause types in LOB/FLOB as a whole (rather than just the progressive) may shed further light on this.

### 3.4 Colloquialization of written language

Space prevents discussion here of the complex changes in British and international society which may have influenced published written language in 1991 to become more 'colloquial' than thirty years earlier. In the corpora themselves evidence of colloquialization comes from the higher incidence of contracted forms in FLOB, both within the corpus as a whole, and within present progressives. By far the majority of contractions occur in quoted speech, but even when all quotations are removed, the FLOB count rises significantly:

**Table 7:** Contracted forms in present progressive

(a) All present progressives (active)

| | **LOB** | | **FLOB** | | **Proportional change** | | **Overall change** | |
|---|---|---|---|---|---|---|---|---|
| | **Freq** | **%** | **Freq** | **%** | **%** | **LL** | **%** | **LL** |
| *be* contractions | 200 | 20.3% | 275 | 21.6% | +1.3% | 0.45 | +37.5% | 11.89 |
| *not* contractions | 5 | 0.5% | 3 | 0.2% | -0.3% | 0.93 | -40.0% | 0.51 |
| all contractions | 203 | 20.6 | 277 | 21.8% | +1.2% | 0.35 | +36.5% | 11.45 |

(b) Excluding quotations

| | **LOB** | | **FLOB** | | **Proportional change** | | **Overall change** | |
|---|---|---|---|---|---|---|---|---|
| | **Freq** | **%** | **Freq** | **%** | **%** | **LL** | **%** | **LL** |
| *be* contractions | 17 | 2.7% | 61 | 7.2% | +4.5% | 14.80 | +258.8% | 26.34 |
| *not* contractions | 0 | 0.0% | 1 | 0.1% | +0.1% | - | - | - |
| all contractions | 17 | 2.7% | 62 | 7.4% | +4.6% | 15.42 | +264.7% | 27.24 |

The general growth of contracted forms can be shown by a comparison of the full form of the negative particle *not* to its contracted variant *n't*.

**Table 8:** *Not* in contracted and full form in LOB and FLOB

| | **LOB** | | | **FLOB** | | | **Change** | | |
|---|---|---|---|---|---|---|---|---|---|
| | ***n't*** | ***not*** | **ratio%** | ***n't*** | ***not*** | **ratio%** | ***n't*** | ***not*** | **ratio%** |
| Press | 162 | 981 | 16.5% | 268 | 870 | 30.8% | +106 | -111 | 14.3% |
| General Prose | 268 | 2330 | 11.5% | 336 | 1942 | 17.3% | +68 | -388 | 5.8% |
| Learned | 16 | 829 | 1.9% | 31 | 932 | 3.3% | +15 | +103 | 1.4% |
| Fiction | 1505 | 1336 | 112.6% | 1847 | 1216 | 151.9% | +342 | -120 | 39.2% |
| **Total** | **1951** | **5476** | **35.6%** | **2482** | **4960** | **50.0%** | **+531** | **-516** | **14.4%** |

Hundt and Mair (1999) have pointed out the varying degrees to which different written genres absorb speech-like habits, including rising use of contractions, but also first and second person pronouns, phrasal verbs with *up*; declining use of more formal features, e.g. passives and the archaic preposition *upon*. They concentrate on the press genres (sections A-C in LOB and FLOB) and academic expository writing (section J), finding the former amenable to such changes, and the latter highly resistant.

One construction which one might expect to support the argument for colloquialization but which in fact does not is the semi-auxiliary *be going to*. Between LOB and FLOB its growth is confined to the journalistic sections of the corpora.[9]

**Table 9:** Semi-auxiliary *be going to* in LOB and FLOB

| | **LOB frequency** | **FLOB frequency** | **Change** |
|---|---|---|---|
| Press | 30 | 46 | +16 |
| General Prose | 59 | 39 | -20 |
| Learned | 5 | 5 | 0 |
| Fiction | 154 | 155 | +1 |
| **Total** | **248** | **245** | **-3** |

It seems that analysis of a wider range of linguistic indicators, together with assessment of social changes in the 1960s-90s, is required to determine if there really has been a general shift towards a more colloquial style.

## 4. Conclusions

The evidence provided by LOB and FLOB for change in the progressive in recent written British English is that the present tense forms have borne most of the increase. The analysis of present forms has not provided complete answers, but pointed to some apparent areas of growth: first, a rise in non-past forms in general, and not just present progressives; secondly, a spreading out of verb types, from the domain of activity to other types, notably mental and communication verbs. There has also been a noticeable increase in main clause use of the present progressive. Two overriding factors that may have influenced these increases are the spread of colloquial speech habits into written language, and (possibly related to this) an increase in subjective/interpretative uses. The corpus evidence provided for each factor is interesting but so far only partial. In future more attention will be given to the areas of meaning not covered here, and a wider variety of corpus data that may impact on written British English, notably spoken material of the same period, and other regional varieties of English, both written and spoken.

## Acknowledgements

This research has been supported by AHRB grant no. MRG-AN5355/APN853. I would also like to thank Geoffrey Leech, Anna Siewierska and Paul Rayson for helpful comments in developing this paper.

## Notes

1 Log likelihood values of 6.63 and above equate to $p < 0.01$, and those at 3.84 and above equate to $p < 0.05$, with 1 d.f.

2 It should be noted also that subjunctives have not yet been separately counted. Retrieval of the progressives was made with Xkwic (Christ 1994), after the corpora had been POS-tagged with CLAWS4 (Leech et al. 1994). Strictly speaking, the counts in Tables 1 and 2 should be normalized because FLOB is very slightly bigger than LOB. In practice, normalizing to 1,000,000 words exactly made very little difference to the percentages and significance values.

3 Differentiating quoted from non-quoted usage had to be done manually and the counts are not completely certain, despite the presence of quotation tags. Similarly, quoted speech could not always be separated from quoted writing, and the counts for 'excluding quotation' given in this paper apply to both kinds of quotation.

4 Although there is a manually corrected version of the LOB corpus (Johansson et al. 1986), it cannot directly be used to extract simple present and progressive forms, because the tagset does not distinguish between auxiliary and main verb uses of *be*, *do* and *have*, nor between infinitival and indicative uses of non-3rd person singular verbs.

5 The ratios presented here are not intended to suggest that progressive and simple present are the only verbal options for describing current situations (modal verbs, for example, are also available). The tense and aspect choices are numerous in past time, although apparently there is a similar pattern in that simple past forms decline in the same categories as the past progressive, although the reverse is not true.

6 Text frequencies of different sub-categories of aspectual meaning have been given by Buyssens (1968), Duskova (1971) and Mindt (2000), but in each case the lack of explicit criteria for choosing between categories makes them difficult to replicate.

7 Undoubtedly this scheme is a little simplistic, and as applied by Biber et al. p.361ff. appears to be based on the most frequent sense of the verb, rather than its use in context. I originally used Dixon's (1991) verb classes – based on both semantic and syntactic principles – but found this too fine-grained to yield many examples in the various categories, and so no overall patterns emerged.

8 The interpretative example discussed in 3.2.1 is not in a main clause; however Wright presents main clauses and private verbs (among other things) as typical rather than criterial properties of subjective/interpretative progressives.

9 However, a brief investigation carried out on matching samples of the Survey of English Usage from 1959–65 and ICE-GB corpora from the early 1990s, did show a clear expansion of the *be going to* construction, from 35 to 162 instances in 80,000 words of spoken data, and from 17 to 48 instances in 100,000 words of written data.

**References**

Allen, W. S. (1955). *Living English structure: a practice book for foreign students.* London: Longman.

Biber, D., S. Johansson, g. Leech, S. Conrad, E. Finegan (1999). *Longman grammar of spoken and written English.* Harlow, UK: Longman.

Buyssens, E. (1968). *Les deux aspectifs de la conjugaison anglaise au XXe siècle.* Bruxelles: Université libre de Bruxelles.

Christ, O. (1994). 'A modular and flexible architecture for an integrated corpus query system'. *Proceedings of COMPLEX'94: 3rd Conference on Computational Lexicography and Text Research* (Budapest, July 7–10 1994). Budapest, Hungary. 23–32.

Denison, D. (1998). Chapter 3 (Syntax), in Romaine, S. (ed.) *The Cambridge history of the English language*, Vol. IV. Cambridge: CUP.

Dixon, R. M. W. (1991). *A new approach to English grammar, on semantic principles.* Oxford: OUP

Dunning, T. (1993). 'Accurate methods for the statistics of surprise and coincidence'. *Computational Linguistics.* Vol. 19, no. 1:61–74.

Duskova, L. (1971). 'Some quantitative aspects of continuous forms in present-day English'. *Prague Studies in English*, 14:7–39.

Hofland, K. and S. Johansson (1982). *Word frequencies in British and American English.* Bergen: Norwegian Computing Centre for the Humanities.

Hundt, M. and C. Mair (1999). '"Agile" and "uptight" genres: the corpus-based approach to language change in progress'. *International Journal of Corpus Linguistics* Vol.4.2, 221–242.

Jespersen, O. (1931). *A modern English grammar on historical principles.* Part IV. Copenhagen: Munksgaard.

Johansson, S., E. Atwell, R. Garside, and G. Leech (1986). *The tagged LOB Corpus: user's manual.* Bergen: Norwegian Computing Centre for the Humanities.

Joos, M. (1964). *The English verb: form and meaning.* Madison: University of Wisconsin Press.

Leech, G., R. Garside, and M. Bryant (1994). 'CLAWS4: the tagging of the British National Corpus'. In *Proceedings of the 15th International Conference on Computational Linguistics (COLING 94)* Kyoto, Japan, 622–628.

Ljung, M. (1980). *Reflections on the English progressive*. Gothenburg Studies in English 46. Göteborg: Acta Universitatis Gothoburgensis.
Mair, C. and M. Hundt (1995). 'Why is the progressive becoming more frequent in English? A corpus-based investigation of language change in progress.' *Zeitschrift für Anglistik und Amerikanistik* 43: 111–122.
Mindt, D. (2000). *An empirical grammar of the English verb system*. Berlin: Cornelsen.
Mossé, F. (1938). *Histoire de la forme périphrastique être + participe présent en germanique*, Vols. 1–2. Paris: Klincksieck.
Ota, A. (1963). *Tense and aspect of present-day American English*. Tokyo: Kenkyusha.
Smitterberg, E. (2000). 'The progressive form and genre variation during the nineteenth century'. In Bermudez-Otero, R., D. Denison, R. M. Hogg, C.B. McCully, *Generative theory and corpus studies: a dialogue from 10 ICEHL*. Berlin: Mouton de Gruyter. 283–297.
Strang, B. (1982). 'Some aspects of the history of the *be* + *ing* construction'. In Anderson, J. (ed.) *Language form and linguistic variation*. Papers dedicated to Angus McIntosh. Amsterdam: John Benjamins. 427–74.
Vendler, Z. (1957). 'Verbs and times'. *Philosophical Review* 56, 143–60.
Visser, F. Th. (1973). *An historical syntax of the English language*. Vol. III. Leiden: Brill.
Wright, S. (1995). 'Subjectivity and experiential syntax'. In Stein, D. and S. Wright, (eds) *Subjectivity and subjectivisation*. Cambridge: CUP. 151–172.

## Contributors

**Paul Baker**
Department of Linguistics
Lancaster University
UK
bakerjp@exchange.lancs.ac.uk

**Magnar Brekke**
Norwegian School of Economics
Bergen
Norway
magnar.brekke@nhh.no

**Peter Collins**
Linguistics Department
University of New South Wales
Australia
p.collins@unsw.edu.au

**Pieter de Haan**
Department of English
University of Nijmegen
Netherlands
P.deHaan@let.kun.nl

**Neil Drave**
Division of Language Studies
City University of Hong Kong
Hong Kong
lsdrave@cityu.edu.hk

**Roberta Facchinetti**
Department of Literature and Philosophy
University of Verona
Italy
roberta.facchinetti@univr.it

**Professor Maurizio Gotti**
Department of Literature and Philosophy
University of Bergamo
Italy
m.gotti@unibg.it

**He Anping**
Foreign Languages Department
South China Normal University
P.R.China
heanping@scnu.edu.cn

**Sebastian Hoffmann**
English Department
University of Zürich
Switzerland
sebhoff@es.unizh.ch

**Professor Janet Holmes**
School of Linguistics & Applied Language
Victoria University of Wellington
New Zealand
janet.holmes@vuw.ac.nz

**Christine Johansson**
Department of English
University of Uppsala
Sweden
christine.johansson@engelska.uu.se

**Göran Kjellmer,**
Department of English
University of Gothenburg
Sweden
kjellmer@hum.gu.se

**Geoffrey Leech**
Department of Linguistics
Lancaster University
UK
G.Leech@lancaster.ac.uk

**Hans Martin Lehmann**
English Department
University of Zürich
Switzerland
hmlehman@es.unizh.ch

**Manfred Markus**
Department of English
University of Innsbruck
Austria
manfred.markus@uibk.ac.at

**Dr Tony McEnery**
Department of Linguistics
Lancaster University
UK
eiaamme@exchange.lancs.ac.uk

**Ilka Mindt**
Department for English and American Studies
University of Würzburg
Germany
mindt@mail.uni-wuerzburg.de

**David Minugh**
English Department
Stockholm University
Sweden
minughd@English.su.se

**Vincent Ooi**
Department of English Language & Literature
National University of Singapore
Singapore
vinceooi@nus.edu.sg

**Nelleke Oostdijk**
Department of Language & Speech
University of Nijmegen
Netherlands
n.oostdijk@let.kun.nl

**Pam Peters**
Department of Linguistics
Macquarie University
Australia
ppeters@ling.mq.edu.au

**Paul Rayson**
UCREL Computing Department
Lancaster University
UK
paul@comp.lancs.ac.uk

**Norbert Schlüter**
Institute of English Philology
Free University of Berlin
Germany
nosch@zedat.fu-berlin.de

**Peter Schneider**
English Department
University of Zurich
Switzerland
pschneid@es.unizh.ch

**Robert Sigley**
Foreign Languages Department
Daito Bunka University
Japan
sigley@ic.daito.ac.jp

**Adam Smith**
Department of Linguistics
Macquarie University
Australia
asmith@ling.mq.edu.au

**Nicholas Smith**
Department of Linguistics
Lancaster University
UK
nick@comp.lancs.ac.uk

**Andrew Wilson**
Department of Linguistics
Lancaster University
UK
eiaaw@exchange.lancs.ac.uk